Anti/Idealism

Anti/Idealism

Re-interpreting a German Discourse

Edited by Juliana de Albuquerque and Gert Hofmann

DE GRUYTER

ISBN 978-3-11-076297-6
e-ISBN (PDF) 978-3-11-058660-2
e-ISBN (EPUB) 978-3-11-058502-5

Library of Congress Control Number: 2019950563

Bibliografic information published by the Deutsche Nationalbibliothek
The Deutsche Nationalbibliothek lists this publication in the Deutsche Nationalbibliografie;
detailed bibliografic data are available on the Internet at http://dnb.dnb.de.

© 2021 Walter de Gruyter GmbH, Berlin/Boston
This volume is text- and page-identical with the hardback published in 2019.
Cover image: Gert Hofmann
Printing and binding: CPI books GmbH, Leck

www.degruyter.com

Acknowledgements

We would like to thank the Department of German and the School of Languages, Literatures and Cultures at University College Cork (UCC) for hosting and funding the activities and conferences of the (Anti-)Classicism & (Anti-)Idealism Research Network. We are especially grateful to our Department's secretaries, Deborah Fitzgibbon and Veronica Forde for their organisational assistance. We would also like to express our gratitude to Mary Venables, Kristie Kachler, Ian Creaner, Hanna Völker and Marcus Bowman for their linguistic and technical support in the process of editing this book.

Table of Contents

Introduction —— 1

Goethe's (Anti-)Classicism and Experientialism

Matthew Bell
Embracing the Enemy: The Problem of Religion in Goethe's "Confessions of a Beautiful Soul" —— 13

Juliana de Albuquerque
"Meine Schwester Natalie ist hiervon ein lebhaftes Beispiel:" *Bildung* **and Gender in Goethe's** *Wilhelm Meisters Lehrjahre* —— 27

Margaret Strair
Mediating Subjectivities: Anti-Classical and Anti-Ideal Impulses in Goethe's *Zur Farbenlehre* **and** *Die Wahlverwandtschaften* —— 49

Christopher Law
Reading Surfaces: Goethe and Benjamin —— 69

Kant-Critique and the Romanticist Movement

Tadahiro Oota
Jakob Friedrich Fries as an Opponent of German Idealism —— 87

Manuel Clemens
Apparent Purposes.
    How Does the Purpose of Purposelessness Operate? —— 103

Víctor Ibarra B.
Antecedents to Hegel's Conception of Judaism in Kant's Practical Philosophy —— 115

Joanna Raisbeck
"Diese Unwissenheit ist mir der unerträglichste Mangel, der gröste Widerspruch": The Search for Pre-rational Knowledge in Karoline von Günderrode —— 131

Nadia Schuman
Romantic Anti-Idealism and Re-evaluations of Gender: Schlegel, Günderrode and Literary Gender Politics —— 147

Joseph Trullinger
The Polymorphous Political Theology of Novalis and Marcuse —— 161

Hölderlin and Nietzsche: The Ecological Complication of Idealist Aesthetics

Gert Hofmann
Hölderlin's Poetics of *Zärtlichkeit:* The Corporeal Turn of Transcendental Idealism —— 175

Ansgar Mohnkern
Grund/Abgrund.
  On Kant and Hölderlin —— 187

Jennifer Anna Gosetti-Ferencei
Nietzsche and Cognitive Ecology —— 209

Annamaria Lossi
Overturning Philosophy:
  Classic and (Anti)-Classic Considerations on Nietzsche's *Ecce Homo* —— 227

Index —— 243

Introduction

The essays in this volume represent a collective attempt to reinterpret a German intellectual tradition by considering the ways in which the fields of literature and philosophy interact with each other from the Enlightenment onwards.

As E. M. Butler explains in her classical study *The Tyranny of Greece over Germany* (1935), one of the consequences of the Reformation on artists and intellectuals in Germany was that they came to see themselves as having to create a literary and thought tradition that could match Luther's rupture of the Catholic world.

The religious conflicts that followed from the Protestant Reformation prompted social and political changes throughout the Holy Roman Empire. Protestantism itself left a profound impression on German creative life as a whole. And while German writers honed their creativity as Luther's linguistic descendants by engaging with philosophy, in turn, philosophy came to be shaped by its interaction with literature.

This exchange is especially important for an understanding of the development of German thought from the late eighteenth century's Enlightenment through to the first half of the twentieth century: Why was it essential for G. W. F. Hegel to discuss Sophocles' ancient tragedy of *Antigone* in the *Phenomenology of Spirit*? Why did Nietzsche emphasise the connection between himself and certain literary figures, such as Heine and Dostoevsky? Why did Freud, who saw himself working ultimately in a philosophical tradition, say that he owed more to the great dramatists than to the psychologists? Or why have Martin Heidegger's references to literary works, from his early mention of *The Death of Ivan Ilych* in his magnum opus *Being and Time* to the interpretation of works by Friedrich Hölderlin, Georg Trakl and Rainer Maria Rilke, had such a defining impact also on schools of literary criticism?

T. J. Reed suggests that these amazingly productive permeations are owed to "the imprecise and permeable lines" of what is only conventionally perceived as defining boundaries between literary, philosophical or theological debates: "Goethe's poetry contains a vital philosophy, some of Kant's essays can be read as dramatic dialogue, Lessing's greatest drama outpreaches orthodox theology. Essential light is cast equally by them all." (Reed, 2013, p. ix)

The late eighteenth century is characterised by two crucial events. On the one hand, it is marked by the rise of Goethe as a dominating literary figure with far-reaching influence on German intellectual life. On the other, it sees the birth and development of Immanuel Kant's approach to enlightenment philosophy as transcendental critique, which became the foundation for the philosophical discourse of German Idealism.

From Friedrich Schiller and the three young thinkers of the Tübingen School (Georg Wilhelm Friedrich Hegel, Friedrich Hölderlin and Friedrich Wilhelm Joseph Schelling) who inaugurated the philosophical tradition of German Idealism in the late eighteenth century, to Freud and Heidegger in the twentieth, much of German thought can be understood as an attempt to establish a synthesis between these two types of world perception epitomised by both Goethe and Kant—between, so to speak, *Dichtung* and *Wahrheit*.

While these three young philosophers concreatively adopted Kant's view of philosophy as a system of pure thought, they also reacted to some extent against his systematising impulse by positing the *equiprimordiality* of "world" and "self," of aesthetic perception and reason, and of experience and pure idea.

This can be seen notably in "The Oldest Systematic Program," dating from around 1797, a fragmentary manifesto of German Idealism presumably co-authored by Hegel, Schelling and Hölderlin, where "beauty" is described as the sole unifying principle between truth (theoretical reason) and goodness (practical reason).

Guided by the idea that all philosophy of *Geist* is an aesthetic philosophy, "The Oldest Systematic Program"[1] argues that we cannot have a truthful perception of anything unless we also employ an "aesthetic sense," and that our understanding of history, instilled with the reasonable principles of transcendental critique, requires an aesthetic sensibility. The aesthetic sense, as a sense of beauty, arises as an independently creative force right out of the Kantian dualism: the annihilating abyss between perceptive objectivity (empirical world) and spontaneous subject (transcendental ego). Beauty, in a clash of the irreconcilable, emerges here as the "only truthful and conceivable creation out of nothingness" ("Schöpfung aus Nichts") (Hegel 1979, p. 234).

Kant's dualism between thought and experience (freedom and necessity) is the source of idealist philosophy's self-referential critique. For Kant, there is no discursive reconciliation possible between idea and experience, only the aporetic statement of their antagonistic co-existence, which is the transcendental condition of his philosophical critique of reason, but also of the poetic impulse to reconcile this antagonism in a trans-conceptual, figurative way. Consequently, in spite of this categorical antagonism, Kant's critique culminates in the "categori-

---

[1] We rely here on the translation of Diana I. Behler, "The Oldest Systematic Program of German Idealism." In: Behler, Ernst (ed.) (1987). *Philosophy of German Idealism: Fichte, Jacobi, and Schelling*. London: A&C Black, pp. 61–63. For the German original see: Georg Wilhelm Friedrich Hegel (1979): *Werke*. Band 1. Frankfurt a. M.: Suhrkamp, pp. 234–237.

cal imperative" as the con-creative *metaphorical* form for the impossible fusion of its constituent discourses (the theoretical and the practical): the "categorical imperative" links the discourses of idea and experience, as of freedom and natural law, ultimately in the "as if" of a metaphorical equation. Kant's categorical metaphor has inspired the *poetic* drift of philosophy and critical theory ever since (cf. Steven Helmling (2009): *Adorno's Poetics of Critique*)—it thus constitutes the *anti*-idealist kernel of any idealist discourse of pure thought. In Kant's own thinking the "oxymoronic monster" of the sketched concept of an "aesthetic idea" as an "idea of aesthetic value" and meaningfulness constitutes "the core of [his] philosophy of art" in his *Critique of Judgement* (Chaouli 2011, p. 56). Kant's "aesthetic idea" instils the impulse of an aesthetic sense into his own discourse of the intelligible, resulting in a productive blur of all conceptual knowledge of transcendental intelligence,[2] but also stirring up the poetic as a trans-conceptual expansion of the philosophical discourse by other means.

Hegel, Schelling and Hölderlin spin this thought out in "The Oldest Systematic Program," where it is suggested that the *aesthetic act* should be seen as the "supreme act of reason" ("höchster Akt der Vernunft") (Hegel 1979, p. 235) since it results in the wholistic "creation" of a lived "world" of beauty rather than in the "spontaneous" emergence of purely abstract intellectual principles and ideas.

Kant's *critique* of reason, as the human faculty of ideas, manifests the intrinsic status of *crisis* of reason in the lived world. Following Schiller's play aesthetics, which first attempted to integrate idea and experience practically, through art, the European philosophical discourse has been both haunted by the intellectual trauma of Kant's crisis, and inspired by the vision of overcoming or at least managing it artistically and poetically. Hölderlin's corporeal turn of the transcendental discourse in a poetically articulated notion of the "apriority of the individual"; Novalis', Schlegel's and Tieck's "progressive universal poetic," which catapults Kant's rigid subject-object antagonism into a transcendental world symphony of poetic events; Nietzsche's philosophy of life as pursuing a more environmental than transcendental "sense of the earth"; and Derrida's deconstruction of the transcendental subject in a discourse that intensely depends on literary inspirations are only some of the most decisive and impactful steps on this route.

---

[2] "Eine ästhetische Idee kann keine Erkenntniß werden, weil sie eine Anschauung (der Einbildungskraft) ist, der niemals ein Begriff adäquat gefunden werden kann." (Kant 1913, *Kritik der Urtheilskraft*, p. 342).

They all bring to the fore the intrinsically ironic signature of all idealist philosophical practice—i.e., the point where the virulence of questions overwhelms all possible answers categorically, and the erratic sediments of a speculative *fantasy* prove to be an irreducible reality for the analysis of philosophical investigation and its conceptual presumptions. This is the point where philosophy's crisis, unfathomably gaping as the in-between space of its mutually exclusive discourses, turns into the stimulating condition of what proves to be the persevering dignity of the human subject even under the condition of its discursive subversion: the freedom of its transcendental creativity and the aesthetic fantasy to configure ideas and experiences, in the modality of the "as if," as metaphorical structures —and as the only non-annihilating response to the "natural antithetics" (Kant 1911, p. 282) of human reason in a poetically induced—as Derrida puts it—"experience of the impossible."[3]

Kant's transcendental idealism is indeed itself triggered by the intellectual *experience* of the "discord and disintegration (Zwiespalt und [...] Zerrüttungen)" of the human use of reason (Kant 1911, p. 282). His system of transcendental critique is rooted in the irreducible confrontation of thought with the antinomies of its own split constitution and consequently attempts to let these antinomies manifest themselves. The *self*-critique of transcendental reflection is intrinsic to the transcendental discourse itself: the *anti*-idealist impulse thus emerges as an aesthetically and poetically productive blur from the discourse of idealism itself.

In a tightrope walk of philosophical artistry par excellence, Kant positions the subject of autonomous human acts right in the abyss between critique and crisis of reason, where neither *topos* nor *logos* of the human discourse apply, but where, however, the a-topical and a-logical construction of a formal metaphor (i.e., the categorical imperative) emerges as the only possible formulation of a lived reality of human freedom.

Both Derrida's deconstructive "experience of the impossible" and Kant's intellectual experience of the "natural antithetics" of human reason suggest the existence of *im*-possible realities of human life that evoke spheres of human responsiveness beyond discursive comprehension and cognitive appropriation. They lead into dynamic and essentially *im*-perfect configurations of awareness that inspire imaginative artistic and poetic forms of expression beyond the transcendental semantics of idealist philosophy.

---

3 Cf. Jacques Derrida on the *event* character of the deconstructive operation, in: Jacques Derrida (1998, p. 38).

Both mark defining moments of a trajectory of philosophical speculation since Enlightenment that relies on decisively *aesthetic* forms of reflection in order to contend an absolute dignity of human presence beyond the reach of discursive comprehension.

Adhering to the self-critical impulse of Kant's philosophy by positing an equiprimordiality of both the empirical world and the intelligible subject, while trying to overcome the problems within the idealist model of *Bildung* espoused by German classicism, "The Oldest Systematic Program" on the one hand argued for the co-extensiveness of the reality of both philosophy (idea) and art (lived world) but concludes, on the other hand, with a radical suggestion concerning the *trans*-philosophical as well as *trans*-historical reach of poetic reflection:

> Poetry thereby obtains a higher dignity; it becomes again in the end what it was in the beginning—*teacher of Humanity*; because there is no longer any philosophy, any history; poetic art alone will outlive all the rest of the sciences and arts.[4]
>
> (Die Poesie bekommt dadurch eine höhere Würde, sie wird am Ende wieder, was sie am Anfang war—Lehrerin der Menschheit; denn es gibt keine Philosophie, keine Geschichte mehr, die Dichtkunst allein wird alle übrigen Wissenschaften und Künste überleben.) (Hegel 1979, p. 235).

It was Goethe's *Wilhelm Meisters Lehrjahre* (published in 1795–1796) that was perceived at the time as a model realisation of poetic art's "higher dignity" to act as "teacher of humanity." Goethe's writing could be seen as both *complement* and *inversion* of Kant's philosophy of transcendental critique. Both relied on the primordiality of human "experience" as a source of empowerment for intellectual *Bildung* and enlightenment. But while for Kant the experience of thought encapsulated the "natural antithetics" of the human intellect, which triggered enlightenment as a process of *critical self-reflection* of the human mind towards the empirical world, for Goethe, in a naturalist challenge of classicist aesthetics, experience as a literary affair reinforces a basic human sense of the *organic integration* of human individual and world, and propagates the inspirational embeddedness of the subject of education in their environmental sphere of social and natural life.

The critical engagement with these divergent traditions of Goethe and Kant enabled the literary and philosophical discourse around 1800 to develop new aesthetic and philosophical impulses which, beyond idealism and classicism, paved the way for the development of a whole range of new traditions of thought

---

4 Trans. Diana I. Behler, with variations by the authors.

and writing in the long nineteenth and twentieth centuries, such as, among others, romanticism, historical materialism, existentialism, Nietzsche's philosophy of life, phenomenology, hermeneutics, and deconstructivism.

In the light of these programmatic divergences and their creative potential between lived experience and speculative autonomy, this volume undertakes a new reading of the protagonists of the literary, aesthetic and philosophical discourse around 1800 and subsequent developments.

This is the basic context illuminating the themes addressed by the essays in this volume, such as: Hegel's preoccupation with Antigone's tragic constitution in his phenomenological approach to the idea of ethical order (*Sittlichkeit*), Hölderlin's late notion of the poetic apriority of the individual, Goethe's psychological realism in his *Wilhelm Meister* trilogy, and Nietzsche's ecological subversion of Kant's philosophical transcendentalism.

* * *

This volume is divided into three sections dealing with topics at the intersection of philosophy and literature in German intellectual history. The first section concentrates exclusively on Goethe as a case of "anti-Classicism within classicism" (Matthew Bell) emerging from a rigorous twist of the idealist orientation of classicist aesthetics towards an almost naturalist and experience-fuelled psychographic poetic and poetic science of the world.

The articles in the second section explore philosophical and aesthetic approaches to a systematic Kant critique, and the Kant-inspired poetic rationalism critique of the Romanticist movement, with a particular focus on Karoline von Günderrode and the gender-normative implications of this critique.

The articles in the last section are dedicated to the poetic philosophy and/or philosophical poetics of Hölderlin and Nietzsche in pursuit of corporeal and environmental complications of the idealist discourse of aesthetics.

The first section begins with an article by Matthew Bell on the problem of religion in Goethe's *Confessions of a Beautiful Soul*. Bell argues that the development of Goethe's Beautiful Soul reflects a set of psychological perspectives already familiar to eighteenth-century thought, and that can be traced back at least as far as Richard Burton's *Anatomy of Melancholy*. Bell suggests that Goethe intends the character's religious melancholy to be understood as the price she pays for not adhering to Spinoza's dictum that "he who loves God cannot demand that God should love him in return."

Exploring the question of autonomy and its relation to the feminine in Goethe's *Wilhelm Meisters Lehrjahre*, Juliana de Albuquerque's article complements Bell's analysis by offering a criticism of some traditional feminist interpretations of *Confessions of a Beautiful Soul*. According to Albuquerque, in order to understand the problem of autonomy in Goethe's novel, we need to compare the characters of the Beautiful Soul and that of her niece, Natalie. Such a comparison shows how the notion of *Bildung* in Goethe's work can be seen as an ideal of self-mastery that is valid for both men and women equally.

The two last articles in this section were written by Margaret Strair and Christopher Law. Both articles are dedicated to a study of Goethe's *Theory of Colours*. Strair focuses on the anti-idealist impulses in Goethe's *Zur Farbenlehre* and *Die Wahlverwandtschaften*. According to Strair, works such as these can be used to study Goethe's reception of and reaction to Kantian idealism. As such, Strair's article is a commentary on the ways in which Goethe understands how the acquisition of knowledge about the world is related to experience and the possibility of self-knowledge. On this note, she concludes that "failing to fully shed some key idealist tendencies endangers aspects of [Goethe's] classical programme, as in the case with *Elective Affinities*."

Lastly, Christopher Law explores the critical reception of Goethe's scientific studies by Walter Benjamin. He argues that the relation between electricity and colour in Goethe's *Theory of Colours* "registers a threshold between classicism and anti-classicism which becomes particularly prominent in the awake of Kant's *Kritik der Urteilskraft*." Law observes that a similar problem appears in Benjamin's early fragmentary work on colour and language, and he concludes that, "despite the intimate proximity between Goethe and Benjamin's theories of surface, it seems plausible to suggest that it was Goethe's attempt to seamlessly enfold the singular event of electricity and the harmonious plurality of colour [...] that Benjamin could not bring himself to accept."

The second section, dedicated to studies on German idealism, romanticism and their reception by twentieth-century literature and philosophy, begins with Tadahiro Oota's article about Jakob Friedrich Fries' systematic critique of Kant's transcendentalism. According to Oota, Fries radicalises Kant's critical methodology through reflecting on the *empirical* implications of Kant's conception of a transcendental *a priori*, extending his criticism on the pure intelligible subjectivism of Fichte and Schelling. Starting from a "standpoint of ordinary experience by analysing 'the ordinary opinions (Beurteilungen) in daily life,'" he attempts to describe "philosophical cognition" as based on the analytical construction of "general presuppositions of opinions."

Manuel Clemens' focus lies on Friedrich Schiller's critical perception of Kant's transcendental antagonism of nature and morality in his letters *On the Aesthetic Education of Man* (*Über die ästhetische Erziehung des Menschen*). He also emphasises the *experiential* impulse in the aesthetic act of play as a "supplementary form" of knowledge, meant to "appeal [...] to the senses" in a poetically productive and ethically effective manner. He points out how Schiller's argument leads to the creative paradox of an artistic (playful) practice that performs "aesthetic purposelessness, in order to examine its purpose."

Victor Ibarra's text is a study of Hegel's conception of Judaism in his early theological writings, with the aim of illuminating Judaism "as a notion within Hegel's practical philosophy." Ibarra argues that Hegel's analysis of the Jewish religion in texts such as "Das Leben Jesu" (1795) was inspired by his early contact with Kant's moral philosophy. He also suggests that, although Hegel rejects Kant's categorical imperative in an early collection of fragments named "Der Geist des Christentums und sein Schicksal" (1798–1800), the constitutive features of his interpretation of Judaism remain the same throughout his writing and are based on Kant's notion of heteronomy.

Gender is a topic of discussion in the articles on Goethe's contemporary, the poet Karoline von Günderrode, written by Nadia Schuman and Joanna Raisbeck.

According to Schuman, Günderrode's prolific philosophical and literary contributions defy the explicit misogyny in the German Idealist and Classicist traditions. Schuman argues that the standards for literature in these traditions are not compatible with the roles they implicitly prescribe for women in society and that, "the implications of these ascriptions include the exclusion of prolific women Romantic writers from the canon of German Romantic texts."

Raisbeck focuses on what she identifies as the "epistemological quest" in Günderrode's literary work and how "traces of Kant are superseded by elements of Platonism" in such texts. According to Raisbeck, although Günderrode is seldom mentioned in narratives about Early Romantic philosophy and literature, her work is representative of this period in its attempt to develop metaphysical and epistemological ideas through poetic discourse.

Joseph Trullinger, in "The Polymorphous Political Theology of Novalis and Marcuse," explores the systematic potential in Novalis' critique of Friedrich Schiller's aesthetic idealism for Herbert Marcuse's ideology-critical utopianism. Discussing Novalis' "extension of Schiller's aesthetic education into a theology of Eros," he examines Novalis' organic anthropology, which envisions the poetic reconciliation of death and life (*Eros* and *Thanatos* in the Freudian context of Marcuse's writing), to suggest that Marcuse was mistaken in his negative reading of Novalis in his dissertation, *The German Artist Novel*.

The last section of the book is dedicated to the writings of Friedrich Hölderlin and Friedrich Nietzsche. Gert Hofmann's article on "Hölderlin's Poetics of *Zärtlichkeit*" investigates the "Corporeal Turn of Transcendental Idealism" in Friedrich Hölderlin's latest poetological writings, to be found, for example, in his letters to Casimir Ulrich Böhlendorff, and in some of his late hymnal fragments. His aesthetic of "tenderness" responds to the *corporeal* conditions of human experience "before being manifested in the transcendental realm of human consciousness." Hölderlin undertakes the poetic inversion, rather than reconciliation, of Kant's transcendental antagonism through conceiving of his poetry as a manifestation of the human "apriority of the individual."

Hölderlin thus establishes the *Abgründigkeit* of a lived human apriority, which is also the subject of Ansgar Mohnkern's essay on "*Grund/Abgrund.* On Kant and Hölderlin." His reading of Hölderlin's elegy "Menons Klagen um Diotima" (1802/03), examines Hölderlin's "poetic version of breaking a fundamental promise of German Idealism, the establishment of a fundament itself, by turning from a language of 'ground' (Grund) towards a language of abyss and 'chasm' (Abgrund)."

Hölderlin's "corporeal turn" of idealist aesthetic anthropology paves the ground for the environmentalist drift in Friedrich Nietzsche's philosophical critique of "anthropocentric views of nature." Jennifer Anna Gosetti-Ferencei's article entitled "Nietzsche and Cognitive Ecology" drafts a new reading of Nietzsche's philosophy as "critical cognitive ecology" that elaborates on the "ecocritical critique of human cognition itself."

The volume concludes with Annamaria Lossi's "Overturning Philosophy: Classic and (Anti)-Classic Considerations on Nietzsche's *Ecce Homo*," which suggests that Nietzsche's genuine self-descriptive and self-ironising style of philosophising on one hand contributes "to Nietzsche's rediscovery as an 'anticlassic'" and, on the other hand, shows him "as a 'classic' *sui generis.*"

Bibliography

Behler, Ernst (ed.) (1987): *Philosophy of German Idealism: Fichte, Jacobi, and Schelling*. London: A&C Black, pp. 61–63.

Butler, E. M. (1935): *The Tyranny of Greece over Germany*. Cambridge: Cambridge University Press.

Chaouli, Michel (2011): "A Surfeit in Thinking. Kant's aesthetic ideas." In: *The Yearbook of Comparative Literature 57: Poetic Thinking*, pp. 55–77.

Derrida, Jacques (1998): "Aus Liebe zu Lacan." In: *Vergessen wir nicht – die Psychoanalyse!* Ed. and trans. Hans-Dieter Gondek. Frankfurt a. M.: Suhrkamp, pp. 15–58.

Hegel, Georg Wilhelm Friedrich (1979): *Werke.* Vol. 1. Frankfurt a. M.: Suhrkamp.

Kant, Immanuel (1911): *Kritik der reinen Vernunft* (2nd edition). Akademieausgabe, vol. 3, Berlin: Reimer.

Kant, Immanuel (1913): *Kritik der Urtheilskraft*. Akademieausgabe, vol. 5, Berlin: Reimer.

Reed, T. J. (2013): *Light in Germany: Scenes from an Unknown Enlightenment.* Chicago: Chicago University Press.

Goethe's (Anti-)Classicism and Experientialism

Matthew Bell
Embracing the Enemy: The Problem of Religion in Goethe's "Confessions of a Beautiful Soul"

Abstract: Book VI of Goethe's *Wilhelm Meister's Apprenticeship*, the "Confessions of a Beautiful Soul," occupies an unusual place in literary criticism: a work by a male author that according to feminist criticism is a paradigm of women's autobiography. Adopting some elements of these feminist readings, but in opposition to crude psychoanalytical interpretations, this paper argues that the Beautiful Soul's development occurs according to a set of psychological processes that are well attested in eighteenth-century thought. As Goethe wrote to Schiller in 1795, the Beautiful Soul transposes "the subjective and the objective"—or in the terms of Goethe's poem "The Divine," she creates a private God by projecting her own moral sense onto creation. In doing so she raises the expectation that God and the world will answer her demands of them. In this way she falls foul of Spinoza's stricture that "he who loves God cannot demand that God should love him in return." When creation and the creator fail to meet her demands of them, as they inevitably must, she pays a psychological price in the form of intense bouts of religious melancholy. In this way Goethe applies his own version of the psychologisation of religion such as was practised by e.g. Hume and Holbach, and had its roots in Burton's *Anatomy of Melancholy*. The "Confessions" are thus typical of Weimar Classicism's treatment of religion: an ideological strategy of reframing whereby the (religious) enemy is re-described as a useful and congenial moral-psychological lesson.

The "Confessions of a Beautiful Soul" ("Bekenntnisse einer schönen Seele"), which make up the entirety of Book VI of Goethe's novel *Wilhelm Meister's Apprenticeship* (*Wilhelm Meisters Lehrjahre*), have come to occupy an unusual position in literary criticism. The first feminist interpretation of the "Confessions of a Beautiful Soul," a 1983 essay by Marianne Hirsch, reads Goethe's text as a prototype of a tradition of women's autobiographical narrative. In this tradition the female subject of the narrative develops quite differently from the male subject of the classic "novel of education" (*Bildungsroman*). Whereas the male subject moves towards a harmonious wholeness, both personally and in his engagement with society, the female subject is "excluded from active participation in culture"

https://doi.org/10.1515/9783110586602-003

and is consequently "thrown back on herself" (Hirsch 1983, p. 23). What results is an "intense inwardness" which "allows her to explore and develop spiritually, emotionally, and morally, but often at the expense of other aspects of selfhood" (Hirsch 1983, pp. 23–24). On Hirsch's reading, Goethe's Beautiful Soul rises to a prominent position within her religious confession, Zinzendorfian Pietism, but what drives her development is her refusal to adapt to the social and sexual roles offered to her by male-dominated society. So whilst she does achieve some social recognition, it is marked by exclusion as much as inclusion. The female subject ends up trapped between the private and the public spheres. Far from engaging harmoniously with society, she develops a radical form of inwardness. Hirsch maintains that the Beautiful Soul's half-achieved or distorted development is a prototype of numerous autobiographical narratives by women in the nineteenth and twentieth centuries. (A selection of these women's narratives are the subjects of the rest of the volume that begins with Hirsch's essay.) What is unusual then is that such prominence within a tradition of women's writing should be accorded to a work by a man.

The oddness is made even odder by the fact that the Beautiful Soul and her radical subjectivity are set within the frame of the *Bildungsroman* of Weimar Classicism—odd because the aesthetic and philosophical objectivity to which Weimar Classicism aspires is the very antithesis of what the Beautiful Soul represents. As Susanne Zantop has observed, this antagonism of male and female narratives in *Wilhelm Meister's Apprenticeship* is highly ideological in nature: it is nothing less than a conflict between the values of Weimar Classicism and the values of Goethe's and Schiller's opponents, notably radical subjectivity and dogmatic Christianity. Indeed the conflict is enacted openly within Book VI, when the Beautiful Soul is challenged by her step-uncle, a Spinozist aesthete, who appears to represent Goethe himself. However, on Zantop's reading, by the close of Book VI the Beautiful Soul has acquired so much independence and force that she ends up, as it were, in rebellion against her author:

> In the Beautiful Soul Goethe creates a literary figure that acquires so much independence that it must revolt against him. Writing as the Beautiful Soul, Goethe writes, as it were, against himself. (Zantop 1986, p. 87).[1]

So we might describe the "Confessions of a Beautiful Soul" as a case of anti-Classicism within classicism.

---

[1] All quotations from German are translated by the author of this paper, except where noted otherwise.

These antitheses are clear to see in the contemporary reception of the novel. Reactions were strongly polarised. Wilhelm von Humboldt, who was sympathetic towards Weimar Classicism, dismissed the Beautiful Soul as "a petty, vain and limited soul (eine kleinliche, eitle und beschränkte Seele)" (MA v, p. 658). Opponents of Weimar Classicism, notably Friedrich von Stolberg, celebrated the Beautiful Soul whilst condemning the sexual immorality of the rest of the novel.[2] Modern criticism of the "Confessions of a Beautiful Soul" may be said to have begun with the first systematic attempt to account for this polarisation, Frederick Beharriel's essay "The Hidden Meaning of Goethe's 'Bekenntnisse einer schönen Seele'" of 1970. Beharriel showed that the polarisation in the reception of Book VI reflected the ambivalence of Goethe's portrayal of the Beautiful Soul. Using evidence from the text and from the contemporary reception, Beharriel showed that the religious discourse of Book VI was psychological in nature (Beharriel 1970, p. 37). For instance, the Beautiful Soul's friend Philo encourages her to read the writings of Graf Zinzendorf, "if only in order to acquaint [herself] with a particular psychological phenomenon" (EG, p. 614) ("und wäre es auch nur, um ein psychologisches Phänomen kennen zu lernen") (MA v, p. 398). Beharriel concluded that Goethe had achieved a finely balanced portrayal of the Beautiful Soul. Her asceticism and independence of spirit are admirable, but she becomes a Christian ascetic because she cannot cope with her own sexuality. Her Pietism is the expression of "a form of sexual neurosis, a sublimation, as Freud would later have said, of neurotically suppressed sexual energy" (Beharriel 1970, p. 48). However, as Zantop rightly observes, Beharriel's Freudian "hidden meaning" is a poor fit for the Beautiful Soul's experience. The sexual dynamics of Book VI are in no sense hidden; the Beautiful Soul is fully aware of them (Zantop 1986, p. 78). Moreover, Philo's reference to a "psychological phenomenon," the only use of the term *psychology* in Book VI, has nothing to do with sexuality and everything to do with religion. Zantop's objection to Beharriel is supported by Goethe's own diagnosis of the underlying psychological dynamic. Writing to Schiller while completing Book VI in March 1795, Goethe emphasises religion and does not mention sexuality: "my novel's religious book," he writes, "rests upon the most noble deceptions and the most delicate confusion of the subjective with the objective" ("das religiöse Buch meines Romans [beruht] auf den edelsten Täuschungen und auf der zartesten Verwechslung des subjektiven und objektiven") (to Schiller, 18 March 1795, MA viii/1, p. 70). This is clearly at odds with the Freudian sexual neurosis posited by Beharriel, which is anything but "noble" and "delicate."

---

[2] See Schiller to Goethe, 23 July 1796 (MA viii/1, p. 222).

Whilst justly criticising Beharriel's Freudian reading, Zantop does not offer a psychological alternative to it and instead takes the "confusion of the subjective with the objective" in a very general sense; it relates to a fundamental ambiguity which she attributes to Goethe, literary critics, and the genre of autobiography in general (Zantop 1986, p. 75). It is certainly true that Book VI has multiple layers of meaning and some delicate ambiguities, but I believe it would be wrong to follow Zantop in overlooking the rather obvious meaning of Goethe's words, or indeed to follow Beharriel in construing the psychology of Book VI in terms of a Freudian sexual neurosis. There is a psychological dynamic at work in Book VI, and it is not Freudian. Rather, the "confusion of the subjective with the objective" refers to the tendency of the Beautiful Soul to project her own powerful subjective moral qualities onto objective reality. In order to make objective reality conform to her subjectivity, she installs her own moral sense in the place normally occupied by objective reality, constructing as she does so a private God, which is essentially just a projection of her subjectivity onto the objective realm. To be sure, the "deceptions" about which Goethe wrote to Schiller are "noble" and the "confusion" is "delicate" because they derive from the lovable and admirable impulse to project onto the world the moral goodness that is in oneself. The Beautiful Soul is in fact an example of the process described by Goethe in his subtle crypto-Spinozist poem "The Divine" ("Das Göttliche"):

> Noble let man be,
> Helpful and good;
> For that alone
> Differentiates
> Him from all beings
> That we know.
>
> Hail to the unknown,
> Loftier beings
> We imagine!
> Let man be like them;
> His example teach us
> To believe in them. (EG, pp. 13–14, adapted).
>
> (Edel sei der Mensch,
> Hülfreich und gut!
> Denn das allein
> Unterscheidet ihn
> Von allen Wesen
> Die wir kennen.
>
> Heil den unbekannten
> Höhern Wesen,
> Die wir ahnden!

Ihnen gleiche der Mensch;
Sein Beispiel lehr uns
Jene glauben.) (MA ii/1, p. 90).

As the second strophe implies, the "higher beings" have no objective existence; they are only intuited ("ahnden"), and in order for them to be believed ("glauben"), humanity must serve as an example ("Beispiel") for them. In other words, we create the divine and fill it with content drawn from our own, human morality. Faith in the divine is a kind of moral trick we play on ourselves, albeit with the noblest motivation.[3] The subjective is confused with the objective.

The present reading of the "Confessions" thus has two aims. In the first place, by describing the psychological dynamic that plays out in the "Confessions of a Beautiful Soul," it supplies a piece that has been missing from the criticism of Goethe's novel. More generally it adds to our understanding of Goethe's thought during the period of Weimar Classicism and indeed of the history of Enlightenment thought at the end of the eighteenth century. The psychology of the Beautiful Soul is connected to the Spinozism that dominates the latter books of Goethe's novel because this psychology is—structurally and in some of its detail—similar to the moral and psychological arguments against religious faith in Spinoza's *Ethics* and *Tractatus*. Goethe's commitment to Spinoza remained deep even in the mid-1790s, as Schings has suggested, and is denied, implicitly at any rate, by Nicholas Boyle.[4] Moreover, the psychological critiques of religion developed by the radical Enlightenment, to use Jonathan Israel's term, persisted right to the end of the eighteenth century. On this reading of the "Confessions," the "confusion of the subjective with the objective" is part of an underlying psychological dynamic that we find also in other works by Goethe and other authors (for instance in Schiller's *Der Geisterseher*). The Beautiful Soul's descent into deep despair, before she eventually discovers the signs of her salvation, follows a pattern that was familiar to Goethe and his contemporaries from Calvinist and Pietist conversion narratives.[5] Hundreds if not thousands of these conversion narratives were produced during the seventeenth and eighteenth centuries, and they attained some prominence in the literature of the period, most famously in Bunyan's *Pilgrim's Progress* and Defoe's *Robinson Crusoe*. Goethe would also have encountered material of this kind at first hand during his Pietist

---

[3] Compare Lange's similar though differently accented Spinozistic reading of the poem (Lange 2009, pp. 168–170).
[4] It is the comparative absence of references to Spinoza that is striking in Boyle 2000.
[5] On German Pietist conversion narratives and their relation to English Puritan literature, see Damrau 2006.

phase in the years 1768 to 1770 and from his friendship with Susanna von Klettenberg—who was, of course, the model for the Beautiful Soul. He made poetic use of the Pietist conversion narrative several times, notably in the poetic fragment "Prometheus" and two passages of *Faust. Part I* written in the late 1790s.[6] Needless to say, Goethe's treatment of the conversion narrative differs in certain crucial respects from the Pietist originals. For example, whereas the Calvinists and Pietists understood the nadir of the Christian's journey to faith in terms of despair, for Goethe it was an instance of melancholia.[7] In rewriting the conversion narrative in this way, Goethe was following a tradition that reached back to Robert Burton's *Anatomy of Melancholy* in which the term "religious melancholy" was coined, in part as a means of stigmatizing low-church enthusiasm. Burton's innovation gave rise to a tradition of psychologizing religious belief, such as we find in Hume's *Natural History of Religion* (1757) and Holbach's *The Sacred Contagion, or Natural History of Superstition* (*La Contagion sacrée, ou histoire naturelle de la superstition*, 1768). That is to say, the Calvinists and Pietists construed their journey in terms of a loss of faith, whereas Goethe, following Burton and the radical Enlightenment, construed it in psychological terms. Another important influence on Goethe's treatment of the conversion narrative was his reading of Spinoza, for as Goethe claims in his autobiography *Poetry and Truth* (*Dichtung und Wahrheit*), it was the teachings of Spinoza that showed him a way out of his own melancholic subjectivity in the early 1770s (MA xvi, p. 667).[8]

The Beautiful Soul's melancholy journey begins in her eighth year, when she suffers a haemorrhage that confines her to bed for nine-months. The convalescence, she says, laid "the foundation for my whole way of thinking" (EG, p. 590). ("Während des neun monatlichen Krankenlagers [...] ward, so wie mich dünkt, der Grund zu meiner ganzen Denkart gelegt.") (MA v, p. 360). During these nine months she is physically inactive and has no direct engagement with external reality. Her father compensates for her inactivity by bringing her dead biological specimens, including "all sorts of [...] anatomical specimens, human skin, bones and mummified objects" (EG, p. 590) ("anatomische Präparaten, Menschenhaut, Knochen, Mumien und dergleichen." (MA v, p. 360). The specimens are significant in two ways. First, they represent death and are at the root of a network of melancholy symbols of death in Book VI, including

---

6 See Bell 2002.
7 On the distinction between despair and melancholia, see Stachniewski 1991, p. 27.
8 On the reception of Spinoza in the *Apprenticeship*, see Schings 1988.

the bloodstained martyred Christ on his cross.⁹ Second, rather than a lived experience of nature, the Beautiful Soul has only indirect, intellectual experience, an experience filtered through consciousness. The weakness of her body is accompanied by a compensating hypertrophy of consciousness, by the kind of natural compensatory economy of forces that Goethe employed in his studies of animal metamorphosis (Bell 1994, pp. 245–251). The hypertrophy of consciousness points again in the direction of melancholia, for as Wolf Lepenies has argued, a hallmark of late eighteenth-century German melancholia is the "enforced hypertrophy of the realm of reflection," such as we find in Goethe's *Werther* (Lepenies 1998, p. 83).

Inactivity and the consequent hypertrophy of consciousness lay the foundations for her confusion of the subjective and the objective. Having developed a powerful sense of her own moral qualities, and being little versed in the ways of the world, she compensates for her lack of experience by projecting her own highly developed moral qualities onto creation and the creator. Even at this early stage her God is an "Invisible Being," that is to say a being that has no relation to objective reality, is separate from his creation, and has only moral attributes.¹⁰ She now begins to project her own moral characteristics onto the world around her. A world that merely exists is not enough for her; the world must have the same moral qualities and loving nature as she has. Hence she demands to be surrounded with things that can reciprocate her love: "I couldn't play with dolls any longer, I wanted objects that would return my love." (EG, p. 590) ("Ich konnte nicht einmal mit Puppen spielen, ich verlangte nach Wesen, die meine Liebe erwiderten.") (MA v, p. 361). This demand for moral reciprocation will turn out to be a problem, for two connected reasons. For one thing, demanding moral reciprocation from the world raises unfulfillable expectations. The world simply does not measure up to our high moral demands of it; it will not return our feelings, but is likely to disappoint us. Other people, with their imperfections and weaknesses, are a repeated source of disappointment. Sinfulness represents a particular challenge. The idea of human sinfulness

---

9 On Goethe's well-known dislike of representations of Christ crucified in medieval and renaissance art, see Luke 1988–89.
10 "unsichtbares Wesen" (MA v, p. 359). The "invisible" God is a consistent feature of her narrative, whether in the form of "the Invisible One" (EG, pp. 591, 593, 600, 609; "der Unsichtbare": MA v, pp. 361, 366, 376, 390), "the Invisible Friend" (EG, pp. 597, 601, 610, 610, 612; "der unsichtbare Freund": MA v, pp. 372, 378, 392, 395, 421), "the Invisible Being" (EG, pp. 590, 602, 628; "das unsichtbare Wesen": MA v, pp. 361, 380, 421) or "the Invisible Guide" (EG, pp. 610, 610; "der unsichtbare Führer": MA v, pp. 391, 392).

is foreign to her; she is not aware of having sinned or of witnessing the sin of others:

> The thing, that evil thing that has never been explained, which separates us from the Being we owe our life to, the eternal Being by whom all that we call Life is sustained, the thing that is called Sin—this I did not yet know. (EG, p. 610).[11]

> (Das Ding, das noch nie erklärte böse Ding, das uns von dem Wesen trennt, von dem wir das Leben empfangen haben und aus dem alles, was Leben genannt werden soll, sich unterhalten muß, das Ding das man Sünde nennt, kannte ich noch gar nicht.) (MA v, p. 391).

However, her French tutor, who somewhat ominously "had seen much of the world" (EG, p. 591) ("hatte die Welt gesehen") (MA v, p. 363), insists on warning her that her romantic daydreams are dangerous. Not only are the kind of romantic fictions she likes prone to turn suddenly into real-life attachments—they can, as he puts it, "soon become quite serious" (EG, p. 593) ("bald ernsthaft werden") (MA v, p. 365)—but also many of the men even in good society are infected with syphilis:

> My teacher had also told me in confidence that most of these disreputable customers constituted a danger not only to a girl's virtue but also to her health. So I cringed at the thought of them and became really concerned if one of them somehow got too close to me. I avoided cups and glasses, and even chairs they had been sitting on. As a result I became completely isolated, both morally and physically, and all the nice things they said to me I proudly took for incense that was scattered out of a sense of guilt. (EG, p. 594).

> (Überdies hatte mir mein Alter einmal vertraulich eröffnet, daß mit den meisten dieser leidigen Bursche nicht allein die Tugend sondern auch die Gesundheit eines Mädchens in Gefahr sei. Nun graute mir erst vor ihnen, und ich war schon besorgt, wenn mir einer auf irgend eine Weise zu nahe kam. Ich hütete mich vor Gläsern und Tassen wie vor dem Stuhle, von dem einer aufgestanden war. Auf diese Weise war ich moralisch und physisch sehr isoliert, und alle die Artigkeiten, die sie mir sagten, nahm ich stolz für schuldigen Weihrauch auf.) (MA v, p. 366–367).

The sudden realisation that she is surrounded by a world of sin and disease, of contagious moral and physical infirmity, leads to an anxious overreaction and to isolation. A pattern for her future behaviour is thus established: the shattering failure of the world to live up to her expectations of it makes her reluctant to engage with the world, so that she endures long periods of reclusiveness that only deepen her sense of her own moral uniqueness.

---

11 See also EG, p. 611 (MA v, p. 394).

Expecting reciprocation is also problematic in the sense that a love that demands reciprocation is ultimately selfish and narcissistic, for the moral reciprocation it demands is only ever a projection of our own moral qualities. No matter how noble these are, they can only ever be ours and therefore imperfect. This is why Spinoza proposed that "he who loves God cannot strive that God should love him in return" (Spinoza 1996, p. 169). In Book XIV of *Poetry and Truth* Goethe quotes this example of Spinoza's "boundless unselfishness": "here I found," he says, "some pacification of my passions, there seemed to open up before me a grand and free vista over the sensuous and moral worlds." ("[...] grenzenlose Uneigennützigkeit [...] ich fand hier eine Beruhigung meiner Leidenschaften, es schien sich mir eine große und freie Aussicht über die sinnliche und sittliche Welt aufzutun)." (MA xvi, p. 667). In the grip of her own subjectivity, the Beautiful Soul expects God to reciprocate her love, in direct contravention of Spinoza's principle. When her marriage to Narcissus comes to depend on his promotion at court, she prays to her "Invisible Friend" for his success. But she receives neither comfort nor indeed any response from her God: "I felt like someone wishing to warm himself in the sun when the shadow obstructs him. [...] I remained unwarmed, felt no reciprocity, could not make out His answer." (EG, p. 601–602) ("Es war mir wie einem, der sich an der Sonne wärmen will, und dem etwas im Wege steht, das Schatten macht. [...] so blieb ich kalt; ich fühlte seine Rückwirkung nicht und konnte seine Antwort nicht vernehmen.") (MA v, p. 378–379). Her God's failure to reciprocate pitches her into a bout of deep melancholia: "I would often go to bed weeping, and get up next morning after a sleepless night with nothing changed. I needed strong support and this was not to be vouchsafed me by God [...]" (EG, p. 602) ("Ich legte mich oft mit Tränen zu Bette, und stand nach einer schlaflosen Nacht auch wieder so auf; ich bedurfte einer kräftigen Unterstützung, und die verlieh mir Gott nicht [...].") (MA v, p. 379).

Her tendency to project her moral purity onto others leaves her once more totally unprepared when her friend Philo reveals his sinfulness to her. The effect of this sudden insight is to cast a melancholy pall of darkness over the Beautiful Soul's whole spirit: "The thought that I was no better than he came over me and descended like a cloud which darkened my mind." (EG, p. 611) ("Der Gedanke, du bist nicht besser als er, stieg wie eine kleine Wolke vor mir auf, breitete sich nach und nach aus und verfinsterte meine ganze Seele.") (MA v, p. 394). Scrutinizing herself, she finds her own salvation in doubt. The way out of her condition is through faith, and Zinzendorf's teaching shows her where to find it—in the death of Christ. But before she can find faith, she must first descend into the deepest religious melancholy:

"Grant me such Faith, oh almighty God!" was the prayer of my heavy heart. I leaned over the little table at which I was sitting, hiding my tear-stained face in my hands. I was in the state that we must be in if God is to hear our prayer; and how rarely are we in that state!

How can I find the proper words to describe what I felt at that moment? A strong impulse lifted my soul to the cross on which Jesus died. I cannot call it other than an impulse, like that which carries one toward an absent friend, someone one loves dearly, making a connection that is more intense, more real than one would have imagined. My soul drew nigh to the incarnate, the crucified One, and at that moment I knew what Faith was. (EG, p. 613).

(Nun, Allmächtiger! so schenke mir Glauben, flehte ich einst in dem größten Druck des Herzens. Ich lehnte mich auf einen kleinen Tisch, an dem ich saß, und verbarg mein beträntes Gesicht in meinen Händen. Hier war ich in der Lage, in der man sein muß, wenn Gott auf unser Gebet achten soll, und in der man selten ist. / Ja wer nur schildern könnte, was ich da fühlte. Ein Zug brachte meine Seele nach dem Kreuze hin, an dem Jesus einst erblaßte; ein Zug war es, ich kann es nicht anders nennen; demjenigen völlig gleich, wodurch unsre Seele zu einem abwesenden Geliebten geführt wird, ein Zunahen, das vermutlich viel wesentlicher und wahrhafter ist, als wir nicht vermuten. So nahte meine Seele dem Menschgewordnen und am Kreuz gestorbenen, und in dem Augenblicke wußte ich, was Glauben war.) (MA v, p. 396).

Her conversion to Pietism comes in the Zinzendorfian form of a vision of Christ's suffering. Having found faith through Christ's passion she becomes an avid churchgoer, and begins to find solace in Zinzendorf's hymns. She even becomes sociable, mixing in the Pietist circles that have come to dominate the city's factional religious life.

With the drama of her conversion now behind her, in the last third of the book the Beautiful Soul faces challenges of a different nature. Goethe told Schiller that the "Confessions" looked backwards to Books I to V of *Wilhelm Meister's Apprenticeship* and forwards to Books VII and VIII,[12] and critics, for instance Hellmut Ammerlahn, have assumed that the first two thirds of the "Confessions" are analeptic and the last third proleptic (Ammerlahn 2003, pp. 215–216). In fact things are not quite that neatly programmatic. The last third of Book VI does introduce a new set of characters, some of whom will feature in Books VII and VIII, among them the wealthy uncle, who arranges the family's future by seeking out a husband for the Beautiful Soul's youngest sister. The marriage is managed in meticulous detail by the uncle at one of his estates, in something of a *Gesamtkunstwerk*, with the architecture, art, music and activities all ordered to the highest aesthetic standards. Part of the function of the last third of the book, then, is to introduce new aesthetic concerns, indeed a form of aesthetic existence that has some similarities with and can even be seen as a prelude to Weimar Classi-

---

[12] To Schiller, 18 March 1795 (MA viii/1, 70).

cism itself. Now for the first time the Beautiful Soul has an experience of art rich enough to match the depth of her spiritual convictions. Art, it is suggested, can match and even replace religion (Boyle 2000, p. 367). Indeed the replacement of positive religion by art is central to the uncle's project. The uncle's opinions on religion are rather less palatable to the Beautiful Soul than his artistic productions, or they would be if she fully understood their purport, for the uncle turns out to be a crypto-Spinozist. What he says seems innocuous enough:

> "If we can imagine," he said to me one day, "that the Creator of the world should take on the form of His creature and inhabit the world for a time in this guise, then this human creation must seem perfect indeed if the Creator Himself could ally Himself so closely with it. In the concept of humanity there cannot be a contradiction with the idea of godhead, and if we often feel remoteness and difference from the godhead, then it is our urgent responsibility not to dwell on our weaknesses and faults like the devil's advocate but to seek out our finest qualities by which we can legitimately confirm our godlikeness." (EG, p. 619).

> (Wenn wir uns, sagte er einmal, als möglich denken können, daß der Schöpfer der Welt selbst die Gestalt seiner Kreatur angenommen, und auf ihre Art und Weise sich eine Zeitlang auf der Welt befunden habe; so muß uns dieses Geschöpf schon unendlich vollkommen erscheinen, weil sich der Schöpfer so innig damit vereinigen konnte. Es muß also in dem Begriff des Menschen kein Widerspruch mit dem Begriff der Gottheit liegen, und wenn wir auch oft eine gewisse Unähnlichkeit und Entfernung von ihr empfinden, so ist es doch um desto mehr unsere Schuldigkeit, nicht immer wie der Advokat des bösen Geistes nur auf die Blößen und Schwächen unserer Natur zu sehen, sondern eher alle Vollkommenheiten aufzusuchen, wodurch wir die Ansprüche unsrer Gottähnlichkeit bestätigen können.) (MA v, p. 406).

This is a lightly veiled but doctrinally pure Spinozist humanism. The mission of Christ is entertained only as an unreal possibility ("if we can imagine [...] that") and is brought into complete conformity with philosophy ("in the concept of humanity there cannot be a contradiction with the idea of godhead"), as in the Spinozan doctrine that there can be no truths in theology that are not also truths in philosophy (see Israel 2001, p. 194). The unspoken (Spinozan) premise is that God is co-extensive with his creation—*deus sive natura*. This dangerous "theology" is sugared with a more palatable though still strongly anti-Pietist moral message: humans should not focus on sin; they should try instead to conform to their own presumptive "godlikeness" and so be the best they can. We return then to Goethe's crypto-Spinozist poem "The Divine." The Beautiful Soul is sharp enough to realise that her uncle is saying something heterodox and dressing it up for her benefit. His philosophy challenges Pietism's melancholy and its focus on the sinfulness of natural man. Our dealings with God should be driven not by a melancholy passion but by a disinterested philosophical appreciation of God's attributes. This is the underlying motive of the uncle's Spinozist challenge to her religiosity. Spinoza's "intellectual love of God" ("amor dei intellectualis") involves no projection of the self onto God, no confusion of subjective and objective.

The structural function of the uncle's crypto-Spinozist discourses is not to put an end to the Beautiful Soul's spiritualism—even in its philosophical moments the novel is far too provisional and dynamic for that. As we see in Books VII and VIII, the uncle and his friends and successors have been engaged in a somewhat makeshift and uncoordinated rear-guard action against the ills of modern society, determined to reform things but unable to agree among themselves what form the reforms should take. Disunity and disagreement are built into the novel's fabric.

Paedagogical theory is a particular source of disagreement. The younger sister's orphaned children are educated under the uncle's supervision by a mysterious French Abbé— a rather obvious allusion to the Savoyard vicar of Rousseau's *Émile*. The Beautiful Soul, to her chagrin, is not allowed any part in their education and makes her disapproval of the Abbé's methods clear:

> But one thing I cannot condone about these educators, is that they deprive children of anything that might lead to their communing with themselves and with their Invisible, and only true Friend. And I am often irritated with my uncle that for this reason he thinks I would be detrimental to the children. Nobody is really tolerant in practice, for however much someone may assure us that he is leaving a person to his own desires and inclinations, in effect he does all he can to exclude them from activities not acceptable to himself. (EG, p. 628–629).
>
> (Aber das, was ich nicht an diesen Erziehern billigen kann, ist, daß sie alles von den Kindern zu entfernen suchen, was sie zu dem Umgange mit sich selbst und mit dem unsichtbaren, einzigen treuen Freunde führen könne. Ja es verdrießt mich oft von dem Oheim, daß er mich deshalb für die Kinder für gefährlich hält. Im Praktischen ist doch kein Mensch tolerant! Denn wer auch versichert, daß er jedem seine Art und Wesen gerne lassen wolle, sucht doch immer diejenigen von der Tätigkeit auszuschließen, die nicht so denken wie er.) (MA v, p. 421).

The uncle's appropriation of the children is part of the proleptic function of Book VI. The children point forwards to Books VII and VIII which are dominated by the question of how the characters are to become socially engaged. An isolated figure, prey to illusions and resistant to socialisation, the Beautiful Soul has to be side-lined: the logic of the novel and the prospects of society require it. Still, as Zantop rightly argues, she is far from being a silent victim of social progress (Zantop 1986, p. 87). Her resistance is made clear when she observes, acerbically but with some justice, that the uncle's tolerance of her views in their earlier conversations was merely theoretical; in practice he is an intolerant as anyone. It is entirely in keeping with her intelligence and independence of mind that she should recognise his shortcomings. It is also important that her resistance features prominently at the end of Book VI. Even if she has no say in the children's education, their memories of her will be mentioned in Books VII and VIII, and her independence of spirit lives on in them: her niece Natalie will voice even sharper criticism of the uncle's educational methods than her aunt did (EG, pp. 693, 697; MA v, pp. 522, 529). The Beautiful Soul's resistance lives on in Natalie and contributes to the diversity of the Society of the Tower (*Turmgesellschaft*) and the polyphony of the novel. Read in this way the "Confessions" add one more to the roster of "difficult" characters whose passions hinder their socialisation to varying degrees and who have to be accommodated within or excluded from the novel's increasingly utopian trajectory: Wilhelm, Mignon, the Harpist, Aurelie, Lothario, Lydie, Natalie. Goethe admitted, and many readers have since found, that *Wilhelm Meister's Apprenticeship* is resistant to its own utopian ambitions (to Schiller, 9 July 1796, MA viii/1, 208). It is in this sense that we should understand Zantop's view that the Beautiful Soul develops and retains her own aesthetic value within the novel, and that the novel of Weimar Classicism contains its own anti-classicism.

Bibliography

Ammerlahn, Hellmut (2003): *Imagination und Wahrheit. Goethes Künstler-Bildungsroman. "Wilhelm Meisters Lehrjahre": Struktur, Symbolik, Poetologie*. Würzburg: Königshausen & Neumann.

Beharriel, Frederick (1970): "The Hidden Meaning of Goethe's 'Bekenntnisse einer schönen Seele'". In: Sammons, Jeffrey L. / Schürer, Ernst (Eds.): *Lebendige Form: Interpretationen zur deutschen Literatur*. Munich: Fink, pp. 37–62.

Bell, Matthew (1994): *Goethe's Naturalistic Anthropology: Man and other Plants*. Oxford: Oxford University Press.

Bell, Matthew (2002): "Faust and the British Tradition of Religious Melancholy." In: Boyle, Nicholas / Guthrie, John (Eds.): *Goethe and the English-Speaking World*. Rochester, NY, and Woodbridge, Suffolk: Camden House, pp. 71–83.

Boyle, Nicholas (2000): *Goethe, the Poet and the Age, vol. ii: Revolution and Renunciation, 1790–1830*. Oxford: Oxford University Press.

Damrau, Peter (2006): *The Reception of English Puritan Literature in Germany*. London: Maney for the MHRA and IGRS.

Goethe, Johann Wolfgang von (1985–98): *Sämtliche Werke nach Epochen seines Schaffens*. Ed. Richter, Karl et al. Munich: Hanser.

Goethe, Johann Wolfgang von (2016): *The Essential Goethe*. Ed. Bell, Matthew. Princeton, NJ: Princeton University Press.

Hirsch, Marianne (1983): "Spiritual Bildung: The Beautiful Soul as Paradigm." In: Abel, Elizabeth / Hirsch, Marianne / Langland, Elizabeth (Eds.): *The Voyage In: Fictions of Female Development*. Hanover, NH: University Press of New England, pp. 23–48.

Israel, Jonathan I. (2001): *Radical Enlightenment: Philosophy and the Making of Modernity 1650–1750*. Oxford: Oxford University Press.
Lange, Horst (2009): "Isaac, Iphigeneia, Christ: Human Sacrifice and the Semiotics of Divine Intentions in Goethe." In: *Publications of the English Goethe Society* 78, pp. 166–188.
Lepenies, Wolf (1998): *Melancholie und Gesellschaft*. Frankfurt a. M.: Suhrkamp.
Luke, David (1988–89): "'Vor deinem Jammerkreuz': Goethe's Attitude to Christian Belief." In: *Publications of the English Goethe Society* 59, pp. 35–58.
Schings, Hans-Jürgen (1988): "Goethes Wilhelm Meister und Spinoza." In: Wittkowski, Wolfgang (Ed.): *Verantwortung und Utopie: Zur Literatur der Goethezeit. Ein Symposium*. Tübingen: Niemeyer, pp. 57–69.
Spinoza, Benedict de (1996): *Ethics*. Trans. Curley, Edwin. London: Penguin.
Stachniewski, John (1991): *The Persecutory Imagination: English Puritanism and the Literature of Religious Despair*. Oxford: Oxford University Press.
Zantop, Susanne (1986): "Eigenes Selbst und fremde Formen: Goethes 'Bekenntnisse einer schönen Seele'." In: *Goethe Yearbook* 3, pp. 73–92.

Abbreviations

EG = Goethe, Johann Wolfgang von (2016): *The Essential Goethe*. Ed. Bell, Matthew. Princeton, NJ: Princeton University Press.
MA = Goethe, Johann Wolfgang von (1985–98): *Sämtliche Werke nach Epochen seines Schaffens*. Ed. Richter, Karl et al. Munich: Hanser.

Juliana de Albuquerque
"Meine Schwester Natalie ist hiervon ein lebhaftes Beispiel:" *Bildung* and Gender in Goethe's *Wilhelm Meisters Lehrjahre*

Abstract: In Goethe's *Wilhelm Meisters Lehrjahre* the famous chapter on the Beautiful Soul is the portrait of an individuality that gradually takes flight from herself into a religious pathology. It has been argued by a number of scholars, including Marianne Hirsch (1983) and Catriona MacLeod (1998), that this is intended by Goethe to be taken as a paradigm of *Bildung* for women, as the best that a woman of exceptional sensitivity could hope to achieve in his society and time. In this paper I challenge this interpretation. I argue that Goethe's notion of *Bildung* is an ideal of self-mastery that is valid for men and women equally. To this end I draw a comparison between the characters of the Beautiful Soul and her niece Natalie, the character Wilhelm seeks throughout the novel and who eventually becomes his wife. Goethe juxtaposes these two figures at several points to contrast images of health and progression with images of illness and paralysis. Goethe's ideal of *Bildung* has deep psychological and therapeutic implications that are still relevant—it offers us the ideal of the individual, whether man or woman, who in the face of the circumstances of their lives learn to master their responses to them, and overcome the constraints imposed by society to achieve a genuine expression of his or her personality.

1 Introduction

Wilhelm Meisters Lehrjahre is the story of a young man who, spurred by the failure of a love affair with an actress, leaves the comfort of a traditional, bourgeois family in pursuit of a life of adventure with an itinerant theatre troupe.

During the time he spends with the traveling players, Wilhelm encounters a kaleidoscope of characters, from many backgrounds. The nature and motivation of some of these characters appear to the reader to be relatively transparent. For example, the disillusioned actor Melina, the flirtatious Philine and her easygoing, misogynistic friend Laertes, the pragmatic theatre manager Serlo, and other lesser characters such as the Abbé and the Doctor.

Others characters, however, are overtly mysterious and remain for a long time hard to pin down. Their nature and history are hidden from us. Characters here include the androgynous child Mignon, the melancholic Harpist, and the Amazon (who we later discover in her true identity as Natalie).

The character who combines both mystery and seeming transparency is the Beautiful Soul. She makes her appearance in the book only as the narrating voice of a manuscript about her own life's confession.

This confession of the Beautiful Soul represents an interruption to the main narrative of Wilhelm Meister and the connection of this with the rest of the story is at first far from clear. Up to this point in the book, Wilhelm's development has been achieved through a restless exchange of experiences with the world in which the inevitable disappointments of life never quell for very long Wilhelm's essentially generous and optimistic nature.

"Bekenntnisse einer schönen Seele" represents the first step into extended self-reflection in the novel, and remains the most sustained exercise of this kind it contains. It also represents in one important respect the antithesis of Wilhelm's experience: the disappointments of life gradually overcome the Beautiful Soul, causing her seek with ever-more determination the world of the spirit divorced from the exigencies of everyday life.

An influential contemporary reading of Wilhelm Meister Lehrjahre associated with scholars such as such as Marianne Hirsch (1983) and Catriona MacLeod (1998) suggests that "Bekenntnisse einer schönen Seele" is a depiction of what Goethe believes to be the inevitably frustrated fate of the exceptional woman in his own society (Hirsch 1983, p. 28).

Hirsch writes that "Bekenntnisse einer schönen Seele" is to be seen as the "paradigm" of female *Bildung* within what she calls Goethe's "androcentric" novel. She maintains that as a prototype of the *Bildungsroman*, *Wilhelm Meisters Lehrjahre* "very clearly reserves Wilhelm's type of development for young men, but it presents in this self-contained insert, Wilhelm's counterpart" (Hirsch 1983, p. 26). Wilhelm she sees as an essentially superficial, lacking in *Innigkeit*, and describes his character as *"unpsychological"* (Hirsch 1983, p. 29). She says that: "in many ways, the Beautiful Soul is the *antithesis* of Wilhelm who has an aversion to reflection, is unable to write his own autobiography, and enjoys living in the present by repressing memory and the past" (Hirsch 1983, pp. 28–29).

Taking a different perspective, Catriona MacLeod argues that Goethe attempts what she calls "an extreme aestheticization" of the female characters in *Wilhelm Meisters Lehrjahre*. She means by this, a development of the female characters into aesthetic types that reflect male desires and fears, but that are nevertheless ultimately devoid of true independence and their own inner life.

MacLeod raises interesting questions about the extent to which Goethe may have remained intellectually and artistically imprisoned in the social prejudices of his day, and whether he remained inhibited by the patriarchal assumptions of his time, perhaps not fully able to see how these condemned women to a restricted autonomy.

There is food for thought here. But I suggest that MacLeod, like Hirsch before her, does not do full justice to the underlying challenge that Goethe offers in his novel to the moral prejudices and hypocrisies of his time. These scholars also, in my view, neglect the ways in which the book looks forward to a new relationship between the sexes of mutual respect based on a shared ideal of autonomy.

As more recent scholarship on Goethe's Wilhelm Meister suggests, he challenges the moral prejudices of his time by describing relationships in terms of elective affinities, a concept that implies a certain degree of fluidity and non-exclusiveness, as noted by Susan E. Gustafson in her book *Goethe's Families of the Heart* (2017).

Gustafson's reading of Goethe is relevant to this paper in two important respects:

First, it stresses the psychological aspects of Goethe's literary writings which are important for an understanding of the question autonomy and gender in his work as a whole, both for society and the individual. In this respect, we should remember that *Wilhelm Meisters Lehrjahre* (1795–6) was published at a moment in the intellectual history of Europe that had witnessed some of the first attempts to understand human psychology in terms of development from childhood to adult life, as well as in terms of the interplay between environment and the individual's psychological make-up.

The formation of individual psychology and the discovery of the individual's inner life can be credited to works of literature such as Jean-Jacques Rousseau's *Confessions* (1782) and Karl Philipp Moritz's *Anton Reiser* (1785-90).

Second, it approaches Goethe as a writer who was more sensitive to the question of gender than McCleod or Hirsch give him credit for. One could even suggest based on Gustafson's reading that Goethe's work contributes to the discussion of women and sex in what the historian Jonathan Israel calls Radical Enlightenment. In his book, Israel argues that the ideas of the Enlightenment had begun to have tangible and visible effects on the social relations between the sexes as early as the 1790s.

According to Israel, the radical philosophy of the seventeenth century that was inspired by Cartesian and Spinozist naturalism, enabled thinkers such as Lambert to question the common assumption of male superiority and write that "the tyranny of men exists by force rather than by natural law"[1] (Lambert

---

[1] My translation.

in Israel 2002, p. 83). This allowed the increasing participation of women in the intellectual debate for the first time as "an audience and an active presence" (Israel 2002, p. 84). One example of such woman is the Princess Sophie Charlotte from the house of Hannover, who had always been a keen advocate for the importance of philosophy: "Leibniz [...] respected her as a philosophical force in her own right, and in later years the two frequently discussed the further evolution of the European philosophical scene, as well as of his own system" (Israel 2002, p. 85).

I suggest that Goethe's notion of *Bildung* is clearly conceived by him as an ideal of self-mastery for each individual, whether man or woman. For Goethe, the crucial question is how far an individual, of either sex, can master his or her pattern of response to the circumstances that life confront them with and overcome the constraints imposed by society upon the fruitful and complete expression of his or her personality. The ideal of *Bildung* developed by Goethe in the novel emphasises the individual's quest to achieve self-realisation through the mastery of psychological traits within oneself and social demands imposed from without. What Wilhelm Meister illustrates is that we only come close to this ideal through living in the world. For example, Wilhelm gets involved with art, but art not as an end but as a means to something. As T.J. Reed comments:

> Wilhelm's education is a profoundly natural process, an unfolding of what is in the character rather than a result of external chance. Much that happens seems fated, even benevolently organized—as often in novels, it turns out to be a small world and a coherent one. Yet these comforting connections are only a quasi-allegorical framework for an inner growth. (Reed 1984, p. 63).

When we consider the female characters in the novel as a whole, it becomes clear, I suggest, that Goethe by no means intended the Beautiful Soul as the inevitable fate of the exceptional woman. As scholars like Jane Brown (2014) and Gustafson (2017) have emphasised, Goethe creates characters that are to be seen as metaphors or partial allegories of each other while portraying unique individuals. Each is potentially in part the others. The Beautiful Soul which contains a story of *Bildung* within the larger story of Wilhelm's own *Bildung* should be seen as potentially Wilhelm's own, just as Wilhelm's own is potentially that of the Beautiful Soul. Goethe develops characters not in order to derive moral lessons from them, but rather to show how each one, encountering different circumstances and possessing different character traits, is nevertheless, to some extent, potentially the others.

This becomes particularly evident when we compare the character of the Beautiful Soul with that of the central figure of Natalie. At several points of the novel, Goethe juxtaposes these two characters to give us contrasting images of different patterns of strength and development while bearing in mind that we are not expected to make absolute judgments of one or the other.

1.1 Goethe's distinction between health and sickness

As Robert J. Richard remarks, the contrast between health and sickness is a familiar theme in Goethe's work. Whether accurately or not, Eckermann famously reports Goethe as saying on 2 April 1829 that: "The classic I call the healthy, and the romantic the sick"[2] (Eckermann 2006, p. 310). ("Das Klassische nenne ich das Gesunde, und das Romantische das Kranke.") We cannot be certain whether Goethe actually made this remark in this form, nevertheless, it it is not incompatible with many other of his remarks scattered throughout his life.

The theme of health and sickness appears to have preoccupied Goethe at different moments works and correspondences, for example: in an entry from the *Italienische Reise* where he compares modernity to a hospital in which every man will become each other's nurse; in the essay about "Winckelmann und sein Jahrhundert" (1805), where the relationship between sickness and health is explained more explicitly, as the juxtaposition of two psychological types; in the record of a conversation with his private secretary Wilhelm Friedrich Riemer dated from 1808, and in an essay called "Klassiker und Romantiker in Italien, sich heftig bekämpfend" (1820) where he writes about how in comparison with the Italians, the Germans had already resolved the classic and romantic divide.[3]

The reconciliation of the classical and the romantic was always very important to Goethe. Nevertheless, we can detect especially in the latter part of his life, a tendency to see romanticism in art as an expression of unhealthy propensities. And he himself, at the end of his life, seems to have quite self-consciously attempted to create a modern classical ideal in his writing and in his habits. Goethe tended to see the classical as a metaphor of psychological robustness, naturalness and harmony, whereas he tended to the romantic as representing its opposite, which for Goethe meant psychological feebleness, unnaturalness and disharmony, or as he tells Riemer: "So-called romantic poetry attracts particularly our young people, since it is arbitrary, tending to disconnectedness— in short, it flatters the inclinations of youth" (Goethe in Richards 2002, p. 458).

The psychological robustness inspired by the classic is related to the ideal of self-realisation and acceptance of our limitations Goethe expresses in poems like

---

2 My translation.
3 See Richards 2002, pp. 458–460.

Zueignung (1784), where he writes: "Erkenne dich, leb mit der Welt in Frieden!" And *Natur und Kunst* (ca. 1800) in which he says: "He who will great things must gird up his loins; only in limitation is mastery revealed, and law alone can give us freedom" (SV, p. 197). ("Wer Großes will, muß sich zusammenraffen; In der Beschränkung zeigt sich erst der Meister, Und das Gesetz nur kann uns Freiheit geben.") (HA 1, p. 245).

The same ideal is found in the works of other writers of the period who interacted with Goethe and who endorsed "the view that classicism was a cure for melancholy" (Bell 2004, p. 85). Among those writers there was notably Karl Philipp Moritz who Goethe became friends with at the time of his journey to Italy, and who edited a journal of empirical psychology whose motto was *Know Thyself* (*Gnothi Sauton*). Moritz was also the author of the psychological novel *Anton Reiser* whose structure resembles a psychological case history and bears similarities to Goethe's story of the Beautiful Soul.

Although Goethe's model for the classic type was inspired by the ideal of the Ancient Greek as an individual whose inner life was harmoniously expressed in the outside world, he did not of course by this mean that such harmony could only be expressed by ancient art or only among ancient men. As Eckermann reports Goethe as saying, the contrast for him between classic and romantic is not one represented by the passage of time, but one expressed by a general disposition: "Most of what is new is not romantic because it is new, but because it is weak, feeble and sick; and the old is not classic because it is old, but because it is strong, fresh, cheerful and healthy."[4] ("Das meiste Neuere ist nicht romantisch, weil es neu, sondern weil es schwach, kränklich und krank ist, und das Alte ist nicht klassisch, weil es alt, sondern weil es stark, frisch, froh und gesund ist.") (Eckermann 2006, p. 310).

The theme of health and sickness recurs under different guises in almost everything Goethe wrote, and I suggest that it is central also to *Wilhelm Meister* (1795–1796), and that one of the focal points for this in the novel is the juxtaposition of the character of Natalie with that of her aunt, who is the Beautiful Soul.

This metaphor of health and sickness is not meant to represent a moral judgment, and does not imply that the classic is unambiguously good or that the romantic is unambiguously bad. As Goethe himself remarks, the definitions of the classic and the romantic are tightly intertwined: "a word, through consequences of its usage, can take on a completely opposite meaning—since in our tradition

---

4 My translation.

nothing lies closer to the romantic than the Greek and Roman" (Goethe in Richards 2002, p. 459).[5]

Goethe was too profound an artist not to see that there is something of health and something of sickness in everything human. In his scientific writings, for instance, in the essay called "Die Lepaden" (1824), Goethe makes the point that abnormal or irregular natural patterns demonstrate nature's creative drive as a guiding principle.

For Goethe health and sickness are both to be understood depending on circumstances as valid and indeed potentially fruitful responses on the part of an organism to what is happening in its environment.[6]

In *Wilhelm Meister* the manuscript entitled "Confessions of a Beautiful Soul" is given to Wilhelm to study by the doctor who is caring for the Harpist after his emotional breakdown. Referring to the manuscript, he remarks to Wilhelm that: "he had found it most beneficial for those with a sickly disposition [i.e., the Beautiful Soul], whose health could not be completely restored, to cultivate religious sentiments" (EG, p. 585).[7]

I suggest that Wilhelm's encounter with the Beautiful Soul at this juncture in the narrative is intended by Goethe as a pivotal point in his development, in his growing sense of self-awareness, as an example of precisely that which Natalie, who becomes his wife, has had the strength and health to avoid. For instance, to quote what the Beautiful Soul says about her niece:

> I could not fail to be amazed at her; I might almost say that I developed respect for her. One could not imagine a more noble presence, a more peaceful disposition, a greater evenness of attention to every kind of goal or object. Never for a moment was she idle, and everything she turned her hands to became a worthy object. (EG, p. 627).

---

[5] Richards writes that "since the notions of the classical and romantic arouse out of both Schiller reflections On the Naïve and Sentimental and the Schlegel Brothers' studies of Greek and Roman poetry, the categories, indeed, had deeply rooted connections." (Richards 2002, p. 459).
[6] An interesting approach to the theme of health and sickness in German Classicism and in Goethe's writing can be found in Cornelia Zumbusch's *Die Immunität der Klassik* (2014). According to the author, one could interpret the themes of health and sickness in German classic literature as a response to the medical discourse of the period, especially in relation to immunisation or vaccination processes.
[7] The doctor here anticipates Freud's frequently expressed view that religion was an important protection against the development of neurotic symptoms. See for example in *Massenpsychologie und Ich-Analyse* (1921) (Freud 1989, p. 132): "even those who do not regret the disappearance of religious illusions from the civilized world of today will admit that so long as they were enforced they offered those who were bound by them the most powerful protection against the danger of neurosis." (Penguin Freud Library, Vol. 12, p. 176).

> ([...] ich konnte das Kind nicht ohne Bewunderung, ja ich darf beinahe sagen, nicht ohne Verehrung ansehn. Man sah nicht leicht eine edlere Gestalt, ein ruhiger Gemüt und eine immer gleiche, auf keinen Gegenstand eingeschränkte Tätigkeit. Sie war keinen Augenblick ihres Lebens unbeschäftigt, und jedes Geschäft ward unter ihren Händen zur würdigen Handlung.) (HA 7, p. 417).

The consistent ability effectively to apply means to ends which is the signal characteristic of Natalie's character in the novel was always throughout his writing identified by Goethe as the mark of healthy individuality. In his profound and subtle psychological portrait of the Beautiful Soul Goethe shows us an individuality of deep sensitivity and intelligence who yet lacks this one crucial capacity to apply means to ends.

In the context of Wilhelm's emotional development, the contrast between the relative health of Natalie and the relative sickness of the Beautiful Soul suggests to us those elements that Goethe regarded as essential for the process of *Bildung* to be successful, in other words, for a healthy individuality to evolve and achieve its potential. For Goethe personally an active participation in all of life's activities was clearly preferable to a withdrawal from it even though he understood perfectly well that circumstances often prevented such a complete engagement as this, for instance, in the case of his own sister who he felt did not achieve a fulfilled life: "Her facial traits neither striking nor beautiful spoke of a being that was neither at one with itself nor could become so"[8] (HA 9, p. 229). We should however underline that it is a female character that Goethe selects to give us his ideal of healthy individuality in the novel. It is clear from this, in contrast to the position adopted by critics like Hirsch and Macleod, that Goethe in no way regarded women as inferior to men in their potential for healthy development.

2 Wilhelm's Emotional Development

Hirsch describes Wilhelm Meister's character as "unpsychological" (Hirsch, p. 29). I do not find this convincing. The novel is punctuated by various episodes in which Wilhelm appears in intimate dialogue with himself, trying to examine his own life, justify his choices and refine his first impressions. For example, in Chapter Fourteen of Book Two, Wilhelm reflects about his own nature and the need to free himself from his present circumstances:

---

8 My translation.

> He recalled the time when his spirit was uplifted by an eager surge of boundless activity [...]. But now, as he realized, he had fallen into a state of continual floundering, sipping at life instead of drinking deeply as before. *He could not perceive clearly that there was an irresistible yearning which nature had imposed on him as a law of his being, and that this was being stimulated, but only half satisfied, and ultimately frustrated by circumstance.* (EG, pp. 452–3).

> (Er erinnerte sich der Zeit, in der sein Geist durch ein unbedingtes hoffnungsreiches Streben emporgehoben wurde [...] Es ward ihm deutlich, wie er letzt in ein unbestimmtes Schlendern geraten war [...] *aber deutlich konnte er nicht sehen, welches unüberwindliche Bedürfnis ihm die Natur zum Gesetz gemacht hatte, und wie sehr dieses Bedürfnis durch Umstände nur gereizt, halb befriedigt und irregeführt worden war.*) (HA 7, p. 141–142. My emphasis).

What Goethe means by this irresistible yearning is nature driving Wilhelm to discover his true character and to realise it.

Wilhelm's encounter with the memoir of the Beautiful Soul can be compared to his discovery of Shakespeare's writings earlier in the novel, above all Hamlet.

It is worth noting that Hegel, who was deeply influenced by Goethe, was later to see in Hamlet a version of the Beautiful Soul. For Hegel, again, the essential thing about Hamlet was inability effectively to coordinate ends and means. In Hegel's view both characters are essentially frustrated by the conditions they encounter in life and *Wilhelm Meister* as a whole can be seen as Wilhelm's struggle to overcome frustrating circumstances rather than falling victim to them as Hamlet and in certain respect—as Hegel argues—the Beautiful Soul also does.

Wilhelm's profound response to Shakespeare and to Hamlet is hardly of an "unpsychological" character. And Shakespeare is brought in specifically by Goethe to underline Wilhelm's need to develop and mature. Because of his youthful restlessness, Wilhelm always finds himself at the mercy of first impressions, as a young man he still lacks the ability to sustain attention and suspend immediate judgement. He often fails to give things a second look. The most striking example of this is his relationship with Marianne and its unhappy conclusion, when he becomes convinced, mistakenly as it happens, that she is having an affair with another man.

In Chapter 16 of Book Four, Aurelie becomes the first character in the novel to warn Wilhelm about his tendency to get carried away by abstractions and first impressions. She tells him that he is constantly misled by his fantasy of others; that when he discusses literature he sounds very wise and sure of himself, however "when [he is] associating with real people, [he seems] like some first child of creation growing up to gape at lions and monkeys, sheep and elephants in strange astonishment and good-natured devotion" (EG, pp. 525–6; HA 7, p.257). What Aurelie perceived in Wilhelm at that stage, is a tendency to escape from reality through fiction. A characteristic that he also shares with the Beautiful Soul and that defines the attitude of the melancholic personality in other novels of the period, such as in Moritz's *Anton Reiser* where the main character escapes from life's unpleasant circumstances by going into periods of fanatic attachment to religion, theatre and literature. Art, however, and this is what Wilhelm will learn by studying Shakespeare, is not supposed to be a means to escape from life, but as a tool to better interact with the world.

Here for the first time Wilhelm admits that he is worried about his maturity, which again reveals that he is increasingly becoming aware of himself.

Hamlet is Wilhelm's first encounter with melancholia treated as a central theme of a major work of art. In retrospect we can see it as preparing him for dealing with the later reality of Aurelie's depressive illness and the Harpist's emotional breakdown, and his encounter with the memoir of the Beautiful Soul. In trying to help in whatever way he can Aurelie and the Harpist, Wilhelm has to confront his own underlying melancholia. In contrast to what happens in the first two books of the novel, when Wilhelm's heart is broken and, rather than of confronting emotional trauma, he defends himself against it, by momentarily abandoning his hopes for the theatre and attempting to conform to his father's wishes to see him take on responsibilities in the family business. Now, however, Wilhelm has no choice other than try to learn how to better understand himself.

It is at this point in his development that Wilhelm is given the manuscript of the Beautiful Soul by the doctor who is helping treat the Harpist after his breakdown (EG, p. 585; HA 7, p. 350). The manuscript serves a double purpose in the narrative: the story of the Beautiful Soul entertains Aurelie on her death bed at the same time as it provokes Wilhelm to begin seriously to contemplate on his own inner life as well as reflect more carefully upon his experiences.

This is the central turning-point in Wilhelm's development. It deepens his empathetic insight and his perspective on the human condition. It also coincides with a new steadiness in his nature which up to this has been undermined by restlessness and by his vulnerability to new experiences.

3 Confessions of a Beautiful Soul

The book within *Wilhelm Meister* entitled "Bekenntnisse einer schönen Seele" recounts the development of a religiously animated woman from childhood into maturity and beyond. It describes her early emotional attachments and intellectual interests, her family life, formal education, religious sensibility, health and psychological make-up. But it is a tale of *Bildung* which is strikingly different from both that of Wilhelm and also that of her niece, Natalie. In contrast to these two other characters in the book, the story of the Beautiful Soul depicts a deeply spiritual personality that is profoundly preoccupied with her relationship with God, even to the expense of her worldly existence.

In this character, like in that of Moritz's *Anton Reiser* which was published five years before *Wilhelm Meister*, in 1785–1790, Goethe give us a description—amongst other things—of the conflict between piety and worldliness within the individual. In his study about Moritz's life and works, Mark Boulby writes that religion plays a paradoxical role in Anton Reiser's life: if on the one hand it warps Anton's early childhood development, on the other hand, it is only through "the self-observation of [its] *praxis pietatis*, 'noting every step, every smile, every expression and every word' (AR, p. 106) which provided the basis for his self-understanding" (Boulby 1979, p. 43). A similar remark could be said about Goethe's Beautiful Soul.

The *Confessions* begin with the Beautiful Soul's recollection of a childhood sickness at the age of eight which keeps her in bed for several months. She recovers physically but the illness causes her to lose all interest in the things of childhood: "After a year I was more or less recovered, but nothing wild remained with me from my childhood. I couldn't play with dolls any longer, I wanted objects that would return my love." (EG, p. 590; HA 7, p. 359).

Remembering her long and difficult convalescence, she describes that period as laying the foundations of her personality:

> During the nine months of convalescence which I bore patiently, the foundations of my present way of thinking were laid—or at least it seems to me now. For during that time my mind received various impulses that helped in the shaping of a specific character. (EG, p. 590).
>
> (Während des neunmonatlichen Krankenlagers, das ich mit Geduld aushielt, ward, so wie mich dünkt, der Grund zu meiner ganzen Denkart gelegt, indem meinem Geiste die ersten Hülfsmittel gereicht wurden, sich nach seiner eigenen Art zu entwickeln.) (HA 7, p. 358).

Throughout this period of her life, the Beautiful Soul receives ambiguous indications as to what is expected from her: her father keeps the ailing child entertained with objects of science and nature but her mother and aunt instil in her a first taste for religion and fantasy. At the first moments of the narrative, the adults in her life seem to be above all concerned to keep her distracted, and to offer her a compensation for her illness, rather than a structured education.

Science, religion, fantasy and romance: she absorbs a bit of everything without making clear distinctions between them. For instance, she writes that: "I often recounted to my father what I had learnt from him. I never took medication without asking where the ingredients came from, what they were called and what they looked like." This deep interest in the natural world existed side by side with a fascination with fantasy: "Nor had my aunt's stories fallen on barren soil. I imagined myself dressed in beautiful clothes and meeting the most charming princes who could not rest till they found out who this unknown beauty was." It appears that this fascination with fantasy reached a point at which the little girl could not make a clear distinction between fantasy and reality: "Then there was a similar adventure with a delightful little angel, in white garments and with golden wings, who was much drawn to me; and this I kept developing in my mind till I almost reached the point that he actually appeared." (EG, p. 590) (Ein ähnliches Abenteuer mit einem reizenden kleinen Engel, der in weißem Gewand und goldenen Flügeln sich sehr um mich bemühte, setzte ich so lange fort, daß meine Einbildungskraft sein Bild fast bis zur Erscheinung erhöhte.) (HA 7, p. 359).

The *Confessions* portray a character's conflict within herself between the need to fulfil her desires as a unique individual and the need to remain loyal to the expectations placed upon her by her family setting and her social context.

In the first part of Book Six, Goethe seems to be looking critically at a certain type of education. Throughout her childhood the Beautiful Soul receives ambivalent instructions about what is expected from her. An ambivalence between activity and idleness then becomes the core of the Beautiful Soul's condition and she learns to think that she can resolve her internal conflict by escaping interaction with the world and by retreating to an intimate relation with a higher, invisible, nonhuman power: God.

In the 19th century a widespread reading of the chapter on the Beautiful Soul was that it was a moral tale redeeming what was widely regarded as an immoral novel.

For example, in the journal of Ralph Waldo Emerson of August the 28th 1833, the young Emerson describes visiting the great romantic poet William Wordsworth in England. Emerson reports: "Goethe's Wilhelm Meister he abused with might & main—all manner of fornication. It was like flies crossing each other in the air. He had never got further than the first book, so disgusted was he. I spoke *for* the better parts of the book and he promised to look at it again" (Emerson in Porte 1982, p. 114).

As Goethe's nineteenth century biographer G.H. Lewes remarks: "the Confessions of the Beautiful Soul which occupied the sixth book have in some circles embalmed what was the corruption of the other books. Stolberg burned all the rest of the work and kept these chapters as a treasure" (Lewes 1858, p. 185).

In the twentieth century, under the influence of Freud, perceptions shifted and the Beautiful Soul came to be seen by some commentators in rather different terms. There is no doubt that "Bekenntnisse einer schönen Seele" can be read a progenitor of Freud's great case studies from the end of the nineteenth and beginning of the twentieth century. For instance, Frederick Beharriel suggests that the religiosity of the Beautiful Soul reflects an inability to come to terms with her sexuality (Beharriel 1970, p. 48).

Nicholas Boyle, emphasising the irony which underlines the entirety of Book Six, suggests that:

> in this narrative tour de force [...] all appearances are deceptive [...] his contemporaries did not see, or did not want to see, what literary criticism has only recently brought to light: the network of motifs which amount to a psychological explanation of all that is overtly Christian in the canoness's religious sensibility. Sickness, her own and others', accompanies her throughout her life and is responsible for her introspection and so at length to celibacy. Bleeding, in particular—a nose bleed, haemorrhages, a head wound—is associated with her moments of affection for men, and from this reminder of her feminine sexuality she turns away to her heavenly 'friend,' whose bloody wounds were a staple topic of pietist hymnody. (Boyle 2002, Vol. 2, p. 340).

More recent decades have seen the rise of feminist analyses of the Beautiful Soul arguing that she is essentially as a victim of a patriarchal society. Hirsch, for example, argues that the primary problem of the Beautiful Soul is not within her but rather without her. She writes that: "the heroine's allegiance to childhood, pre-oedipal desire, spiritual withdrawal, and ultimately death is not neurotic but a realistic and paradoxically fulfilling reaction to an impossible contradiction" (Hirsch 1983, p. 28).

Hirsch's interpretation is problematic for a number of reasons. First of all, she never gives us a clear definition of what she understands by "pre-oedipal desire." Secondly and more significantly, she fails to give a definition of neurosis which we can contrast with what she calls "a realistic and paradoxically fulfilling reaction to an impossible contradiction."

Goethe's text is subtler than Hirsch acknowledges. The confusion between science, religion and fantasy becomes a constant theme in the life of the Beautiful Soul. As a child, she learns not only for her own satisfaction and cultivation but for deeper emotional reasons.

Gustafson, for instance, interprets the Beautiful Soul's early interest in nature as a response to her attachment to her father: "her fixation on dismembered bodies parallels her idealization of her own ailing body, allows her to bond with her father, and reveals how truly disturbing her desires are" (Gustafson 2017, p. 88). It is notable also how readily her early interest in religion and fantasy turn into flights of imagination about love and sexuality. As I have noted above, at the beginning of the Confessions, the Beautiful Soul writes that, as a child: "[she] wanted objects that would return [her] love" (EG, p. 590; HA 7, p. 359).

In the relationships she develops with the opposite sex—for example, her early teenage infatuation with the Chamberlain's sons and her later relationship with Philo—she tends to become detached from the world of flesh and blood, preferring the world of pure abstraction. There is no question of the emotional importance of this abstract realm to her, it is however striking how devoid her religious sensibility is of traditional Christian iconography. As Nicholas Boyle points out, the religion of the Beautiful Soul is rarefied to a high degree and aspires to be within the limits of reason alone (Boyle 2002, Vol.2, p. 342).

Apart from its other functions within the context of the novel, "Bekenntnisse einer schönen Seele" can surely also be seen as an implicit criticism of the place of women in society at this time, reflected not least in the education—or lack of it —offered to them. Written at a time when women were trapped in what was still a hierarchical and patriarchal society, as a result of which essential aspects of their nature were inevitably frustrated, they fell victim to conflicts within the self and to illness.[9]

Matthew Bell has suggested that the character of the ailing melancholic woman represents within the context of the literature of Storm and Stress literature, the psychology of revolt. In this literature, melancholia and what was at the time perceived as its opposite, hypochondria, are typically portrayed as a response to intolerable circumstances in life. Bell comments that "the *leidendes Weib* symbolizes the dissatisfactions of eighteenth-century society, exposed as she is to male sexual predation, the constraints of a stratified society, and unfeeling bourgeois Christian morality" (Bell 2004, p. 55).

In my view, when we compare it with the other discussions and examples of education in the novel as a whole—for instance, Wilhelm's own trajectory, Mignon's attempts to learn to read, the Uncle' and the Abbé's model of instruction, Natalie and Therese resource to discipline, and Frederick and Philine's autodidacticism—"Bekenntnisse einer schönen Seele" takes on the look of a tale of development in which something appears to have gone awry. This at least was how one of Goethe's friends reacted to it.

In a letter to Schiller dating from the 4th of December 1795, Wilhelm von Humboldt comments that:

---

[9] See for example the description of the Mary Lamb case (1796) given by Lisa Appignanesi in *Mad, Bad and Sad: A History of Women and the Mind Doctors from 1800 to the Present* (Appignanesi 2010, pp. 15–56).

Clearly, Goethe has chosen, admittedly with energy, an only very inaccurately named beautiful and more accurately petty, vain and narrow-minded soul, which only has a few larger aspects. [...] Although equally I shall always read the Confessions with great interest, and it will not annoy or irritate me to follow the development of the character with effort, nevertheless the individual is to me still an extremely fatal figure, which in all her metamorphoses displeases equally strongly and always in the same way (which to me is a proof of the great art with which Goethe has painted the character).[10]

(Offenbar hat Goethe wohl mit Fleiß eine nur sehr uneigentlich schön genannte und mehr kleinliche, eitle und beschränkte Seele, die nur einige größere Seiten hat, gewählt. [...] Ob ich gleich die Bekenntnisse immer mit großem Interesse lesen werde und es mich nicht verdrießen lasse, dem Gange des Charakters auch mit Mühe nachzugehen, so ist mir das Individuum doch immer eine höchst fatale Gestalt, die mir in allen ihren Metamorphosen gleich stark und (was mir ein Beweis der großen Kunst ist, mit der Goethe den Charakter souteniert hat) immer auf gleiche Weise missfällt.) (HA 7, pp. 657–658).

We need therefore to consider why it was that Goethe gave such a prominent place in the novel to this comparatively unhappy narrative which at first sight appears to have so little connection with the rest of the book.

I suggest that that the connection is revealed in the links between the Beautiful Soul and her niece, Natalie. At three points in the novel Goethe juxtaposes these two characters This, I suggest, gives us a clue to the secret importance of the *Confession* for the rest of the novel.

The first occurs at the conclusion of the narrative of the Beautiful Soul herself, when she refers to her niece Natalie's personal inclination to do good to others, which she compares this to herself:

The eldest daughter claimed the greater part of my affection, probably because she looked like me and, of all the four, it was she who clung to me most. But I must say that the more I observed her growing up, the more she put me to shame. I could not fail to be amazed at her; I might almost say that I developed respect for her. *One could not imagine a more noble presence, a more peaceful disposition, a greeter evenness of attention to every kind of goal or object. Never for a moment was she idle, and everything she turned her hands to became a worthy object. Nothing troubled her so long as she could do what was demanded of her by circumstances, and she could be quite content when she did not find anything that needed doing at the moment.* This ability to remain active without feeling the need for some particular occupation, was something that I never again encountered. Her behaviour toward the needy and suffering was exemplary. I must confess that I myself had never had the ability to make an occupation out of my works of charity. I was not parsimonious in my gifts to the poor, and often gave more than I should have in my circumstances, but in a way I was buying myself off, and if someone were to receive my full care and attention, this would have to

---

10 My translation.

be someone of my own flesh and blood. But with my niece it was just the opposite, and I admired her for this. (EG, p. 627).

(Die älteste Tochter hatte meine ganze Neigung gefesselt, und es mochte wohl daher kommen, weil sie mir ähnlich sah, und weil sie sich von allen vieren am meisten zu mir hielt. Aber ich kann wohl sagen, je genauer ich sie beobachtete, da sie heranwuchs, desto mehr beschämte sie mich, und ich konnte das Kind nicht ohne Bewunderung, ja ich darf beinahe sagen, nicht ohne Verehrung ansehn. Man sah nicht leicht eine edlere Gestalt, ein ruhiger Gemüt und eine immer gleiche, auf keinen Gegenstand eingeschränkte Tätigkeit. Sie war keinen Augenblick ihres Lebens unbeschäftigt, und jedes Geschäft ward unter ihren Händen zur würdigen Handlung. Alles schien ihr gleich, wenn sie nur das verrichten konnte, was in der Zeit und am Platz war, und ebenso konnte sie ruhig, ohne Ungeduld, bleiben, wenn sich nichts zu tun fand. Diese Tätigkeit ohne Bedürfnis einer Beschäftigung habe ich in meinem Leben nicht wieder gesehen. Unnachahmlich war von Jugend auf ihr Betragen gegen Notleidende und Hülfsbedürftige. Ich gestehe gern, daß ich niemals das Talent hatte, mir aus der Wohltätigkeit ein Geschäft zu machen; ich war nicht karg gegen Arme, ja ich gab oft in meinem Verhältnisse zu viel dahin, aber gewissermaßen kaufte ich mich nur los, und es mußte mir jemand angeboren sein, wenn er mir meine Sorgfalt abgewinnen wollte. Gerade das Gegenteil lobe ich an meiner Nichte.) (HA 7, pp. 417–418. My Emphasis).

In my view this passage is the key to understanding the significance of the character of the Beautiful Soul in the novel as a whole. By making the contrast with Natalie, the character of the Beautiful Soul is highlighted as someone who, for better or for worse, has turned away from practical activity in the world. Each reader must judge for herself weather she views this as the portrait of a fulfilled or unfilled individuality. Goethe himself is too great an artist to moralise on this question.

Two paragraphs preceding this quotation, she says: "I felt that, with my infirmity, I was not in a position to do much for these children, if indeed anything" (Goethe 2016, p. 627). As Gustafson argues, taking a rather critical view of the character, this way of thinking is problematic and reveals the ambivalence of the Beautiful Soul's actions, after all, at the same time that she tries to protect herself from the influence of a patriarchal family structure, she also delivers her beloved nephews to the care of her uncle who, as such, may be seen to represent an ideal of patriarchal family based upon social and economic benefit (Gustafson 2017, p. 95).

The second juxtaposition with Natalie occurs in Book Eight, when, after his first night at Natalie's house, Wilhelm is struck by the similarity between a portrait of the Beautiful Soul and her niece:

"I've been looking at that portrait," he said, "and am amazed that the artist could be so true and false at the same time. It is a good general likeness of you, a very good one really, but it does not capture either your features or your character."

"What is still more amazing," Natalie replied, "is that it is such a good likeness, for it is not a picture of me, but of an aunt who, even as an old lady, resembled me as a child. It was painted when she was about the age I am now, and most people, when they first see it, think it is a picture of me. I wish you had known this splendid person, for I am indebted to her for so much. Her delicate health, along with perhaps too much concern about herself, and in addition an extreme moral and religious reserve, prevented her from becoming for the world what, in other circumstances, she might well have been." (EG, p. 691).

("Ich habe das Porträt hier angesehen," sagte er zu ihr, "und mich verwundert, wie ein Maler zugleich so wahr und so falsch sein kann. Das Bild gleicht Ihnen im allgemeinen recht sehr gut, und doch sind es weder Ihre Züge noch Ihr Charakter."
"Es ist vielmehr zu verwundern," versetzte Natalie, "daß es so viel Ähnlichkeit hat; denn es ist gar mein Bild nicht; es ist das Bild einer Tante, die mir noch in ihrem Alter glich, da ich erst ein Kind war. Es ist gemalt, als sie ungefähr meine Jahre hatte, und beim ersten Anblick glaubt jedermann mich zu sehen. Sie hätten diese treffliche Person kennen sollen. Ich bin ihr so viel schuldig. Eine sehr schwache Gesundheit, vielleicht zu viel Beschäftigung mit sich selbst, und dabei eine sittliche und religiöse Ängstlichkeit ließen sie das der Welt nicht sein, was sie unter andern Umständen hätte werden können.") (HA, Band 7, p. 517).

In this contrast between Natalie and her aunt, so it seems to me, Goethe clearly intends to draw a comparison between a happy practical engagement with the world and an unhappy withdrawal from it. But again the sophistication of Goethe's portrayal of these two characters is such that any sensitive reader must experience sympathy for both.

The third and most unequivocal comparison of the two characters occurs in Lothario's last lines in the novel, in which he praises the personality of his sister:

It is beyond belief what a cultivated man can achieve for himself and others [...] My sister Natalie is a living example of this. The ideal of human activity which Nature has prescribed for her beautiful soul will always remain unattainable. She deserves this name more than many others—more even than, if I may say so, than our noble aunt, who, when our good doctor assembled that manuscript, was the most beautiful personality we knew. (EG, p. 747–748).

(Unglaublich ist es, was ein gebildeter Mensch für sich und andere tun kann [...] Meine Schwester Natalie ist hiervon ein lebhaftes Beispiel. Unerreichbar wird immer die Handlungsweise bleiben, welche die Natur dieser schönen Seele vorgeschrieben hat. Ja sie verdient diesen Ehrennamen vor vielen andern, mehr, wenn ich sagen darf, als unsre edle Tante selbst, die zu der Zeit, als unser guter Arzt jenes Manuskript so rubrizierte, die schönste Natur war, die wir in unserm Kreise kannten.) (HA 7, p. 608).

Lothario's speech scarcely supports Hirsch's interpretation of the Beautiful Soul as "the paradigm" of female *Bildung* within the novel. So far from being confined to men, Lothario's speech makes plain Goethe's view that the ideal *Bildung* is in fact universal and that it can be attained by both men and women alike. Had the type of cultivation esteemed by the *Turmgesellschaft* "been developed for young men" (Hirsch 1983, p. 26) as Hirsch insists, one would hardly have been able to cite Natalie as its highest example.

In contrast to what Hirsch suggests, the universe of *Wilhelm Meisters Lehrjahre* does not simply replicate the structure and the morality of Goethe's society. The atmosphere of sexual freedom that characterises the book, the free association between men and women both in the context of the theatre and in the context of the *Turmgesellschaft* illustrates a subversion of established patriarchy and is in conflict with Hirsch's suggestion that there must be a different paradigm of *Bildung* for men and women.

4 Goethe's Philosophy of Gender

The views on gender that we find in Goethe's fictional work cannot be considered in isolation from his broader views on science and on philosophical and ethical questions.

German Literature in the eighteenth and nineteenth centuries is in general characterised by a significant overlapping and interchange between science, philosophy and fiction. As E. M. Butler explains, after the Reformation the ascetic ideals of early protestant leaders removed the Germans from the tradition of Catholic mythology and its rich heritage of liturgical art and music. Consequently, the German writers of the period had to find other sources of inspiration, in particular: history, the natural sciences and philosophy (Butler 1935, p. 4).

In addition, although Goethe's pre-eminence was, of course, in the realm of poetry, the novel, drama, and literature generally, Goethe was himself also engaged in natural science. He discovered the inter-maxillary bone and was a significant precursor of evolutionary theories which were to emerge later in the nineteenth century (he was acknowledged as such by Charles Darwin). When we consider a poem like the "Metamorphosis of Plants," we see how freely Goethe moved between science and literature, happily blurring any distinction between the two.

Goethe believed that we could learn about ourselves by studying nature and by drawing parallels and analogies from nature to the observation of human phenomena. In this regard, Astrida Orle Tantillo suggests that, in his scientific works, "Goethe presents a theory of gender that is not based upon sexual organs [that] describe[s] the relationship between the masculine and the feminine as complex and not strictly hierarchical [where] genders are often portrayed as equals that compete for control" (Tantillo 1998, p. 123).

Tantillo explains that Goethe's concept of Nature is fluid. As a consequence of that fluidity, the boundaries between nature and culture are not clear. Culture emerges from nature, as an expression of man as part of nature.

As part of this ceaseless dynamic, in Goethe's observations about nature, the relation between the sexes loses the rigid and hierarchical structure traditionally embraced by philosophy, from Plato to Kant.

As observed by Tantillo, Goethe views the relationship between the sexes as a non-hierarchical dynamic between polarities. Due to that, Tantillo explains that:

> Goethe's hierarchy reflects a fluid, creative vision of nature [...] Goethe's organisms...participate in striving toward something higher through creativity generally—not only through reproductivity, but in creating new or beautiful forms for themselves, whether or not these forms are capable of further reproduction. Goethean organisms, like Aristotelian ones, strive towards ends. For Goethe, however, these ends may constantly change—for individuals as well as for each generation of species—as organisms strive to overcome their previous restraints of environment or bodily form. (Tantillo 1998, p. 126).

For Goethe hierarchy hinges not on sexuality but on the autonomy of the self. Thus, the suggestion of Hirsch that Goethe was thinking in terms of a fundamentally different paradigm of *Bildung* for men and women must be rejected.

Through the education she receives from her uncle and the Abbé, Natalie blossoms into a truly cultivated individual. She is able to do good to others because of the sense of harmony she has reached in herself. Such harmony allows Natalie to know the limits of her own nature and to act according to an economy of means that ultimately leads all her actions to express freedom, beauty and moral perfection.

The same cannot be said about her aunt. In spite of her intellectual curiosity and deep moral sensibility, the education given to the Beautiful Soul is deficient and inappropriate to her own nature. It encourages a flight from self and reality instead of an engagement with them.

The universe of Wilhelm Meister is more challenging of conventional morality than it may now seem. Goethe's ideal of *Bildung* is in no way a justification for conformity with the existing norms or customs of society.

It is not Goethe's ambition to portray docile individuals who conform to their social environment and this is not what he achieves. Rather than being a tool for social control, Goethe's ideal of *Bildung* has deep psychological implications—it is a provocation by a great artist to each of his readers to *master* his or her own circumstances and overcome the constraints imposed by society upon the fruitful and complete expression of his or her personality. A careful reading of *Wil-*

helm Meisters Lehrjahre reveals Goethe to have been far removed from the contemporary view of a complacent upholder of eighteenth century patriarchy.

5 Conclusion

In *Wilhelm Meisters Lehrjahre* Goethe uses parallel narratives and poetry in order to interrupt and slow down the book, allowing the reader to see different perspectives and, consequently, achieve a deeper understanding of the plot.

These interruptions are there to remind the reader to take the novel as an experience, and as an experiment. As one of the most important interruptions to Wilhelm's narrative, the place and purpose of the "Bekenntnisse einer schönen Seele" in *Wilhelm Meisters Lehrjahre* is to offer a new perspective or point of departure to understand the dynamic of Wilhelm's emotional development. It also allows us think about the effects of different ideals of *Bildung* on the lives of different individuals, whether male or female.

In this paper I have argued that Goethe's ideal of *Bildung* as an ideal of self-mastery and self-possession of the individual can be attained by both men and women alike. I suggested that the interpretations of Goethe's *Wilhelm Meisters Lehrjahre* focusing on a single gendered perspective fail to acknowledge the socially subversive potential of Goethe's novel.

Of course, *Wilhelm Meisters Lehrjahre* is not intended to be read as a utopia of sexual equality. However, it is equally unfair to Goethe's spirit and letter to read the novel as a mere reproduction of eighteenth century prejudices.

In spite of Goethe's early rise to celebrity and long-lasting influence on German society and culture, neither his life nor his work should be seen as justifications of the *status quo*. As Goethe tells Eckermann toward the end of his life, an allegiance to the current state of society had always been unimaginable to him:

> If the status quo were in everything excellent, good and just, so I would have nothing against it; since, however, besides much that is good there is also at the same time much bad, unjust and imperfect, so a friend of the status quo can be called often not much less than a friend of the obsolete and the bad.[11]
>
> (Wenn das Bestehende alles vortrefflich, gut und gerecht wäre, so hätte ich gar nichts dawider; da aber neben vielem Guten zugleich viel Schlechtes, Ungerechtes und Unvollkommenes besteht, so heißt ein Freund des Bestehenden oft nicht viel weniger als ein Freund des Veralteten und Schlechten.) (Eckermann 2006, p. 511).

---

[11] My translation.

In *Wilhelm Meisters Lehrjahre*, for example, he examines some of the psychological conflicts generated by contemporary social conditions as well as some of the possible ways these conflicts can be transcended by strong and persisting individuals. It is striking furthermore that Goethe chooses precisely a female character as the one deserving of the highest praise for her personal development.

Goethe's work is characterised by a consistent focus on the individual in her struggle to achieve autonomy and harmony despite the obstacles placed in her way by the constraints of society. A truly cultivated person is somebody who develops a strong sense of autonomy and self-awareness despite her circumstances: "Only in limitation is mastery revealed, and law alone can give us freedom" (SV, p. 197). ("In der Beschränkung zeigt sich erst der Meister, und das Gesetz nur kann uns Freiheit geben.") (HA 1, p. 245).

Bibliography

Appignanesi, Lisa (2010): *Mad, Bad and Sad: a History of Women and the Mind Doctors from 1800 to the Present*. London: Virago.
Bell, Matthew (2004): *The German tradition of psychology in literature and thought, 1700–1840*. New York: Cambridge University Press.
Boulby, Mark (1979): *Karl Philipp Moritz: At the Fringe of Genius*. Toronto: University of Toronto Press.
Boyle, Nicholas (2003): *Goethe: the poet and the age*, Vol. 2. Oxford: Oxford University Press.
Brown, Jane K (2014): *Goethe's Allegories of Identity*. University of Pennsylvania Press.
Butler, Eliza Marian (1935): *The Tyranny of Greece over Germany a study of the influence exercised by Greek art and poetry over the great German writers of the eighteenth, nineteenth and twentieth centuries*. Cambridge: Cambridge University Press.
Eckermann, Johann Peter / Bergemann, Fritz / Weitz, Hans-J. (2006): *Gespräche mit Goethe in den letzten Jahren seines Lebens*. Frankfurt a. M.: Insel Verlag.
Emerson, Ralph Waldo / Porte, Joel (1982): *Emerson in his journals*. London: Harvard University Press.
Freud, Sigmund (1989): "Massenpsychologie und Ich-Analyse (1921)." In: *Werkausgabe – Studienausgabe in zehn Bänden mit einem Ergänzungsband*, Band 9. Frankfurt a. M.: Fischer.
Goethe, Johann Wolfgang von (2000): "Gedichte." In: Trunz, Erich (Ed.): *Werke* (Hamburger Ausgabe in vierzehn Bänden), Band 1. München: Deutscher Taschenbuch Verlag.
Goethe, Johann Wolfgang von (2000): "Italienische Reise." In: Trunz, Erich (Ed.): *Werke* (Hamburger Ausgabe in vierzehn Bänden), Band 11. München: Deutscher Taschenbuch Verlag.
Goethe, Johann Wolfgang von (2000): "Naturwissenschaft 1." In: Trunz, Erich (Ed.): *Werke* (Hamburger Ausgabe in vierzehn Bänden), Band 13. München: Deutscher Taschenbuch Verlag.

Goethe, Johann Wolfgang von (2000): "Wilhelm Meisters Lehrjahre." In: Trunz, Erich (Ed.): *Werke* (Hamburger Ausgabe in vierzehn Bänden), Band 7. München: Deutscher Taschenbuch Verlag.

Goethe, Johann Wolfgang von (2000): "Aus meinem Leben. Dichtung und Wahrheit Buch 1–13" In: Trunz, Erich (Ed.): *Werke* (Hamburger Ausgabe in vierzehn Bänden), Band 9. München: Deutscher Taschenbuch Verlag.

Goethe, Johann Wolfgang von (2016): *The Essential Goethe*. Ed. Bell, Matthew. New Jersey: Princeton University Press.

Goethe, Johann Wolfgang von, and Luke, David (1964): *Goethe: Selected Verse*. Harmondsworth, England: Penguin.

Gustafson, Susan E. (2017): *Goethe's Families of the Heart*. Bloomsbury Academic.

Hegel, Georg Wilhelm Friedrich (2001): *Hegel on tragedy*. Eds. Paolucci, Anne / Paolucci, Henry. Smyrna, DE: Griffon House Publications, for The Bagehot Council.

Israel, Jonathan I (2003): *Radical Enlightenment: Philosophy and the Making of Modernity, 1650–1750*. Oxford: Oxford University Press.

Lewes, George Henry (2010): *The Life and Works of Goethe: with Sketches of His Age and Contemporaries, from Published and Unpublished Sources*. Vol. 2, Cambridge: Cambridge University Press.

MacLeod, Catriona (1998): *Embodying ambiguity: androgyny and aesthetics from Winckelmann to Keller*. Detroit: Wayne State University Press.

Moritz, Karl Philipp: *Anton Reiser*. Frankfurt a. M.: Fischer Klassik. Kindle Edition.

Reed, Terence J. (1984): *Goethe*. Oxford: Oxford University Press.

Richards, Robert J. (2004): *The Romantic Conception of Life: Science and Philosophy in the Age of Goethe*. Chicago: University of Chicago Press.

Rousseau, Jean-Jacques (2007): *The Confessions of Jean-Jacques Rousseau*. Ed. Cohen, J. M. London: Penguin.

Tantillo, A. O. (1998): "Goethe's Botany and His Philosophy of Gender." In: *Eighteenth-Century Life*, vol. 22, no. 2, pp. 123–138.

Zumbusch, Cornelia. (2012): *Die Immunität der Klassik*. Berlin: Suhrkamp Verlag.

Abbreviations

AR = Moritz, Karl Philipp: *Anton Reiser*. Frankfurt a. M.: Fischer Klassik. Kindle Edition.

EG = Goethe, Johann Wolfgang von (2016): *The Essential Goethe*. Ed. Bell, Matthew. New Jersey: Princeton University Press.

HA = Goethe, Johann Wolfgang von (2000): *Werke*. Ed. Trunz, Erich (Hamburger Ausgabe in vierzehn Bänden). München: Deutscher Taschenbuch Verlag (followed by volume).

SV = Goethe, Johann Wolfgang von, and Luke, David (1964): *Goethe Selected Verse*. Harmondsworth, England: Penguin.

Margaret Strair
Mediating Subjectivities: Anti-Classical and Anti-Ideal Impulses in Goethe's *Zur Farbenlehre* and *Die Wahlverwandtschaften*

Abstract: As noted in recent scholarship, knowledge of an unknowable, inner life permeates some of Goethe's fictional works, reflecting the influence of Kant's idealism on his conception of the self. These issues manifest in Goethe's scientific texts in the relationship between subject and object, which involves reconsidering the issue of subjectivity and psychological depth in terms of observation and scientific methodologies. In other words, his scientific texts show an interest in how inner life can be mediated in terms of empirical knowledge of outer life in ways that react with and against Kant's idealism. This paper considers ways in which the attempt at or desire for a smooth mediation between inner and outer, between subject and object, is complicated in key texts of Goethe's. It also examines the epistemological orientation to this question of mediation by highlighting anti-ideal and anti-classical impulses in Goethe's fictional and scientific texts.

Published within a year of one another, his *Theory of Colours* and his novel *Elective Affinities* both deal with questions of experiential knowledge and demonstrate ways in which acquiring this knowledge is closely related to the possibility of self-knowledge. While these questions of knowledge and self-knowledge resonate with the experiential overtones of each text, the actual parameters of knowledge in these texts diverge, revealing a lack of uniformity in Goethe's reaction to Kant's idealism. In one, empiricism proves to be revealing about both the experimenter and its objects of observation, and in the other it is not; the senses are able to effectively mediate in one, and ultimately fail to do so in the other. Viewing these texts together highlight different anti-classical and anti-ideal impulses in Goethe's works. It can be argued that failing to fully shed some key idealist tendencies endangers aspects of his classical program, as in the case of *Elective Affinities*.

1 Introduction

In the wake of Kant's Copernican Turn, the unsettling prospect of a world by and large empirically inaccessible haunts Goethe. With the subject torn from the material world via Kant's idealist program, he warns in his 1792 essay "The Experiment as Mediator Between Object and Subject" ("Der Versuch als Vermittler von Objekt und Subjekt") of "innere Feinde" or "inner enemies" such as abstraction that obfuscate and distract us from true, unmediated knowledge of phenomena. As vestiges of idealism, these "inner enemies" become both essential points of combat and engagement for Goethe in his scientific and fictional writings. To this end, Goethe's *Elective Affinities* (*Die Wahlverwandtschaften*, 1809) and his *Theory of Colours* (*Zur Farbenlehre*, 1810), published within a year of one each other, are useful if not complicated interlocutors for one another.[1] For their shared depiction of experimental projects, the two works diverge from one another in their attempts at combatting the "inner enemies" and the means available for doing so. In *Theory of Colours* we find a Goethean "Augenmensch," whose empiricism and its anti-Newtonian contours take form in an observer who can trust his senses to serve as the foundation for his knowledge of light and colour, and critically, himself. Conversely, in *Elective Affinities*, an experiment of affections guided by an "indescribable, almost magical attraction" (EA, p. 308) ("unbeschreibliche, fast magische Anziehungskraft") (SW 8, p. 516) that drives the four main characters' attraction for one another requires a different means of observation. In this story's experiment, the characters' "own senses" are "insufficient to observe" and their "reason too weak to follow." (EA, p. 43). ("Sinne kaum genügend fühlen [...] zu beobachten [...] Vernunft kaum hinlänglich, [...] zu fassen.") (SW 8, p. 306).

Analogous issues have been raised in scholarship by Jane K. Brown, who identifies in Goethe's fictional corpus allusions to language that prefigures psychoanalytic theory and introduces an early notion of depth psychology to representations of subjectivity of its characters. Specifically, her monograph *Goethe's Allegories of Identity* explores the differences and commonalities between the knowable and unknowable dimensions of the self. Drawing on earlier models of the allegory from theatrical performance, Brown views Goethe's understanding of the symbol as a revision of this older model of allegory for the post-Kantian world.[2] The symbol serves as a possible model for subjectivity by adding an unknown depth to subjective, intellectually-constituted life of the individual

---

[1] Connections between *Theory of Colours* and *Elective Affinities* have been discussed by Bell (1994, pp. 287–324) by utilizing methodologies in *Theory of Colours* to explain the outlooks of the protagonists in *Elective Affinities*, Brodsky (1982) regarding representational systems in Goethe's scientific texts and the novel, Moore (2015, pp. 242–252) on the issue of the gaze and its boundaries in them, and Tantillo (2000, p. 313) on polarity and productivity.

[2] Brown (2014, pp. 9–11) offers an overview of the shifts in Goethe's thought from earlier paradigms, Currie (2013, pp. 40–41) for discussion on link between eighteenth-century thought and psychoanalysis.

characters, that is, the unknown is repositioned "into the human breast" (Brown 2014, p.10). Attention to the model of the symbol reflects an increasing interest in the contours of the self, and knowledge of this self as contained in Goethe's fictional writings is also present in his scientific writings.[3] This interest manifests in the fluctuating status of empirical knowledge across his works: introducing and discussing the unknown depths of the subject calls to question the empirical means by which these things are measured.

Termed differently, the issue is as follows. In divergent ways, *Theory of Colours* and *Elective Affinities* illuminate his maxim that: "All that is in the subject is in the object and also something more. All that is in the object is in the subject and also something more." (MR, p. 174) ("Alles was im Subject [sic] ist, ist im Object [sic] und noch etwas mehr. Alles, was im Object ist, ist im Subject und noch etwas mehr.") (SW 13, p. 219). They both depict attempts at a seamless incorporation of inner and outer, sharing an interest in how unknown dimensions of the self can be understood and mediated. However, they bump up against different challenges of mediation between the two that at times halt this incorporation. At a time where knowledge of the self and knowledge of the empirical world are entwined with one another in complicated, if not messy ways, Goethean science and key fictional works of his delineate how the two can be understood and visualised through the relationship between subject and object.[4] But taken in the context of scientific experiments, much more is at play than subjective and objective spheres in these questions of mediation. Rather, the issues that inform Goethe's attempts at chiselling away at the previously seen as insurmountable separation between subject and object are also epistemological.[5] These concerns seek equivalence between the subject and object by attempting to understand the ungraspable, inner-self to varying extents as connected to the observable, graspable phenomena. Critically, *Theory of Colours* and *Elective Affinities* illustrate ways in which Goethe's anti-ideal impulses inform the at times stunted mediation between subject and object, and at the same time, operate contrary to his classical aesthetics.

---

3 Dawson (2016), Wahl (2005, p. 59) and Holdrege (2005) offer overviews of science during Romanticism with respect to the relationship between the observer and scientific process.
4 The issue of subject/object is taken up extensively in secondary scholarship, notably Amrine (1998), Rehbock (1995), Stephenson (1995), and Zajonc (1998). More specific references on this topic are in notes 8 and 21.
5 Hensel (1998) explores the relationship of sensory experience to phenomenology in Goethean science. Dawson (2016) deals explicitly with the question of Goethe's epistemology of science and Romantic science. Bell (1994, pp. 88–90) traces the epistemological and ontological concerns giving rise to Newton and then Goethe's reaction.

2 Anti-Idealism, Goethean Science, and Mediation[6]

Elsewhere in his writings, Goethe notes the significance of and relationship between the graspable and the ungraspable for the purpose of conducting scientific experiments: "Man must persist in the faith that the incomprehensible can be understood; otherwise he would not pursue research. Every particular thing that can be applied in any way is comprehensible. In this way what is incomprehensible can become useful" (WM, p. 705) ("Der Mensch muß bei dem Glauben verharren, daß das Unbegreifliche begreiflich sei; er würde sonst nicht forschen. Begreiflich ist jedes Besondere, das sich auf irgend eine Weise anwenden läßt. Auf diese Weise kann das Unbegreifliche nützlich werden.") (SW 10, p. 577). The known and the unknown, the graspable and ungraspable, as he terms it, are not in diametric opposition to one another, but rather are understood in terms of one another in a dialectical fashion: the ungraspable may in itself be graspable at some point, the possibility of which drives research.[7] In exploring the milieu out of which *Theory of Colours* and *Elective Affinities* emerge, "The Experiment as Mediator Between Object and Subject," invokes a similar question of mediation. Though in this text, the issue of mediation is not resigned exclusively to the graspable and ungraspable, but rather between subject and object. That is, the subject and the object may be understood in such ways that play with and pare away at the barrier between them Kant erected in his critical philosophy.[8] As the title of his 1792 essay suggests, Goethean science is prefaced on a question of mediation between subject and object that struggles for an epistemological equivalence between the two and immediately turns back to the question of method. Though a continuation of the scientific method,[9] it is a refinement that demands knowledge of the self in order to be knowledgeable of the world in ways that strict adherence to an idealist program would not allow.

---

[6] Dawson (2016, p. 691) offers this description of Goethean science as "mediatory" rather than "verificatory" in analysis of "The Experiment as Mediator Between Object and Subject" (Dawson 2016, pp. 690–695); see also Brodsky (1982, p. 1152 and p. 1162) on mediation.

[7] Dawson (2016, p. 694) provides discussion and explanation of the dialectical features of Goethean science, particularly regarding how the concrete and the abstract transform into one another through research.

[8] Rehbock (1995, p. 308) and Amrine (1998, p. 44) note this relationship between subject and object, I also emphasise their distinctness even in being brought into proximity with one another.

[9] Holdrege (2005, p. 12) and Wahl (2005, p. 59) identify Goethe's empiricism within existing scientific paradigms at the time.

To return to Goethe's warning of "inner enemies," the problem Goethean science attempts to remedy is structured by a separation between subject and object. That separation is maintained by the presence of these "inner enemies," which divorce the subject from the material world:

> For here at this pass, this transition from empirical evidence to judgment, cognition to application, all the inner enemies of man lie in wait: imagination, which sweeps him away on its wings before he knows his feet have left the ground; impatience, haste; self-satisfaction; rigidity; formalistic thought; prejudice; ease; frivolity; fickleness—the whole throng and its retinue. Here they lie in ambush and surprise not only the active observer but also the contemplative one who appears safe from all passion. (EM, p. 943).
>
> ([...] denn beim Übergang von der Erfahrung zum Urteil, von der Erkenntnis zur Anwendung ist es, wo dem Menschen gleichsam wie an einem Passe alle seine inneren Feinde auflauern, Einbildungskraft, Ungeduld, Vorschnelligkeit, Selbstzufriedenheit, Steifheit, Gedankenform, vorgefasste Meinung, Bequemlichkeit, Leichtsinn, Veränderlichkeit und wie die ganze Schar mit ihrem Gefolge heißen mag, alle liegen hier im Hinterhalte und überwältigen unversehens sowohl den handelnden Weltmann als auch den stillen, vor allen Leidenschaften gesichert scheinenden Beobachter.) (SW 25, p. 30).

Internal to the scientist, the "inner enemies" lead him to favour the "Vorstellung" / "idea" over "die Sache" / "thing"[10] such that "the thing must fit his character, no matter how exalted his way of thinking" (EM, p. 944) ("sie muß in seine Sinnesart passen, und er mag seine Vorstellungsart noch so hoch über die gemeine erheben") (SW 25, p. 31). Ideas over things, as well as subjective or abstracting processes belonging to the observer over the objective and concrete situate the observer at a critical point where objective, empirical facts are subsumed by the wild workings of imagination and abstraction. We are aware of what the observer can inject into a given process, but as Goethe implies through pointing at the danger involved in this, the subject and the object are epistemologically different from one another in that the subjective, abstracting tendencies of the observer fail to appropriately match the objects with which they work. One is absorbed into the other without attention to the inherent differences between the two, and the different ways of knowing demanded by the status of objects versus the way the subject has come to know.

However, there isn't as strong a rejection of Kant's idealism as it may at first appear in this configuration.[11] Rather, there are strong concessions to the sub-

---

10 For the whole sentence in German, see SW 25, p. 30.
11 The question of where Goethe sits in relation to idealism is taken up in the *Goethe Yearbook* 18 in Millán/Smith (2011), Amrine (2011), and Nassar (2011). Cassirer (1963) looks directly at Kant and Goethe, Cunningham/Jardine (1990, p. 4) view Romantic science not necessarily as an out-

ject, and its "inner enemies" that obfuscate observation. These must be curbed in order to erode the irreconcilable differences between the subject and the object, between the experimenter and the world, but not eliminated. Even a decade into Kant's post-critical world and its Copernican Turn,[12] the basic tenants on which Goethe's thought are prefaced provide us with a rethinking of this very turn. For Goethe, encounters in the natural world are a model for, and mirror through which to view his conception of human subjectivity.[13] Goethe's human subject recognises the interconnectedness of physical phenomena, and in doing so, essentially moves away from ultimate unknowability of things in themselves on which Kant's Copernican turn pivots (Rintelen 1972, p, 472). There is depth to both subjects and objects, each of which is dependent on recognising partitions and limitations, but partitions and limitations that can be understood in terms of one another. Ceasing with a complete "subjectification of knowledge" (Nassar 2011, p. 75) allows for a reflection of the two.[14]

Additionally, his perspective shares Kant's investment in the subject and what the subject imposes on objects of observation, prefacing the essay with a reminder that the human will always put phenomena in relation to himself (EM, p. 940) ("betrachtet er sie in Bezug auf sich selbst") (SW 25, p. 26). Even so, this affinity to Kant's philosophy does not fully encompass Goethe's project: to ascribe to this the limitations that Kant has in the *Critique of Pure Reason* via the intuitions of space and time would be to overlook Goethe's main objective, that is, the emphasis on processes of observation and experimentation. The problem is not one of noumena and phenomena, but rather a problematic subject-object relationship in which the task for the observer is to "find the measure for what he learns, the data for judgment, not in himself, but in the sphere of what he observers" (EM, p. 941) ("den Maßstab zu dieser Erkenntnis, die Data der Beurteilung nicht aus sich, sondern aus dem Kreise der Dinge nehmen die er beobachtet") (SW 25, p. 26).[15] Thus, Goethe asserts the independence of a sphere that Kant has previously shifted away from. He moves against Kant by

---

right rejection of previous schools of thought. Rehbock (1995, pp. 353–356) offers a thorough overview of the relationship between Kant and Goethe on the subject/object division.
12 See Kant (1998, p. 110, B xvi) in which the exact language of the Copernican Turn isn't one of mediation in this sense, but rather one of how objects conform to the subject.
13 Amrine (2011), Nassar (2011), and Dawson (2016) address related points. See note 16 for Brown (2014) on issue.
14 Nassar (2011, p. 86) identifies Goethe as an interlocutor for Novalis, noting that Goethe as scientist-poet "did not wish to construct a system of knowledge." While he may not have developed a comprehensive system, there are distinct, guiding ideas.
15 Amrine (1998, pp. 37–38) elucidates this methodology.

considering ways in which this world can be knowable or unknowable as the subject must attune itself to it.[16] This requires a different kind of knowing: the subject cannot look solely inward, and thus the challenge is to make two epistemologically different spheres equivalent by combatting certain inward-oriented parts of the subject and turn outward.

The importance of this text lies in the question of self-knowledge and empiricism, how the lines of inquiry uniting the two operate with similar considerations in mind, and become a question of mediation. Playing with an idealist program in the way that Goethe seizes on certain anti-idealist impulses, and creates an awareness of the self that is needed in to make abstract thought concrete and viewable through experimentation.[17] After all, to be "clever" / "klug" (SW 25, p. 27) as Goethe puts it, is operating with an awareness of knowledge to one's self (EM, p. 941). He strives for transparency of the self that accompanies a shift in methodology and reorients our thinking about science as a task of mediation. For Goethe, self-knowledge enables the objective world to be recognised as separate from the subject as something that demands a different way of knowing than the subject knows itself and its depths. And yet, the different kinds of knowing suggested by the need for self-knowledge reinforce the separation between subject and object and affirm their distinctness, even if in close epistemological proximity.

3 *Theory of Colours*, Mediation and the Senses

Other examples of Goethe's scientific theory focus similarly on ways in which abstraction is not to be combatted, but rather reconciled with external phenomena. While readable as a theoretical and practical continuation of "The Experiment as Mediator Between Object and Subject," *Theory of Colours* redirects discussion of the problematic subject/object relationship to how knowledge of observable phenomena provides knowledge of the self, as opposed to exclusively on how knowledge of the self aids in knowledge of the world. His discussion of colours, which includes their symbolic meanings, is based on a discussion of perception, marking the decentring of vision from the eye itself and incorporating the entire

---

16 This is a key point for rethinking Kant's turn, in that by turning to the objective sphere, there is an increased focus on grasping "the infinite." Brown (2014, pp. 79–81) cites this change as allowing the observer to escape the limits of his own subjectivity.
17 Millán/Smith (2011) survey Goethe's relationship to idealism. Dawson (2016, p. 709) summarises related trends in Romantic science more broadly.

experience of the viewer.[18] It involves empiricising largely subjective experiences through illustrating what objects and observable phenomena can expose about dimensions of the subject.

The theoretical underpinnings guiding his experiments with colour invoke a Copernican Turn of their own kind by dismantling what Goethe views as the ossified theory and practice of Newtonian science.[19] Goethe likens Newtonian science in the preface to his *Theory of Colours* to a superfluously constructed "fortress" ("Burg") in which "it became necessary to connect all these incongruous parts and additions by the strangest galleries, halls, and passages" (TC, p. xx) ("Alle diese fremdartigen Teile und Zutaten mußten wieder in die Verbindung gebracht werden durch die seltsamsten Galerien, Hallen, und Gänge") (SW 23.1, p. 15). Adherents to the increasingly dogmatic and untested methodology embodied by the fortress are "invalids," caught under the delusion of their ability to defend the fortress and their practice: "Meanwhile, the building itself is already abandoned; its only inmates are a few invalids, who in simple seriousness imagine that they are prepared for war" (TC, p. xx). ([...] das Gebäude bereits leer steht, nur von einigen Invaliden bewacht, die sich ganz ernsthaft für gerüstet halten") (SW 23.1, p. 16). The imagery of the Newtonian fortress and its followers is a warning against the kinds of dangers akin to the "inner enemies": left unchecked, these abstracting powers become ever more divorced from the observable, physical world and locked up in a fortress that has become "uninhabitable" (TC, p. xx) ("unbewohnbar") (SW 23.1, p. 15).

The intervention Goethe offers involves stepping out of the theoretical confines of this fortress. He offers an opportunity for reflection more so than a corrective of our natural tendencies in observation, which is a challenge to Newton's dogmatic institution. These natural tendencies involve a close proximity of the observer's empirical and conceptual apparatuses, recognising that seeing and theorising are not far removed from one another in the observer:

> Every act of seeing leads to consideration, consideration to reflection, reflection to combination, and thus it may be said that in every attentive look on nature we already theorise. But in order to guard against the possible abuse of this abstract view, in order that the practical deductions we look to should be really useful, we should theorise without forgetting

---

[18] Crary (1992, p. 69) considers Goethe's study of optics and colours as containing a reconfiguration of the observer and observed, marking a subjectification of vision. Moore (2015, p. 238) relatedly notes subject-hood for Goethe as "a dialectical process between observer and observed."

[19] Dawson (2016) and others have likened the anti-Newtonian tendencies with general movement against Kant's thought. For additional discussion on this, see Brown (2014, pp. 80–81), Amrine (1998, p. 38), Heitler (1998, p. 58), and Stephenson (1995, pp. 25–27).

we are so doing, we should theorise with mental self-possession, and, to use a bold word, with irony. (TC, p. xix).

(Jedes Ansehen geht über in ein Betrachten, jedes Betrachten in ein Sinnen, jedes Sinnen in ein Verknüpfen, und so kann man sagen, daß wir schon bei jedem aufmerksamen Blick in die Welt theoretisieren. Dieses aber mit Bewußtsein, mit Selbstkenntnis, mit Freiheit, und um uns eines gewagten Wortes zu bedienen, mit Ironie zu tun und vorzunehmen, eine solche Gewandtheit ist nötig, wenn die Abstraktion, vor der wir uns fürchten, unschädlich und das Erfahrungsresultat, das wir hoffen, recht lebendig und nützlich werden soll.) (SW 23.1, p. 14).

To theorise with irony, as Goethe suggests, does not mean to combat theorising entirely, but rather to proceed with an awareness that enables self-reflection over self-correction (Zajonc 1998, p. 24).[20] The danger lies in the observer who lacks mental self-possession ("Selbstkenntnis") since "in every attentive look on nature we already theorise." The imbrication of theorising and observation is stronger in this essay, suggesting that the observer's task here is less focused on the experiment as a way of mediating the distance between subject and object, but rather on relocating this task into the subject. That is, the subject becomes the locus where the issue of mediation manifests and where it becomes complicated.[21]

Part of the significance of the attention to the subject's capabilities, both empirical and conceptual, is that it too raises a question about interface between subject and object, adding another critical dimension to the question of mediation. As light displays itself to the senses, Goethe describes an understanding of nature initiated by phenomena,[22] revealing a capacity of phenomena to shape the subject. The configuration Goethe uses is based on a vital nature that reveals itself to the observer in a chiefly sensuous fashion:

> Nature speaks to other senses—to known, misunderstood, and unknown senses: so speaks she with herself and to us in a thousand modes. To the attentive observer she is nowhere dead nor silent; she has even a secret agent in inflexible matter, in a metal, the smallest portions of which tell us what is passing in the entire mass. However manifold, complicat-

---

[20] Cassirer (1963, pp. 82–83) notes this tendency in Goethe in relation to Kant's philosophy.
[21] Amrine (1998, p. 44) describes this as a blurring of the boundary between subject and object, which Rehbock (1995, p. 308) examines. Stephenson (1995, p. 49) notes a "medium of the senses," Bell (1994, p. 295) calls this "ironic naturalism," and Zajonc (1998, p. 18) addresses related issues on the question of what Goethean science demands of the subject. Here, however, the nature of colour also plays into this via Crary (1992). Brodsky (1982, p. 1157) relatedly states that "formal perceptions are colored by activity of cognition."
[22] Amrine (2011, p. 45) examines the status of phenomena in nature, specifically via Goethe's indebtedness to Spinoza in its conception.

ed, and unintelligible this language may often seem to us, yet its elements remain ever the same. (TC, p. xviii).

(So spricht die Natur hinabwärts zu andern Sinnen, zu bekannten, verkannten, unbekannten Sinnen; so spricht sie mit sich selbst und zu uns durch tausend Erscheinungen. Dem Aufmerksamen ist sie nirgends tot noch stumm; ja dem starren Erdkörper hat sie einen Vertrauten zugegeben, ein Metall, an dessen kleinsten Teilen wir dasjenige, was in der ganzen Masse vorgeht, gewahr werden sollten. So mannigfaltig, so verwickelt und unverständlich uns oft diese Sprache scheinen mag, so bleiben doch ihre Elemente immer dieselbigen.) (SW 23.1, p. 13).

In acknowledging the "misunderstood and unknown senses" to which nature speaks, the capacities of the subject are expanded in order to be receptive to an array of phenomena presented by nature.[23] In short, nature is able to define the subject through the subject's direct empirical encounter with nature: features of phenomena reveal or broaden empirical capacities of subjects. Even though the issue of mediation is primarily phrased in terms of the subject and relocated back into the subject, the process depends on phenomena. Not only are phenomena needed, but a mirroring between subject and object is additionally revealed through this depiction of the subject's senses: if there are capacities of the subject that are unknown and expanded, then the objects contain a related unknown array of its properties. Any other methodology that is divorced from this largely empirical encounter does not acknowledge the possible expanse of the senses, and fails to acknowledge how subject and object can mutually reflect one another both in terms of what is known and what is unknown about each.

Goethe echoes this idea in establishing how light and colour, like phenomena of nature, appeal most directly to the sense of sight, which in turn reveals a proximity to sense and phenomenon. It reinforces the importance of restoring perceptual truth as a basis for understanding natural phenomena in a move contra Newton,[24] showing an equivalence between subject and object:

Effects we can perceive, and a complete history of those effects would, in fact, sufficiently define the nature of the thing itself. We should try in vain to describe a man's character, but let his acts be collected and an idea of the character will be presented to us. The colours are acts of light. [...] Colours and light, it is true, stand in the most intimate relationship to one another, but we should think of both as belonging to nature as a whole, for it is nature as a whole which manifests itself by their means in an especial manner to the sense of sight. (TC, p. xvii).

---

[23] Hensel (1998, p. 78), Seamon (1998, p. 3), Stephenson (1995, p. 51), and Zajonc (1998, p. 18) note the question of the senses, their expanded capacities, and cultivating them.

[24] Moore (2015), Dawson (2016), and Amrine (2011) highlight the importance of the perception more broadly and importance of its restoration in scientific investigations.

(Wirkungen werden wir gewahr, und eine vollständige Geschichte dieser Wirkungen umfaßte wohl allenfalls das Wesen jenes Dinges. Vergebens bemühen wir uns, den Charakter eines Menschen zu schildern; man stelle dagegen seine Handlungen, seine Taten zusammen, und ein Bild des Charakters wird uns entgegentreten. Die Farben sind Taten des Lichts, Taten und Leiden. […] Farben und Licht stehen zwar unter einander in dem genausten Verhältnis, aber wir müssen uns beide als der ganzen Natur angehörig denken: denn sie ist es ganz, die sich dadurch dem Sinne des Auges besonders offenbaren will.) (SW 23.1, p. 12).

It seems that here, more so than in his other writings, the senses and phenomena attain a status nearly identical with one another in which nature reveals itself in a comprehensive manner to the eye. And yet, terming colours as acts of light is an admission that they are appearances. This reinforces certain perceptual and hence epistemological limitations on the subject and furthermore underscores the difference between the two.[25]

Theory of Colours addresses the demands the external world places on the subject, suggesting a model of mediation that is in part driven by how nature has shaped the subject. Methodologically, *Theory of Colours* sets out to make the inner workings of the self in objective terms, as a corrective to prior schools of thought.[26] But most importantly, it sets up an equivalence between subject and object that is aided by the observer's self-awareness and possession, in which an anti-ideal status of phenomena must work with the subject's indebtedness to certain tendencies of idealism. The already theorising gaze of the subject that is shaped by the phenomena of nature shows a co-existence of competing impulses in the attempts at equivalence between subject and object.

4 *Elective Affinities*, Mediation, and the anti-Classical

In "The Experiment as Mediator Between Object and Subject" and *Theory of Colours*, fissures in Kant's idealism are viewable through a tempering of the abstract and ungraspable by reorienting ourselves towards the graspable, though vestiges of that idealism remain in the difference between subject and object. A related issue of understanding the graspable with the ungraspable, the known with

---

[25] Brodsky (1982, p. 1149) addresses the issue of colour as appearance, Rehbock (1995) presents a comprehensive overview of the status of phenomena in Goethe's science and theory of colour.
[26] Brown (2014, pp. 77–94) handles related issues more broadly in the construction of a "Scientific Self" in Goethe's writings.

the unknown, resonates with rhetorical issues described by Goethe elsewhere in his writings. In his maxims on rhetoric and literature, the respective models of symbol and allegory operate through similar means, though produce different outcomes. For allegory, transparency[27] is key, which suggests a degree of accessibility through the relationship between the particular that is graspable and the general that is ungraspable.[28] At least some of this model is reflected in his scientific writings: there is a sense that self-knowledge and knowledge of the empirical world are tied together in ways that allow for a better understanding of the both the subject and the object. In other words, what is ungraspable can be termed as graspable with careful attention to the ways in which subject and object are understood in terms of one another. However, in an attempt to empiricise and quantify the depths of the human soul, *Elective Affinities* opens up complications to this. More so than in his scientific writings, self-knowledge and empiricism fail to align with one another, reasons for which are reflected in the experiential philosophy that guides the characters in the novel. If Goethean science is "mediatory rather than verificatory" (Dawson 2016, p. 691) then the verificatory nature of experimentation that some protagonists initially ascribe to is weakened throughout the story.[29] It is precisely this failure of a verifictory approach that leads to some of the moments that run counter to parts of Goethe's classical aesthetics.[30]

One need to look no further than the outcome of the experiment of affections that guides the four protagonists into opposing pairs to see where a verificatory science fails.[31] Initial and erroneous attempts at equating human emotions with chemical experiments are predicated on the assumption that emotions function

---

27 Seyhan (1999, pp. 152–154) offers a discussion of how the rhetorical figures of symbol and allegory work together in Goethean thought, and their respective genesis.
28 See SW 13, p. 207, in which maxims on "Allegorie und Symbol" illustrate this point further, highlighting how the symbol has a quality of inexpressibility. See Müller-Sievers (1997, pp. 22, 140–141) on symbol, allegory, and scientific discourse.
29 The question of which scientific framework is appropriate for the conflation between science, literature, and life, including a Newtonian one, is discussed in Adler (1990, p. 265). Adler (1987) contains a broader overview of discourses on chemistry during the period surrounding *Elective Affinities* and its applications in the novel.
30 Atkins (1980) and Schwartz (2005, pp. 216–229) analyse the novel in terms of its connections to aesthetic discourses, and aspects of classicism; Brodsky (1982, p. 1150) locates conflicting aesthetic discourses in the text. Bersier (1988, pp. 409–410) notes departures from classical values.
31 Tantillo (2001, pp. 195–198) addresses the contemporary reception of this work in the context of Goethe's scientific thought.

like atoms.[32] As Charlotte puts it in the incipient stages of the experiment: "'[...] in these simple forms, one sees people one is acquainted with; one has met with just such things in the societies amongst which one has lived'." (EA, p. 39) ("'[...] so sieht man in diesen einfachen Formen die Menschen, die man gekannt hat; besonders aber erinnert man sich dabei der Sozietäten, in denen man lebte'.") (SW 8, p. 302). In this respect, designating the characters as "autonomous but not quite whole" as Brown does,[33] "partially" resonates with Charlotte's construction of themselves: Charlotte sees the individuals as autonomous agents, but fails to see the whole and entirety of the depth of the subjective interior as relevant for the experiment.

The chemical metaphor and the implications of and reasons for Charlotte's initial remark in relation to others by Eduard have been taken up in the scholarship of Jeremy Adler, Claudia Brodsky, Helmut Müller-Sievers and Astrida Orle Tantillo, each addressing the discursivity and failure of certain scientific, aesthetic, and social discourses in the text.[34] To expand on these readings with an eye to Matthew Bell's that considers thought processes and language rather than scientific discourses in the text,[35] Charlotte's remark doesn't consider the importance of mediation, failing to acknowledge that the ability to view similarities between human and atoms are actually upheld by a separation between the two. In short, in equating emotions with atoms, she does not initially consider what is at stake in aligning the two together. However, the language used throughout the story by both the characters and the narrator alludes to ways in which there is an awareness to certain differences between the emotional depth of humans and the atoms of their chemical metaphor. A relevant example of this language occurs early in the novel and is perhaps articulated most clearly through Charlotte's misgivings about the introduction of a third party into her and Eduard's company. Unsure of the possible outcomes of this introduction,

---

[32] See Tantillo (2000, p. 318) on projecting one's "own characteristics on natural theory," Adler (1990, p. 264) on chemical and social theory, Stephenson (1989, p. 387) on other gaps in discourses throughout the novel, Vogl (1999, pp. 145–147, 155) on representations of knowledge in the novel more broadly.
[33] Brown (2014, p. 69) offers this description of the characters in relation to the chemical conceit at the heart of the novel.
[34] Tantillo (2001 pp. 197–198) summarises Adler's, Brodsky's, and Müller-Sievers's arguments. Müller-Sievers (1997, pp. 151–155) discusses different ways of knowing belonging to each character, more broadly using epigenesis, self-generation, and Kant's philosophy as primary interlocutors for understanding the conflation of discourses in the novel and the experiment in it. See Brodsky (1982, pp. 1148–1149), also Tantillo (2000, p. 318).
[35] Bell (1994, pp. 299–302, 307, 317–318) discusses *Theory of Colours and Elective Affinities* along these lines, especially regarding the perspectives of characters, and the issue of language.

she speaks of "these dim sensations" ("die dunklen Anregungen") that are "the result of unconscious recollections of unhappy consequences which we have experienced following our own or others' actions" (EA, p. 8) ("unbewußte Erinnerungen glücklicher und unglücklicher Folgen, die wir an eigenen oder fremden Handlungen erlebt haben.") (SW 8, p. 277). The reliance on such "inchoate feelings" (Brown 2014, p. 171) throughout the story portrays an interior that is defined in largely difficult to quantify terms. But most importantly, this reveals a division between the inner life of the characters and what fails to be quantified or accounted for in the external world: awareness of these instincts does not translate into knowledge of their own actions or those of others. The inward fails to be reoriented outward in a critical and reflective way, suggesting an epistemological divide that is not easily smoothed over or mediated.

The omniscient narrator, however, is aware of the extent of the characters' interiors and their actions.[36] At one point, the narrator invokes a hypothetical, careful observer who in turn could identify through the "Betragen" or "behaviour" of individual members of the group their "inner thoughts and feelings" (EA, p. 103) ("innere Gesinnungen und Empfindungen") (SW 8, p. 353). This subtle but present distinction between inner and outer exists in ways that lack a fixed word, but can be demonstrated through action of the well-known "indescribable, almost magical attraction" (EA, p. 308) ("unbeschreibliche, fast magische Anziehungskraft") (SW 8, p. 516) that inexplicably draws Eduard and Ottilie together. Knowledge of this magical force of attraction eludes the characters in ways that merely gesture towards but are not squarely aligned with an anti-idealist impulse. Compared to the narrator, the characters experience a depth that is not easily rendered in language,[37] and it becomes apparent that the protagonists gesture towards an anti-idealist impulse through some awareness of the depths of the self. However, they never quite allow these depths and their influences on their actions to be fully transparent to one another throughout most of the novel.

This separation of knowledge of the self and empirical knowledge of the world around them seen here is destabilising. The disastrous conclusion to the novel results from the inability to contain the excess of emotion and unquanti-

---

[36] Adler (1987, pp. 141–145, at 142) addresses the issue of the narration, also see Moore (2015, p. 247) for a narrator who is "a stand in for the scientist," and "projects objectivity." (Moore 2015, p. 250) further indicates a "dialectical relationship between observer and observed" in the narration.

[37] Cp. Brodsky (1982, pp. 1151–1152), for the significance of figuration and how "linguistic meaning should be turned upon nature's phenomenality," and Müller-Sievers (1997, pp. 22, 140–141) for language and representation at the time.

fiable depths of the human subject, showing a departure from classical aesthetics, which as noted elsewhere, is supposed to "chain the feelings" (IP, npg) ("fesselt die Gefühle") (MA 6.2, p. 19).[38] Never quite reaching the point where empirical knowledge and knowledge of the self can be effectively mediated in terms of one another, *Elective Affinities* illustrates and exposes additional dangers of a verificatory approach to science[39] that fails to be ultimately productive for cultivating the senses and observational capacities of the protagonists. At least in terms of the subjects' own view of themselves and others, they fail to grasp a wholeness of things as they are, resigned to an unproductive state (Atkins 1980, p. 1; Tantillo 2000, pp. 318–319).

5 Conclusion: Anti-Classical and Anti-Ideal in the Question of Mediation

However divergently *Elective Affinities* and *Theory of Colour* depict experiments and their agents, both texts illustrate the meshing of subject and object through different means. Both engage with the dangers of "inner enemies" when they prevent possible mediation between the subject and the object, and show the stakes in the proximity of self-knowledge and empirical knowledge. On the issue of mediation, Goethe never quite fully departs from the framework set by Kant, but when he does, he finds ways of critically reworking and acknowledging how the subject and the object establish distance between one another and how they, while epistemologically different, are nonetheless structured in similar ways. Taken together, they reveal how epistemological considerations and differences drive attempts at mediation. These in turn reveal anti-ideal and anti-classical fissures in Goethe's scientific and fictional writings, demonstrating a chiastic relationship between the two: the anti-ideal seems to promote classical values, whereas the anti-classical emerges where some idealist-inflected separation between subject and object remains. It may be proposed that Goethean science and his classical aesthetics share certain natural affinities in their desire for smooth mediation, for restraining

---

38 Richter (2005, pp. 3–44, at 9) provides an overview of Weimar Classicism, including its aesthetic features that stress form and containment of a violent undercurrent. Bell (1994, p. 5) describes this classicism as "an attempt at harmony and mediation."
39 Tantillo (2005, pp. 324–327, 342) discusses classical conceptions of science, the question of their applicability to Goethean science, and issues of applying the term "Weimar Classicism" to Goethe's scientific views. Tantillo additionally highlights the dynamism of Goethean science in comparison to the static ideals of Platonism.

the subjective, and assuming a measurable connection between subject and object, though this may not always be possible.

Bibliography

Adler, Jeremy (1987): *„Eine fast magische Anziehungskraft:" Goethes ‚Wahlverwandtschaften' und die Chemie seiner Zeit*. Münich: CH Beck.

Adler, Jeremy (1990): "Goethe's Use of Chemical Theory in His Elective Affinities." In: Cunningham, Andrew / Jardine, Nicholas (Eds.): *Romanticism and the Sciences*. New York: Cambridge University Press, pp. 263–279.

Amrine, Frederick (1998): "The Metamorphosis of the Scientist." In: Seamon, David /Zajonc, Arthur (Eds.): *Goethe's Way of Science: A Phenomenology of Nature*. Albany, NY: State University of New York Press, pp. 33–54.

Amrine, Frederick (2011): "Goethean Intuitions." In: *Goethe Yearbook* 18, pp. 35–50.

Atkins, Stuart (1980): "Die Wahlverwandtschaften: A Novel of German Classicism." In: *The German Quarterly* 53. No. 1, pp. 1–45.

Bell, Matthew (1994): *Goethe's Naturalistic Anthropology: Man and Other Plants*. Oxford: Clarendon Press.

Bersier, Gabrielle (1988): "Sinnliche Übermacht – übersinnliche Gegenmacht: Die dämonische Verwandlung des klassischen Eros in der Epoche der ‚Wahlverwandtschaften'." In: Wittkowski, Wolfgang (Ed.): *Verantwortung und Utopie: Zur Literatur der Goethezeit*. Tübingen: Max Niemeyer Verlag, pp. 405–418.

Brodsky, Claudia (1982): "The Coloring of Relations: Die Wahlverwandtschaften as Farbenlehre." In: *MLN 97*, pp. 1147–1179.

Brown, Jane K. (2014): *Goethe's Allegories of Identity*. Philadelphia: University of Pennsylvania Press.

Cassirer, Ernst (1963): "Goethe and the Kantian Philosophy (1945)." In: *Rousseau, Kant, Goethe*. Gutman, James / Kristeller, Paul Oskar (Trans.). New York, Evanston, London: Harper & Row, pp. 61–98.

Crary, Jonathan (1992): *The Techniques of the Observer: On Vision and Modernity in the Nineteenth Century*. Cambridge: MIT Press.

Cunningham, Andrew / Jardine, Nicholas (1990): "Introduction: The Age of Reflexion." In: Cunningham, Andrew / Jardine, Nicholas (Eds.): *Romanticism and the Sciences*. New York: Cambridge University Press, pp. 1–9.

Currie, Pamela (2013): *Goethe's Visual World*. London: Legenda.

Dawson, Benjamin (2016): "Science and the Scientific Disciplines." In: Hamilton, Paul (Ed.): *The Oxford Handbook of European Romanticism*. New York: Oxford University Press, pp. 684–710.

Goethe, Johann Wolfgang von (1872): *The Elective Affinities*. New York: Henry Holt and Company.

Goethe, Johann Wolfgang von (1909): "Introduction to the Propyläen (1798)." In: Eliot, Charles W. (Ed.): *Prefaces and Prologues To Famous Works*, Vol. XXXIX. New York: Harvard PF Collier and Sons, no page numbers. https://www.bartleby.com/39/34.html.

Goethe, Johann Wolfgang von (1982): *Wilhelm Meister*. Trans. Waisdon, H.M. London: One World Classics.

Goethe, Johann Wolfgang von (1988): "Einleitung in die Propyläen (1798)." In: Goethe, Johann Wolfgang von: *Sämtliche Werke nach Epochen seines Schaffens*. [Münchner Ausgabe. Vol. 6.2]. Eds. Lange, Victor/Becker, Hans K. München: Carl Hanser Verlag, pp. 9–26.

Goethe, Johann Wolfgang von (1989a): "Der Versuch als Vermittler von Objekt und Subjekt (1792)." In: Johann Wolfgang Goethe: *Sämtliche Werke, Briefe, Tagebücher, und Gespräche*. Vol 25. Eds. Engelhardt, Wolf von / Wenzel, Manfred. Frankfurt a. M.: Deutscher Klassiker Verlag, pp. 26–36.

Goethe, Johann Wolfgang von (1989b): "Wilhelm Meisters Wanderjahre (1829)." In: *Johann Wolfgang Goethe: Sämtliche Werke, Briefe, Tagebücher, und Gespräche*. Vol. 10. Eds. Neumann, Gerhard / Dewitz, Hans-Georg. Frankfurt a. M.: Deutscher Klassiker Verlag, pp. 9–774.

Goethe, Johann Wolfgang von (1991): "Zur Farbenlehre (1810)." In: Goethe, Johann Wolfgang: *Sämtliche Werke, Briefe, Tagebücher, und Gespräche*. Vol. 23.1. Ed. Wenzel, Manfred. Frankfurt a. M.: Deutscher Klassiker Verlag, pp. 9–1040.

Goethe, Johann Wolfgang von (1993): "Maximen und Reflexionen." In: *Johann Wolfgang Goethe: Sämtliche Werke, Briefe, Tagebücher, und Gespräche*. Vol. 13. Ed. Fricke, Harald. Frankfurt a. M.: Deutscher Klassiker Verlag, pp. 9–455.

Goethe, Johann Wolfgang von (1994): "Die Wahlverwandtschaften (1809)." In: Goethe, Johann Wolfgang: *Sämtliche Werke, Briefe, Tagebücher, und Gespräche*. Vol 8. Ed. Wiethölter, Waltraud. Franfurt a. M.: Deutscher Klassiker Verlag, pp. 269–529.

Goethe, Johann Wolfgang von (1998): *Maxims and Reflections*.Trans. Stopp, Elisabeth, Ed. Hutchinson, Peter. London: Penguin Books.

Goethe, Johann Wolfgang von (2006): *The Theory of Colours. 1840*. Trans. Eastlake, Charles Locke. Mineola: Dover Publications.

Goethe Johann Wolfgang von (2016): "The Experiment as Mediator Between Object and Subject." In: *The Essential Goethe*. Ed. Bell, Matthew. Princeton: Princeton University Press, pp. 940–46.

Heitler, Walter (1998): "Goethean Science." In: Seamon, David / Zajonc, Arthur (Eds.): *Goethe's Way of Science: A Phenomenology of Nature*. Albany, NY: State University of New York Press, pp. 55–70.

Hensel, Herbert (1998): "Goethe, Science, and Sensory Experience." In: Seamon, David /Zajonc, Arthur (Eds.): *Goethe's Way of Science: A Phenomenology of Nature*. Albany, NY: State University of New York Press, pp. 71–82.

Holdrege, Craig (2005): "Editorial." In: *Janus Head* 8. No. 1, pp. 12–13.

Kant, Immanuel (1998): *Critique of Pure Reason* (1787). Guyer, Paul / Wood, Allen W.(Trans.). New York: Cambridge University Press.

Millán, Elizabeth / Smith, John H (2011): "Introduction: Goethe and Idealism-Points of Intersection." In: *Goethe Yearbook* 18, pp. 2–9.

Moore, Evelyn K. (2015): *The Eye and the Gaze: Goethe and the Autobiographical Subject*. Bern: Peter Lang.

Müller-Sievers, Helmut (1997): *Self-generation: Biology, Philosophy, and Literature around 1800*. Stanford: Stanford University Press.

Nassar, Dalia (2011): "'Idealism is nothing but genuine empiricism': Novalis, Goethe, and the Ideal of Romantic Science." In: *Goethe Yearbook* 18, pp. 67–95.

Rehbock, Theda (1995): *Goethe und die "Rettung der Phänomene": Philosophische Kritik des naturwissenschaftlichen Weltbilds am Beispiel der Farbenlehre*. Konstanz: Verlag am Hockgraben.

Richter, Simon (2005): "Introduction." In: Richter, Simon (Ed.): *The Literature of Weimar Classicism*. Rochester: Camden House, pp. 4–44.

Rintelen, Fritz-Joachim (1972): "Kant and Goethe." In Beck, Lewis White (Ed.): *The Proceedings of the Third International Kant Congress*. Dordrecht: D. Reidel Publishing Company, pp. 471–479.

Schwartz, Peter (2010): *After Jena: Goethe's Elective Affinities and the End of the Old Regime*. Lewisburg: Bucknell University Press.

Seamon, David (1998): "Goethe, Nature, and Phenomenology: An Introduction." In: Seamon, David / Zajonc, Arthur (Eds.): *Goethe's Way of Science: A Phenomenology of Nature*. Albany, NY: State University of New York Press, pp. 1–14.

Seyhan, Azade (1999): "Allegorie der Allegorie: Romantische Allegorese als Kulturelle Erinnerung." In: Helfer, Martha (Ed.): *Rereading Romanticism*. Amsterdam, Atlanta: Rodopi, pp. 151–169.

Stephenson, R.H. (1989): "Theorizing to Some Purpose: 'Deconstruction' in the Light of Goethe and Schiller's Aesthetics—the Case of *Die Wahlverwandtschaften*." In: *Modern Language Review* 84. No. 2, pp. 381–92.

Stephenson, R.H. (1995): *Goethe's Conception of Knowledge and Science*. Edinburgh: Edinburgh University Press.

Tantillo, Astrida Orle (2000): "Polarity and Productivity in Goethe's Wahlverwandtschaften." In *Seminar: A Journal of Germanic Studies* 36. No. 3, pp. 310–325.

Tantillo, Astrida Orle (2001): *Goethe's Elective Affinities and the Critics*. Rochester: Camden House.

Tantillo, Astrida Orle (2005): "Goethe's 'Classical' Science." In: Richter, Simon (Ed.): *The Literature of Weimar Classicism*. Rochester: Camden House, pp. 323–245.

Vogl, Joseph (1999): "Mittler und Lenker: Goethes 'Wahlverwandtschaften'." In: Vogl, Joseph (Ed.): *Poetologien des Wissens um 1800*. Munich: Wilhelm Fink Verlag, pp. 145–161.

Wahl, Daniel (2005): "'Zarte Empirie': Goethean Science as Way of Knowing." In: *Janus Head* 8. No. 1, pp. 58–76.

Zajonc, Arthur (1998): "Goethe and the Science of His Time." In: Seamon, David / Zajonc, Arthur (Eds.): *Goethe's Way of Science: A Phenomenology of Nature*. Albany: State University of New York Press, pp. 15–30.

Abbreviations

EA = Goethe, Johann Wolfgang von (1872): *The Elective Affinities*. New York: Henry Holt and Company.

EM = Goethe, Johann Wolfgang von: "The Experiment as Mediator Between Object and Subject." In: Bell, Matthew (Ed.): *Essential Goethe*. Princeton: Princeton University Press, pp. 940–946.

IP = Goethe, Johann Wolfgang von (1909): "Introduction to the Propyläen (1798)." In: Eliot, Charles W. (Ed.): *Prefaces and Prologues To Famous Works*, Vol. XXXIX. New York: Harvard PF Collier and Sons, no page numbers. https://www.bartleby.com/39/34.html.

MA = Goethe, Johann Wolfgang von (1988): "Einleitung in die Propyläen (1798)." In: Goethe, Johann Wolfgang von: *Weimarer Klassik:1798–1806*. [Münchner Ausgabe. Vol. 6.2]. Eds. Lange, Victor/Becker, Hans K. München: Carl Hanser Verlag, pp. 9–26.
MR = Goethe, Johann Wolfgang von (1998): *Maxims and Reflections*. Trans. Stopp, Elisabeth, Ed. Hutchinson, Peter. London: Penguin Books.
TC = Goethe, Johann Wolfgang von (2006): *The Theory of Colours*. 1840. Trans. Eastlake, Locke Charles. Mineola: Dover Publications.
WM = Goethe, Johann Wolfgang von (1982): *Wilhelm Meister*. Trans. Waisdon, H.M. London: One World Classics.
SW = Goethe, Johann Wolfgang (1989): *Sämtliche Werke, Briefe, Tagebücher, und Gespräche*. Frankfurt a.M.: Deutscher Klassiker Verlag.

Christopher Law
Reading Surfaces: Goethe and Benjamin

Abstract: In Johann Wolfgang von Goethe's *Zur Farbenlehre*, the idea of electricity plays a significant role in the generation of surfaces, which Goethe considers necessary for the plurality of colours to attain to visibility. This paper proposes that the relation between electricity and colour registers a threshold between classicism and anti-classicism, which becomes particularly prominent in the wake of Kant's *Kritik der Urteilskraft*. By arguing that this problem was also present in Walter Benjamin's early, fragmentary work on colour and language, the paper suggests that Benjamin's critical reception of Goethe's scientific studies may be reconsidered.

1

In the 854th section of *Zur Farbenlehre*, one of a series of remarks advanced under the heading "Helldunkel" or chiaroscuro, Goethe sketches a distinction between the rotundity of natural objects and the planar quality of artistic surfaces:

> As its most natural example, the sphere would be auspicious for forming a general concept of chiaroscuro, but would not be sufficient for its aesthetic use. The fleeting unity of such a rotundity leads to the nebulous. In order to bring about the effects of art, surfaces must be generated on it, so that the elements of the shadow-side and the light-side separate themselves more distinctly.
>
> (Zum natürlichsten Beispiel für das Helldunkel wäre die Kugel günstig, um sich einen allgemeinen Begriff zu bilden, aber nicht hinlänglich zum ästhetischen Gebrauch. Die verfließende Einheit einer solchen Rundung führt zum Nebulistischen. Um Kunstwirkungen zu erzwecken, müssen an ihr Flächen hervorgebracht werden, damit die Teile der Schatten- und Lichtseite sich mehr in sich selbst absondern.) (Goethe 1989, p. 249).[1]

Beneath its explicit concern with the respective virtues of natural and artistic mediums, Goethe's distinction betrays the lasting influence of Immanuel Kant's *Kritik der Urteilskraft* on his colour theory and other scientific investigations. In the very act of proposing that the sphere can serve as the "most natural example" of chiaroscuro and can hence exemplify a "general concept" thereof,

---

1 Translations are my own, unless otherwise stated. Where I have used or consulted existing translations, references to these are given alongside references to the original.

Goethe casts doubt on this form's capacity to be an object of aesthetic judgement —that is, a judgement not mediated by concepts, and of which there can be no incontestable, or "natural", example. If Goethe's claim does not therefore turn on the relative aesthetic qualities of natural spheres and planar surfaces (Fläche), it stands that only with the development of the latter can the "aesthetic use" of the technique of chiaroscuro be promoted and the "effects of art" sufficiently aligned with the state of "purposiveness without end" (Zweckmäßigkeit ohne Zweck) that is said to characterise the free lawfulness of judgements of taste (Kant 1971, p. 241). Insofar as it seeks to fend off the nebulous transience of a merely "fleeting unity," Goethe's affirmation of the planar surface, at the same time, evinces a hallmark of classicism: if variation in colour is natural, it is nonetheless only in art that nature's multiplicity may achieve a sufficient representational form. As Paul Celan would put it in his "Meridian" speech a century and a half later, though not without a pronounced distancing from the expressed sentiment, the task is "to capture the natural as natural by means of art (das Natürliche als das Natürliche mittels der Kunst zu erfassen)" (Celan 1983, p. 46).

In so affirming the enduring character of the aesthetic surface, however, Goethe also hits upon a problem that further discloses the complexity of his inheritance of Kant's third Critique: if aesthetic judgements of taste are singular, yet not merely nebulous, this is because the pleasure or displeasure arising from the free play of the imagination and understanding corresponds to a "feeling of life (Lebensgefühl)" whose temporality is best described as a "lingering (Verweilung)" (Kant 1971, p. 204, p. 222). An aesthetic use of the chiaroscuro should last, but without the means of "general concepts": the problem of art in the wake of the third Critique—itself indexed by Kant's claim that claims about art are not pure but rather "logically conditioned (logisch-bedingtes)" aesthetic judgements (Kant 1971, p. 312)—is precisely the nature of this duration. For Kant, the state of lingering describes the phenomenological peculiarity of reflective judgement insofar as the subject catches him or herself in the act of judgement itself, rather than merely subsuming the particular under the universal. Precisely how this duration might lend itself to Goethe's distinction between natural and artistic forms, however, remains open to question, not least because—as Goethe, like any reader of the *Kritik der Urteilskraft* would have registered—the place of colour in Kant's text is anything but clear.[2]

---

[2] For Kant's most explicit arguments about colour, see Kant 1971, pp. 224–25 and pp. 324–25.

2

If classicist modes of representation survived an array of anti-mimetic modernisms and continued to bear influence on innovative poetic methods, such as Celan's, well into the twentieth century, it owes to the fact that, in the wake of Kant's third Critique, the mimetic representation of nature was inflected by an emphasis on art's irreducibly singular character. Only singular presentations could adequately express that which is natural about nature, because every general concept of nature fails to account for nature's own dynamism. Walter Benjamin's sporadic but persistent engagement with Goethe's theory of art demonstrates the extent to which this idea—which can be provisionally conceived as a threshold between classicism and anti-classicism—continued to be experienced as a problem in the first half of the twentieth century. Goethe's influence on Benjamin also exposes, however, the potential faultlines of this idea. And in light of Benjamin's protracted and often marginalised encounters with Goethe, an enquiry into the latter's own claim for the specificity of art, as opposed to nature, is important for the following reason: Benjamin claims time and again that Goethe fails to adequately distinguish between art and nature, and that his entire theory of art hangs, proceeds and ultimately fails on the basis of this ambiguity. Indeed, this claim might constitute the primary issue that prevents Benjamin from identifying with Goethe's theory of art at a fundamental level.

This line of critique is opened in Benjamin's doctoral dissertation, *Der Begriff der Kunstkritik in der deutschen Romantik* (submitted at the University of Bern in 1919), or more accurately in the afterword to the academic work, which Benjamin distributed privately among friends (Benjamin 1974a, pp. 110–119); it finds its most sustained elaboration in the essay "Goethes Wahlverwandtschaften," composed between 1919 and 1922. In the later text, Benjamin emphasises how Goethe's intricately constructed novel presents itself as a natural artefact: in destroying the drafts of *Die Wahlverwandtschaften*, Goethe deliberately obscured evidence of the "constructive technique of the work (konstruktive Technik des Werkes)" (Benjamin 1974, p. 146). This presentation of the work as a natural, rather than constructed, entity corresponds, in Benjamin's reading, to an ambiguity in the concept of nature itself, which *Die Wahlverwandtschaften* manifests for the first time:

> Thus, a fundamental motive for Goethean research into nature emerges only here. This study rests upon an ambiguity—sometimes naive, sometimes doubtless more meditated—in the concept of nature. For it designates in Goethe at once the sphere of perceptible phenomena and that of intuitable archetypes. (Benjamin 1996, p. 314).

(So erscheint ein Urgrund Goetheschen Forschens in Natur nur hier. Dieses Studium beruht auf bald naivem, bald auch wohl bedachterem Doppelsinn in dem Naturbegriff. Er bezeichnet nämlich bei Goethe sowohl die Sphäre der wahrnehmbaren Erscheinungen wie auch die der anschaubaren Urbilder.) (Benjamin 1974, p. 147).

The lack of clarity regarding whether the so-called ur-phenomena are to be understood as empirically observable natural phenomena or as intuitable ideas is said by Benjamin to exemplify an illegitimate overlap between Goethe's literary and scientific work—particularly the *Farbenlehre*, whose composition, Benjamin notes, touches closely on that of the novel. From this perspective, Goethe's distinction between natural rotundity and artistic surface is posited only on the basis of a more fundamental failure to differentiate nature and art.

3

Although the references to the *Farbenlehre* in "Goethes Wahlverwandtschaften" are the first to be found in Benjamin's surviving body of writing, Benjamin was already occupied in the mid-1910s by his own fledgling project on colour.[3] Rather than culminating in anything like a theory or doctrine (*Lehre*) of colour, however, Benjamin's project was to remain unfinished. And despite the fact that the surviving texts evidence, like the *Farbenlehre*, a subtle engagement with Kant's critical philosophy, they more or less sideline the obvious question of whether or not colour has formal qualities that make it a suitable object for aesthetic judgement. Benjamin's entire project is oriented less by these outstanding issues raised by the third Critique than by the major claim of the "Transcendental Aesthetic" of the *Kritik der reinen Vernunft:* that human experience is delimited to the sensible reception of objects as forms in space and time. For Benjamin, instead, colour is a "medium," which is only reduced to a secondary quality of spatio-temporal objects for those who have lost the capacity for perceiving colour purely, namely "adults, productive people" (Benjamin 1985, p. 111). On the other hand, "colour in the life of children is the pure expression of (their) pure receptivity (Empfänglichkeit), insofar as it is directed at the world" (Benjamin 1985, p. 111). Just as determining, conceptually-mediated judgements, by definition, do not "reflect" on their own status as judgements, the spatio-tem-

---

[3] The question of precisely when Benjamin read Goethe's *Farbenlehre* is a contested one. For an overview of the stance taken by the editors of the *Gesammelte Schriften* (Benjamin read the text no earlier than 1919) and for a convincing counterview (Benjamin read the text at some point in the mid-1910s), see Fenves 2011, pp. 266–267, n. 27.

poral forms of perception that govern adult life—so Benjamin argues—fail to acknowledge colour as a medium; colour is dampened when the world is perceived as a progression of spatio-temporal forms, an insight that accords with Goethe's *Farbenlehre*.

Indeed, according to Goethe, the colour wheel "on paper" manifests a diversity and makes possible a harmony compared to which even the rainbow (lacking as it is in "pure red") appears to be poor in world (Goethe 1989, p. 240). Two texts from Benjamin's early complex of writings on colour and fantasy—"Der Regenbogen: Gespräch über die Phantasie" and "Der Regenbogen oder die Kunst des Paradieses: Aus einer alten Handschrift"—concern themselves with nothing other than this "natural" constellation of colour. The former text, a dialogue occasioned by a vivid experience of colour occurring in the dreams of one character, Margarethe, and communicated to her interlocutor, Georg, demonstrates the extent to which the pure reception of colour displaces human subjects from their status as autonomous subjects capable of knowing the world through judgements upon spatio-temporal phenomena:

> GEORG: I felt myself to be quite light in those hours. Of everything around me I was aware only of that through which I was in the things: their qualities, through which I penetrated them. I myself was a quality of the world and floated over it. It was filled with me as though with color. (Benjamin 2011a, p. 215).

> (GEORG: Ich fühlte mich ganz leicht in diesen Stunden. Von allem nahm ich nur das wahr, wodurch ich in den Dingen war: ihre Eigenschaften, durch die ich sie durchdrang. Ich war selbst Eigenschaft der Welt und schwebte über ihr. Sie war von mir erfüllt wie von Farbe.) (Benjamin 1989a, p. 20).

Colour, according to the dialogue, is the purest expression of the imagination because no creative capacity corresponds to it: whereas we "taste" when we perceive taste or "smell" when we perceive smell, we do not "colour" when perceiving colour. Rather: "Colors see themselves; in them is the pure seeing, and they are its object and organ at the same time. Our eye is colored" (Benjamin 2011a, p. 218; 1989a, p. 23). Benjamin here appears to adopt, without hesitation, one of Goethe's most forceful insights: "One may look so strongly at a perfectly yellow-red surface, that the colour seems to actually penetrate the organ" (Goethe 1989, p. 233). Not only does colour exceed the strictly defined limits of spatio-temporal objects, it also violently affects the organs that perceive it.

As Peter Fenves notes in an exacting commentary, the extremity of Benjamin's thought is inseparable from the form in which it is presented (Fenves 2011, pp. 79–102). As the last surviving dialogue written by Benjamin, the text arguably marks the exhaustion of this particular mode of writing; once a dialogue undertakes the task of recalling a dream, after all, it is already testing the limits of what the form can do: "A dream can't be told," as Margarethe tells Georg in the text's opening lines (Benjamin 2011a, p. 214; 1989a, p. 19). Moreover, the end of the dialogue can be read as marking the exhaustion or impasse of the argument itself, if ever one existed. Throughout the exchange, Margarethe seems to imply that the reception of nature and the production of art are in essence the same activity; Georg that there must remain a distinction between imaginative colour (or colour in fantasy), and colour in any existent picture. Yet, with the appearance of a rainbow at the text's conclusion, the dialogue ends in a call for silence (Fenves 2011, pp. 79–80). This question is of the utmost significance for considering the relationship between the two "Rainbow" texts. As Fenves again notes, an inconsistency governs the kinship between "Der Regenbogen: Gespräch über die Phantasie" and "Der Regenbogen oder die Kunst des Paradieses." In the latter text, what promises to be an enquiry into an ageless and "difficult question: where the beauty of nature comes from" gives up this task as soon as it is posed, weaning itself off the dialogue whose insights it appears to presuppose (Benjamin 1989b, p. 562). Beyond its pseudepigraphic title, there is no further mention of a "rainbow" in the text, which considers instead the forms of configuration appropriate to different forms of art.

Indeed, reflecting on cases when the spatial quality of nature is foregrounded, Benjamin distances himself from the question of beauty in nature by means of a sly parody of Kant: "Wherever it is a matter of such spatial properties, nature is beautiful not in light of mere perception but only in some sentimental and edifying regard, as when one pictures the Alps or the immensity of the sea" (Benjamin 2011b, p. 224; 1989b, p. 562). What might for Kant be paradigmatic objects of disinterested pleasure for judging subjects—the Alps, the sea—become, for Benjamin, repositories of sentimental desires. In contrast, only those who "are able to dwell in nature" find it truly beautiful: "above all, children" (2011b, p. 224; 1989b, p. 562). Benjamin's short piece turns, accordingly, not on beauty in nature, but on art, whose task is that of "generation" (Erzeugung) (1989b, p. 562). By this, Benjamin means (without any explicit reference to Kant) that space must be generated in such a way that it is no longer merely a pure form of intuition in which objects can be formed by judging subjects: "The space of nature, in this view, is undimensional, torpid, a nothing, if it is not animated by humble empirical means" (Benjamin 2011b, p. 225; 1989b, p. 562). As hinted by this passage, Benjamin sees art, and particularly sculpture, to be a process of "animation (Belebung)" or of "spiritual appearance (geistige Erscheinung)"; art establishes a "generated spirit (erzeugten Geist)." Despite the playful register of the text's relation to the third Critique, it is impossible to miss the influence of Kant's definition of "Geist" as the "animating principle (belebende Princip)" of a work (Kant 1971, p. 313).

The next paragraph begins with the assertion that painting also involves the spiritual generation of space. However, Benjamin writes:

> The spatial depth that is generated in painting concerns the relation of space to objects. This relation is mediated through the surface. The surface, the spatial nature of things is developed in itself, as something unempirical, concentrated. Not the dimension but the infinity of space is constructed in painting. This happens through the surface, in that, here, things develop not their dimensionality, their extension *in* space, but their being *toward* space. (Benjamin 2011, p. 225).

> (Die Raumtiefe, die in der Malerei erzeugt wird, betrifft die Beziehung des Raumes zu Gegenständen. Diese wird durch die Fläche vermittelt. In der Fläche entwickelt sich an sich die raumhafte Natur der Dinge, unempirisch, konzentriert. Nicht die Dimension, die Unendlichkeit des Raumes wird in der Malerei konstruiert. Dies geschieht durch die Fläche, indem die Dinge nicht schlechthin ihre Dimensionalität entwickeln, nicht ihre Ausdehnung im Raume, sondern ihr Dasein *zum* Raume.) (Benjamin 1989b, p. 563).

Benjamin then claims that the required "form of appearance" should express not the "dimensionality" of objects, which would correspond to their "extension in space (Ausdehnung im Raume)," but rather their "contural tension (konturale Spannung)," the minimal strain which generates space each time anew. Here, Benjamin's claims seem to dovetail with Goethe's: without this form of appearance, he notes, the surface "remains two-dimensional and attains only a graphic, perspectival, illusionary depth" (Benjamin 2011, p. 225; 1989b, p. 563; translation modified). And as in Goethe's depiction of that most graphic style, chiaroscuro, the form of appearance to counteract this illusionary depth is said to be colour.

4

Before dissolving into "clouds,"[4] the fragment makes a final distinction between the colour of fantasy and the colour of art:

> In painting, a color cannot be considered as standing in itself alone; it stands in relation and has substance as surface or ground, in one way or another is shaded and connected to light and darkness. Color as conceived by children exists entirely in itself, and can be related to no higher concept (through development). (Benjamin 2011, pp. 226–27).

---

[4] The fragment breaks off with a new paragraph that begins and ends with the words "Die Wolken" (Benjamin 1989b, p. 564).

(Die malerische Farbe kann nicht für sich gesehen werden, sie hat Beziehung, ist substantiell als Oberfläche oder Grund, irgendwie schattiert und auf Licht und Dunkel bezogen. Die Farbe im Sinne der Kinder steht ganz für sich, auf keinen übergeordneten Farbbegriff (durch Entwicklung) zu beziehen.) (Benjamin 1989b, p. 564).

This paragraph follows an attempt to schematically oppose "the beauty of nature and of the child" on the one hand, and "the beauty of art" on the other (Benjamin 2011, p. 226; Benjamin 1989b, p. 563). Is it indeed the case, then, that Benjamin's text ends with the inscription of an impassable dualism? Whereas direct references to Goethe are entirely absent from these remarks, Benjamin's insistence on the centrality of "tension" and "contour" for the generation of surface echoes one of the main insights of the *Farbenlehre*, as the explicit reference to "light and darkness" makes clear. Whereas Benjamin proposes that only children may access colour as a pure medium, Goethe—as is clear from the sections on *Helldunkel*—is far more optimistic about the potential for artistic surfaces to present chromatic differentiation in an aesthetically significant yet persisting form. A surface, as the passages that introduced this contribution make clear, is a perceptual or phenomenological apparatus in which colour is not necessarily dampened in order that an object be perceived as a form in space and time. Despite fundamental differences in approach, the two thinkers appear to agree on the fact that surfaces must be artistically generated. How is this generation to be achieved for Goethe, however?

Goethe has insisted that the "aesthetic use" of chromatic differentiation diverges from the "most natural example" of such, the sphere. It is, however, in another phenomenon—which, in the period around 1800 was considered reducible neither to the organic nor inorganic realm—that Goethe identifies the emergence of a surface of chromatic differentiation.[5] In the 742nd section of the *Farbenlehre*, he writes of electricity:

> It is for us a nothing, a zero, a null-point, a point of indifference, which, however, dwells in all appearing natures, and is at the same time a point of origin, from which, on the slightest occasion, a double appearance emerges, which appears only insofar as it once again disappears.
>
> (Es ist für uns ein Nichts, ein Null, ein Nullpunkt, ein Gleichgültigkeitspunkt, der aber in allen erscheinenden Wesen liegt, und zugleich der Quellpunkt ist, aus dem bei dem geringsten Anlaß eine Doppelerscheinung hervortritt, welche nur insofern erscheint, als sie wieder verschwindet.) (Goethe 1989, p. 223).

---

5 See Holland 2009.

Just as Benjamin argues that surfaces manifest "existence toward space" rather than "extension in space" (whereby space is conceived as an *a priori* form), Goethe's surfaces interrupt any preconception of what a surface is, leaving the emergent space wholly determinable. Thus the apparently paradoxical statement that although the phenomenon of electricity "particularly follows the surface (Oberfläche), it is in no way superficial (keinesweges oberflächlich)" (Goethe 1989, p. 223). And in the same way that Benjamin emphasises how, as a mode of the appearance of objects, surfaces manifest their "contural tension," Goethe reduces the dimensionality of space to the generation of a single "point." This point is figured as a "point of indifference," not because its generality determines every conceivable instance of its appearance, but because its emergence is of such a singular nature—only "on the slightest occasion" does such an event occur—that it may not enter into any comparative framework according to which any one point may be considered different from any other. The irreducible occasionality of surfaces, moreover, means that they appear only to disappear, leaving behind nothing but a trace of their appearance, a trace which is named "a nothing."

If surfaces fail to yield the lasting significance that would be necessary for a comparative framework and thus for an overarching concept of the surface, they can, likewise, never be followed back to a discrete source. As in the famous claim put forward apropos of the word origin (*Ursprung*) in the "Epistemo-Critical Prologue" to Benjamin's *Ursprung des deutschen Trauerspiels*, the word *Quellpunkt* here denotes not an identifiable root or source, but a singularity which nevertheless "dwells" in every manifestation of electricity. As Benjamin writes, the dialectic appropriate to origin dictates that "singularity and repetition (Einmaligkeit und Wiederholung)" condition one another (Benjamin 1974c, p. 226). If it is not apparent here exactly what electricity is—a field, force, or energy—it is clear enough what it is not: substantial. Electricity is not mined like a substance that remains forever identical to itself, but is instead induced in a field, its origin generated only on the occasion of its repetition. As Kevin McLaughlin has compellingly argued of literary appeals to electricity in John Ruskin and Marcel Proust, this mode of generation also effects a subtle diagnosis of aesthetic judgement in the wake of Kant's third Critique and a transformation in the self-understanding of "classicism" that occurs around 1800 (McLaughlin 1999, p. 969). No longer determined by a set of criteria that may or may not be detected in discrete artistic artefacts, aesthetic judgement sees the object withdrawing itself to be merely the occasion (*Anlaß*) of its own appearance, and—by extension—the occasion of the free play of the faculties, experienced, because universally communicable, as pleasure. Whereas such a claim continues to haunt readers of Kant's work, insofar as it appears to entirely erase the object in favour of its ephemeral appearance (a *double* appearance in Goethe's parlance: appearing only to disappear), its implications appear to be far less troublesome for Goethe. It is precisely through such an appearing and disappearing "nothing"—a nothing which is substantialised by means of an indeterminate article and, as if to drive the point home, repeated with variation ("ein Null, ein Nullpunkt, ein Gleichgültigkeitspunkt")—that artistic surfaces appear in the first instance. The appearance which emerges on the surface is a double one, then, not only because it is also a disappearance, but, moreover, because it generates a momentary depth of the kind that renders the surface "in no way superficial." Determined neither by mathematics nor by its illegitimate appropriation in the realm of colour theory by optics, this is a depth that cannot be mined for lasting substantial content and which thus forms the site of a new relation between poetry and truth.

5

With the recent surge of critical interest in Goethe's late journals on morphology, this insight along with much else in *Zur Farbenlehre* has fallen by the wayside. Not only scientifically dubious, the book is, at a textual level, too systematic and, at a philosophical and scientific one, too indebted to a transcendental account of difference to be able to account for the real plurality that the truly curious scientist encounters in natural phenomena.[6] As Amanda Jo Goldstein has argued in vivid detail, Goethe's scattered writings on morphology express a concern not with the "double appearance" of surfaces—their simultaneous generation and withdrawal—but with their irreducible multiplicity, conceived along Epicurean and Lucretian lines of fragmentation, dispersal, and metamorphosis (2017, pp. 72–135). This corresponds, in Goldstein's reconstruction, to a rejection of Kant's third Critique, not only insofar as aesthetic judgements claim the subject (contra Goethe's "vulnerable" scientific observer) to be "indifferent to the very *survival* of the object" (Goldstein 2017, p. 128) but also to the extent that Kant is said to uphold an antinomy between the "power" of singular organic life and the mechanism of non-organic nature (Goldstein 2017, pp. 78–82). With morphology, on the other hand, the watchword is not singularity but multiplicity. It would be impossible to sufficiently engage with the sophistication of this thesis in the present contribution. Instead, in moving toward a conclusion, I will simply agree with one of its claims: the difference between nothing and something, in-

---

[6] For an investigation of the textual and compositional state of the morphology notebooks in comparison to the *Farbenlehre*, see Geulen 2008, especially pp. 53–54.

dexed by Goldstein's emphasis on the term "power," is precisely what is at stake, from Goethe's theory of electricity in the early nineteenth century to the neo-Kantian accounts of "origin" that are revised by Benjamin in the first decades of the twentieth. This is not to concede, however, that the insight of the *Farbenlehre* is entirely reducible to this point. According to Goethe, as this contribution has emphasised, the phenomenon of electricity does indeed function as the condition of possibility for the multiplicity and harmony of colours sought by the *Farbenlehre*. No sooner is a surface developed, however, does it becomes another space for the emergence of difference. The colour wheel "on paper" is the site not only of potential harmony, but also of the always attendant possibility of discord; this uncertainty arises from Goethe's recognition of the link between colour and language.

This is not a merely local problem, but rather comes to inflect Goethe's own presentation and organisation of his material throughout the *Farbenlehre*. In the "Concluding Observations on Language and Terminology" that bring the fifth part of the text to a close, Goethe obliquely addresses the theme of symbolism raised in the *Kritik der Urteilskraft*. For Kant, symbolism sees judgement assuming a "double enterprise (doppeltes Geschäft)," not only of linking concepts to intuitions, but also of reflecting upon that application in order adopt the object of this intuition as the symbol for an "entirely different object" (Kant 1971, p. 352). Perhaps picking up on Kant's subsequent remark that "our language is full of such indirect presentations (Unsere Sprache ist voll von dergleichen indirecten Darstellungen)," Goethe recognises symbolism to pervade all forms of linguistic communication:

> One never reflects enough that a language is really only symbolic, only figurative, and that the objects are never expressed immediately, but only in reflex. This is particularly the case when the talk is of things which only approach experience and which one can more easily call activities than objects, like those, in the realm of the doctrine of nature, that are forever in movement. They cannot be held, and yet one should talk of them; one therefore seeks out all kinds of formulas in order to get at them, even if only by way of analogy.
>
> (Man bedenkt niemals genug, daß eine Sprache eigentlich nur symbolisch, nur bildlich sei und die Gegenstände niemals unmittelbar, sondern nur im Widerscheine ausdrücke. Dieses ist besonders der Fall, wenn von Wesen die Rede ist, welche an die Erfahrung nur herantreten und die man mehr Tätigkeiten als Gegenstände nennen kann, dergleichen im Reiche der Naturlehre immerfort in Bewegung sind. Sie lassen sich nicht festhalten, und doch soll man von ihnen reden; man sucht daher alle Arten von Formeln auf, um ihnen wenigstens gleichnisweise beizukommen.) (Goethe 1989, p. 226).

Quickly following this insight, Goethe asks after the possibility of a "diversified language (mannigfaltigen Sprache)" that could preserve the writer from the kind of "predilection" that usually befalls scientific writing (Goethe 1989, p. 227). In the next section, he comments on the challenges of such a task: "Yet how difficult it is to avoid putting the sign in place of the thing, to keep the essence always living before us, and not to kill it through the word" (Goethe 1989, p. 227). Finally, in the closing paragraphs of the text, Goethe makes a "mystical allusion (mystische Deutung)," suggesting that colour "could also serve as a language, when one wants to express primordial relations, which do not meet the senses so powerfully and variously (als einer Sprache, auch da bedienen könne, wenn man Urverhältnisse ausdrücken will, die nicht eben so mächtig und mannigfaltig in die Sinne fallen)" (Goethe 1989, p. 263). Colourful language stands in, Goethe proposes, where both language and sense experience fail to capture the living quality of chromatic difference.

It is not because it has immediate access to the totality of colours, however, that such a "language" can express primordial relation. Goethe does admit that, upon seeing a colour, our desire to create another initiates a relation which "encompasses the totality of the whole circle of colour" but this remains no more than a "striving after universality (Streben nach Allgemeinheit)," whose satisfaction is precisely what remains in question throughout the entirety of the *Farbenlehre* (Goethe 1989, p. 238). On the contrary, colour expresses the character of linguistic reference precisely because it is a site where every direct relation between word and thing breaks down: "Add to this that all colours can be more or less besmirched (beschmutzt), can be made to a certain degree unrecognizable and so combined, partly with themselves, partly with pure colours" (Goethe 1989, p. 244). Only by being estranged from their self-identity can colours be varied to infinity; only colour's fall into a "besmirched" language, where every colour can be predicated of every other, allows it to be conceived as a language in the first place.

Perhaps in this way, if in no other, Benjamin's and Goethe's projects on colour enter into the closest proximity. To emphasise the non-creative relation that humans have to colour, Benjamin's dialogue frequently employs the term reception (*Empfängnis*), which is of central significance to his own theory of naming. In his 1916 text "Über Sprache überhaupt und über die Sprache des Menschen" the human is said to perform the task of naming things when "he receives the mute, nameless lanuage of things and, in the name, carries them over into sounds (er die stumme namenlose Sprache der Dinge empfängt und sie in den Namen in Lauten überträgt)" (Benjamin 1977, p. 151). Likewise, the name is said to be nothing but a "receptive (empfangend)," rather than spontaneous or creative, material sounding. In employing variations of the term *Empfängnis*, Benjamin's essay brackets the idea that a subject is affected in its receptivity to a world of phenomena in favour of an objectivity that arises only insofar as the name uncreatively receives other non-human languages. Yet, as many of Benjamin's readers have sought to demonstrate through close readings of the text, no sooner is a thing named than it is "overnamed": Benjamin's retelling of the fall of paradisal naming language into predicative language signals not a historical genesis of language, but rather the impossibility of the reduction of language's heterogeneity to any such story (Jacobs 1999, p. 106; Weber 2008, p. 45). Such a fate also befalls the language of the *Farbenlehre*. In seeking an example of "a language of signs where the elementary sign expresses the appearance itself," Goethe offers the term "polarity" before immediately noting that this sign is replaceable by the terms "plus and minus" (Goethe 1989, p. 228). It is as if, exactly when a non-predicative "elementary sign" appears to be at hand, the desire for it is immediately disappointed. Nowhere is this better expressed than when, after detailing the phenomenological intricacies of colour variations (*Gelb*, *Rotgelb*, *Gelbrot*, *Blau*, *Rotblau* and *Blaurot*), Goethe writes under the heading "Rot": "One excludes by this denomination everything in the red that might give an impression of yellow or blue. One thinks of a pure red, a perfect carmine left to dry on a white porcelain dish (ein ganz reines Rot, einen vollkommenen, auf einer weißen Porzellanschale aufgetrockneten Karmin)" (Goethe 1989, p. 236). Pure red is thinkable only as a stain on white porcelain, by which time it is not "red" at all but "carmine."

As with electricity, then, so with reading. In the former, a differential field is generated only by a momentary difference that is held as a "nothing," while in the latter, the horizontal field of semantic differentiation that generates meaning is opened, closed and transformed by the vertical movement that occurs every time a reader puts eyes, hands or ears to a text. And as Benjamin was aware, reading is determined by interstices—silences, punctuation, ellipses and enjambment—which generate meaning from a text's empty spaces as much as from its positive content. Benjamin's scepticism about Goethe's failure to distinguish between nature and art is inseparable from his insistence that Goethe also failed to adequately attend to such linguistic problems. His diagnosis of the ambiguity in Goethe's concept of nature highlights the "studies in magnetism" (Benjamin 1974b, p. 147). Quoting Goethe's preface to the first edition of the *Farbenlehre*, Benjamin suggests that it is not the scientific theory itself that is at issue as much as Goethe's attribution of a voice to nature: in so enforcing his worldview, Goethe contravenes the objective role played by language. And it is easy to see how the passages under consideration in this contribution could be likewise interpreted. After suggesting that the electrical generation of a surface, rather than the abundance of the natural world, is the condition of possibility for perceiving the genuine diversity of colour, Goethe reflects that: "To encompass and enclose the appearances of colour in this series, in this circle, in this wreath of phenomena: that was the goal of our undertaking. What we have failed to do, others will complete" (Goethe 1989, p. 223). Despite the intimate proximity between Goethe and Benjamin's theories of surface, it seems plausible to suggest that it was Goethe's attempt to seamlessly enfold the singular event of electricity and the harmonious plurality of colour into one comprehensive "series," "circle," or "wreath" that Benjamin could not bring himself to accept. Nevertheless, in demonstrating the inextricability of this aim from the decidedly non-circular operations of language, Goethe exposes his project to an uncertain future, rather than to a predetermined fulfilment.

Bibliography

Benjamin, Walter (1974a): "Der Begriff der Kunstkritik in der deutschen Romantik." In: *Gesammelte Schriften*. Vol. 1. Tiedemann, Rolf / Schweppenhäuse, Hermann (eds.). Frankfurt a. M.: Suhrkamp, pp. 7–122.
Benjamin, Walter (1974b): "Goethes Wahlverwandtschaften." In: *Gesammelte Schriften*. Vol. 1. Tiedemann, Rolf / Schweppenhäuser, Hermann (eds.). Frankfurt a. M.: Suhrkamp, pp. 123–202.
Benjamin, Walter (1974c): "Ursprung des deutschen Trauerspiels." In: *Gesammelte Schriften*. Vol. 1. Tiedemann, Rolf / Schweppenhäuse, Hermann (eds.). Frankfurt a. M.: Suhrkamp, pp. 203–430.
Benjamin, Walter (1977): "Über Sprache überhaupt und über die Sprache des Menschen." In: *Gesammelte Schriften*. Vol. 2. Tiedemann, Rolf / Schweppenhäuse, Hermann (eds.). Frankfurt a. M.: Suhrkamp, pp. 140–157.
Benjamin, Walter (1985): "Die Farbe vom Kinde aus Betrachtet." In: *Gesammelte Schriften*. Vol. 6. Tiedemann, Rolf / Schweppenhäuse, Hermann (eds.). Frankfurt a. M.: Suhrkamp, pp. 110–112.
Benjamin, Walter (1989a): "Der Regenbogen: Gespräch über die Phantasie." In: *Gesammelte Schriften*. Vol. 7. Tiedemann, Rolf / Schweppenhäuse, Hermann (eds.). Frankfurt a. M.: Suhrkamp, pp. 19–23.
Benjamin, Walter (1989b): "Der Regenbogen oder die Kunst des Paradieses: Aus einer alten Handschrift." In: *Gesammelte Schriften*. Vol. 7. Tiedemann, Rolf / Schweppenhäuse, Hermann (eds.). Frankfurt a. M.: Suhrkamp, pp. 562–564.
Benjamin, Walter (1996): "Goethe's Elective Affinities." In: *Selected Writings*. Vol. 1. Bullock, Marcus / Jennings, Michael W. (eds.). Cambridge, MA; London: Harvard University Press, pp. 297–360.
Benjamin, Walter (2011a): "The Rainbow: A Conversation about Imagination." In: *Early Writings: 1910–1917*. Eiland, Howard (trans.). Cambridge, MA; London: Harvard University Press, pp. 214–223.
Benjamin, Walter (2011b): "The Rainbow, or The Art of Paradise." In: *Early Writings: 1910–1917*. Eiland, Howard (trans.). Cambridge, MA; London: Harvard University Press, pp. 224–227.
Celan, Paul (1983): *Der Meridian und andere Prosa*. Frankfurt a. M.: Suhrkamp Verlag.

Fenves, Peter (2011): *The Messianic Reduction: Walter Benjamin and the Shape of Time*. Stanford, CA: Stanford University Press.

Geulen, Eva (2008): "Serialization in Goethe's Morphology." In: *Compar(a)ison: An International Journal of Comparative Literature* 2, pp. 53–70.

Geulen, Eva (2016): *Aus dem Leben der Form: Goethes Morphologie und die Nager*. Berlin: August Verlag.

Goethe, Johann Wolfgang von (1989): "Die Farbenlehre." In: *Sämtliche Werke*. Münchner Ausgabe. Vol. 10. Richter, Karl (ed.). Munich: Carl Hanser.

Goldstein, Amanda Jo (2017): *Sweet Science: Romantic Materialism and the New Logics of Life*. Chicago, London: University of Chicago Press.

Holland, Jocelyn (2009): *German Romanticism and Science: The Procreative Poetics of Goethe, Novalis, and Ritter*. New York; London: Routledge.

Jacobs, Carol (1999): *In the Language of Walter Benjamin*. Baltimore, MD; London: John Hopkins University Press.

Kant, Immanuel (1971): "Kritik der Urteilskraft." In: *Kants Werke*. Akademie-Textausgabe. Unaltered photocopy reprint of the text from the publication series of Kant's complete works initiated by the Prussian Academy of Sciences 1900 ff. Vol. 5. Preussische Akademie der Wissenschaften (ed.). Berlin, New York: De Gruyter, pp. 165–485.

McLaughlin, Kevin (1999): "The Coming of Paper: Aesthetic Value from Ruskin to Benjamin." In: *MLN* 114. No. 5, pp. 962–990.

Weber, Samuel (2008): *Benjamin's–abilities*. Cambridge, MA; London: Harvard University Press.

Kant-Critique and the Romanticist Movement

Tadahiro Oota
Jakob Friedrich Fries as an Opponent of German Idealism

Abstract: Jakob Friedrich Fries (1773–1843) was a nineteenth-century German philosopher, contemporaneous with so-called "German Idealism," who is best known for his main work, *New Critique of Reason* (1807/1828–1831).[1] Fries regards Kant's philosophy as incomplete and tries to revise and renew it. Since he adopts Kant's spirit of criticism, he emphasises the finitude of human cognition and in this respect he criticises his contemporaneous opponents: Reinhold, Fichte, and Schelling.

Fries criticises Kant's conception of transcendental cognition as follows: Although transcendental cognition concerns cognitions *a priori*, transcendental cognition itself can be acquired only in an empirical way because human cognition always begins with experience. Hence Kant was in error to regard it as *a priori*. German Idealists elaborated on Kant's mistake and interpreted mere inner perception as cognition *a priori*, which led them to adopt the "synthetic method" as a means of philosophising. Fries corrects them by assuming the "analytical method," whereby he starts from the standpoint of ordinary experience by analysing "the ordinary opinions (*Beurtheilungen*) in daily life" in order to reveal the philosophical cognitions constructing the general presuppositions of opinions. He calls such a project "Critique of Reason." Kuno Fischer (1824–1907), however, contradicts Fries's approach by defending German Idealists, arguing that the cognition *a priori* can never be acquired in an empirical way. Otto Liebmann (1840–1912) also follows Fischer and criticises Fries's approach as a "retrogression to Locke."

In this article I deal with Fries's conception of the "Critique of Reason" and respond to the objections above. Fries's method is an analysis of *opinions*, which are neither mere experience nor logical judging (*urtheilen*). The philosophical cognitions constructing the presuppositions of opinions belong to "reason," which is to be distinguished from "understanding," which conducts the "analysing" operation by relying on arbitrary reflection.

---

1 *New and Anthropological Critique of Reason* (NaKV) is the 1828–1831 revised edition of *New Critique of Reason* (NKV).

1 Introduction

1.1 Outline of Fries's Critique of Reason

In this article, I treat Jakob Friedrich Fries's conception of the "Critique of Reason" and reveal how Fries's philosophical method ensures the apodicticity of philosophical cognition.

Jakob Friedrich Fries (1773–1843) had a great influence on the philosophical discourse of his time, which led to his contemporaries arguing about his ideas, and there was a "Friesian-School," which published its own magazine in the 1840's (cf. Beiser 2014, p. 25).

Fries's philosophy is principally based on Immanuel Kant's method of critique.[2] On the one hand, he adopts many of Kant's grounds of criticism, emphasising the finitude of human cognition. He approves of Kant's thematisation of the *method* of philosophy (SM, p. 90) to gain philosophical cognition within this constraint and also to make philosophy a science open to all (SPh, p.VI. Cf. SM, p. 89).[3]

On the other hand, Fries regards Kant's critique as incomplete and thus attempts to complete it (cf. SM, p.123, RFS, p. 276). He criticises Kant's conception of transcendental cognition. According to Fries, Kant's way of critique included a significant defect.

> For Kant, transcendental cognition means the cognition of the possibility and applicability (*Anwendbarkeit*) of the cognitions *a priori* [...]; here he talks about transcendental mental faculties and what he calls transcendental are those from which principles of cognitions *a priori* arise. [...] Whoever wants to compare [existent disciplines] exactly can find that by his 'transcendental cognition' Kant meant in fact the psychological or, better, the anthropological cogniti4on, whereby we recognise which cognitions our reason possesses *a priori* and how they arise from it. [...] / However, Kant made a great mistake that he regarded tran-

---

2 Fries notes, "while this [philosophical] viewpoint has been changed by Kant, the whole transcendental critique and the success of all Kantian philosophical works based on this viewpoint arises. Its success is no longer doubted now" (VePM, p. 157). "What matters most is that I have contributed to it by describing the scientific system, so that the Kantian clear investigations in the methodology are recognised better and more generally, regarding its product" (SL, p. IIX). In addition "hence, from a historical viewpoint, my work follows Kant's great works and their decisively important investigations" (NaKV, I, p. XII).

3 According to Fries, because the science to which philosophy belongs is "no ingenious product of reason" (SPh, p. VI), "philosophy is a product of the independent self-activity of reason" (SPh, p. VI).

scendental cognition as a kind of cognition *a priori* and, namely of philosophical cognition, and misjudged its empirical-psychological nature. [...]

(Transcendentale Erkenntniß heißt ihm die Erkenntniß von der Möglichkeit und Anwendbarkeit der Erkenntnisse *a priori* [...]; er spricht von transcendentalen Gemüthsvermögen, und nennt diejenigen so, aus denen Principien von Erkenntnissen *a priori* entspringen [...]. Wer hier genau vergleichen will, der wird bemerken, daß Kant mit seiner transcendentalen Erkenntniß eigentlich die psychologische, oder besser anthropologische Erkenntniß meinte, wodurch wir einsehen, welche Erkenntnisse *a priori* unsre Vernunft besitzt, und wie sie in ihr entspringt. [...] / Kant aber machte den großen Fehler, daß er die transcendentale Erkenntniß für eine Art der Erkenntniß *a priori* und zwar der philosophischen hielt, und ihre empirische psychologische Natur verkannte.) (NKV, I, p. XXXVf.; NaKV, I, p. 29, translated by the author).

According to Fries, although transcendental cognition is concerned with cognitions *a priori*, the transcendental cognition itself can only be acquired in an empirical way, because "all human cognition begins properly with sensible perceptions, although it doesn't arise from them in respect to general and necessary truth" (SM, p. 80).

In this regard, Fries calls Kant's "mistake" the "Kantian preconception" (NKV, I, p. XXXV; NaKV, I, p. 28). According to Fries, the German Idealists, too, extended Kant's mistake.

> Because of this [Kantian] preconception every conventional way of critique of reason has a defect, and the greatest mistake was made from the natural conclusion that the inner perception was regarded as the source of the cognitions *a priori*. Hence, *the immediate consciousness* in Reinhold and others, the Fichtean *inner* and *intellectual intuition*, and the total retrogression to dogmatical rationalism by Schelling.
>
> (An diesem Vorurtheil kränkelt jede bisherige Behandlung der Vernunftkritik, und die größten Fehler wurden alle durch die natürliche Folge desselben gemacht, daß man die innere Wahrnehmung für den Quell von Erkenntnissen *a priori* hielt. Daher *das unmittelbare Bewußtseyn* bey Reinhold und andern, daher die Fichtische *innere* und *intellektuelle Anschauung*, und der völlige Rückschritt zum dogmatischen Rationalismus bey Schelling.) (NKV, I, p. XXXVII; NaKV, I, p. 30, translated by the author).

According to Fries, it was their first mistake, that "through the apriority of transcendental cognition, they converted the inner perception into a cognition *a priori*" (NKV, I, p. XXXVII) as the highest principle from which they started philosophising.

Such a mistake led them into a false method of philosophy, i.e. the "progressive or synthetic method" (RFS, p. 257; SM, p. 96).[4] The "synthetic method" refers

---

4 It is also called the "dogmatic method" (cf. SM, p. 96).

to the philosophising process, which starts from a general principle and deduces particular principles from it. Fries calls this method's standpoint a "rationalist preconception" (NKV, I, p. XXVIII; NaKV, I, p. 21) and criticises it as follows.

> Among the best known philosophers, it was Reinhold who, as he intended to acquire the unity missing from the Kantian system, determined the rationalist preconception again under the following formula: it may be the purpose of all the theoretical science and speculation to deduce all our knowledge from a highest principle. At first this principle was supposed to be a basic proposition in a logical sense, however it was converted into one in a metaphysical sense, and became the idea of the universe and the godhood. [...] However, humans can neither grasp nor comprehend the essence of godhood, nor even less the essence of things from it [...].
>
> (Unter den Philosophen, die am meisten gehört wurden, brachte Reinhold, indem er die fehlende Einheit zum Kantischen System hinzu suchen wollte, das rationalistische Vorurtheil unter der Formel wieder bestimmt in Anregung: es sey der Zweck aller theoretischen Wissenschaft und Spekulation, alles unser Wissen aus einem höchsten Princip abzuleiten. Dieses Princip sollte anfangs logisch ein Grundsatz seyn, wandte sich aber bald metaphysisch herum, und wurde zur Idee des Universums oder der Gottheit. [...] daß aber der Mensch das Wesen der Gottheit weder fassen noch begreifen könne, noch viel weniger also das Wesen der Dinge aus ihm [...].) (NKV, I, p. XXII; NaKV, I, p. 16, translated by the author).

According to Fries, "philosophical cognition is not a kind of cognition that must be investigated and learned anew by one person for the first time, but everyone possesses these cognitions and adapts them daily by thinking" (SM, p. 89). In this respect, Fries adopts the "regressive or analytical method" (RES, p. 258; SM, p. 95f.; VePM, p. 176. Cf. Beiser 2014, p. 29).[5] He starts from the standpoint of an "ordinary experience" (VePM, p. 176; RFS, p. 260), in other words, "the ordinary opinions (*gemeine Beurtheilungen*) in daily life" (SM, p. 91. Cf. NKV, I, p. 14; NaKV, I, p. 9). He finds a way to reveal the general principles in the "analysing process of thought (*der zergliedernde Gedankengang*)" (SM, p. 91; NaKV, I, p. VI) of the opinions, by which one can find the philosophical cognitions that construct the general presuppositions of such opinions (SM, p. 101f. Cf. RFS, p. 264f.).[6] He calls such a method the "art of philosophising (*Kunst zu philosophiren*)" (SM, p. 88. Cf. RFS, p. 257f.), and the analysing operation "philosophising (*philosophiren*)" (SM, p. 105. Cf. RFS, p. 261, p. 269).

---

[5] Fries defines analytical method as a "method that regressively climbs from the particular to the general, from the consequence to the next reason" (SM, p. 99).

[6] According to Fries, such an operation corresponds to the "groundwork (*Grundlegung*)" of Kantian philosophy (NaKV, II, p. VI; SM, p. 119).

According to Fries, the place of such philosophical cognitions is "reason" as a mental faculty, from the standpoint of Kantian transcendental idealism (RFS, p. 270).[7] In this respect, the analysing process can be identified with so-called transcendental cognition, as it concerns a mental faculty of cognition. From this viewpoint, he identifies this process with self-cognition (SM, p. 105; NKV, I, p. XLVIII; NaKV, I, p. 41) and calls it "speculation (*Spekulation*)" (SM, p. 105; NKV, I, p. 321; NaKV, I, p. 384). The purpose of the speculation is to find the philosophical cognitions, bringing them to consciousness[8] and *exhibiting* (*aufweisen*) them as the "immediate cognitions of reason" (NKV, I, p. XXXVIII; NaKV, I, p. 31). He calls such an operation "deduction (*Deduktion*)" (NKV, I, p. 283; NaKV, I, p. 342; SM, p. 112)[9] in reference to Kant (NaKV, I, p. XXI).[10] Finally, he names the discipline to which this process belongs as "philosophical anthropology:"

> So then we ask: What is the requirement of speculation in our time? The answer is the same as ever: self-cognition in regard to cognition, investigation of our faculty of cognition, investigation of reason. Locke, Leibniz and Hume called it an investigation of human under-

---

[7] However, Fries hardly uses these words in his later work. Instead, he tends to use the term "theory of reason." (SM, p.110; NKV, I, p. 284; NaKV, I, p. 342).

[8] Fries defines the term "consciousness" as follows: "Consciousness in the narrowest sense of the word means the inner self-cognition of cognitions, i.e. the cognition of the cognitions which we possess" (SPh, p. 54). Elsewhere he defines it as "the inner cognition that such a cognition is lying in me" (SPh, p. 47). He also uses the word "re-consciousness (*Wiederbewußtsein*)" with respect to the philosophical cognitions, in order to emphasise that the philosophical cognitions are brought to consciousness only as mediated by an analysing operation. (SPh, p. 47, p. 57; NKV, I, p. 94; NaKV, I, p. 136).

[9] Fries gives an example: "For example, I say that every substance persists, every change has a cause and all simultaneity is determined by the exchange of the substance. Or, I judge of justice and injustice, virtue and vice and I say first and foremost that every reasonable existence should be treated as a purpose in itself according to its personal dignity. Or finally, I insist that there should be a god and the will should be free. On what do I base my judgment on in such cases? I recognise the laws of nature in the first case, the laws of freedom in the second case, and the laws of eternal order of the things in the third case, without appealing to the intuition. However, these very laws, of which I become re-conscious only in judgment, must be in my reason as immediate cognitions. I only use the judgment to become conscious of them. Hence, we can justify (*begründen*) our judgment only by exhibiting which original cognition of reason underlies our judgment, but without being able to put the cognition immediately next to the judgment and defend it by the judgment. Such a way to justify a principle is called its *deduction*." (NKV, I, p. 283; NaKV, I, p. 342).

[10] "The anthropological justification of all philosophical basic truth seems to me to be a main task. Now Kant called the justification of use of categories 'deduction'. I have kept this name because my justification had the same purpose and also adopted the meaning at the correct understanding of the transcendental verification (*Beweis*). However, my deduction of course differs [from Kant] in its performance." (NaKV, I, p. XXI).

standing. For Eclecticists it was the task of empirical psychology, for Kant the critique of reason, and we would like to call it *philosophical anthropology*.

(Fragen wir also: was ist unsrer Zeit das Bedürfniß der Spekulation? so ist die Antwort noch immer die nämliche wie ehedem: Selbsterkenntniß in Rücksicht des Erkennens, Untersuchung unsers Erkenntnißvermögens, Untersuchung der Vernunft. Locke, Leibnitz und Hume nannten es die Untersuchung des menschlichen Verstandes, den neuern Eklektikern war es die Aufgabe der empirischen Psychologie, Kanten die der Vernunft=Kritik, wir wollen es *philosophische Anthropologie* nennen.) (NKV, I, p. XXXVIII; NaKV I, p. 31, translated by the author).

Fries calls his whole project a "critique of reason" (SM, p. 104. Cf. RFS, p. 267). Hence, the "critique of reason" means the *method* of philosophy, and is identified with "philosophical anthropology" or "empirical psychology" (NKV, I, p. XXXVI; NaKV, I, p. 29) with respect to the discipline to which it belongs.

1.2 Conventional Evaluation of Friesian Philosophy

After his death Fries's philosophy was regarded as "psychologism" or a "psychological approach to Kant" (Beiser 2014, p. 24). Due to this estimation, his philosophy has been forgotten in the "legitimate" history of philosophy.

Kuno Fischer, a Hegelian and first great opponent of Fries's philosophy, thematised and criticised Fries's philosophy in his 1862 lecture. He characterised Fries's contention that the cognition *a priori* could be recognised in an empirical way as his decisive doctrine. Fischer then clearly denied this doctrine and refuted Fries's philosophy as follows:

[As Fries bases the critique of reason on empirical psychology,] now, if the critique of reason is only psychological and therefore merely empirical, how can the objects of its insight be *a priori*? [...] / Fries counters: What the critique of reason discovers is *a priori*, however the investigation itself is *a posteriori*. The object of its cognition is *a priori*, its cognition itself is empirical. [...] / Here is the πρῶτον ψεῦδος of Friesian philosophy: *What is a priori can never be recognised a posteriori*. I don't know anyway to make a distinction between *a priori* and *a posteriori* without referring to our cognition. I don't understand how something *a priori* can exist (*sein*) independently from cognition. Equally I don't understand how cognition is supposed to be *a priori* in ourselves, when the same can only be recognised through experience.

(Wenn nun die Vernunftkritik blos psychologisch und darum lediglich empirisch ist: wie können die Objekte ihrer Einsicht *a priori* seyn? [...] / Fries entgegnet: was die Vernunftkritik entdeckt, ist *a priori*; aber die Entdeckung selbst ist *a posteriori*. Der Gegenstand ihrer Erkenntniß ist *a priori*, ihre Erkenntniß selbst ist empirisch.[...] / Und eben hier liegt in der friesischen Philosophie das πρῶτον ψεῦδος. *Was a priori ist, kann nie a posteriori erkannt werden.* / Ueberhaupt weiß ich den ganzen Unterschied von *a priori* und *a posteriori* auf nichts anderes zu beziehen als auf unsere Erkenntniß. Ich verstehe nicht, wie unabhängig von der Erkenntniß etwas *a priori* seyn kann. Ich verstehe eben so wenig, wie in uns eine Erkenntniß *a priori* seyn soll, welche selbst nur durch Erfahrung erkannt wird.) (Fischer 1862, p. 18, translated by the author).

Otto Liebmann followed Fischer's conclusion[11] and criticised Fries's philosophy as "no improvement [of Kantian philosophy], but only a retrogression to Locke" (Liebmann 1865, p. 150). Wilhelm Windelband (1848–1915) also accepted Liebmann's estimation and asserted that Fries's philosophy was "an attempt to translate a critical principle of self-cognition of human reason into the words of empirical psychology" (Windelband 1880, p. 386).[12]

With these characterisations Fries's philosophy disappeared from the "legitimate" genealogy of nineteenth-century German philosophy.

2 Response from a Friesian standpoint

2.1 Response by Leonard Nelson (1882–1927)

Now we will reconsider the objections to Fries from the standpoint of his own philosophy.

Leonard Nelson finds the solution to these criticisms by making a distinction between *critique* and *metaphysics*. Nelson points out that in agreement with Kant, Fries claims that metaphysics consists of cognitions *a priori*, in other words, apodictic cognitions (Cf. NKV, II, p. 11; NaKV, II, p. 8; SM, p. 114; VePM, p. 170). However, the critique which investigates its cognitions *a priori* can be accomplished in an empirical way. Fries bases this distinction on another distinction he made in his earliest work in 1798 between the *object* of critique and the *content*.

> It is therefore the business of transcendental critique to find the nature (*Inbegriff*) of our cognition *a priori* and reduce it to its principles. This investigation of what kind of cognitions we possess *a priori* and how they are obtained, obviously belongs now completely to a type of psychological cognition. [...] / Its object (*Gegenstand*) is cognitions *a priori*, however its content is mostly *empirical* cognitions. The judgments which constitute the contents of critique are only *assertoric*; *apodictic* judgments belong to the object of critique.

---

[11] He regarded the philosophy of Fichte, Schelling and Hegel as "the idealist way (*Richtung*)" (Liebmann 1865, p. 70), and Fries's philosophy as "an empiricist way" (Liebmann 1865, p. 140).
[12] Finally, he characterised Fries's philosophy with Beneke as a kind of "psychologism."

> (Es ist also das Geschäft der transcendentalen Kritik, den Inbegriff unsrer Erkenntniß *a priori* aufzusuchen und auf seine Prinzipien zurückzuführen. Diese Untersuchung, was für Erkenntnisse *a priori* wir besitzen und wie dieselben beschaffen sind, gehört nun offenbar ganz zur psychologischen Erkenntnißart. [...] / Ihr Gegenstand sind Erkenntnisse *a priori*, ihr Inhalt aber meist empirische Erkenntnisse. Die Urtheile, welche den Inhalt der Kritik ausmachen, sind nur assertorisch; apodiktische gehören zum Gegenstand derselben.) (VePM, p. 180 f., translated by the author).

Nelson emphasises this distinction and here finds the essence of Fries's "deduction." First Nelson answers Liebmann's objection by explaining that the contents of critique can be empirical, but do not imply the denial of the possibility of cognitions *a priori* (Nelson 1905, p. 43).

In addition, Nelson emphasises the character of Fries's deduction to answer Fischer's objection. Nelson argues that Fischer regarded the relation between content and object as a logical relation of the verification (*Beweis*) between reason and consequence. However, Fries does not regard the relation as verification, but rather calls it deduction. Therefore, unlike what Fischer noted, the content of critique can still be empirical (Nelson 1905, p. 42 f.).

However, it does not appear that Nelson's answer changed the perception of Fries. Fischer did not reject the justification of this distinction because he considered it to be based on the relation between reason and consequence. He denied the possibility of the distinction, on which Nelson's answer itself is based, because such a distinction implies an existence independent from our cognition. Hence, Fischer's objection is concerned with the validity of deduction itself. Nelson's answer is not a refutation of Fischer's objection, but rather merely a denial of it.[13]

2.2 Another Form of Response

We can find another solution in Fries's thought itself. In fact, Fries himself ceases to explain such a distinction after 1798.

The critique of reason means the *method* of philosophy. However, the critique as a method itself contains two aspects: (I) study of the method itself, and (II) the application of the method. (I) The former deals with the methodology of critique, i.e. the way in which the act of philosophising or critique should be carried out, and on which presuppositions this method would be based, espe-

---

[13] While Nelson's answer to Liebmann is also based on this distinction, it would not be valid until this problem is solved.

cially in relation to the mental faculties. (II) The latter deals with the philosophical cognitions acquired through philosophising, which constitute the presuppositions of our opinions or the conditions of our experience in a wider sense. This distinction replaces the previous distinction Fries made in 1798 and corresponds to the differing contents of the first book and the second to third books of his *New Critique*. As the critique is now based on such a distinction, Fries claims *apriority* and *apodicticity* for philosophical cognition.[14] This distinction is based on the concept of the *opinions (Beurtheilungen)* as objects of philosophising, and the precise distinction between *reason* and *understanding*, which arose only after 1798.

2.2.1 Turning from an Empiricism Standpoint by Focusing on Opinions

In his paper in 1798 and his first book *Reinhold, Fichte and Schelling*, Fries adopts the analytical method. However, he mentions here that we must start from ordinary experience (*gemeine Erfahrung*), and through observing that, we can find the philosophical cognitions (RFS, p. 260; VePM, p. 176) that belong to reason and are valid for the condition of our experience. Regarding this standpoint, his theory was distinguished mainly from dogmatism (VePM, p. 157f.; RFS, p. 301f.).

In contrast to that, and following the *New Critique*, Fries finds the object of the analysing operation in *opinions in daily life* (*Beurtheilungen im täglichen Leben*) (SM, p. 91. Cf. NKV, II, p. 14; NaKV, II, p. VI, p. 9). These opinions are distinguished from mere experience or so-called sense data, because they already include the cognitions in the shape of real relations (*reelle Verhältnisse*) of representations (SL, p. 125, p. 159).[15] Thus they are not included in sensible intuitions,[16] but arise from another one of our mental faculties.[17] They are also dis-

---

[14] Fries tends to use the word "apodictic" instead of "a priori" in his *New Critique*. "Such a distinction between the 'assertoric' and 'apodictic' corresponds exactly to the Kantian distinction of 'a posteriori' and 'a priori'" (NKV, I, p. 249), because "such a distinction [between 'a priori' and 'a positeriori'] is [...] often misleading" (NKV, I, p. 250), since, when the concept "a priori" is related to cognition, it could be mistaken for the innateness of cognition, although "all actual cognition is [only] given to us through and with the perception for the first time" (NKV, I, p. 250). This doesn't mean, however, that the form on which such a cognition is based on arises from the experience (NKV, I, p. 250). However, he also admits the apriority of such philosophical cognitions (SM, p. 80).

[15] Such real relations, whose representations the reason contains as immediate cognitions, are called also "categories" (SL, p. 159; GPh, II, p. 600f.).

[16] NKV, II, p. 14; NaKV, II, p.VI, p. 9.

tinguished from logical judging (*urtheilen*), because they include no cognitive content, but are valid only for the mere *form* of re-cognition.[18] This change of the object of analysis distinguished Fries's standpoint from both dogmatism and empiricism.[19] For Fries, the purpose of philosophising is identified by analysing the opinions to find the philosophical cognitions which constitute the presuppositions of *all our opinions*.

2.2.2 Distinction between Reason and Understanding

This distinction above is based on the other distinction between two mental faculties, i.e. reason and understanding, and also the two "lines of thought," which are thematised in his second philosophical book *System of Philosophy as Evident Science* in 1804.

The philosophical cognitions that construct the presuppositions of opinions belong to "reason" as a mental faculty, which is distinguished from "understanding" that fulfils the "analysing" operation by arbitrary reflection through logical form.

2.2.2.1 Reason

According to Fries, if philosophical cognitions are valid for the presuppositions of *all our* opinions, they must have their origin in our reason as a mental faculty.[20] Reason is supposed to be a faculty that contains the philosophical cognitions to be adapted to the experience in the shape of "opinions" (NaKV, p. VI). While the cognition of understanding is mediated, (*mittelbar*) because the philosophical cognitions are brought into consciousness for the first time through the logical form of understanding (NKV, I, p. 188f., 198ff.; NaKV, II, p. 236f., 247ff.), the cognitions of reason must immediately belong to reason without consciousness (NKV, I, p.199f.; NaKV, II, p.248f.). As such immediate cognitions of reason are always dark (*dunkel*) and without consciousness (NKV, I, p.199f.; NaKV, II, p.248f.), they must be distinguished from the intuitive cognitions of sensibility (NKV, I, p. 199f.; NaKV, II, p. 248f.), which are already evident.

---

17 NaKV, II, p. VI.
18 NKV, I, p. 188; NaKV, p. 236; SL, p. 97f.
19 NKV, I, p. XXIII; NaKV, I, p. 17.
20 In relation to the actuality of the synthetic cognitions *a priori*, Fries takes the same standpoint as Kant. Nelson calls such a standpoint "the acknowledgment of the inevitable actuality of metaphysical presuppositions" (Nelson 1905, p. 57).

What philosophising must do is to show that these presuppositions are the immediate cognitions of reason. Fries calls this process of exhibiting the immediate cognition of reason "deduction" (NKV, I, p. 283; NaKV, I, p. 342; SM, p. 112) and regards it as a process of justification for philosophical cognitions. Hence, it is reason as a mental faculty that ensures the apodicticity of philosophical cognitions with respect to their possession. He calls this theory the "theory of reason (*Theorie der Vernunft*)" (NKV, I, p. 284; NaKV, I, p. 342, SM, p. 110).

2.2.2.2 Understanding

Such a precise determination of reason enables Fries to set out the peculiar characteristics of understanding which is to be an agent of the philosophising operation.

This understanding is a faculty of reflection (NKV, I, p. 190; NaKV, I, p. 239), to which "the arbitrary, mediated and logical representing in concept, judgment and reasoning" belongs (NKV, I, p. 199; NaKV, I, p. 248). It analyses opinions, reveals their presuppositions, and brings them to consciousness by comprehending and formulating them through concept and judgment (Cf. NKV, I, pp. 188, 199; NaKV, I, pp. 236, 248). With this reflection, such presuppositions that belong to reason are conceptualised and brought into judgments for the first time, and hence, brought to the consciousness as well.[21] Such concepts, judgments, and re-consciousness (Cf. NKV, I, p. 188; NaKV, I, p. 236) are the field where the analysing process, i.e. speculation[22], arises.

2.2.2.3 Line of Thought

With respect to the process of delineating judging (*urtheilen*) and forming opinions (*beurtheilen*), Fries distinguishes between two different "lines of thought

---

[21] This is valid, both for the cognitions of reason and the forms of sensibility. For example, space and time are the conditions of experience, and we have "the representation of them," but we become conscious of them for the first time when they are acquired as representations through the analysing process, i.e. abstraction (cf. SPh, p. 69; NKV, II, p. 29).

[22] Gary Hatfield explains Fries's method as follows: "He [Fries] did, in fact, call his theory of reason a 'physical' theory, but that meant only that he considered it to rest on inductive grounds, in the same manner as physics" (Hatfield 1990, p. 115). He refers here to NKV, II, p. 72 and I, p. 25–26. However, Fries mentions that speculation as a philosophising method must be distinguished from induction which can never ensure the apodicticity of cognitions. Fries finds here a similarity between philosophy and physics, only in the sense that the philosophy also adopts the regressive or analytic method (NaKV, II, p. 26) and it is based on the experience (NaKV, II, p. 72), which, however, does not mean that the philosophy is essentially based on such induction.

(*Gedankenlauf*)." He defines "lines of thought" as "those which [...] belong to the empirical state of mind except for some representations [i.e. spontaneity and sensible intuitions]" (NKV, I, p.93; NaKV, I, p. 134) and claims it to be a "standpoint from which our anthropological investigation starts" (NKV, I, p. 92; NaKV, I, p. 133). He distinguishes between two "lines of thought": "line of memorised thought (*gedächtnißmäßiger Gedankenlauf*)" and "line of logical thought (*logischer Gedankenlauf*)" (NKV, I, p. 94; NaKV, I, p. 135).[23] Fries notes that "the memory, inner perception of representations, the recollection and the peculiar law of imagination" (NKV, I, p. 94; NaKV, I, p. 135) belong to the former. Hence, the opinions which the analysing process targets are supposed to belong to the line of memorised thought. In contrast, the "arbitrary determination of representations" (NKV, I, p. 94; NaKV, I, p. 135) belong to the line of logical thought, which is constituted by "the understanding effecting them by the will" (NKV, I, p. 94; NaKV, I, p. 135). Due to such arbitrariness, the understanding is able to make representations of any kind, cooperating with the imagination (*Einbildungskraft*) (NKV, I, p. 145ff., 235ff.; NaKV, I, p. 190ff., 289ff.), which enables the investigation of the presuppositions that accords with the immediate cognition of reason. It is the arbitrariness of the analysing operation that enables the *apodicticity* of cognitions from the viewpoint of the philosophising process.

2.3 Role of Psychology: Against "Psychologism"

As is now evident, Nelson's understanding of Fries's philosophical standpoint is different from that of Fries's. A similar difference also appears in their understanding of the role of "psychology." Nelson regards Fries's critique as a psychological one, because it is concerned with reason as a mental faculty, and, in this respect, he defines psychology in the wider sense: a science of inner experience (Nelson 1905, p. 23f.).

However, Fries's standpoint differs from Nelson's. According to Fries, the act of having opinions (*beurtheilen*) belongs to inner experience, and, in this sense, Fries acknowledges that the analysing process could be a matter of empirical psychology.

> Every particular fact, that I know this or that thing, that I recognise this or that particular object, is an object of inner experience. Therefore for every cognition there is a twofold standpoint of observation. For a start, every cognition corresponds (*zukommen*) to an object which should be recognised in that cognition, and then, if I am able to judge (*urtheilen*)

---

[23] Fries owes this distinction to Ernst Platner (cf. Platner 1795, p. 40).

about that cognition, I must become conscious of the cognition itself again (*wieder bewußt*) [...].

(Jede einzelne Thatsache, daß ich dies oder jenes weiß, daß ich diesen oder jenen einzelnen Gegenstand erkenne, ist ein Gegenstand der innern Erfahrung. Es giebt also für jede Erkenntniß einen zweyfachen Standpunkt der Betrachtung, einmal kommt jeder Erkenntniß ein Gegenstand zu, welcher in ihr erkannt werden soll, und dann muß ich mir der Erkenntniß selbst erst wieder bewußt werden, wenn ich über sie soll urtheilen können [...].) (NKV, I, p. XLV; NaKV, I, p. 37, translated by the author).[24]

Hence, the opinions (*Beurtheilungen*) belong to inner experience, in addition, to inner perception[25] in the sense that we must be able to become *conscious* of the opinions.[26]

In this respect, Fries also recommends using the word "philosophical anthropology" instead of "psychology" to avoid misunderstanding.[27] He makes use of the product of psychology for philosophising[28] but carefully restricts its role in order to avoid falling into "psychologism."

---

[24] Fries claims the same thing in *System of Metaphysics:* "Every recognising is an activity of our spirit (*Geist*). Hence, all cognitions are objects of inner experience [...]" (SM, p. 104).

[25] He defines "inner perception" as "cognition of cognitions" in 1787 (VePM, p. 178). Afterwards, he defines it as follows: "a representation of which we are re-conscious is called 'perception (*Perzeption*)'" in *System of Philosophy* (SPh, p. 57). In addition, "we [...] can achieve [philosophical knowledge] only from inner consciousness of ourselves. The character of this inner perception is that it expresses itself in every particular case: 'I think' 'I recognise', 'I feel', 'I desire', 'I will'" (NKV, I, p. 6), "A clear representation is called 'perception (*Perzeption*)' in contrast to the dark one" (NKV, I, p. 90) in *New Critique*. "Perception is the consciousness of sensible intuitive cognitions" in *System of Metaphysics* (SM, p. 29).

[26] In this respect, Fries criticises Kant by noting: "Hence, his [Kant's] self-contradictory concept of 'transcendental faculties of mind' arose, which were not only supposed to be a source of cognitions *a priori*, but also he regarded their functions as recognisable *a priori*, as if we had another source of self-cognition except inner experience" (SL, p. 32). Fries's standpoint rests on the criticism that emphasises the finitude of human cognitions on which the critique itself is also based.

[27] In addition, he carefully avoids the word "psychology" as he determines his method. "[Because critique of reason concerns a human mind as an object of inner experience,] hence, it could be the science which is commonly called 'psychology', but we avoid such a use of the word for some reasons" (NKV, I, p. XLIII; NaKV, I, p. 36). "The original self-activity of reason in recognising is the task (*Räthsel*) of psychology in the ordinary sense, but in fact it is not our topic" (NKV, I, p. 310; NaKV, I, p. 372. Cf. Leary 1982, p. 231ff.).

[28] We can find an example in his distinction of mental faculties. "[...] the better theory about consciousness and distinction between self-activity (spontaneity) of reason and arbitrariness of thinking understanding is already known more generally" (SM, p. 73). As we have seen, this definition of mental faculties plays a vital role in Fries's philosophy.

3 Conclusion

Fries's philosophy is based on the standpoint that *a priori* cognitions can be acquired in an empirical way. From this standpoint he adopts a regressive or analytical method; he locates the method of "philosophising" in the process of analysing "the ordinary opinions in daily life," which reveal the philosophical cognitions that constitute the general presuppositions of opinions. Such an operation aims to exhibit philosophical cognitions as the immediate cognitions of reason, i.e. "deduction." From this standpoint, Fries emphasises both empirical psychology and "philosophical anthropology" (1.1).

However, Fries's philosophy has been unjustly considered as psychologism, ever since Kuno Fischer claimed that the cognitions *a priori* can be only recognised *a priori* and criticised Fries's philosophy, especially its emphasis on psychology (1.2). Leonard Nelson attempted to answer this objection by emphasising the distinction between object and content of critique, which Fries proposes in his earliest work (2.1).

However, Fries himself responded to this objection in another way, in his *New Critique*, which is more relevant than his earliest work. First, he avoids the viewpoint of empiricism by finding the object of philosophising in opinions, instead of experience (2.2.1). Secondly, he confirms the apodicticity of philosophical cognitions by finding the agent of philosophising in "understanding" as a faculty of arbitrary reflection, which brings the cognitions to consciousness to its logical form, and which is distinguished from reason that possesses immediate cognitions (2.2.2). In addition, Fries carefully restricts the role of psychology itself. (2.2.3)

In conclusion, it is evident that Fries investigated his way into metaphysics as a system of knowledge that is made of apodictic philosophical cognitions *a priori*, while remaining within the constraint of criticism in a Kantian sense. In this, he appeared to offer an alternative to German Idealism during the development of the Kantian philosophy in the nineteenth century.

Bibliography

Beiser, Frederick (2014): *The Genesis of Neo-Kantianism, 1796–1880*. Oxford: Oxford University Press..

Hatfield, Gary (1990): *The Natural and the Normative: Theories of Spatial Perception From Kant to Helmholtz*. Cambridge: MIT Press.

Hegel, Georg Wilhelm Friedrich (1971): *Werke in zwanzig Bänden: Theorie-Werkausgabe, Band. 7*. Hrsg. v. Moldenhauer, E. u. Michel, K. M., Frankfurt am Main: Suhrkamp Verlag.

Leary, David E (1982): "The Psychology of Jakob Friedrich Fries (1773–1843): Its Context, Nature, and historical Significance." In: *Storia E Critica Della Psicologia*, Vol. 3, No.2, pp. 217–48.

Liebmann, Otto (1865): *Kant und die Epigonen: Eine kritische Abhandlung*, Stuttgart: Karl Schoder.

Nelson, Leonard (1905): "Jakob Friedrich Fries und seine jüngsten Kritiker." In: Hessenberg, Gerhard, Kaiser, Karl, Nelson, Leonard (Eds.): *Abhandlungen der Friesschen Schule. Neue Folge*, Band 1, Heft 2. Göttingen: Vandenhoek & Ruprecht, pp. 233–319.

Platner, Ernst (1795): *Lehrbuch der Logik und Metaphysik*. Leipzig: Schwickertschen Verlag.

Windelband, Wilhelm (1880): *Die Geschichte der neuern Philosophie in ihrem Zusammenhange mit der allgemeinen Curtur und den besonderen Wissenschaften, Zweiter Band: Von Kant bis Hegel und Herbart.* Leipzig: Breitkopf und Härtel.

Abbreviations

VePM =	Fries, Jakob Friedrich (1798): "Ueber das Verhältniß der empirischen Psychologie zur Metaphysik." In: *Psychologisches Magazin*, Band III. Ed. Schmid, Carl Christian Erhard. Jena: Cröckerscher Verlag.
RFS =	Fries, Jakob Friedrich (1803): *Reinhold, Fichte und Schelling*. Leipzig: August Lebrecht Reinicke.
SPh =	Fries, Jakob Friedrich (1804): *System der Philosophie als evidente Wissenschaft.* Leipzig: Johann Conrad Hinrichs.
NKV, I–III =	Fries, Jakob Friedrich (1807): *Neue Kritik der Vernunft*, Band I–III. Heidelberg: Wohr und Zimmer.
SL =	Fries, Jakob Friedrich (1819): *System der Logik. Ein Handbuch für Lehrer und zum Selbstgebrauch*. zweite Auflage. Heidelberg: Wohr und Zimmer.
SM =	Fries, Jakob Friedrich (1824): *System der Metaphysik. Ein Handbuch für Lehrer und zum Selbstgebrauch*. Heidelberg: Christian Friedrich Winter.
NaKV, I–III =	Fries, Jakob Friedrich (1829 ff.): *Neue oder anthropologische Kritik der Vernunft*, Band I–III, zweite Auflage. Heidelberg: Christian Friedrich Winter.
GPh, I–II: =	Fries, Jakob Friedrich (1837 ff.): *Die Geschichte der Philosophie dargestellt nach den Fortschritten ihrer wissenschaftlichen Entwicklung*, Band I-II. Halle: Verlag der Buchhandlung des Waisenhauses.

Manuel Clemens
Apparent Purposes.
How Does the Purpose of Purposelessness Operate?

Abstract: One field of idealism in combination with anti-idealism is aesthetic education, since it combines the idea of an aesthetic idealist sphere with its intervention into the real world. Friedrich Schiller's letters *Über die ästhetische Erziehung des Menschen* [*On the Aesthetic Education of Man*] (1795) express this ambivalence prominently. His *Aesthetic Letters* articulate a cultural critique around the 1800s, stating that, on the one hand, his contemporaries are only able to think in terms of economic benefits as it relates to all aspects of existence, rendering human existence one-dimensional and unhappy, and that, on the other, theoretical projects on the grand scale of the Enlightenment and the French Revolution cannot be fully realised since they appeal to human beings —once again one-dimensionally—only through reason.[1] As a result, while Enlightenment ideas are considered and taught, they cannot be implemented properly (if at all) since they do not correspond to the reality of human action. Schiller therefore brings a form of aesthetic education into play, one which he locates in art. Since Enlightenment constructs, such as Kant's categorical imperative, appeal only to reason, a supplementary form of aesthetic knowledge is introduced, intended to appeal ethically to the senses as well.

In Schiller's terminology from the *Aesthetic Letters* the basic idea of aesthetic education is expressed as follows: the dominance of rational thinking is the result of an overpowering "Formtrieb" (Schiller 1975, p. 605), or "formal impulse" (cf. Schiller 1965, Letter 12, p. 65). While the rational "formal impulse" is useful, since it gives form to existence (i.e., structure, duration, moderation), it also overpowers the human developmental process and dominates the other basic human drive, "Stofftrieb" (Schiller 1975, p. 609), or "material impulse" (cf. Schiller 1965, Letter 13, p. 70). The latter is originally in a balanced relationship with the former, since as mere substance (unformed matter, the senses, and irrationality) it absolutely requires form for its shaping. But if the formal impulse takes over, the sensing, material part becomes suffocated, and the result is the unfor-

---

[1] Understanding Schiller as an early cultural critic builds on ideas found in: Bollenbeck 2007a, pp. 11–26; Bollenbeck 2007b, p. 76–111.

https://doi.org/10.1515/9783110586602-008

tunate attempt to realise pure ideas from the realm of reason as described above. To solve this problem, Schiller proposes art in the form of an aesthetic education: if the formal and material impulses are unbalanced, then they must be brought into harmony. Since this cannot be achieved on its own but rather requires a facilitating mechanism, this is where art comes in. It brings form and matter into the desired balance, for which Schiller coined the term "Spieltrieb" (Schiller 1975, p. 612)," or "play impulse" (cf. Schiller 1965, Letter 14, p. 74). By means of the play impulse, human beings are now able to realise their theoretical constructs, since they are no longer trying to implement these ideals unilaterally controlled by reason. Aesthetic education translates the theory of the categorical imperative into a practical impulse and thus transforms it into something human beings can implement in society. Schiller describes this method of achieving Enlightenment ideas through art as an aesthetic detour, because reason is no longer seen as powerful enough to implement its plans directly, but rather must do so with the aid of art:

> In a word, there is no other way to make the sensuous man rational than by first making him aesthetic. (Schiller 1965, p. 108).

> (Mit einem Wort: es gibt keinen andern Weg, den sinnlichen Menschen vernünftig zu machen, als daß man denselben zuvor ästhetisch macht.) (Schiller 1975, p. 641).

1 Schiller: Apparent Purposes

Along this detour, what also unfolds is what we will now turn to: aesthetic purposelessness, in order to examine its purpose. The idea of aesthetic education brought into play by Schiller, being directed against the world of purposefulness, could certainly be understood to be "useless," for the aesthetic realm of education is constituted by leisure, obstinacy, and impertinence (and as such it can be understood in relation to the working world as being without purpose); however, in spite of everything, it is not purposeless, since it is supposed to produce something: namely, education. Therefore, the purpose-free pursues a task, and we want to examine in greater detail the benefits created and shaped by purposelessness. Since we are arriving at a threshold that is difficult to define with this oscillation between purposelessness and purpose, the term "apparent purpose" ("Zweckscheinbarkeit") is introduced here to clarify the following.[2] It leads to a contradictory connection between beauty and education—or between

---

[2] This notion of "apparent purpose" is addressed in greater detail in: Clemens 2015, pp. 55–58.

purpose and purposelessness—built upon the fundamental question: How can something that is free of any purposeful purpose still develop a purpose, namely, to shape the aesthetic education of man? How does this special purpose of purposelessness work?

Schiller's *Aesthetic Letters* initially propose for humans a state that promises to bring little benefit: the play impulse should place unilaterally, rationally, determined human beings in a "zero state" in which they once again obtain the possibility of "zero determined outcomes"—that is, none determined by one-sided consequences of reason, theory and economy, in order to rebalance the impulses between form and matter. This situates a person in a purposeless relationship with the world, since within these socioeconomic freedoms one can pursue one's own needs, which are purposeless in the sense that they allow persons to free themselves from the demands that are otherwise placed upon them.

Since this negation is based on the desire to reduce the purposeful but has nevertheless an aim, it is an exemplary illustration of the contradiction inherent in purposelessness: On the one hand, this "zero state" distinguishes itself by leaving the subject indefinite, and on the other hand, it prepares the subject for something which determines it anew—and better than before. And this is exactly where our question comes in; if purposelessness can negate and shape at the same time, how can this be represented, how can we talk about it, and what happens in this intangible state, which assumes:

> In the aesthetic state, then, Man is *Zero*, insofar as we are considering an isolated result and not the whole capacity, and are regarding the absence of any particular determination inside him. (Letter 21).[3]
>
> (In dem ästhetischen Zustande ist der Mensch also *Null*, insofern man auf ein einzelnes Resultat, nicht auf das ganze Vermögen achtet und den Mangel jeder besondern Determination in ihm in Betrachtung zieht.) (Schiller 1975, p. 635).

For the description of this 'annulled' or purposeless field, we use the term "apparent purpose," which will serve as a key concept for understanding purposelessness. It can be used to sketch the outlines of purposelessness, making it clear that the aesthetic "zero state" that arises in this regard is neither useful nor useless. The purposeless occurs in our understanding of aesthetic education, namely only *seemingly:* appearances are indeed detached from the sphere of clear purpose, initially rendering them without obvious purpose. But purposes are also present, though destined for a subjective sphere, which they arrive at only when they abandon their immediate purpose. Clear and distinct purposes are in-

---

[3] Translation with alterations by the author based on Schiller 1965, p. 101.

itially turned into apparent purposes in order to escape a constraining reality. This happens through the revaluation of purposes in aesthetic appearance. Their freedom of purpose therefore consists in the fact that the subject can choose its own purposes. Purposeful freedom operates as a setting of purposes within freedom, and hereby create an aesthetic counter-world. It appears that in aesthetic worlds, rational purpose is refined, and via aesthetic appearance its purposes become apparent. Art inhibits the constant spread of a purposeful *and* subjective world orientation and thus replaces it not with one that is utterly without purpose, but rather with purposeful thinking, planning, and action in the realm of *appearances*, whereby the distinctions between purpose and objective constraints are suspended. These purposes are no longer opposed to the subject, and purposes with alienating characteristics are kept at a safe distance. After the aesthetic period in education, the subject itself can decide whether the development from the realm of appearances should be activated in reality or not.

Schiller mentions very briefly that "idleness" ("Müßiggang") (Schiller 1965, p. 54, Schiller 1975, p. 596) could be the moment in which the journey of aesthetic education can begin.[4] In regard to our understanding of apparent purposes, idle moments in an educational setting grant playfulness generously, but also seek to develop them into something concrete. They are apt to engage not only seemingly with the (pragmatic) world, but in the moment of their development, idleness blurs the distinction between play and seriousness, as well as between contemplation and action. Disinterested play has not decided yet if it remains in the realm of the play or transforms its play into something more worldly, i.e. enlightened aesthetic judgments. Nonetheless, despite their appearance, apparent purposes are not less active then real purposes. Idleness and aesthetic experiences require action, but subjective action is not yet ready to engage with the world outside of this realm.

However, because apparent purposes are still apparent and not real, the important question is: how they can be activated if this does not happen automatically? Since Schiller describes man dominated by formal impulses, these kind of people are not all too open for aesthetic experiences and its detours. For this reason, Schiller imagines a fictional art educator and delegates to him the task to educate the people when he encounters them in idle moments. He explicitly warns him to not be too serious and confront them with all his idealism:

---

[4] A further investigation on Schiller's notion of idleness in regard to his project of aesthetic education can be found in Clemens 2015, pp. 31–35.

> The gravity of your principles will scare them from you, but in play they will continue to tolerate them [...] In vain you will assail their maxims, in vain condemn their deeds; but you can try your fashioning hand upon their idleness. Drive away lawlessness, frivolity and coarseness from their pleasure [...] (Schiller 1965, p. 54).

> (Der Ernst deiner Grundsätze wird sie [= die Zeitgenossen] von dir scheuchen, aber im Spiele ertragen sie sie noch [...] Ihre Maximen wirst du umsonst bestürmen, ihre Taten umsonst verdammen, aber an ihrem Müßiggange kannst du deine bildende Hand versuchen. Verjage die Willkühr, die Frivolität, die Rohigkeit aus ihren Vergnügungen [...]) (Schiller 1975, p. 596).

The quoted passage describes the beginning of Schiller's idealistic process. This beginning, however, is very concrete and not highly idealistic. It respects the dominance of formal impulses: With idleness, Schiller found a moment to circumvent such domination and locates the subject in the moment where it is structurally already in the desired aesthetic state. Here, idleness has temporarily weakened the formal impulse, and constitutes therefore the best moment to foster aesthetic experiences. This moment of idleness could be called a 'pre-aesthetic state', because it is a valid beginning towards the development of the play impulse.

The main part of the *Aesthetic Letters* subsequently discusses how to develop these idle moments into a fully balanced "aesthetic state" ("ästhetischer Zustand") (Schiller 1965, Schiller 1975, pp. 570–669). This development depends on change and can never be planned like a professional education. Schiller relies on the subject's desire to develop the experience of idleness. And after the problem of the development of the aesthetic state, another problem needs to be addressed: Even when the subject achieves this state, the aesthetic balance also needs to be translated back into real life (or into the "moral state" ("moralischer Zustand") (cf. Schiller 1965, pp. 99, 109, 113, Schiller 1975, pp. 633, 642, 675) as Schiller puts it). Idleness was the moment of a positive distance from real life and the aesthetic state the deeper development of this distance. But since Schiller desires not only an aesthetic subject, but also one that acts socially, the subject needs to have the skill and the desire to translate the ideal perspective into real life and action.

Thus, the development of apparent moments is confronted with three difficulties: First, the subject needs to find itself in idle moment of a pre-aesthetic state. Secondly, it needs the desire to develop these idle experiences into the balance of the aesthetic state, and finally, the subject undertakes the task to translate this playful balance back into social action.

2 Kant: Aesthetic Judgment and the *Bildungsroman*

In a common sense discourse "purposelessness" or the "purpose-free" always occurs when there is talk of experiences that critically oppose and compensate for the purposeful demands of everyday life, and accordingly, in a sense, are "useless" (such as art, work-life balance, or going to the theatre). By this simple mechanism, "purposelessness" becomes something very vague, which one can always call on without really having to understand it or comprehend the difficulty of the relation between the purposeless and the purposeful.

Our investigation contradicts the ease and vagueness of the purpose-free. In dealing with Schiller's *Aesthetic Letters*, we have already introduced a concept, namely "apparent purpose," which better expresses the ambivalence of purposelessness and does not lose itself in vague ideas. We defined apparent purpose as a process that does not do away with purposes, but allows them to be placed in a sphere which does not run contrary to the needs of the subject. Kant, on the contrary, strives for a pure aesthetic judgment. His desire for pure aesthetics is opposed to the idea of aesthetic education, since Kant rendered the aesthetic judgment utterly speechless and imageless, whereas Schiller combines purposes and aesthetics by means of appearances.

As Kant writes at the beginning of the *Critique of Judgment*, an aesthetic judgment is based on a feeling of pleasure that does not refer back primarily to the intellect and its conceptual instruments for cognitive judgments, but rather to a special relationship between reason and intuition (Kant 1987, §§ 1–9).[5] Intuition perceives the beautiful object, but it does not enter into unity with a concept. This repression of concepts renders Kant's judgment of taste disinterested, which means that the feeling of pleasure elicited by looking at a beautiful object is not connected with any interest in the material existence of that object. Instead, all that arises is a pleasure that Kant situates "in the realm of pure contemplation" (Kant 1987, p. Ak 204), that is, in the lingering of this intuition. Thus, aesthetic perception is distinguished from the agreeable, which Kant subordinates to an interest in a real object, and also from the good, which returns to a concept owing to its universality—that is, where reason and intuition form a clearly defined unity. As such, Kant can conclude, with regard

---

[5] For further discussions on Kant's notion of aesthetic judgment see Guyer 1997, pp. 85–86; Heinrich 1994, pp. 40–52; Makkreel 1990, pp. 49–58; Bell 1987, p. 87; Crowford 1974, pp. 88–89; Crowther 1989, pp. 55–56.

to disinterestedness that: "Taste is the judgment of an object or a mode of thinking by a pleasure without interest. The object of such pleasure is the beautiful" (Kant 1987, p. Ak 211). And once again with regard to the concept-less: "The beautiful is that which pleases without concept" (Kant 1987, p. Ak 219). The independence of reason and imagination leads to "free play" (Kant 1987, p. Ak 217) between these two poles, which gives the subject the pleasure of the beautiful object. And this is exactly where the greatest difficulty of Kant's aesthetic theory lies, because it is not clear what happens to concepts in the course of judgment, since, when reason is in play, it cannot simply disappear.

A judgment of taste—as in the case of a conceptual-logical judgment—is universally pleasing, which for Kant means that individuals necessarily universalise their subjective pleasure in aesthetic judgment, assuming that others hold the same opinion in regard to the same beautiful object. A logical judgment—that the meadow is green, for example—is based on a concept, and thus assumes its general validity as a judgment. However, the logical verifiability does not apply if the judgment is aesthetic, since it no longer refers back to a concept. If the green meadow is found to be pleasing in aesthetic judgment, then this statement cannot be further proven. The fact that this preference nevertheless has the appearance of universality—thus producing apparent concepts—is due to reason, which is in a state of play and still is 'somehow' present, although it does not impose any concepts upon intuition. (To clarify, it could also be said in a figurative and more simplified way, that one produces experimental concepts which are tentatively formulated but can also be dissolved again.) For Kant, the third point of aesthetic judgment is this: "The beautiful is that which *universally* pleases without concept" (Kant 1987, p. Ak 229).[6]

At this point, we return to the difficulty already indicated in Kant's aesthetics and ask: What happens to the concepts in this interplay? Kant's statements are anything but clear. Kant himself once said that *no* concept-formation occurs in the judgment of taste (Kant 1987, pp. Ak 211f., p. Ak 219),[7] but also that play arises "without presupposing a *fixed* concept" (Kant 1987, p. Ak 217),[8] and finally, that it comes about because "imagination *schematizes* without a concept" (Kant 1987, p. Ak 287).[9] It should come as no surprise, given these different formulations, that the exploration of concepts is also controversial within the field of Kant studies. In order to challenge Kant's variably defined notion of the concept-less, which always receives a different shading and with the relationship of

---

6 Emphasis mine.
7 Cf. Kant 1989, p. Ak 229: "Free beauty does not presuppose a concept."
8 Emphasis mine.
9 Emphasis mine.

the resulting distinct elements not immediately made clear, we must ask the following question: How can reason, which automatically produces concepts, refer to the imagination in "free play" without determining the latter by concepts? Aesthetic judgment does not simply shut off reason, but rather comes about only through the imagination, so long as it is situated in a play between imagination and reason. However, this means that reason, so to speak, still 'plays along', and the play carries features of a design that cannot spring forth from imagination alone. Kant writes that imagination and reason must "harmonize" (Kant 1987, p. Ak 218), i.e. finding the required "harmony" can be found "only where imagination in its freedom awakens reason," and where such awakening "without concepts puts the imagination into standard play" (Kant 1987, p. Ak 296). Imagination finds within this interplay "its freedom," however it is somehow shaped into "standard play." In other words, here is a heretofore unknown "free regularity of the imagination" at work, which gives imagination an autonomous status, and can thus be considered self-regulating. However, we must again ask: Can imagination render unto itself its laws, given that reason is the sole legislator; and how, as could be asked inversely, can reason be present without being able to exercise its conceptual purpose?

The standard solution to this circular reasoning is to propose that the imagination here does not enter into unity with a particular concept, but only with the general ability to form concepts (cf. Guyer 1997, Henrich 1994, Makkreel 1990). Thus, intuition is not formed to the point of ultimately being tied to a concept, but rather is determined in a content-less state—in the sense of a formal concept formation—merely by being brought together with the general schematism of the categories. According to our reading then, "purposefulness" could also be called "conceptual-ness," since categorically schematised intuitions contain the mere possibility of specific concept formations without, however, their realisation.

This emptiness in Kant's explanation of disinterested artistic experience is also reflected in his fondness for floral patterns and in the purely ornamental nature of his imagery: "flowers, sketches, intertwined traits, under the name of foliage" (Kant 1987, p. Ak 207).Therefore, his pure aesthetic has sometimes been decried by critics as a "wallpaper pattern aesthetic" (Strube 1979, p. 170. Trans. by the author). And if education describes the effort of bringing art and world experience together, then we see very well here that this cannot be done with Kant. In the beginning of Goethe's Bildungsroman *Wilhelm Meisters Lehrjahre*, a similar complaint about the difficulty of unifying art and world experience is made, in the scene where Wilhelm gets angry upon regarding the patterned wallpaper in his parents' living room:

When Wilhelm greeted his mother the next morning, she informed him that his father was very angry and would soon forbid him from those regular visits to the theater. "I, too, would like to go to the theater sometimes," she continued, "but I am often annoyed at the way our domestic peace and quiet are disturbed by your wild addiction to this pleasure. Your father is always saying, "What the use of this? Why waste one one's in the theater"?
"I've often heard him say that," said Wilhelm, "and I may have answered him too rudely; but for goodness' sake, Mother, why is everything useless that doesn't bring in money or enlarge our property? Didn't we have enough room in the old house? Was it necessary to build a new one? Doesn't my father spend a sizable amount of his profits every year in decorating these rooms? All these silk wallpapers and this English furniture, do we need all that? Couldn't we do with less? These striped walls, with their endless rows of flowers, their scrolls and baskets and figures, seem so unpleasant, like a stage curtain in our own house. It's different in a real theater where you know that the curtain will go up and reveal all sorts of things to entertain, enlighten and elevate us." (Goethe 1995, pp. 2–3.)[10]

(Als Wilhelm seine Mutter des andern Morgens begrüßte, eröffnete sie ihm, daß der Vater sehr verdrießlich sei und ihm den täglichen Besuch des Schauspiels nächstens untersagen werde. "Wenn ich gleich selbst", fuhr sie fort, "manchmal gern ins Theater gehe, so möchte ich es doch oft verwünschen, da meine häusliche Ruhe durch deine unmäßige Leidenschaft zu diesem Vergnügen gestört wird. Der Vater wiederholt immer, wozu es nur nütze sei, wie man seine Zeit nur so verderben könne."
"Ich habe es auch schon von ihm hören müssen", versetzte Wilhelm, "und habe ihm vielleicht zu hastig geantwortet; aber um's Himmels willen, Mutter! Ist denn alles unnütz, was uns nicht unmittelbar Geld in den Beutel bringt, was uns nicht den allernächsten Besitz verschafft? Hatten wir in dem alten Haus nicht Raum genug? Und war es nötig, ein neues zu bauen? Verwendet der Vater nicht jährlich einen ansehnlichen Teil seines Handelsgewinnes zur Verschönerung der Zimmer? Und diese seidenen Tapeten, diese englischen Mobilien, sind sie nicht auch unnütz? Könnten wir uns nicht mit geringeren begnügen? Wenigstens bekenne ich, daß mir diese gestreiften Wände, diese hundertmal wiederholten Blumen, Schnörkel, Körbchen und Figuren einen durchaus unangenehmen Eindruck machen. Sie kommen mir höchstens vor wie unser Theatervorhang. Aber wie anders ist's, vor diesem zu sitzen! Wenn man noch so lange warten muß, so weiß man doch, er wird in die Höhe gehen, und wir werden die mannigfaltigsten Gegenstände sehen, die uns unterhalten, aufklären und erheben.") (Goethe 1965, pp. 11–12).

The mother's wish for "domestic peace" is contrasted with Wilhelm's discomfort, provoked by the sight of the wallpaper and expressed in his objections to his parents' diffidence, which does not seek to experience art, but constrains it to these same private four walls. The useless nature of the luxurious furnishings is, at least with regard to the wallpaper, at most an aesthetic prelude for Wilhelm, which refers to a future promise in the form of the theatrical realm. However, the walls cannot simply be opened like a theatre curtain and fall away, leading

---

10 From *Wilhelm Meister's Apprenticeship*.

into another world. Considering William's later enthusiasm for the theatre and for Shakespeare, it is easy to comprehend how insignificant the "striped walls, with their endless rows of flowers, their scrolls and baskets and figures" are in relation to his upcoming educational journey. In William's eyes, the wallpaper pattern intermingles with the emptiness present in his parents' home, while his own striving for education seeks out "all sorts of things" that "entertain, enlighten and elevate us" —all that is not permitted by Kant's understanding of the beautiful.

Accordingly, Wilhelm Meister's purposeless education is based on his experiences in this journey from pure (and dull) beauty to his new life as an actor—in other words, as he ventures in the course of the novel from a boring and almost meaningless aesthetic sphere into encounters with a social context. Thus, in understanding this question in the context of this article, literature can be regarded as a playground for initially world-less ideas (Kant's aesthetics), which receive a specific task in the course of their development (Schiller's educational idea), and then, via apparent purposes, become concretised in the Bildungsroman and the journey of its protagonist. This journey begins with the desire to follow idealistic aspirations and recounts the negotiation between these hopes and worldly constraints, while also providing an account of the journey's transitory character. At the beginning, Wilhelm finds himself in Schiller's pre-aesthetic state of idleness and the rest of the novel will tell the story of his attempt to intensify his aesthetic aspirations (Schiller's aesthetic state so to speak) and finally ask the question how to combine them with a bourgeois life and social action (Schiller's moral state and the goal of the *Aesthetic Letters*). If we compare Wilhelm Meister's development with Schiller's letters, it goes without saying that Wilhelm's first theatrical aesthetic aspirations in front of the wallpapers of his parents are less successful then the utopia of appearances that Schiller invents.

3 Conclusion: Apparent Concepts

The conceptual abstractions of purposelessness in Kant, with their pictorial quality on the level of wallpaper patterns, appeal to our imagination. We should not be misled by his intended precision nor be bored by his imagery, however. As such, we can conclude that the question of concepts in the aesthetic judgment of Kant cannot be conclusively answered, and consequently, through the aim of apparent purpose, *apparent concepts* can be established. This means that, on the one hand, it seems as though there are concepts—or at least forms of conceptual-ness—but, on the other hand, the supposed concept formation can go beyond itself into the concept-less.

In our inability to distil the question of the presence of concepts and our need to leave it in the order of the apparent, we are not—unlike Kant and many of his interpreters—in search of *pure* aesthetic judgments,[11] for the following reason: For Kant, aesthetic perception is something static, which identifies a brief moment that does not actually exist in the empirical—and anti-idealist—world. We are, in fact, always situated within a process constituted by *impure* aesthetic perceptions, such as the process of an aesthetic form of education. Only in the rarest of cases does one make either purely aesthetic or purely unaesthetic judgments; usually, judgments occur in a shifting ratio between these two poles. Kant's aesthetics only allow for contemplation within a silent enclave, because only in this place (as in his theory) they are constructed without context.

The pictures and wallpaper games (as well as birdsong and flowers), which serve for Kant as examples of his theory, bear no features of the environment in which they appear to the subject. Their free play, which for Kant is the central moment of the aesthetic experience, is harnessed by Schiller into a larger project which strives for aesthetic freedom in a more worldly setting. Our concept of apparent purpose thus views the aesthetic as well as its undecidedness in a social context. Kant's aesthetic experience, inversely, is always only a brief moment absent of a social environment. Schiller's aesthetic theory is, in fact, idealistic as well, but he aims to realise some of its aspiration. This is the reason why he is looking for a combination of (pure) idealism and (impure) idleness. Goethe's *Bildungsroman* takes both seriously and provides an account of the possibilities and failures of apparent purposes.

Bibliography

Bell, David (1987): "The Art of Judgment." In: *Mind*, Vol. 96.
Bollenbeck, Georg (2007a): "Von der Universalgeschichte zur Kulturkritik." In: Ehrlich, Lothar / Bollenbeck, Georg (Eds.): *Friedrich Schiller. Der unterschätzte Theoretiker*. Vienna – Cologne – Weimar: Böhlau, p. 11–26.
Bollenbeck, Georg (2007b): *Eine Geschichte der Kulturkritik. Von Rousseau bis Günther Anders*. München: C.H. Beck.
Clemens, Manuel (2015): *Das Labyrinth der ästhetischen Einsamkeit: eine kleine Theorie der Bildung*. Würzburg: Königshausen & Neumann.
Crowford, Paul (1974): *Kant's Aesthetic Theory*. Madison, WI: Wisconsin University Press.
Crowther, Paul (1989): *The Kantian Sublime*. Oxford: Oxford University Press.

---

[11] For a detailed discussion of Kant's aesthetic judgment see Kern 2000.

Goethe, Johann Wolfgang (1965): *Goethes Werke*, Bd. VII. 6. Auflage. Ed. Trunz, Erich. Hamburg: Christian Wegner Verlag.
Goethe, Johann Wolfgang (1995): *The Collected Works*, vol. 9. Trans. Blackhall, Eric. Princeton: Princeton University Press.
Guyer, Paul (1997): *Kant and the Claims of Taste*. Cambridge, MA: Cambridge University Press.
Heinrich, Dieter (1994): *Aesthetic Judgment and the Moral Image of the World*. Stanford, California: Stanford University Press.
Kant, Immanuel (1987): *Critique of Judgment*. Trans. Pluhar, Werner S. Indianapolis, Indiana: Hackett.
Kern, Andrea (2000): *Schöne Lust. Eine Theorie der ästhetischen Erfahrung nach Kant.* Frankfurt am Main: Suhrkamp.
Makkreel, Rudolf (1990): *Imagination and Interpretation in Kant*, Chicago: Chicago University Press.
Schiller, Friedrich (1965): *On the Aesthetic Education of Man*. Trans. with an Introduction by Snell, Reginald. New York: Frederick Ungar.
Schiller, Friedrich (1975): *Sämtliche Werke*. Band V. Eds. Fricke, Gerhard / Göpfert, Herbert G. 5. Auflage. München: Carl Hanser Verlag.
Schiller, Friedrich (1982): *On the Aesthetic Education of Man. In a Series of Letters*. Trans. Wilkinson, M. / Willoughby, L. A. New York: Oxford University Press.
Strube, Werner (1979): "Interesselosigkeit. Zur Geschichte eines Begriffs in der Ästhetik." In: *Archiv für Begriffsgeschichte* (23).

Víctor Ibarra B.
Antecedents to Hegel's Conception of Judaism in Kant's Practical Philosophy

Abstract: This article examines the Kantian antecedents to Hegel's conception of Judaism. I show that Hegel's treatment of Judaism is based on his early reception of Kant's practical philosophy. In order to exhibit this relationship, the article presents the notion of heteronomy in Kant's *Grundlegung zur Metaphysik der Sitten* (1785) and then examines the fragment of Hegel's called "Das Leben Jesu" (1795). In this fragment, it is clear how Kant's moral philosophy influenced the young Hegel. This is relevant because the constitutive features of the notion of Judaism remain the same—i.e., based on Kant's notion of heteronomy—throughout Hegel's philosophy.

In this paper, I would like to argue that Hegel's treatment of Judaism is based on his early reception of Kant's practical philosophy. To do so, I will (1) analyse which elements from Kant's practical philosophy are relevant to understand Hegel's reception of it. Later, I will address one of the early fragments, "Das Leben Jesu" (1795), to show (2) how Hegel's rejection of Judaism is grounded in Kant's practical philosophy. In this fragment, it is clear how Kant's moral philosophy has influenced the young Hegel. This is relevant because, despite the fact that Hegel openly rejects Kant's categorical imperative ever since the group of fragments known as "Der Geist des Christentums und sein Schicksal" (1798–1800), the constitutive features of the notion "Judaism" remain the same—i.e. based on Kant's notion of heteronomy—throughout Hegel's philosophy.

I would like to state that my exposition of Hegel's critique of Judaism does not imply that I endorse his critique, which may be considered anti-judaic. The main purpose of this chapter is to conceptually reconstruct *Judaism* as a notion within Hegel's practical philosophy. Therefore, Judaism is taken here as a conceptual inquiry, within a determined frame of thought.

1 The Kantian Frame

If we follow the trail of reflections on Judaism in Hegel's work, we see that the notion coheres well within his system. Every time Hegel refers to the Judaic relation to God, he uses the same constitutive features, namely, a powerful, separate and absolute God in the face of a weak, finite and servile humanity.

It is true that Hegel's rejection of Judaism is part of a larger tradition of Protestant thinkers, and that we find the opposition between Judaism not only in philosophy, but also in literature—in Hölderlin and Novalis, for example. However, in order to understand Hegel's specific way of conceiving Judaism and Christianity, we must focus on his early writings, and on how he develops his own opinion of Judaism by reading Kant's practical philosophy. Here lies the specificity of Hegel's refusal of Judaism, namely, how he interprets the Kantian notion of *heteronomy*.

The most adequate way to understand Kant's conception of heteronomy is through his reflections on freedom and, hence, by analyzing *Grundlegung zur Metaphysik der Sitten* (GMS, 1785), insofar heteronomy is defined within the frame of the exposition of the categorical imperative, which is fully developed in this text. GMS is divided into a prologue, three chapters and a final observation. Each of these chapters supposes some sort of interdependence. Kant starts with the most vague and common notions of morality until a full isolation of the *a priori* components that define and determine moral freedom. He aims to show how morality should not be grounded by experience, but precisely by *a priori* principles. This would be the only possible way to deduce a solid principle of morality, because "[e]xperience teaches us that a thing is so and so, but not that it cannot be otherwise" ([e]rfahrung lehrt uns zwar, daß etwas so oder so beschaffen sei, aber nicht, daß es nicht anders sein könne) (KrV B3). Necessity and universality can only be assured through *a priori* sources. For this reason, Kant's conclusions with regard to morality extend not only to humankind, but to every rational being.

Kant fully addresses *Heteronomie* only at the end of the second chapter, in AA, IV, GMS 432–433. Here, he describes it only in negative terms, i.e. it can be understood solely as the opposite to another term: the principle of *autonomy*. Therefore, we need to understand what autonomy is if we want to comprehend the particularities of heteronomy. In this first mention, according to Kant, so far, practical philosophy has considered humankind as tied to law, but this law seemed to be nevertheless external to humankind. In this sense, Kant would consider himself to be a pioneer in thinking a moral law to which we are related through *duty*, as humankind's *internal* law, as a law given by humankind's *will* to itself. *Will* and *duty* must still be clarified, however.

1.1

Kant speaks directly about *a good will* already in the first chapter of *GMS*, though he does not fully explain it. In the introduction, he openly states that metaphysics of morals should research "the idea and principles of a possible *pure* will" (die Idee und die Prinzipien eines möglichen reinen Willens) (AA, IV, GMS 390–391), but he does it without giving any proper characterisation of the *will*. It is complicated to reconstruct the concept due to its vagueness, as Paton has openly expressed: "the conception is necessarily vague, and it is deliberately left so by Kant. We might, perhaps not improperly, describe it as 'a moral will,' but this might have misleading associations" (Paton 1971, p. 34). Only until the second chapter of the book, Kant gives a *positive* account of it:

> Every thing in nature works in accordance with laws. Only a rational being has the faculty to act in accordance with the representation of laws, i.e., in accordance with principles, or a will. Since for the derivation of actions from laws reason is required, the will is nothing other than practical reason.[1]
>
> (Ein jedes Ding der Natur wirkt nach Gesetzen. Nur ein vernünftiges Wesen hat das Vermögen, nach der Vorstellung der Gesetze, d.i. nach Prinzipien, zu handeln, oder einen Willen. Da zur Ableitung der Handlungen von Gesetzen Vernunft erfordert wird, so ist der Wille nichts anders als praktische Vernunft.) (AA, IV, GMS, 412).

At the beginning of the quotation, Kant refers to a specific characteristic of the rational being, namely, the fact that it has the power, property or capacity to act by following the representation of a law *or* a will. Therefore, *the capacity to act by following the representation of a law = will*. This capacity would be distinct to the rational being when considering all other things in nature: all things in nature would act according to laws, but only the rational being is able to mediate its relationship with the law through a representation of such a law.

Moreover, thanks to the will, the rational being can also *conceive* and *act through* a different type of causation, and also follow a different type of law. This second kind of causation requires, on the one hand, a law to be followed, namely, a practical principle in general; and, on the other hand, a rational being that acts in accordance with this principle *thanks to a representation* of it. This representation of the law can be understood solely in terms of what Kant calls

---

[1] Throughout this paper, Kant's quotations are given in both, German and English. As the English translations of Kant (see bibliography) include the pagination of the Akademie-Ausgabe (AA), only the reference to AA is given in the running text. In the only reference to *Kritik der reinen Vernunft*, I use the regular abbreviation *KrV*, because in the case of the three critiques it is traditional to indicate their abbreviations instead of AA.

a *maxim*, namely, the subjective representation of the law through which the rational agent decides her action, called by Kant himself "the subjective principle of volition" (to use Timmermann's translation), opposed—but still complementary—to the practical law (AA, IV, GMS 401).

The maxim is how the agent represents the law to herself in order to act; it is "a proposition, which specifies the will of the agent" and characterises her intentional and rational behavior (Ormeño 2004, 15).[2] This rationality says something also regarding the moral law in comparison to the law of gravity, for instance. This kind of law does not involve an agent whose rationality is capable of following the rules grouped by the law. It cannot be broken. The moral law must be something else, whose command can—but also cannot—be followed by a rational agent. The agent, in this case, *decides*. This is precisely why for Kant the moral value resides in the maxim, not in the purpose, i.e., in the *Prinzip des Wollens*.

In the second part of AA, IV, GMS 412, after having established the equivalence *will = capacity to act by following the representation of a law*, Kant states that the deduction of actions from laws *demands* the use of reason, and this would justify the equivalence *will = practical reason*. I believe this equivalence has to do precisely with the fact that to act according to maxims requires a specific rationality behind our decisions. It is the use of reason that allows the rational being to be able to *conceive* a representation of the law, and to decide to follow that law, or to break it.

Kant describes other relevant features of this will: "The will is thought as a faculty of determining itself to action *in accord with the representation of certain laws*" (Der Wille wird als ein Vermögen gedacht, der Vorstellung gewisser Gesetze gemäß sich selbst zum Handeln zu bestimmen) (AA, IV, GMS 427). In this quotation, there is a new element: the rational being conceives this mediation with the law as self-determination. From this, the agent can be responsible for her decisions, namely, she can call her decisions *her own*. Thanks to the maxim, our relation to the law can be thought as something self-given and self-chosen.

Immediately after this nuance, Kant gives more specific characteristics of the will: it has ends and means. An end is the objective determination of the will, namely, "the object at which one's choice is directed, for the sake of which one acts" (Timmermann 2007, p. 175). A means, on the contrary, is what allows the rational being to accomplish her ends, i.e. it is nothing more than the "ground of the possibility of an action." When the rational being acts, her will is directed toward an end, and accomplishes that end through certain means.

---

[2] The translation is mine.

The will can also ground its desire to act in two different bases: a subjective ground, called *motive* (*Triebfeder*), and an objective one, called *motivating ground* (*Bewegungsgrund*).³ According to Kant therefore, the rational being can have subjective ends if her desire to act is grounded in motives, and objective ends if her desire to act is grounded in motivating grounds. The former cannot claim universality; the latter can.

It is relatively easy to comprehend an action based on motives. Let's think of one of the favorites examples of Kant, the false promise. Two women hold hands at the beach. They are a couple and they seem happy, but one of them, the oldest one, has decided to leave her partner. Not for a moment, not because she is hungry and wants to go to the store to get something to eat or because she needs cigarettes. She does not love the woman next to her anymore, and wants to leave her for good. "How should I proceed?" she asks herself. "Should I tell the truth, that is, should I tell her *I do not love you anymore, I won't come back?*" She considers her options. Laura, her partner, will ask for an explanation. "Maria, why?" Laura will probably scream and cry. That would be uncomfortable. "But if I do not give any reasons, if I leave and say *sweety, I'll come back in a minute*, I won't have to witness her pain, and she eventually will notice that I'm not coming back. Once at home, she will realize that my stuff is gone. It will be easier." She leaves, she promises to come back, but she does not return.

What has determined Maria's *Prinzip des Wollens*? We can clearly identify a rational agent in the example, because there are logical markers, namely, a *reasoning* behind Maria's decision—hence, she has recognised a law (*do not make false promises, do not lie*) and conceived a representation which guided her decision and determined her will, namely, a maxim (*it is convenient for me, now, to lie and to promise something that I can no longer fulfill*). This maxim, though, cannot claim universality, that is, it could not be conceived as a valid law for every rational being without destroying itself. Maria makes a decision. However, she was taken by her impulses, namely, she was driven by her *motives* to break the law, to accomplish certain *end* that is not the law itself, but a material object (namely, *not to witness crying, to not be responsible, to run away*). Maria is not free for breaking the law and achieving the represented end (*running away without scandal*); breaking the law shows on the contrary that Maria proceeded bound by something *else, motivated by an end* whose fulfillment required Laura to be treated as a *means*. Maria's will has not really being *self-determined*; therefore, there is no freedom in the Kantian sense.

---

3 I choose this translations by following Timmermann's comments on Kant's GMS.

How could Maria's action be really free? If her action would have been based on motivating grounds, if her *end* would have been based solely on formal grounds, if she would have been able to *free* herself from the subjective motives which guided her action, then the *end* of her action would have been objective and, therefore, the maxim under which she represented the law to herself would have been able to become universal.

Why did Maria lie? Why did Maria make a false promise? Maria lied because the end of her action was concerned with the *effect* of the action, namely, with the material consequences and not with the pure formality of the action. If Maria would have told the truth to Laura *regardless of the consequences* of her confession, then the *end* would have been objective, based on motivating grounds and not on motives. This would be a moral action according to Kant, namely, to act out of *duty* with disregard to the constraint implied in our relation to the law or, in other words, despite the constraint that tempt us to think of the *effects* of the action.

1.2

Why do we relate to the law by means of constraint? According to AA, IV, GMS 412–413, after specifying the two equivalences that characterise the will (as *the capacity to act by following the representation of a law* and as *practical reason*), Kant affirms that this will, in the case of rational and *finite* beings, is not always determined by pure practical reason, but on the contrary, because of its finitude, this will is also submitted to contingency and, if it is determined by motives, the objectivity of the practical principles *appears* to it as a *constraint*. That is to say, the will of humans cannot be 'good without limitation,' i.e. it cannot relate solely to the practical law; it must also deal with the inclinations toward which it is driven by its motives—if it is determined by them.

> i.e., the relation of objective laws to a will which is not thoroughly good is represented as the determination of the will of a rational being through grounds of reason to which, however, this will in accordance with its nature is not necessarily obedient.
> The representation of an objective principle, insofar as it is necessitating for a will, is called a "command" (of reason), and the formula of the command is called an **imperative.**
>
> (d. i. das Verhältnis der objektiven Gesetze zu einem nicht durchaus guten Willen wird vorgestellt als die Bestimmung des Willens eines vernünftigen Wesens zwar durch Gründe der Vernunft, denen aber dieser Wille seiner Natur nach nicht notwendig folgsam ist.
> Die Vorstellung eines objektiven Prinzips, sofern es für einen Willen nötigend ist, heißt ein Gebot (der Vernunft), und die Formel des Gebots heißt **Imperativ.)** (AA, IV, GMS 413).

The relationship between the rational and finite being's action with regard to the law always expresses a tension in the form of an *ought*. The law commands, the moral agent follows the law, the agent is moral only insofar she follows the command of the moral principle, and what the moral principle of reason commands is, as Kant recognises, not more than "how the need of inclination is to be supplied" (wie dem Bedürfnisse der Neigung abgeholfen werde) (AA, IV, GMS 414). It is important to have in mind, though, that not every imperative constitutes the moral law: imperatives can command "*hypothetically* or *categorically*" (AA, IV, GMS 414), i.e., in the first case, the action can be conceived as a means for an end, namely, the end of the action is in the *effect* or the *consequence* of the action (using the previous example, Maria's way of leaving Laura by lying and making the false promise of coming back, because she wants to avoid a scene), and, in the second case, the action is represented without other end but itself (Maria telling the truth regardless of the consequences).

If we act because we think a certain action is good to accomplish something *else*, then the imperative is hypothetical. But returning to the example, if Maria does what she must, if she tells the truth, she is obeying a law that, in her case, takes the form of a constriction. For her, telling the truth is the duty that practical reason should indicate in order to determine her will, in order to free her will from the influence of her inclinations. Only by following the categorical imperative we are free from these inclinations. This type of imperative constitutes the moral law, and it has no other purpose but the action itself. This action cannot be a *medium* to get anything else, namely, the end is the action itself, not the effect or the consequences of it. In this sense, the moral law is not concerned with the matter of the action, but only with the form (the pure imperative). Kant gives three different formulations of this principle attending precisely to the fact that, in order to be universal, this law must be free from content. I will refer only to the first one: "*So act as if the maxim of your action were to become through your will a* **universal law**" (handle nur nach derjenigen Maxime, durch die du zugleich wollen kannst, daß sie ein allgemeines Gesetzt werde) (AA, IV, GMS 421). I have already shown that *Maxime* is a particular representation of the subject, precisely the representation through which the agent relates to the law, what Kant calls the subjective principle of volition. If I cannot claim universality for my own principle of volition, then the representation through which I decide my action does not relate itself with the moral law, i.e., it is not moral, but works only as a hypothetical imperative. According to Kant, the agent should ask whether her maxim can be universal; that is to say, the agent should ask if this representation of her decision to act can be held by all other agents, and at the same time preserve the possibility of a community. In the case of Maria, can the maxim *lie if necessary, regarding your convenience* be universally held? Obviously not. If everyone lies, how can we trust each other? Namely, if Maria's maxim becomes universal, out relation to others would be always mediated by doubts;[4] our action would always remain suspicious and, therefore, any community becomes unthinkable.

Therefore, our autonomy exists insofar as we act for the sake of duty, namely, insofar as the maxim of our will can claim universality. Only in this case can the idea of a self-legislative will make sense.

1.3

Now that we understand what Kant means with autonomy, it is possible to address the main reference to heteronomy in GMS:

> If the will seeks that which should determine it *anywhere else* than in the suitability of its maxims for its own universal legislation, hence if it, insofar as it advances beyond itself, seeks the law in the constitution of any of its objects, then *heteronomy* always comes out of this. Then the will does not give itself the law but the object through its relation to the will gives the law to it. Through this relation, whether it rests now on inclination or on representations of reason, only hypothetical imperatives are possible: "I ought to do something *because I will something else*." By contrast, the moral, hence categorical, imperative says: "I ought to act thus-and-so even if I did not will anything else." E.g., the former one says: "I ought not to lie, if I want to retain my honorable reputation;" but the latter says: "I ought not to lie, even if I did not incur the least disgrace." The last must therefore abstract from every object to the extent that it has no *influence* on the will, hence practical reason (will) does not merely administer some other interest, but merely proves its own commanding authority as supreme legislation. Thus, e.g., I should seek to promote someone else's happiness, not as if its existence mattered to me (whether through immediate inclination or any satisfaction indirectly through reason) but merely because the maxim that excludes it cannot be comprehended in one and the same volition as a universal law.

> (Wenn der Wille irgend worin anders, als in der Tauglichkeit seiner Maximen zu seiner eigenen allgemeinen Gesetzgebung, mithin, wenn er, indem er über sich selbst hinausgeht, in der Beschaffenheit irgend eines seiner Objekte das Gesetz sucht, das ihn bestimmen soll, so kommt jederzeit Heteronomie heraus. Der Wille gibt alsdann sich nicht selbst, sondern das Objekt durch sein Verhältnis zum Willen gibt diesem das Gesetz. Dies Verhältnis, es beruhe nun auf der Neigung, oder auf Vorstellungen der Vernunft, läßt nur hypothetische Imperativen möglich werden: ich soll etwas tun darum, weil ich etwas anderes will. Dagegen

---

4 In the example of Maria and Laura, Laura's rational dimension is denied insofar she is treated only as a means, not as an end in herself. This relates directly to the second formulation of the categorical imperative, namely, to use humanity always as an end in itself. I cannot expand this subject here, but for an interesting reading of this problem through an aesthetical approach, see Garrido 2012.

sagt der moralische, mithin kategorische Imperativ: ich soll so oder so handeln, ob ich gleich nichts anderes wollte. Z. E. jener sagt: ich soll nicht lügen, wenn ich bei Ehren bleiben will; dieser aber: ich soll nicht lügen, ob es mir gleich nicht die mindeste Schande zuzöge. Der letztere muß also von allem Gegenstande so fern abstrahieren, daß dieser gar keinen Einfluß auf den Willen habe, damit praktische Vernunft (Wille) nicht fremdes Interesse bloß administriere, sondern bloß ihr eigenes gebietendes Ansehen als oberste Gesetzgebung beweise. So soll ich z.B. fremde Glückseligkeit zu befördern suchen, nicht als wenn mir an deren Existenz was gelegen wäre (es sei durch unmittelbare Neigung, oder irgend ein Wohlgefallen indirekt durch Vernunft), sondern bloß deswegen, weil die Maxime, die sie ausschließt, nicht in einem und demselben Wollen, als allgemeinen Gesetz, begriffen werden kann.) (AA, IV, GMS 441).

Here, *Heteronomie* characterises any action in which the subjective principle of volition is determined not by the pure practical reason, namely, not by the call of duty, but by the object (*Objekt*) of the action. We should understand *object* in this quotation as what I have above called the *effect*. In this case, the rational agent is not free from the sensible influences to which she is exposed, as we saw, because of her finitude. Her *Neigungen*, therefore, drive her decision to act, and the action itself is grounded in *Triebfedern*, namely, in subjective ends, not objective ones. Therefore, heteronomy is directly related not to the categorical imperative, but only to hypothetical ones. The way in which the will addresses action, then, by means of heteronomy, implies not self-legislation, but being bound to one's inclinations.

In order to decide freely, the will must free itself from the virtual objects that its action can produce, namely, it must not use its action only as a means to get something else, i.e., an end other than the law itself. Only by freeing itself from the virtual objects or effects that its action can produce is its maxim able to claim universality.

2 The early Hegel and the problem of Judaism

In what follows, I would like to focus on the fragment called "Das Leben Jesu," and to show how Hegel's first notions of practical philosophy and his conception of Jesus are based on Kant's morality; here the focus will be the notion of autonomy as something incarnated by Jesus, a figure who is built up in contrast to the Judaic religion, meaning it is the notion of heteronomy that distinguishes Judaism.

If we take a look at the context in which Hegel's concerns rise, Fichte already linked moral autonomy to Christianity with his *Versuch einer Kritik aller Offenbarung* (VKO) in 1792. According to him, the moral feeling and Christianity are in tune. In fact, Christianity would be a religion of reason. Kant will also say so one year later in *Die Religion innerhalb der Grenzen der bloßen Vernunft*, where he applies the results of his second *Critique* to the realm of religion, with the aim of proving the affinity between his conception of the moral law and Christianity.

Within this framework, for Kant, the early Fichte and for the Hegel of "Das Leben Jesu," Jesus incarnates the figure of the virtuous man, namely, the one who follows the law out of duty. This is to say, Jesus behaves in an autonomous way, as already defined in 1.; he is able to free himself from his inclinations and his will is entirely determined by pure practical reason, although he is tempted by his inclinations. Jesus is, then, the perfect example of practical freedom. Specifically in "Das Leben Jesu," Hegel applies Kant's conception of the categorical imperative to the life of Jesus, narrated as a biography, but leaving out any trace of miracle. "Miracle" would be problematic for this tradition of thought. According to Fichte in VKO, for instance, a miracle is beyond the possibilities of our knowledge; therefore, for him, regarding revelation we will only be capable to say that *it is possible*, not that *it is real*. For Kant, miracles belong solely to superstition.

Hegel's Jesus does not experience any multiplication of the loaves or fishes; he turns no water into wine. It is necessary for Hegel, following a Kantian path, to present Jesus as a human, not as God, nor as saint. The saint would not be able to experience his relationship with the moral law as a constraint, namely, his will is always conceived as a completely good will, i.e., as concurring with the law. As seen in 1., the moral law appears to the humans, as finite rational beings, through the form of the imperative and, therefore, as an ought. The saint is beyond the finite rational being, and has a will that always deals with the inclinations aroused by his sensible and hence finite relation to the world. This is why not only for Hegel, but also for Kant, Jesus must be shown as a moral human, i.e., as a man who freely chooses to follow the moral law, not as an entity whose will coincides immediately with the law. Jesus, as the origin of Christianity, would entail the exigency of duty.

In this context, divinity is always linked to reason (Hegel 1989, p. 207). Therefore, Jesus obeying God is actually an ordinary man following the law, which is given from pure practical reason. A religion of reason in Kant's terms should conceive the law as something emerging from humanity, and reason as something belonging to humanity, namely, humankind participates of the divinity (of reason) and, therefore, the law that this reason commands us to follow is a law that we give to ourselves:

> Among the Jews John reawakened the people to this, their own dignity—not as to something alien, but rather as to something they should be able to find within, in their true

Antecedents to Hegel's Conception of Judaism in Kant's Practical Philosophy — 125

self. They were not to seek in their lineage, nor in the desire for happiness, nor by devoting themselves to some dignitary, but rather in the cultivation of the spark of divinity allotted them—their proof of descendance, in a higher sense, from the Godhead itself. The cultivation of reason is the sole source of truth and tranquility; and John, never pretending to possess reason exclusively or as something rare, insisted that all men could uncover it in themselves. (Hegel 1984, p. 104).

(Unter den Juden war es Johannes, der die Menschen wieder auf diese ihre Würde aufmerksam machte – die ihnen nichts fremdes sein sollte, sondern die [sie] in sich selbst, ihrem wahren Selbst, nicht in der Abstammung, nicht in dem Triebe nach Glückseligkeit, nicht darin suchen sollten, Diener eines großgeachteten Mannes zu seyn, sondern in der Ausbildung des göttlichen Funkens der ihnen zu theil geworden ist, der ihnen das Zeugnis gibt, daß sie in einem erhabnern Sinne von der Gottheit selbst abstammen – Ausbildung der Vernunft ist die einzige Quelle der Wahrheit, und der Beruhigung, die Johannes etwa nicht ausschliessend, oder als eine Seltenheit zu besitzen vorgab, sondern die alle Menschen in sicht selbst aufschliessen können.) (Hegel 1989, p. 207).

In this quotation, it is possible to see in which terms Hegel translates Kantian morality. Firstly, the idea that reason (namely, the origin of law, which according to Kant is pure practical reason) is something not strange to humankind, but belongs to humanity. As we saw regarding heteronomy, Kant was the first philosopher who thought a law related to humankind not as something external, but as something emerging from humankind itself, insofar as the source of this law is within the rational being. The constraint in this relation is only due to our finitude. In Hegel's quotation, John represents the very same movement by reminding his people that this dignity, namely reason, should not be understood as strange to humanity, as being *outside of it*. Hence, this dignity should be found within humanity, not in the ancestry, neither in the appetite for happiness, nor through serving a great man (Hegel 1989, p. 207). All these grounds are subjective ends (*Triebfedern*), not proper responses to the inner compelling law of morality.

One of the strongest ways in which Hegel firstly interpreted Kant's categorical imperative was through the spatial idea of receiving the law from outside or giving ourselves the law from within. In this sense, inclinations would be the external *temptations* that takes us far away from our inner freedom. We can clearly see this in "Das Leben Jesu" when Hegel refers to Jesus's temptation in the desert:

But reflecting further on the conditions under which one could attain these, even supposing one intended to make use of them only for the well-being of mankind— realizing that he would have to subject himself / to his own and others' passions, forget his higher worth and relinquish his self-respect—he rejected the notion of bringing such wishes to fruition and gave no further thought to the matter. Determined to remain forever true to what was indelibly written in his heart, i.e. the eternal law of morality, he revered only him whose sacred will can be swayed by nothing but this law. (Hegel 1984, p. 106).

(Als er aber weiter über die Bedingungen nachdachte, unter welchen diß alles nur erworben [werden] kann, selbst wenn man dessen Besitz nur zum Wohl der Menschheit gebrauchen wollte, nemlich seiner höhern Würde zu vergessen, der Selbstachtung zu entsagen, so verwarf er ohne sich zu bedenken den Gedanken jene Wünsche je zu den seinigen zu machen, entschlossen, dem ewig getreu zu bleiben, was unauslöschlich in seinem Herzen geschrieben stand, allein das ewige Gesez der Sittlichkeit, und den zu verehren, dessen heiliger Wille unfähig ist, von etwas anderm affiziert zu werden, als von jenem Gesez.) (Hegel 1989, p. 210).

What we see here is clearly the determination of the will by disregarding every possible object or effect involved in the action; therefore this is an example of Kantian autonomy. The determination of Jesus's will cannot be contaminated by any other condition but the *eternal law of morality*, which he carries in *his heart*, internally. In this example, Jesus's will is determined by nothing more than the law emerging from the pure practical reason. At the same time, Hegel's analysis emphasises that Jesus's decision venerates the one whose sacred will can be affected only by the law, namely not by the inclinations, i.e. the good will. This emphasis is relevant because it states a difference between Jesus's relationship to law, and the perfect good will's relationship to law. As Jesus is no saint, he experiences law as a commandment. Therefore, in the desert, he actually ponders the possibility of taking the sensuous offers, i.e., he is *tempted* in his finite condition to decide his action with regard to the possible effects that these possessions could have in the world, for humanity. Nonetheless, he does what he *ought* to.

In fact, Hegel's fragment on the life of Jesus makes even more explicit references to Kant's practical philosophy:

'To act only on principles that you can will to become universal laws among men, laws no less binding on you than on them'—this is the fundamental law of morality, the sum and substance of all moral legislation and the sacred books of all peoples. (Hegel 1984, pp. 115–116).

(Was ihr wollen könnt, daß als allgemeines Gesez unter den Menschen, auch gegen euch gelte, nach einer solchen Maxime handelt – diß ist das Grundgesez der Sittlichkeit – der Inhalt aller Gesezgebungen, und der heiligen Bücher aller Völker.) (Hegel 1989, p. 221).

This is clearly a paraphrase of the first formulation of the Kant's categorical imperative. This way of approaching legality proves that Hegel's conception of freedom, at this very early stage of his thought, is completely Kantian.[5] By admitting the categorical imperative so openly, Hegel must also assume with Kant that the moral law appears as a constraint to free ourselves from our inclinations, which is to say, humankind must face the fact that because of its finitude, its relationship with the law will be experienced in this way:

> Do you really believe that the Deity threw the human species into the world and left it at the mercy of nature without a law, without awareness of the purpose of its existence, and without the possibility of discovering within itself how it might become pleasing to him? [...] As for myself, I cling only to the untained voice of my heart and conscience [...] This inner law is a law of freedom to which a person submits voluntarily, as though he had imposed it on himself. (Hegel 1984, p. 127).

> (Glaubt ihr etwa, die Gottheit habe das menschliche Geschlecht in die Welt geworfen, der Natur überlassen, ohne ein Gesez, ohne ein Bewustseyn des Endzwecks ihres Daseyns, ohne die Möglichkeit in sich selbst es zu finden, wie es der Gottheit wohlgefällig werden könne [ref. Goethe] – es sei eine Sache des Glücks – [...] Ich halte mich allein an die unverfälschte Stimme meines Herzens und Gewissens [...] dieses innerliche Gesez ist ein Gesez der Freiheit, dem sich als von ihm selbst gegeben, der Mensch freiwillig unterwirft.) (Hegel 1989, pp. 233–234).

Thus for Hegel, the constraint implied in the law is no impediment to conceive this law as something that the rational agent gives to herself. As with Kant, the obedience to this practical principle would be the only possibility of freedom, that is to say, of being autonomous.

It appears to be clear that Jesus, faced with his inclinations—for instance, the temptations in the desert—always chose the rule given by the moral law coming from within. The inclinations, in this way, seem to be the external factors that can influence the moral decision with sensous *temptations*. Jesus's decision was driven not by the temptations, asociated with sensibility, but by the law, emerging from pure practical reason within him. The Judaic people, on the contrary, are depicted in the fragment precisely associated with sensibility, namely, as incapable of freely choosing the law:

> John felt that he was called upon to awaken his countrymen to purposes higher than mere pleasure, to expectations better than the restoration of the former splendor of the Jewish nation (Hegel 1984, p. 105).

---

[5] This way of depicting Jesus is also related to the Kantian idea of radical evil, presented in the Religion, as well as to the Hegelian attempt to present Jesus as a redemption of this inclination to sin. I cannot however develop this problem further here.

(Dieser Johannes fühlte den Beruf in sich, seine Landsleute auf höhere Zwecke, als blossen Genuß, auf bessere Erwartungen, als die Wiederherstellung des ehemaligen Glanzes des Jüdischen Reichs aufmerksam zu machen) (Hegel 1989, p. 208).

According to this quotation, the Judaic people did not know other ends but mere pleasure. Hence, for Hegel, they are conceived as a community driven by sensibility, not by reason.

The Judaic people are represented as subdued to the necessity of nature, opposed to what is relevant—according to the author—for determining the possibility of freedom for humankind: "realizing that it is beneath man's dignity to strive for this sort of power when he already has within himself a sublime power transcending nature altogether, one whose cultivation and enhancement is his true life's calling" (Hegel 1984, p. 106) (da er in sich eine über die Natur erhabene Kraft besitzt, deren Ausbildung und Erhöhung die wahre Bestimmung seines Lebens ist) (Hegel 1989, p. 209). This inner force, capable of facing nature, is the capacity to reject temptations, namely, the faculty of freely and purely determining the will, fighting the inclinations just as Jesus did. However, Hegel seems to insist in the fact that the Judaic people are incapable of relating to the law autonomously. According to him, Judaism implies the notion of a law that is given to humankind, not of a law that rises from humankind itself. Namely, as the Judaic people follow their inclinations and not their duty, they are not self-determined by the moral law, but driven by *Neigungen*. Hence, it is pure heteronomy.

He found that his teaching had an effect on many people; but since he was keenly aware of the Jews' attachment to deep-rooted national prejudices and their lack of a sense for anything higher than this, he did not seek closer dealings with them or place much confidence in their conviction. On the whole he did not deem them capable of such, did not believe them to be cut from a cloth from which something greater could be fashioned. (Hegel 1984, p. 107).

(Er fand viele, bei denen seine Lehre Eingang hatte – er kannte die Anhänglichkeit der Juden, an ihre eingewurzelte NationalVorurtheile, und ihren Mangel an Sinn für etwas höheres zu gut – als daß er sich mit ihnen näher eingelassen, Vertrauen in ihre Überzeugung gesezt hätte, er hielt diese nicht für fähig, nicht für von der Art, daß etwas grösseres darauf gebaut werden könnte.) (Hegel 1989, p. 211).

Do not believe for an instant that I have come to declare that the laws are no longer valid. I have not come to annul what the laws demand, but rather to make them complete, to breathe spirit into these lifeless / bones. Heaven and earth may pass away, but not the demands of the moral law nor the obligation to obey them. Whoever absolves himself from adherence to them is unworthy to be called a citizen of God's realm, while he who not only complies with them himself but teaches others to honor them will be highly esteemed in the heavenly realm. The one basic condition that I add, in order to make the entire system of laws complete, is this: You must not remain satisfied, like the scribes and Pharisees among you, with observing the mere letter of the law; although human tribunals may have this alone as their object, you must act out of respect for duty and in the spirit of the law. (Hegel 1984, p. 111).

(Glaubt nicht, daß ich etwa gekommen sei, Ungültigkeit der Geseze zu predigen, nicht die Verbindlichkeit zu denselben aufzuheben, bin ich gekommen, sondern sie vollständig zu machen – diesem todten Gerippe Geist einzuhauchen – Himmel und Erde mögen wohl vergehen, aber nicht die Forderungen des Sittengesezes, nicht die Pflicht, ihnen zu gehorchen – wer sich und andere von Befolgung derselben freispricht, ist unwürdig, den Namen eines Bürgers des Reiches Gottes zu tragen; wer sie aber selbst erfüllt, und noch andere sie ehren lehrt, der wird angesehen sein in dem Himmelreich – Aber was ich um das ganze System der Geseze auszufüllen hinzusetze ist die Hauptbedingung, daß ihr euch nicht mit der Beobachtung des Buchstabens der Geseze begnügt, wie die Pharisäer, und die Gelehrten eures Volks, sondern im Geiste des Gesezes aus Achtung für die Pflicht handelt.) (Hegel 1989, p. 216).

In the first quotation, we can clearly see a contrast between Jesus and the Jewish people. According to Hegel, the Jews are incapable of 'higher things', and their faith cannot be trusted. Apparently, implicit in this opposition of higher and lower is the Kantian distinction between autonomy and heteronomy. It seems that, for Hegel, whereas Jesus' character acts in accordance with the law, the Judaic one is governed by an agency based on relative ends. This appears more clearly in the second quotation: Jesus invites us to follow the law in its 'spirit, out of respect to the duty', not out of written formalism. According to Hegel, for the Pharisee the obedience to the law is based on external authority, therefore, on a heteronomous principle. He obeys the written law because he fears the consequences of disobeying the word of Moses. In this sense, Hegel introduces an important difference between written command and moral law. Written law takes us to positivity, to a mere and, above all, external formalism.

For it to be followed, this written command needs to be invigorated from within, otherwise it is nothing but a heteronomous principle, as we can see in the quotation. Judaism is, according to Hegel, captured by this external heteronomy. The Pharisee is incapable of recognising his duty. He will blindly follow the positive command, which of course takes him away from the true moral law, since that law must come from within and be followed only out of respect, not out of fear. The law must be "spiritualized," that is to say: *the law must be followed not because it is written, but because I ought, innerly, to follow it.*[6] That's

---

6 This is direcly related to Kant's notion of moral feeling. As Garrido affirms, "it is through the moral feeling that humankind—and even the worst of men—represents the moral constraint of its will" (2012, p. 36) (The translation is mine). I cannot however develop this problem further here.

why Jesus disobeys the Judaic precepts and heals people on Saturday, contrary to the written prohibition. That's why he breaks the written law, but fulfills the moral one.

Bibliography

Fichte, Gottlieb F. (1998): *Versuch einer Kritik aller Offenbarung* [VKO]. Norderstedt: Meiner Verlag.
Garrido, Juan M. (2012): *El imperativo de la humanidad. La fundamentación estética de los derechos humanos en Kant*. Santiago: Orjikh Editores.
Hegel, G. W. H. (1984): *Three Essays, 1793–1795: The Tubingen Essay, Berne Fragments, the Life of Jesus*. Indiana: University of Notre Dame Press.
Hegel, G. W. H. (1989): *Frühe Schriften I*. Würzburg: Meiner Verlag.
Kant, Immanuel (1929): *Critique of Pure Reason*. London: Macmillan and Co.
Kant, Immanuel (1967): *Kritik der reinen Vernunft* [KrV]. Hamburg: Meiner Verlag.
Kant Immanuel (2002): *Grundwork for the Metaphysics of Morals*. New Haven and London: Yale University Press.
Kant, Immanuel (2017a). *Die Religion innerhalb der Grenzen der bloßen Vernunft*. [Religion] Göttingen: Meiner Verlag.
Kant, Immanuel (2017b): *Grundlegung zur Metaphysik der Sitten*. [GMS] Stuttgart: Reclam.
Ormeño K., Juan (2004): "Notas sobre la *Fundamentación de la metafísica de las costumbres* de Immanuel Kant". In: *Aproximaciones al debate sobre ética*. Santiago: Universidad Academia de Humanismo Cristiano, pp. 11–32.
Paton, Herbert J. (1971): *The Categorical Imperative. A study in Kant's Moral Philosophy*. Pennsylvania: University of Pennsylvania Press.
Timmermann, Jens (2007): *Kant's Groundwork of the Metaphysics of Morals. A Commentary*. New York: Cambridge University Press.

Abbreviations

AA = reference to the pagination of: *Kant's Gesammelte Schriften* "Akademieausgabe" (1900 ff.). Ed. Königlich Preußische Akademie der Wissenschaften. Berlin: Reimer / de Gruyter.
GMS = Kant, Immanuel (2017b): *Grundlegung zur Metaphysik der Sitten*. Stuttgart: Reclam.
KrV = Kant, Immanuel (1967): *Kritik der reinen Vernunft*. Hamburg: Meiner Verlag.
Religion = Kant, Immanuel (2017a). *Die Religion innerhalb der Grenzen der bloßen Vernunft*. Göttingen: Meiner Verlag.
VKO = Fichte, Gottlieb F. (1998): *Versuch einer Kritik aller Offenbarung*. Norderstedt: Meiner Verlag.

Joanna Raisbeck
"Diese Unwissenheit ist mir der unerträglichste Mangel, der gröste Widerspruch": The Search for Pre-rational Knowledge in Karoline von Günderrode

Abstract: The epistemological quest is a recurrent theme in Günderrode's literary oeuvre. This concern with epistemology has an indirect Kantian heritage, as is demonstrated through an examination of her early philosophical studies and how these give rise to an epistemological paradox discussed in her letters. Traces of Kant are superseded by elements of Platonism in Günderrode's literary work: Platonic concepts such as *eros* and *anamnesis* are adopted as means to recover pre-rational knowledge lost to the individual upon birth, where birth (and the emergence of consciousness) is understood as a splitting from a primordial unity. The difficulty of this epistemological quest is poetically expressed by its apparent impossibility and, even if successful, how it is self-defeating as it may necessarily eliminate the individual.

Introduction

While it has been argued by scholars such as Frederick C. Beiser that Early Romantic metaphysics and epistemology function as a response to Kantian and Fichtean subjective idealism (Beiser 2003, p. 66), this is primarily, if not exclusively, with reference to the Jena Romantic circle. The poet and philosopher Karoline von Günderrode is seldom included in this narrative in Early Romantic philosophy and literature. Günderrode's poetically expressed metaphysics are indeed informed by a response to Kantian philosophy, and specifically to Kantian epistemology. Underpinning Günderrode's metaphysics is the conviction that there must be some higher reality beyond phenomenal reality, but how this higher reality can be accessed is itself a vexed question.

Prior to her engagement with Schelling's *Naturphilosophie* from 1804, one recurrent theme within Günderrode's literary oeuvre is that of the epistemological quest, which was itself a common motif in literature around 1800 (Kastinger Riley 1986, p. 95). An epistemological quest does not denote a specific theory of knowledge, but rather involves the process where an individual attempts to have nature—understood in vital or productive terms as *natura naturans*—disclose its fundamental secrets or truths, which, for Günderrode, are ultimate truths in a Platonic sense. Any epistemological quest is inherently conditioned by the limitations of the human faculty for knowledge, and the paradoxical question that I wish to address is the following: if the human capacity for knowledge is limited by consciousness, by the process of individuation, and by rationality, how, and by what cognitive means, can metaphysical truths be disclosed to the individual?

Günderrode's reception of Kantian epistemology

While there is no evidence to suggest that Günderrode read any of Kant's critiques, she certainly had acquired indirect knowledge of Kantian ideas. Günderrode's first exposure to philosophical logic and, by extension, philosophy as a discipline was through an acquaintance with the local pastor at Butzbach, Johann Georg Diefenbach, in 1800. He encouraged her to study Johann Gottfried Kiesewetter's *Grundriss einer reinen allgemeinen Logik nach Kantischen Grundsätzen: zum Gebrauch für Vorlesungen* (1795),[1] and corresponded with Günderrode to help her refine her understanding of Kiesewetter's—and by extension Kant's—concepts.[2] Whilst his work is not as well-known as Karl Leonhard Reinhold's *Briefe über die kantische Philosophie* (1786–1787), Kiesewetter was one of Kant's pupils, was himself a philosopher and professor of philosophy and logic in Berlin, and ranks as "der eigentliche Modephilosoph des Kantianismus" (Rosenkranz 1987, p. 249).

Whilst these studies of Kantian philosophy served as a grounding for further philosophical study, manuscript evidence suggests that Günderrode's own thoughts on epistemology were in part influenced by this exposure to Kantianism. In the *Günderrode-Nachlass* is a theological tract, written in Diefenbach's hand,[3] which deals primarily with the question of revelation. Revelation is un-

---

[1] These studies are reproduced in truncated form in Günderrode 2006, II, pp. 302–349. The manuscript of the studies ends at §202, page 92 of Kiesewetter's *Grundriss einer reinen allgemeinen Logik nach Kantischen Grundsätzen*.
[2] The only known extant letter from Diefenbach to Günderrode discusses the distinction that Kiesewetter draws between "Verstand" and "Vernunft," in: Günderrode 2006, III, p. 335.
[3] There is circumstantial evidence to support this claim. An entry in Günderrode's *Studienbuch* is an extract from one of Diefenbach's sermons, entitled *Bruchstück aus einer Predigt vor einer Landgemeinde*, in Hopp/Preitz 1975, pp. 273–274. The sermon is written in the same hand as the theological tract, and this hand is, bar the letter from Diefenbach to Günderrode, not present anywhere else in the *Nachlass*.

derstood in propositional terms as something that is rationally demonstrable, in accordance with the common perception of revelation in the eighteenth century (Perovich Jr. 2010, p. 260). It also discusses the shared belief in divine providence between the author and interlocutor—presumably Günderrode.

The final part of the manuscript is concerned with the question of how the existence of God can be inferred. To address this question, Diefenbach proceeds in a quasi-Kantian fashion, since the universal maxims that underpin moral law are equated with the concept of God. To make this argument, Diefenbach, following Kant, debunks both empirical and rational approaches to acquiring knowledge of God. One basis for the cosmological argument is invoked only to be dismissed, because any form of empirical observation cannot reliably establish a chain of causality that would lead to a creator:

> We notice, for example, alterations in nature everywhere, which we, however, never grasp in their full scope. So these are only alterations of its parts, where one part acts in the others. When we notice the majority of these partial alterations, we can also see other parts of nature that have been set in motion, which either, as a cause, brought about those alterations or, as an effect, depended on them. And so one interacts with another, and continues in an eternal cycle without us coming to a first cause.[4]
>
> (Wir bemerken z. B. überall Veränderungen in der Natur, die wir aber nie in ihrem ganzen Umfang umfassen. Es sind also nur Veränderungen ihrer Theile, wo einer in den anderen wirket. In den meisten Theilsveränderungen welche wir bemerken, sehen wir auch andere in Bewegung gesetzte Naturtheile, die als Ursache entweder jene Veränderungen hervorbrachten oder als Wirkung von derselben abhiengen. Und so greift eins ins andere, und geht in einem ewigen Kreislauf fort ohne daß wir auf eine erste Ursache kommen.) (Ms. Ff. K. v. Günderrode Abteilung 2 A2: 85r–88r, 87r).

The complexity of natural phenomena could lead the observer to mistake interdependent processes for a linear chain of causality. It follows, therefore, that any pattern of cause and effect cannot lead to the first principle. What cannot be empirically perceived is the Aristotelian unmoved mover, a first cause, the *prima summa*. Diefenbach then moves on to discuss the limitations of reason in pursuit of the creator:

> But nor do I yield a creator from the laws of thought (and from immediate consciousness). I have become aware of that holy being not as a creator, but as a law-giver in me. I must assume that nature has no power over him, because otherwise his commands in me would be folly, but they cannot be that, because they are necessarily part of reason [...] But reason only leads me this far with certainty, not to a concept of the creation—which may admitted-

---

[4] English translations are by the author.

ly be true, but cannot be perceived from nature or from reason, and, if creation is to be believed, this can only be on the authority of immediate divine communication.

(Aus den Gesetzen des Denkens (und dem unmittelbaren Bewußtsein) bring ich aber ebensowenig einen Schöpfer hervor. Jenes heiligen Wesens bin ich mir nicht als Schöpfer, sondern als Gesetzgeber in mir bewußt worden. Daß die Natur nichts gegen ihn vermöge, muß ich annehmen, weil sonst seine Gebote in mir Thorheit seyn mussten, das sie aber doch nicht seyn können, weil sie der Vernunft nothwendig angehören. [...] Aber auch nur soweit führet mich die Vernunft mit Gewißheit, nicht bis zu einer Schöpfung – welche zwar wahr seyn kann, aber weder aus der Natur noch aus der Vernunft erkannt wird, und, wenn sie geglaubt wird, nur auf der Autorität einer unmittelbaren göttlichen Benachrichtigung geglaubt werden kann.) (Ms. Ff. K. v. Günderrode Abteilung 2 A2: 87v–88r).

Here, Diefenbach wants to make space for revealed religion, for the aspect of revelation that does transcend the laws of nature and therefore, even if it were rationally demonstrable, could not be inferred by reason. Belief in the creator and creation can be established "nur auf der Autorität einer unmittelbaren göttlichen Benachrichtigung." Faced with the limitations of subjective perception and inquiry, Diefenbach falls back onto the notion that the internal, rational moral law alone proves the existence of God. The moral imperative is apodictic, and has a source beyond the individual's nature, as the "Gesetzgeber." The individual possesses the freedom to obey the moral imperative, since if an individual's natural inclinations could not be overcome, then they would be useless ("Daß die Natur nichts gegen ihn vermöge, muß ich annehmen, weil sonst seine Gebote in mir Thorheit seyn mussten").

Whilst Diefenbach's tract is little more than indicative of the kind of questions that interested Günderrode, traces of Kantianism can also be found in Günderrode's letters. In a letter to Gunda Brentano in 1802, what becomes a concern for Günderrode is an epistemological *aporia*, and one that is close to Diefenbach's statement of "Wir bemerken z. B. überall Veränderungen in der Natur, die wir aber nie in ihren ganzen Umfang umfassen." Günderrode examines a Spinozist or Leibnizian problem: how can one establish a first cause if only the chain of events is perceptible?

In any case, it is completely incomprehensible to me that we have no other consciousness than perceptions of effects, never of causes. All other knowledge—as soon as I consider this—seems not worthy of knowing to me, as long as I do not know the cause of this knowledge, my capacity for knowledge. This ignorance is the most unbearable deficiency, the greatest contradiction. And I think if we do indeed cross a boundary into a second life, so one of the first internal phenomena that occurs must be that our consciousness expands and becomes clearer; for to take this limitation into a second life would be unbearable.

(Überhaupt ist mirs ganz unbegreiflich daß wir kein anders Bewustsein haben, als Wahrnehmungen von Wirkungen, nirgends von Ursachen. Alles andere Wissen scheint mir (sobald ich dies bedenke) nicht wissenswürdig, solang ich des Wissens Ursache, mein Wissensvermögen, nicht kenne. Diese Unwissenheit ist mir der unerträglichste Mangel, der gröste Wiederspruch. Und ich meine wenn wir die Gränze eines zweiten Lebens wirklich betretten, so müßte es eine unsrer ersten innern Erscheinungen sein, daß sich unser Bewustsein vergrösere und verdeutlichere; den es wäre unerträglich, diese Schranke in ein zweites Leben zu schleppen.) (Preitz 1964, p. 168).

The epistemological problem here is twofold: perceiving only effects, rather than causes, could lead to an infinite regress of effects—that is, never being in the position to establish the underlying cause and therefore extract the causal structure that would lead to an underlying truth. But this also takes a Kantian turn for Günderrode—that is, Kant's Copernican turn. The missing cause is not the *prima summa* as in Diefenbach's theological tract, but rather a subjective faculty: the individual understanding that generates knowledge in the first place: "solang ich des Wissens Ursache, mein Wissensvermögen, nicht kenne." The danger here is that this thought could develop into a radical scepticism that tips into all-encompassing doubt about any conscious experience. Conscious experience could be dismissed as subjectively constructed to the extent that no objective knowledge can be discerned. The individual capacity for knowledge would be self-defeating if it cannot reliably yield any knowledge at all.

The culmination of this thought contains a paradoxical tension: Günderrode concludes with the intriguing thought about sensory expansion after death, about how consciousness can be heightened to circumvent this epistemological problem: "Und ich meine wenn wir die Gränze eines zweiten Lebens wirklich betretten, so müßte es eine unsrer ersten innern Erscheinungen sein, daß sich unser Bewustsein vergrösere und verdeutlichere." The paradox is that sensory expansion can only occur *in* and *through* death, rather than through any other cognitive and perceptual leaps. Whilst there is the putative expansion of consciousness, in this case it is understood as an impossibility within life itself.

"Deus sive natura" and Platonism

This problem of human capacity for knowledge, as well as the paradox of sensory expansion upon death, colour the search for the first cause, which itself is a narrative strand in Günderrode's literary oeuvre. In her prose and poetry, this first cause is figured not as a subjective faculty, but as the generative force that gives rise to the phenomenal world. This force is not to be understood as any version of the Christian God, as in Diefenbach's tract addressed to Günderrode, but rather as a form of divinised, animate nature. This is founded philosophically on a dual-aspect monism, a stable concept throughout Günderrode, and one that adapts the Spinozist concept of "deus sive natura," where the phenomenal world is dependent on and derives from *natura naturans*, the productive aspect of nature. As early as 1800, an entry in Günderrode's *Studienbuch* on Ludwig Gotthard Kosegarten's translation of Vanini's ode *Deo* (Hopp, Preitz 1975, pp. 274–275) indicates an interest in this idea of a divine, all-encompassing principle. But the entry is no copy: it re-writes Kosegarten's translation. This is unusual for Günderrode's early studies around 1800, although she did also produce a literary re-writing of Novalis's "Lied der Toten" (Gölz 2000, pp. 89–130). In her adaptation of Kosegarten, Günderrode shifts the form of the address from third-person to second-person and omits entire strophes. Around 1800, this ode, and indeed Vanini in general,[5] were interpreted through the prism of Herder's dynamic interpretation of Spinoza in *Gott. Einige Gespräche* (1787), since Herder appended the Latin original to the first *Gespräch*. Herder reforms the ode into an expression of panentheism, where God inheres in the world, but also extends beyond it.[6]

Günderrode does not approach the epistemological question of how to gain knowledge of this generative force behind phenomenal reality in Kantian terms, but rather it is framed by elements of Platonism. Whilst there is no direct evidence that Günderrode was familiar with the works of Plato, the concepts of *eros* and *anamnesis*, which frequently manifest in a dialectic, are so common as structural elements to suggest an awareness of Platonic concepts. There was also a resurgence of interest in Plato in the second half of the eighteenth century, indeed what Michael Franz has called the discovery of Plato in the spirit of *Empfindsamkeit* (Franz 1996, p. 77). Of particular interest were the dialogues concerned with love—*Phaedon* and the *Symposium*. The latter was accorded special status as the most poetic of Plato's works (Matuschek 2002, p. 85), and together they were the most frequently published, translated, and imitated Platonic dialogues in the latter half of the eighteenth century (Auerochs 1996, p. 163). One mediator for this resurgence of interest in Platonic ideas, alongside Rousseau and Shaftesbury, was the Dutch philosopher Frans Hemsterhuis, whose writings drew particular attention to the Platonic conceptions of the soul and *eros* (Erler 2007, p. 542). Whilst Günderrode did make excerpts from Hemsterhuis's *Simon ou des facultés de l'âme* (1787), Platonic ideas were sufficiently widespread around 1800 that this is only one of many sources.

---

5 Compare Hölderlin's ode "Vanini" (1798).
6 Panentheism was coined by the nineteenth-century philosopher Karl Christian Friedrich Krause to address the diffuseness of the concept of pantheism, which could simply conflate nature and God.

How do these Platonic concepts of *eros* and also *anamnesis* serve an epistemological function for Günderrode? *Eros* is, as laid out in the first of a series of aphoristic notes in the *Nachlass*, the expression of impersonal love and striving for unattainable perfection: "Perfection is a whole; we do not possess it, it is, as it were, like the blue of the sky above us, and our perfection is only striving towards it, the visual perception of it; therefore there is no personal love, only love for perfection (Die Vortreflichkeit ist ein Ganzes wir haben sie nicht, sie ist gleichsam wie die Bläue des Himels über uns, u unsere Vortreflichkeit, ist nur ein Streben zu ihr, eine Ansicht von ihr; drum ist keine Persöhnliche Liebe, nur Liebe zum Vortreflichen)" (Günderrode 2006, I, p. 436). Whilst perfection cannot be achieved by the individual, it can be perceived, and the introduction of this aesthetic element points to the conflation of perfection and beauty.

It is this understanding of *eros* as striving for that which it cannot ever possess that is developed further in the poem "Liebe und Schönheit." In "Liebe und Schönheit," the figure of the artist is also explicitly the creator, as Prometheus. But the image of the artist-as-creator is not simply one of valorisation. As in the mythological account,[7] Prometheus crafts and ensouls man with a spark of sunlight: "Yet this spark, it ignites in the image | In which the artist's wisdom cloaks it. (Doch dieser Funke, er entflammt im Bilde | In das des Künstlers Weisheit ihn verhüllte.)" (Günderrode 2006, I, p. 377, ll.5–6). Prometheus, it appears, has moulded a perfect synthesis of soul and corporeal form: the artist-as-creator is thus capable of mediating between the divine and the earthly, which reflects the kind of praise of bestowed upon the artist (however ironically) by Socrates in Plato's *Ion*.

But in "Liebe und Schönheit," this act of creation results in the rupture between the individual and the totality. This does not assume a moral dimension as in the Christian sense of the fall into sin. Rather, Günderrode interprets the Promethean creation myth through the lens of the primordial split and draws attention to this layering of mythological narratives through a curious transposition to startle the reader. Prometheus ensouls man with both sunlight and a droplet of absolute beauty: "Until he [Prometheus] had stolen a spark from the sun; | (A drop that fell from the sea of beauty). (Bis er [Prometheus] der Sonne Funken hat entwendet; | (Ein Tropfe der der Schönheit Meer enttroff).)" (Günderrode 2006, I, p. 377, ll.3–4). The individual retains an awareness of the trauma of this primordial split in its birth, and this awareness manifests itself as *eros*:

---

[7] For a contemporary account of the myth, see Karl Philipp Moritz's *Götterlehre oder mythologische Dichtungen der Alten* (1791).

> Life sprang forth from beauty
> But it does not forget its high origin;
> It strives towards it, and love is this desire,
> That eternally strives for the sunlight.
> For love is desire, remembrance of the beautiful,
> Love's longing wishes to behold beauty
> [...]
> But oh! endless is the realm of beauty,
> So endless too is our love's longing.
>
> (Von Schönheit ist das Leben ausgegangen,
> Doch es vergißt den hohen Ursprung nicht;
> Es strebt zu ihm, und Lieb ist dies Verlangen
> Die ewig ringet nach dem Sonnenlicht.
> Denn Lieb ist Wunsch, Erinerung des Schönen,
> Die Schönheit schauen will der Liebe Sehnen.
> [...]
> Doch ach! unendlich ist das Reich des Schönen,
> So auch unendlich unserer Liebe Sehnen.) (Günderrode 2006, I, p. 377, ll.7–18).

Here Günderrode combines the Platonic idea of *anamnesis*, the unconscious remembrance of a past state—here, the state of absolute beauty—"Lieb ist [...] Erinerung des Schönen," and *eros*, the desire towards and to behold this beauty—"es strebt zu ihm [dem hohen Ursprung]." What Günderrode develops is a dialectic between *anamnesis* and *eros*, similar to that which is proposed by Socrates in Plato's *Phaedrus*, where it is embodied by the man who, by perceiving earthly beauty, seeks hopelessly to strive towards true beauty (Plato 2002, 249d). For Günderrode, *anamnesis* is simply innate, not provoked by any external stimulus. The tension of the poem stems from the soul's remembrance of the pure beauty in its "hohen Ursprung," and from its inability to ascend to this primal unity. And it is a tension that necessarily remains unresolved, which is exemplified by the elegiac tone of the closing couplet. The syntactic parallels of the couplet underscore the cleavage between the "Reich des Schönen," which cannot be directly experienced, and "unserer Liebe Sehnen"—the thwarted erotic desire. With the phrase "unserer Liebe Sehnen"—a contrast to "der Liebe Sehnen" at the end of the preceding stanza,—*eros* is stripped of a degree of abstraction, and is instead formulated as a universal human affliction. Thus what "Liebe und Schönheit" presents is the desire for transcendence, here grounded in the awareness of absolute beauty, but the individual cannot, in keeping with *eros*, rise above its material reality to perceive anything on the metaphysical plane.

The epistemological quest and overcoming individuation

The sense of limit that is introduced by "Liebe und Schönheit"—that the individual cannot transcend its own material reality, but that this limit is necessary to perpetuate *eros*—forms the primary tension within "Des Wandrers Niederfahrt" and *Ein apokaliptisches Fragment*. These texts, where *eros* is understood as the drive for knowledge, function as thematic companion pieces in Günderrode's first published collection, *Gedichte und Phantasien* (1804). Both concern the attempt to transcend individual and conscious limits to access the metaphysical reality that structures the phenomenal world, but the question that drives both texts is what form of cognition can be adopted to look beyond contingent reality.

"Des Wandrers Niederfahrt" answers this question in the negative: it charts a failed attempt to seek truth. The eponymous *Wandrer* attempts to seek out fundamental truth through a journey into the underworld, where the descent into the world of the dead also functions as an initiation into arcane knowledge. The *Wandrer*, however, has a false conception of what this profound knowledge may be:

> I wish to lift the unadulterated treasures
> Which the light of the overworld has not touched
> The primordial force, that leads, like the pearl, from life,
> The sea of existence, into its depths.

> (Die unvermischten Schätze wollt' ich heben
> Die nicht der Schein der Oberwelt berührt
> Die Urkraft, die, der Perle gleich, vom Leben
> Des Daseyns Meer in seinen Tiefen führt.) (Günderrode 2006, I, p. 72, ll.88–92).

What the *Wandrer* envisages in the "Urkraft" is a tangible, generative force from which all existence derives—the terminology of "Urkraft" here has parallels with Herder's vitalist reading of Spinoza's God (Timm 1974, p. 235)—or it is at least a perceptible womb, the incubator for all potential life.

How is this conception incorrect? The *Erdgeister* encountered by the *Wandrer* confirm that a ground of being does exist and that it gives rise to appearances. This is no active "Urkraft," but rather functions like a static version of Jakob Böhme's *Ungrund* (Mayer 1999, pp. 21–22). It is a negative form of existence that only exists insofar as it contains the potential to exist: "The unborn rests here, mysteriously | Enshrouded, until its time has come. (Das Ungeborne ruhet hier verhüllet | Geheimnißvoll, bis seine Zeit erfüllet.)" (Günderrode 2006, I, p. 73, ll.110–111). It is *un*human, whereas the metaphors the *Wandrer* employs to describe original being reveal the logical fallacy to which he succumbs: "How it [life] wraps itself around its mother, like a child; | To behold nature at work in its domain (Wie es [das Leben] sich kindlich an die Mutter schlingt | In ihrer Werkstadt die Natur erschauen)" (Günderrode 2006, I, p. 72, ll.93–94). The *Wandrer*, therefore, is thinking of the ground of being in terms of *imago hominis*, which presupposes the human capacity to perceive, even to comprehend it. However, this ground of being exists in both an unconscious— "Its existence is still a dream (Ihr Daseyn ist noch Traum)" (Günderrode 2006, I, p. 73, l.101)—and a preconscious state, and therefore the *Wandrer* is barred from accessing it. The *Erdgeister* elaborate that all existence is determined in such a way that the original separation from the ground of being and the subsequent development of individual consciousness cannot be reversed:

> Too late! You have been born to the day,
> Separated from the element of life.
> We dictate Becoming, not Being,
> And you have split from the mother's womb
> Separated from dreams by your consciousness.
>
> (Zu spät! Du bist dem Tage schon geboren;
> Geschieden aus dem Lebenselement.
> Dem Werden können wir, und nicht dem Seyn gebieten
> Und du bist schon vom Mutterschoos geschieden
> Durch dein Bewußtseyn schon vom Traum getrennt.) (Günderrode 2006, I, p. 73, ll.119–123).

As with "Liebe und Schönheit," birth is a destructive act that fragments primordial unity, and prevents it, in this case, from being reinstated. It is consciousness, and the splitting of unity, in a philosophical sense, between subject and object, that becomes here a problem of cognition. The *Erdgeister* then tantalise with one possibility of circumventing the barrier of consciousness:

> But look down, in the depths of your soul,
> What you seek here you will find there,
> You are but the sighted mirror of the universe.
>
> (Doch schau hinab, in deiner Seele Gründen
> Was du hier suchest wirst du dorten finden,
> Des Weltalls seh'nder Spiegel bist du nur.) (Günderrode 2006, I, p. 73, ll.24–26).

Günderrode neatly sums up the paradox of the *Wandrer's* position: "Des Weltalls seh'nder Spiegel bist du nur." The mirror metaphor draws on a trope in the mystical tradition in which the individual soul is the reflective mirror of God, but also refers to Leibniz's concept of the monad. Whilst the individual is indeed reflective of the cosmos and thus generates an image of the cosmos, this remains invisible to its physical sense of sight. The task at hand is, therefore, to penetrate beyond the individual's spatial, temporal, and sensory limits to the ground of being which the *Wandrer* not only postulates but knows to exist, yet cannot perceive. Thus the text ends at a point of failure, but indicates how an expansion of individual consciousness can occur.

Günderrode takes up this thought of "des Weltalls seh'nder Spiegel" and develops it to its logical conclusion in the short prose text *Ein apokaliptisches Fragment*. It is a positive counterpart to "Des Wandrers Niederfahrt." The text traces the expansion of an individual consciousness to the point at which it experiences its inherent connection to the totality: the speaker escapes the limitations of its subjectivity, but without having to surrender its individuality.

In *Ein apokaliptisches Fragment,* Günderrode does not suggest that dreams offer a visionary form of cognition, but rather that conscious and unconscious states dialectically interact and generate a higher form of consciousness and insight. The text is written as a series of scriptural verses, and on the theme of apocalypse—understood as the revelation of a previously hidden truth through cognition and perception, not as the millennial anticipation of a golden age. The revelation is of an abstract nature. By purging itself of individual consciousness, and therefore undoing the process of individuation which is a barrier to knowledge in "Des Wandrers Niederfahrt," the speaker is able to experience how everything in the universe is interconnected. The question this raises is whether undoing individuation results in the destruction of the self, that is, if it is possible to overcome individuality and reconcile the individual with a divine totality without complete self-dissolution.

The beginning of *Ein apokaliptisches Fragment* finds the speaker separated from the totality of nature, but driven by a desire to unite with this totality: "I wanted to plunge into the red of dawn, or dive into the shadows of the night (Ich wollte mich hinstürzen in das Morgenroth, oder mich tauchen in die Schatten der Nacht)" (Günderrode 2006, I, p. 52). And the only means to resolve this frustrating separation is through dream-cognition. The speaker's dream offers a refracted image of its conscious position: a vision of the vast, fermenting sea, but this does not give any cognitive insights, rather it results in the speaker forgetting itself through loss of memory: "until my memory was extinguished (bis meine Erinnerung erlosch)" (Günderrode 2006, I, p. 53). Awakening brings with it the remembrance of the self: "Then but as I awoke again, and began to know of myself (Da ich aber wieder erwachte, und von mir zu wissen anfieng)" (Günderrode 2006, I, p. 53). And these dreams, though not in themselves revelatory, give rise to a dynamic, conscious and unconscious cognition. From the transition between the dream and conscious states, the speaker becomes aware, however tentatively, of its own hidden origin: "9. But there was a dark feeling in me, as if I had rested in the womb of this sea and had emerged from it, like the other forms. (9. Aber es war ein dunkles Gefühl in mir, als habe ich geruht im Schoose dieses Meeres und sey ihm entstiegen, wie die andern Gestalten.)" (Günderrode 2006, I: p. 53). Here the speaker develops a form of Platonic *anamnesis*, coming to the intuitive realisation that it can recall its own origins. But how this realisation coalesces is significant: Günderrode, like Leibniz and Lessing, stresses how emotion, the "dark feeling (dunkles Gefühl)" that is pre-rational and pre-conceptual, generates true ideas (Allison 1966, pp. 72–75). The subjunctive "as if I had rested (als habe ich geruht)" is not indicative of the unreality of this thought, but rather of the (non-rational) process of cognition at work.

What follows is a dream-like transfiguration of phenomenal reality—whether the remaining verses take place within a dream or not is left ambiguous—in which the speaker appears to itself as a dew-drop and playfully communes with the elements. This state of free play generates another Platonic concept—*eros*, the longing towards divine perfection or beauty from which the individual derives, although this initially lacks an object: "But there was a longing in me that did not know its object (Aber eine Sehnsucht war in mir, die ihren Gegenstand nicht kannte)" (Günderrode 2006, I, p. 53). It is immediately conceptualised as the desire to return to the source of life. This return, however, is figured as death, but it is not death as a loss of self, but rather, death as a transition towards a higher form of consciousness that frees the speaker from its own limitations:

> 12. At one point I became aware that all the beings that had arisen from the sea returned to it again and were created again in changing forms. I was disconcerted by this phenomenon, for I had not known of any end. Then I thought that I too longed to return to the source of life.
>
> 13. And as I thought of this, and felt almost more alive than all of my consciousness, my mind was surrounded all of a sudden by benumbing mists. But these soon disappeared, and I seemed no longer myself, and yet more than I otherwise was, I could no longer find the limits of myself, my consciousness had transcended them, it was larger, different, and yet I felt myself in it.

> (12. Einst ward ich gewahr, daß alle die Wesen, die aus dem Meere gestiegen waren, wieder zu ihm zurückkehrten, und sich in wechselnden Formen wieder erzeugten. Mich befremdete diese Erscheinung; denn ich hatte von keinem Ende gewußt. Da dachte ich, meine Sehnsucht sey auch, zurück zu kehren, zu der Quelle des Lebens.
> 13. Und da ich dies dachte, und fast lebendiger fühlte, als all mein Bewußtseyn, ward plötzlich mein Gemüth wie mit betäubenden Nebeln umgeben. Aber sie schwanden bald, ich schien mir nicht mehr ich, und doch mehr als sonst ich, meine Gränzen konnte ich nicht mehr finden, mein Bewußtseyn hatte sie überschritten, es war größer, anders, und doch fühlte ich mich in ihm.) (Günderrode 2006, I, pp. 53–54).

No longer can the speaker understand itself as an independent being—it remains grammatically so, and yet is not by having ascended to a higher plane of being beyond conscious limits. Death is not an absolute endpoint, since there is no linear end to time in the text: the speaker was previously liberated from a linear understanding of temporality to a fluid, continuous, indeed timeless, present: "The past was lost to me! I belonged only to the present. (Die Vergangenheit war mir dahin! ich gehörte nur der Gegenwart.)" (Günderrode 2006, I, p. 53). Death functions as a threshold, that, when passed, generates deeper cognitive insights, since what the subject has achieved is a state of productive reciprocity between itself and the rest of nature: "I was released from the narrow limits of my being [...] I was restored to everything, and everything was a part of me. (Erlöset war ich von den engen Schranken meines Wesens [...] ich war allem wiedergegeben, und alles gehörte mir mit an.)" (Günderrode 2006, I, p. 54). The implication here is that individuation, as in a Manichean understanding, constitutes the Fall. The lyrical, and increasingly oracular Biblical tone of the text suggests that "Erlöset" is just as much redemption as it is liberation; or at least that the limitations of individuation have been overcome so that the speaker has returned to the vitalising totality.

The final verse of *Ein apokaliptisches Fragment* brings with it a change in perspective with an ecstatic declamation and the only explicit allusion in the text to the Book of Revelation:[8]

> Therefore, whoever has ears, let them hear: it is not two, not three, nor a thousand, it is one and all, it is not that body and spirit are separated, that one belongs to time, the other to eternity, it is one, belongs to itself, and is both time and eternity, visible and invisible, constant in change, an infinite life.
>
> (Drum, wer Ohren hat zu hören, der höre! Es ist nicht zwei, nicht drei, nicht tausende, es ist Eins und alles; es ist nicht Körper und Geist geschieden, daß das eine der Zeit, das andere der Ewigkeit angehöre, es ist Eins, gehört sich selbst, und ist Zeit und Ewigkeit zugleich, und sichtbar, und unsichtbar, bleibend im Wandel, ein unendliches Leben.) (Günderrode 2006, I, p. 54).

What is revealed is not the end of times as the apocalypse, and eternal life is not the preserve of the kingdom of heaven. Rather, there is no eschatology since eternal life is immanent and present, but imperceptible to the external senses. In a riposte to metaphysical dualism, what the speaker proclaims is dual-aspect monism, in which time and eternity, permanence and transience co-exist within the

---

[8] "Drum, wer Ohren hat zu hören, der höre!" echoes a refrain from Revelation 2.7; 2.11; 3.6; 3.13. The formulation here is closer to Matthew 11.15; 13.9, and Luke 8.8.

all-encompassing "unendliches Leben." What has been previously overlooked about this revelation is the weight of the rhetorically stressed "Eins und alles": this is the Spinozist formula *hen kai pan*, which gained prominence following the pantheism dispute instigated by Friedrich Heinrich Jacobi (Beiser 2003, p. 175), and became a popular maxim among the Early Romantic generation.

But in the context of the tension between the individual and the totality, what Günderrode enacts in *Ein apokaliptisches Fragment* is an extension of her reading of Schleiermacher's *Reden über die Religion* (1799). As Ruth Christmann has noted (Christmann 2005, p. 84), at the end of the second *Rede*, Schleiermacher argues that one can experience the infinite within a moment of reality: "To become one with the infinite in the middle of the finite [...] that is the immortality of religion. (Mitten in der Endlichkeit Eins werden mit dem Unendlichen [...] das ist die Unsterblichkeit der Religion.)" (Schleiermacher 2004, p. 74). Günderrode's study of Schleiermacher's second *Rede*, however, makes a significant alteration: Günderrode rules out the possibility of transcendent experience within life—it occurs only through death and self-dissolution:

> Strive even here to destroy your individuality and to live in the One and All, strive to be more than yourself so that you lose little when you lose yourself; if you have coalesced with the universe in this way, then there is no death for you, you belong to infinity. That is the immortality of religion.
>
> (Strebt darnach schon hier eure Individualität zu vernichten u zu leben im Einen u Allem, strebt mehr zu sein als ihr selbst, damit ihr wenig verliehrt wenn ihr euch verliehrt; seid ihr so zusamengeflossen mit dem Universum, so ist kein Tod für euch, ihr gehört der Unendlichkeit. Das ist die Unsterblichkeit der Religion.) (Günderrode 2006, II, pp. 285–286).

What emerges here is the same paradox first highlighted in Günderrode's letter to Gunda Brentano. Any expansion of consciousness, any overcoming of the self, however successful this process may be in *Ein apokaliptisches Fragment*, only occurs through the cessation of individuation. This expansion of knowledge exemplifies, therefore, the ultimate form of defeat for the individual's desire to know.

Bibliography

Allison, Henry E. (1966): *Lessing and the Enlightenment: his philosophy of religion and its relation to eighteenth-century thought*. Ann Arbor: University of Michigan Press.

Auerochs, Bernd (1996): "Platon um 1800. Zu seinem Bild bei Stolberg, Wieland, Schlegel und Schleiermacher." In: *Wieland-Studien* 3, pp. 161–193.

Beiser, Frederick C. (2003): *The Romantic Imperative: The Concept of Early German Romanticism*. Cambridge, MA: Harvard University Press.
Christmann, Ruth (2005): *Zwischen Identitätsgewinn und Bewußtseinsverlust. Das philosophisch-literarische Werk der Karoline von Günderrode (1780–1806)*. Frankfurt a. M.: Peter Lang.
Erler, Michael (2007): *Die Philosophie der Antike: Platon 2/2*. Basel: Schwabe.
Franz, Michael (1996): *Schellings Tübinger Platon-Studien*. Göttingen: Vandenhoeck und Ruprecht.
Gölz, Sabine I. (2000): "Günderrode Mines Novalis." In: Block, Richard / Fenves, Peter (Eds.): *"The Spirit of Poesy": Essays on Jewish and German Literature and Thought in Honor of Géza von Molnár*. Evanston, IL: Northwestern University Press, pp. 89–130.
Günderrode, Karoline von (2006): *Sämtliche Werke und ausgewählte Studien*. Ed. Morgenthaler, Walter, 3 vols. Frankfurt a. M. / Basel: Roter Stern.
Hopp, Doris / Preitz, Max (eds.) (1975): "Karoline von Günderrode in ihrer Umwelt, III. Karoline von Günderrodes Studienbuch." In: *Jahrbuch des freien deutschen Hochstifts*, pp. 223–323.
Kastinger Riley, Helene M. (1986): *Die weibliche Muse: Sechs Essays über künstlerisch schaffende Frauen der Goethezeit*. Columbia, SC: Camden House.
Matuschek, Stefan (2002): "Die Macht des Gastmahls. Schlegels Gespräch über die Poesie und Platons Symposion." In: Matuschek, Stefan (Ed.): *Wo das philosophische Gespräch ganz in Dichtung übergeht. Platons Symposion und seine Wirkung in der Renaissance, Romantik und Moderne*. Heidelberg: Winter, pp. 81–96.
Perovich Jr., Antony N. (2010): "Fichte, Hegel, and the Senses of 'Revelation'" In: Breazeal Daniel / Rockmore, Tom (Eds.): *Fichte, German Idealism and Early Romanticism*. Amsterdam: Rodopi, pp. 259–274.
Plato (2002): *Phaedrus*. Trans. Waterfield, Robin. Oxford: Oxford University Press.
Preitz, Max (1964): "Karoline von Günderrode in ihrer Umwelt. II. Karoline von Günderrodes Briefwechsel mit Friedrich Karl und Gunda von Savigny." In: *Jahrbuch des freien deutschen Hochstifts*, pp. 158–235.
Rosenkranz, Karl (1987): *Geschichte der Kant'schen Philosophie*. Dietzsch, Steffen (Ed.). Berlin: Akademie.
Schleiermacher, Friedrich Daniel Ernst (2004): *Über die Religion. Reden an die Gebildeten unter ihren Verächtern*. Hamburg: Meiner.
Timm, Hermann (1974): *Gott und die Freiheit*. Frankfurt a. M.: Vittorio Klostermann.

Abbreviations

The manuscript sources used in this article are taken from the *Günderrode-Nachlass*, which is held in the Universitätsbibliothek J. C. Senckenberg (SUF), Frankfurt am Main. The abbreviations used for these sources are given in accordance with the archival shelfmarks. The *Nachlass* is designated Ms. Ff. K. v. Günderrode overall, separated into sections ("Abteilungen") and then subsections that are ordered alphabetically, and within those numerically.

Nadia Schuman
Romantic Anti-Idealism and Re-evaluations of Gender: Schlegel, Günderrode and Literary Gender Politics

Abstract: Idealist and classicist thought are woven throughout German romanticism. Idealist explorations of binarily posited metaphysical and ontological enquiries, classical aesthetics and social ideologies shape romantic discourse, including ascriptions of gender normativity and intersexual interactions. The romantic response is at times rebellious and resistant, at others, expansive. In romantic literature, particularly the novel, distinct dualisms are challenged— often boundaries betwixt are destroyed—as various literary forms are synthesised to create a *progressive Universalpoesie*, challenging previous philosophical and aesthetic paradigms and their consequential contemporary social implications. For instance, Friedrich Schlegel's *Lucinde* aspires to redefine *Weiblichkeit*, prompting re-evaluation of intersexual relations. Still, even therewithin the romantics are reproachable, as this crux of the movement recycles misogyny, giving new form to old material. Thus, while the romantics challenge some pre-existing patriarchal paradigms they reproduce others; prolific women writers are affected when reality reflects theory. Karoline von Günderrode exemplifies the impact of this ironic irreconcilability of romantic ideals within literature, and between literature and life. This essay establishes that Günderrode, arguably the embodiment of romantic *Weiblichkeit* as depicted, for instance, in *Lucinde*, exquisitely fuses intellectual and creative aptitude; however, in the context of inextricable socially-interpolated attitudes surrounding gender, her writership and her womanhood cannot be reconciled. Günderrode's adeptness and her profound intellectual and philosophical explications render her antithetical to idealist standards of feminine virtue which the romantics seemingly decry, yet subtly uphold, despite Schlegel's blueprint for an *ursprüngliche Harmonie* between the sexes.

Introduction

German romanticism at times confronted and problematised, at others expounded upon, classical and idealist approaches to aesthetics and ontology, and consequently the social and intellectual implications and applications. One such challenge pertains to gender discourse and the qualitative and characteristic delineations between the sexes. Friedrich Schlegel's *Lucinde*, a foundational text of the romantic movement, redefines *Weiblichkeit, Männlichkeit,* and thus, *Menschheit*, prompting new evaluations of cross gender relations. However, in spite of its problematisation of preceding and contemporary approaches thereto, remnants of ingrained misogyny lead the text to replicate harmful binary contradistinctions between men and women. The novel contributes to and reflects the romantic skopos—creating a *neue Mythologie* grounded in love—and it elevates and liberates the feminine in many ways. Yet it still posits the woman as accessorial to male self-actualisation, essentially repackaging misogyny.

This textual contradiction accentuates one of many complications and paradoxes of the romantic movement. Eleanor Ter Horst writes that in *Lucinde*, "[o]ne of the transformations that Schlegel seeks is a redefinition of gender roles and gendered aesthetics. [...] Schlegel [...] advances an aesthetic that is based on a mixing of conventionally masculine and feminine attributes in both biological males and females" and in doing so, it seems he "anticipated a cultural setting where men and women would be free to develop as individuals without conforming to stereotyped patterns of male and female behavior" (2016, p. 126; Flavell 1975, p. 551). At first glance this alleviates men and women from dualistic and constraining determinacies, yet greater scrutiny reveals otherwise. Peter Firchow recognises that "in Schlegel's conception, women are wholly passionate and consequently incapable of Platonic disinterestedness"; in spite of the sexual and intellectual freedoms *Lucinde* affords women, and the emotional liberties it grants men, it does not firmly discredit eighteenth-century denigration of women that renders them somehow incapable of the same social competencies as men and prone to sexual lasciviousness (1971, p. 24).

The fallibility of this presentation is especially magnified by the function of the text. Firchow notes, "one of Schlegel's most important objectives in this novel is to define man's relation to woman, and, in doing so, implicitly to contrast it with the attitude of the Enlightenment" (1971, p. 24). Schlegel accomplishes the former, and only partially the latter; the man comes out on top; thus, "the novel [accurately] illustrates [...] the relation between romantic theory and practice" (Firchow 1971, p. 22). Arguably, theoretical flaws in romantic ideology are evident when considering lapses in its application, as is perceptible in the reception of romantic women writers. Of problems inherited by the romantics from their theoretical forefathers, often contemporaneous with the movement, the scant recognition of women writers and the constraints placed upon those recognised, warrants criticism. Karoline von Günderrode is one author who experienced the professional and social implications of the complex romantic relationship with gender discourse, which adversely impacted women at the core of the movement.

This essay surveys classical and idealist aesthetics as pertaining to romanticism, after which it discusses the roles and characteristics attributed to and prescribed for women, as delineated by Kant. The fullness of aesthetic and gender discourse cannot be covered herewithin. The overview balances concision and precision, providing the necessary information to illustrate the conundrum of being a woman writer. [1] The essay then considers Schlegel's challenge to gender binarism, as posited in *Lucinde*, comparative analysis shows the anti-idealist approach taken by Schlegel's quasi-autobiographical text and its shortcomings. Schlegel's program seeks to overturn misogynistic and puritanical attitudes regarding women and gender relations but falls short as a foundation for truly progressive gender politics due to male-centrism and the reproduction of toxic misogyny. Reviewing the mutual exclusivity of being an estimable woman and being a meritorious writer highlights applicational flaws implicit in theoretical fallibility, illuminating the plight of women romantics such as Karoline von Günderrode, who by default epitomises romantic rebellion by being the writer worthy of canonisation. Nonetheless, she meets with resistance even in the sphere of the revolutionary romantics, evincing that even they could not escape the biases they sought to disavow.

Aesthetics

In Antiquity, what would later be termed aesthetics, was of great social and intellectual import; "naïvete," "noble simplicity (edle Einfalt), silent grandeur (stille Größe)," and emphasis on form and beauty, are lauded by neo-classicists and the romantics (Ter Horst 2016, p. 122). Inextricable from nearly all aspects of life, beauty becomes synonymous with truth and freedom, signifying harmony, goodness, and morality. Art was more than entertainment, it was charged with the purpose of educating and informing. Johann Joachim Winckelmann, who "historicised universal beauty in art (das universal Kunstschöne historisiert)," determined that "[t]here is but one way for the moderns to become great, and perhaps unequalled; [...] [it is] by imitating the ancients[,] especially the Greek[s]" (Meier 2008, p. 119; Winckelmann 1765, p. 8). Concurrence with this

---

[1] See Winckelmann's *Gedanken über die Nachahmung der Griechischen Werke in der Malerei und Bildhauerkunst* (1755), Lessing's *Laocoon* (1766), Kant's "Über das Gefühl des Schönen und Erhabenen" (1766) and *Kritik der Urteilskraft* (1790), Karl Philipp Moritz' *Über die bildende Nachahmung des Schönen* (1788), Schiller's *Über die ästhetische Erziehung des Menschen* (1795) and *Naive und sentimentalische Dichtung* (1795–6), and Hegel's *Vorlesungen über die Ästhetik* (1835–1838) amongst other sources.

perspective is nonunanimous amongst modern thinkers yet traces and praise of the classical aesthetic and its function persist in modern philosophy, literature, and criticism. However, the idealist discourse of aesthetics diverges from that of the classical. Beauty, for Kant, takes on a less utilitarian role—*Zweckmäßigkeit ohne Zweck* (Kant 1793, p. 44).

Idealism's shift in thinking places the "I" at the centre; intellect takes precedence over imagination, and reason over emotion, altering the approach to art. Simon Gikandi states that "the production of a unique and self-reflective human subject was closely aligned with the project of rationality and the autonomy of aesthetic judgment [...]" (2011, Kindle Location 286). Aesthetic autonomy liberated beauty from all purposes other than beauty in-itself; a judgement of beauty had to be disinterested. Kant asserts that "[i]f we wish to decide whether something is beautiful or not, we do not use understanding [...]; rather, we use imagination" (Kant 1987, p. 44). The idealist approach to aesthetics differs vastly from the classical; it separates art from philosophy and further distances itself by distinguishing the beautiful from the sublime. Each gendered and hierarchised, the beautiful is feminised becoming superficial and the sublime is masculinised becoming profound. The harmoniousness of the classical aesthetic is then lost. Philosophy's problems remain enigmatic as reason fails to adequately address ontological concerns. Modernity's empiricism thrusts man into a moral crisis for which philosophy has no resolution.

Post-Kantian idealists and romantics sought the solution in the synthesis of sense and reason through art. The romantics saw that "among the ancient Greeks the harmony between nature and human volition enabled their culture to develop spontaneously and organically to an ideal realisation of this harmony [...]. In the post-antique world the human will is at odds with nature" (Immerwahr 1980, p. 379). Rectification of this discrepancy, and restoration of harmony between humanity and nature was crucial to the movement. Andrew Bowie describes idealist and romantic philosophies noting that "the former seeks a philosophical account of how unity can be articulated through division, whereas the latter sees such unity as only accessible [...] in our sense of failure when we strive to achieve definitive unity" (Hamilton 2017, p. 190). The romantics, recognising the ineptitude of idealism to properly address ontology, turn to art to think metaphysics, namely, poetry. This *höhere Poesie* re-establishes antiquity's unity by elevating philosophy beyond the bounds of reason. The romantic aim to unify dualisms and eliminate discontinuity, restores pensiveness, and purpose to poetry, culminating at the novel fusion of genres in the *Roman*.

Classicism and idealism contribute to a contiguous, often-indiscrete, developmental trajectory toward romanticism, where both aesthetic approaches coalesce in their creative and intellectual endeavours. Albert Meier asserts that "classic and romantic are better comprehended in their cooperation than in their competition: as complementary styles of German language poetry circa 1800 (Klassik und Romantik besser in ihrem Miteinander als in ihrer Konkurrenz zu begreifen [sind]: als komplementäre Stilvarianten der deutsch sprachigen Poesie um 1800)" (2008, p. 9). Azade Seyhan adds: "the source of early German Romantic inspiration for raising the cognitive and expressive potency of poetry to ever-higher levels [is] transcendental idealism" (Saul 2009, p. 10). Romanticism, borne of both movements, synthesises aspects of each.

Romantics long for Antiquity's perfection but recognise its limitations and inaccessibility. Transitioning through post-Kantian idealism, they declare art the realisation of philosophy and restore duty to beauty. Only through allegory, or *Poesie*, can the limitations of reason be transcended and the reunification of man and woman, mankind and nature, reason and sensation, intellect and creativity begin. Schlegel's œuvre traces this transition and establishes this ambition, for "[r]omantic poetry," is "capable of the highest and most variegated refinement, [it] opens up a perspective upon an infinitely increasing classicism," it "is in the arts what wit is in philosophy, and what society and sociability, friendship and love are in life" (Firchow 1971, p. 175). The *Athenaeum* journal and *Fragmente*, cornerstones of the romantic movement, and *Lucinde*, the Bible of Schlegel's *neue Mythologie*, are keystones interlocking romanticism into its transcendent, or expansive relation to idealism and classicism. In each, one finds blueprints of Schlegel's plan to reunite what modernism had torn asunder. However, the analysis of idealist and romantic gender discourses evince that even within the blueprints Schlegel errs, and reconstructs idealist misogyny.

The Ideal Woman and Romantic Redefinitions

Idealist standards of literary exceptionalism contrast with intellectual limitations they impose upon women. A qualitative gender divide between the sexes is solidified in Kant's "Observations on the Feeling of the Beautiful and Sublime." Seemingly his physiological comparison of the two sexes equates to physiognomological assertions of qualitative gender differences. He elaborates: "there lies in the character of the mind of [the fair sex,] features peculiar to it which clearly distinguish it from [the noble sex,] and which are chiefly responsible for her being characterised by the mark of the beautiful" (Frierson and Guyer 2011, p. 35). Having established the beautiful as a matter of taste, sense-related and pleasure-based, and the sublime as an awe-inspiring matter even transcendent of reason, the ascription of these characteristics ostensibly implies quantitative valuation, the manifestation of which can be observed in the treatment of women. Kant attempts to avoid quantifying, adding that "[t]he fair sex has just as much understanding as the male, only it is a beautiful understanding, while [that of the male] should be a deeper understanding"; however, the matter of purposiveness carries with it implications of worth in a free-market (Frierson and Guyer 2011, p. 36). His assertions regarding the adverse effect of education on a women's charm promote the imposition and expectation of ignorance, translating to intellectual repression and economic oppression.

> A woman who has a head full of Greek [...], or who conducts thorough disputations about mechanics, [...] might as well wear a beard. [...] The woman will accordingly not learn geometry; she will know only so much about the principle of sufficient reason or the monads as is necessary in order to detect the salt in satirical poems which the insipid grubs of our sex have fabricated (Frierson and Guyer 2011, p. 37).

Women are excluded from intellectual endeavours; those exhibiting philosophical prowess, mathematical aptitude, or other forms of extensive knowledge, relinquish their feminine charms and beauty; they are depicted as less attractive, perverted, even boorish and brutish. Kant pretentiously presupposes general superficiality as natural to women, yet his charge for men to actively quelch their intellectual spirit reveals his argument's inanity.

Schlegel, in the thirty-first of the *Athenaeum Fragmente*, makes a scathing critique of the patriarchal oppression of women. Decrying Kant's position, Schlegel writes:

> Prüderie ist Prätension auf Unschuld, ohne Unschuld. Die Frauen müssen wohl prüde bleiben, so lange Männer sentimental, dumm und schlecht genug sind, ewige Unschuld und Mangel an Bildung von ihnen zu fordern. Denn Unschuld ist das Einzige, was Bildungslosigkeit adeln kann (Schlegel 2018, p. 80).

> Prudishness is pretension to innocence, without innocence. Women will probably have to remain prudish for as long as men remain sentimental, stupid, and bad enough to demand eternal innocence and ignorance from them. For innocence is the only thing which can ennoble ignorance (Firchow 1971, p. 165)

In this aphorism, Schlegel associates sexual repression, puritanical concepts of innocence, and the intellectual ignorance into which women have been forced by their male counterparts. To link innocence and ignorance with beauty is to elevate oppression, and is an unethical, self-serving act that conceals the fragility driving it. In Schlegel's *Lucinde*, this is further addressed.

Forging new understandings of *Weiblichkeit*, in ways *Lucinde* challenges gender dualism and the resulting hierarchy established between the sexes. Richard Littlejohns writes that by the mid-twentieth century, "it had become customary to view *Lucinde* as a novel committed to politically progressive ideas, as some kind of gospel of feminism[,] [...] [with] the figure of Lucinde as a prototype of the emancipated woman" (1977, p. 605–606). Lucinde's seeming emancipation coincides with the liberation of the protagonist from the rigid confines of pure reason, creating a *Männlichkeit* that permits sensitivity and creativity. Lucinde, the focus of immense adulation emanating from protagonist Julius, is clever; Julius is creative. Lucinde is "untouched by the faults that custom and caprice call female"; in her, Julius sees "true pride and womanly modesty (Firchow 1971, p. 47). In ways, *Lucinde* appears to rupture from cultural misogyny and to contest systematic oppression of women. However, Littlejohns challenges the reception of the text as indicative of Schlegel's feminism.

While *Lucinde* depicts a strong, independent female protagonist who, in her complementarity completes her male counterpart, numerous aspects of the text remain problematic recyclings of toxic gender stereotypes, rendering it hardly progressive. The woman is still accessorial to the male, her significance is tied to a property of reflection—just as beauty in Kant, so woman in Schlegel. Julius begins his acclaim of Lucinde by declaring to her: "In you [my most cherished and secret intention has] [...] come to fruition and I'm not afraid to admire and love *myself* in such a mirror. Only here do I see *myself* complete and harmonious" (Firchow 1971, p. 46). [2] The implication is that Julius and Lucinde do not come together as two equals forming a whole; rather, Julius exists as a fragment, and Lucinde enables his self-actualisation. He acknowledges that he worships her, adding "that it's good [...] to do so. [They] are one, and man only becomes a man and completely himself when he thinks and imagines himself as the center of all things" (Firchow 1971, p. 118). In worshiping Lucinde, he worships the image of himself reflected by her.

At no point is Lucinde exempted from objectification or subordination. While permitted intellectual empowerment, she is still dominated by a man. Lucinde, though able to be sensual is coaxed, even forced, by her husband into sexual intimacy. In one selection Lucinde resists Julian's advances. He calls her "very obedient" but adds "this isn't the time to quarrel" (Firchow 1971, p. 69). Julius offers her some accommodation, but as a means to his end. He presses: "Now if this time you don't ... then you'll have no excuse at all" (Firchow 1971, p. 70). Lucinde inquires modestly: "'Aren't you going to let the curtain down first[,]'" focused only upon his lust, Julius replies: "You're right. The light is so much more enticing that way" (Firchow 1971, p. 70). He feels her disinterest and her coldness. She requests that he move hyacinths, seeking to distance herself. His retort? "How firm and solid, how smooth and fine! *This* is a well-rounded education" (Firchow

---

[2] My emphasis.

1971, p. 70). Stripped of real agency, she exclaims pleadingly: "'Oh no, Julius! Don't, I beg you; I don't want to[,]'" leading Julius to ultimately force himself upon and gaslight a wife who afterward seems ashamed and traumatised (Firchow 1971, p. 70). Clearly, woman is not liberated in Schlegel's *Lucinde*. Littlejohns notes that

> nowhere in the novel is there the slightest suggestion that women should be granted equal legal or political rights. [...] Schlegel never deals explicitly [...] with the economic or legal position of women in marriage or with their status in society as a whole: it is only their emotional and intellectual emancipation which he seeks. (Littlejohns 1977, p. 606).

Schlegel takes a stance regarding women's rights within marriage, only it is patriarchal. *Lucinde* frees man from morality, to succumb to his own sexual impulses and needs for gratification on all levels; he is able to enjoy same sex intimacy, open flirtation, sexual dominance, and sensitivity all at once. Gender binarism is not destroyed, nor is the oppression of women. Man is able to become, and woman is tasked with aiding his development. This reveals Schlegel's failure to break from the patriarchy of his predecessors.

Günderrode and The Plight of the Woman Writer

Reason, intelligence, even sexual agency modelled by romantic literary figures such as Hoffmann's Clara, Hölderlin's Diotima, Goethe's Gretchen, Novalis' Mathilde, and Schlegel's Lucinde send conflicting messages. Ironically, it is here that art and life meet. If in theory male romantics advocated equality, their literature and lives did not. Women writers felt the brunt of this; they encountered an oppressive barricade built by centuries of misogyny "that predefined [their] sense of self and predetermined their range of activities [, for ...] the societal boundaries between 'unnatural' and 'natural', proper and improper female behaviour became internalised, domesticating not only women but women's writing" (Blackwell and Zantop 1990, p. 10). Regardless of talent and connections, the most successful women never saw the fame of their male counterparts. Even Goethe, who

> appeared to support the concerns of women and the efforts of women writers [...] did so by restricting their sphere of activity[,] [suggesting that] '[...] intelligent and talented women [should] be able to acquire intelligent and talented male friends to whom they could show their manuscripts, so that all unfeminine traits would be expunged. (Goodman and Waldstein 1992, p. 17).

Men worked to preserve the feminine traits of their counterparts in life and art; yet, while appreciating the value of feminine attributes they ascribed worth to male virtues, devaluing the very traits that they imposed upon the literature of women. In eliminating masculine traits from women's texts, they eliminated women's texts from the intellectual sphere. Gesa Dane argues that

> [m]any [women writers] became 'women of the romantic school' only thanks to the constructions of literary historians [one-hundred] years later. Their contemporary Heinrich Heine recognises no such grouping. [...] [I]f these women played any role at all, then it was only insofar as they were linked with a well-known man. (Saul 2009, p. 134).

Romantic women writers often published under male, or gender-neutral pseudonyms. Karoline v. Günderrode published as Tian, Sophie Mereau and Dorothea Schlegel published anonymously, Therese Huber, under the name of a significant other. The privileges of literacy and publication were often matrilineal inheritances, as is the case of Sophie La Roche's granddaughter, Bettina von Arnim. When published by husbands, women's work was frequently feminised. Trailblazers like Günderrode challenged the boundaries, aspiring toward greater social and literary liberties. The rebellious romantic is anti-idealist, in that she engages classical metaphysical concerns and idealist philosophy.

Günderrode's classical affinities, historical knowledge, and metaphysical contemplations, are examples of how she broaches topics taboo for women. Though she addresses "feminine" themes, her explication upon the profound is a prominent characteristic of her and her writing. Günderrode unabashedly admires ferocity, valour, and nobility and her œuvre reflects neo-classical leanings. Poems, including "Orphisches Lied," "Adonis' Totenfeier," and "Ariadne auf Naxos" reveal her affinity for mythology. "Die Manen" fuses mythology and philosophy when addressing death, continuity, and transmutation. In the dialogue between student and teacher, the youth nostalgically laments to his instructor, over "life, death, and the activities of Gustav Adolph II (das Leben, den Tod, and die Tätigkeiten des Gustav Adolphs II)," seventeenth century king and founder of Sweden (Günderrode 1998, p. 19). As the student mourns the greatness of a leader long gone, the teacher consoles him, reminding him that "we must not overlook the infinite chain from the original source to all its effects (unser Auge vermag die lange unendliche Kette von der Ursache zu allen Folgen nicht zu übersehen)" (Günderrode 1998, p. 19). Here, Günderrode offers a discourse of continuity, adjoining the past and the present through a national identity and a common people. Through one's legacy, the text implies, one lives continuously, and through the existence of one's predecessors—one has always been.

Günderrode's metaphysical postulations place her in the company of the classicists and idealists, as she engages the timeless and profound philosophical contemplations of her male contemporaries. Zealously, prompted by ancient philosophy and orientalist enquiries, Weimar classicists and romantics including Wieland, Sophie La Roche, and Goethe, explored *Fortdauer* and *Seelenwanderung* as reincarnation, metempsychosis, and transmutation (Kurth-Voigt 1999). In "Ein apokalyptisches Fragment" the narrator insists:

> There is not two, not three, not thousands, there is one and all; there is not body and spirit divorced, one belonging to time and the other to eternity, there is one, it belongs to itself and it is time and eternity simultaneously, it remains visible and invisible in change, an infinite Life.[3]
>
> (Es ist nicht zwei, nicht drei, nicht Tausende, es ist eins und alles; es ist nicht Körper und Geist geschieden, daß das eine der Zeit, das andere der Ewigkeit angehöre, es ist eins, gehört sich selbst, und ist Zeit und Ewigkeit zugleich, und sichtbar, und unsichtbar bleibend im Wandel, ein unendliches Leben.) (Günderrode 1998, p. 29).

Günderrode's depth of knowledge gains her the admiration of her contemporaries. Dagmar von Gersdorff writes that "Goethe [...] found her poems amazing (Goethe [...] fand ihre Gedichte erstaunlich)" (Gersdorff 2006, p. 11). Günderrode's writing depicts the chain of philosophical and aesthetic development. For instance, Schelling "seeks further to erase all forms of discontinuity between the conscious mind and objective nature by setting up a dialectic wherein nature becomes the objectified self and the self the reflected nature [...] render[ing] subject and object identical in the Absolute" (Saul 2009, p. 9,10).

In "Ein apokalyptisches Fragment," Günderrode engages this dialectic. The fifteen fragments illustrate *ursprüngliche Harmonie*. The narrator observes with awe as "multifarious figures [...] arose from the womb of the deep sea (mancherlei Gestalten [...] herauf stiegen, aus dem Schoß des tiefen Meeres)[,]" which symbolises a primordial womb, or the Absolute, where the separation, or "discontinuity" that divides subject from object is erased (Günderrode 1998, p. 26). The ever-changing forms emerging from this chora, unnamed and shape-shifting, are imperceptible by the conscious intellectual mind and cannot be understood in the representative and symbolic system alone. The narrator undergoes an awakening of a higher consciousness. Helene M. Kastinger Riley points out that

---

3 Author's translation.

[t]he first-person narrator explains the mystical experience of being simultaneously one and all, at the sight of the Mediterranean Sea. Günderrode demonstrates the development of this ego-consciousness, whose chararacter is not described in more detail, as if it was learnt from Nature's secrets.[4]

([d]as erzählende Ich [...] erklärt die mystische Erfahrung, zugleich Eins und Alles zu sein, beim Anblick des Mittelmeers [...] Günderrode legt die Entwicklung der Erkenntnis dieses Ich, welches nicht näher in seiner Persönlichkeit beschrieben wird, als ein der Natur abgelauschtes Geheimnis dar.) (Kastinger Riley 1986, p.104).

The moment of self-actualisation is rooted in the newly-perceived unification found in non-signification. The narrator recognises that "all the beings that had arisen from the sea, returned to it, re-creating themselves in varying forms (alle die Wesen, die aus dem Meer gestiegen waren, wieder zu ihm zurückkehrten, und sich in wechselnden Formen wieder erzeugten)," concluding that "they also longed to return to the source of life ([ihre] Sehnsucht sei auch, zurück zu kehren, zu der Quelle des Lebens)" (Günderrode 1998, p. 28). Günderrode reveals how "[...] the path of absolute idealism ultimately leads to art, where human consciousness finds expression in sensuous form"; her writing epitomises the romantic philosophy stemming from idealist influence—the aesthetic, which reaches outside of the limitations of language and reason, actualises philosophy and consciousness through sensual experience (Saul 2009, p. 10).

Well-known, well-liked, and praised within the circle of prominent romantic writers, Günderrode never received the accolades of these men, though she received the lustful admiration of suitors, with no proposals; perhaps this is because her meditations misaligned with her gender.

> Friedrich von Savigny was set ablaze when he became acquainted with the nineteen-year-old. Clemens Brentano sought in her the erotic partner, who he lavished with passionate proposals. Achim von Arnim gave to her, in his novella *Isabella von Ägypten*, a poetic memorial. [...] Friedrich Creuzer finally, the scholar from Heidelberg, was carried away by this woman, she was his mistress. (Gersdorff 2006, p. 10–11).[5]

> (Friedrich von Savigny fing Feuer, als er die Neunzehnjährige kennenlernte. Clemens Brentano suchte in ihr die erotische Partnerin, die er mit leidenschaftlichen Anträgen überschüttete. Achim von Arnim setzte ihr in seiner Novelle *Isabella von Ägypten* ein poetisches Denkmal. [...] Friedrich Creuzer schließlich, der Gelehrte aus Heidelberg war hingerissen von dieser Frau, sie war seine Geliebte.) (Gersdorff 2006, p. 10–11).

---

4 Translated by Gert Hofmann unless otherwise indicated. Here author's translation.
5 Author's translation.

Though she and her literature were praised, Günderrode received no real recognition of her talent. The autodidact was simultaneously admired and admonished; like Schlegel's Lucinde, in lieu of her grace and intellect, she only received the most superficial and least useful of accolades. She could not be liberated from the bondage of her gender; her attempts to transcend it left her suffering. Despite her melodiously poetic literary aesthetics and the ephemeral beauty for which she was well known, she neither gained appropriate recognition as a writer, nor did she achieve normative social success for a woman of her time. Günderrode's anti-idealist approach to life led to immense internal and relational conflicts.

Conclusion

Proclivity toward intellectual activity, in tandem with the glass ceiling that prevented it, heaved upon Günderrode melancholic despondency; she expresses this in her epistolary writing. Günderrode, consumed with "great virulence" by "the archaic wish to die a heroic death (der alte Wunsch einen Heldentod zu sterben)," was pleased only by "savage greatness and glory (das Wilde Große, Glänzende)"; she grappled with being a woman who felt "desires just like a man, without his virility (Begierden wie ein Mann, ohne Männerkraft)" (Günderrode 1998, p. 103). She was suffocated as woman and writer due to the gender-based limitations imposed upon her. Her correspondences reveal the "vehement despair [which she felt] at the limitations of a female writer's existence" (Blackwell and Zantop 1990, p. 5). Günderrode can be recognised as having taken an anti-idealist approach to literature and life; however, the philosophically attuned poet, playwright, and writer, like the heroines of many romantic novels and her female colleagues, was nonetheless constrained by the gender-binarism and the wall between the sexes that the romantic movement failed to properly dismantle.

Bibliography

Blackwell, Jeannine and Zantop, Susanne (1990): *Bitter Healing: German Women Writers from 1700 to 1830*. Lincoln: University of Nebraska Press.

Firchow, Peter (Trans.) (1971): *Friedrich Schlegel's Lucinde and the Fragments*. Minneapolis: University of Minnesota Press.

Flavell, M. Kay (1975): "Women and Individualism: A Re-Examination of Schlegel's 'Lucinde' and Gutzkow's 'Wally die Zweiflerin'". In: *Modern Language Review* 70, pp. 550–566.

Frierson, Patrick and Guyer, Paul (eds.) (2011): *Observations on the Feeling of the Beautiful and Sublime and Other Writings*. Cambridge: Cambridge University Press.

Gersdorff, Dagmar von (2006): *Die Erde ist mir Heimat nicht geworden: Das Leben der Karoline von Günderrode*. Frankfurt am Main und Leipzig: Insel Verlag.
Gikandi, Simon (2011): *Slavery and the Culture of Taste*. Princeton: Princeton University Press.
Goodman, Katherine R. and Waldstein, Edith (1992): *In the Shadow of Olympus*. New York: State University of New York Press.
Günderrode, Karoline von (1998): *Gedichte, Prosa, Briefe*. Stuttgart: Philipp Reclam.
Hamilton, Paul (2017): "Freedom, Reason, and Art in Idealist and Romantic Philosophy." In: *The Oxford Handbook of European Romanticism*. Oxford: Oxford University Press.
Immerwahr, Raymond (1980): "Classicist Values in the Critical Thought of Friedrich Schlegel". In: *The Journal of English and Germanic Philology*, 79: 3, pp. 376–389.
Kant, Immanuel (1793): *Kritik der Urtheilskraft*. Berlin: F.T. Lagarde.
Kant, Immanuel (1987): *Critique of Judgment*. Werner S. Pluhar (Trans). Indianapolis: Hackett Publishing Company.
Kastinger Riley, Helene M. (1986): *Zwischen den Welten. Ambivalenz und Existentialproblematik im Werk Caroline von Günderrodes*. New York: Camden House.
Kurth-Voigt, Lieselotte E. (1999): *Continued Existence, Reincarnation, and the Power of Sympathy in Classical Weimar*. Rochester: Camden House.
Littlejohns, Richard (1977): "The 'Bekenntnisse Eines Ungeschickten': A Re-Examination of Emancipatory Ideas in Friedrich Schlegel's 'Lucinde'." In *The Modern Language Review* 72, pp. 605–614.
Meier, Albert (2008): *Klassik-Romantik*. Stuttgart: Philipp Reclam.
Saul, Nicholas (ed.) (2009): *The Cambridge Companion to German Romanticism*. Cambridge: Cambridge University Press.
Ter Horst, Eleanor (2016): "The Classical Aesthetic of Schlegel's *Lucinde*". In: *Goethe Yearbook* 23, pp. 123–137.
Winckelmann, Johann Joachim (1765): *Reflections on the Painting and Sculpture of the Greeks*. Henri Fusseli (Trans). London: A. Millar.
Wood, Allen W. (1991): *Elements of the Philosophy of Right*. Cambridge: Cambridge University Press.

Joseph Trullinger
The Polymorphous Political Theology of Novalis and Marcuse

Abstract: In this paper I have two aims: 1) to demonstrate the mistakenness of Marcuse's negative reading of Novalis in his dissertation on *The German Artist Novel*, and 2) to reconstruct how Marcuse's utopianism would benefit from something like Novalis' theory of Eros as divine. Because Novalis is tackling the theory of the drives that animates the central letters of Schiller's *Aesthetic Education of Man*, and because Marcuse is dealing with a similar problematic in Freud's theory of the struggle between Thanatos and Eros, Novalis proves to be a useful figure for illuminating overlooked possibilities for reconciling that problematic. I argue that Novalis puts forth a kind of "theology of Eros" that—as an elaboration of Schiller's idea that "energetic beauty" follows from the play drive—allows an organism to perpetually progress in desire toward an ideal without exhaustion. This then allows us to conceive of Eros as similarly keen and self-evolving without devolving into self-denial. Such a conception would correct Marcuse's metaphysics of mortality that undercuts his politics of life-affirming Eros.

When Herbert Marcuse aims to rethink the relationship between Eros and Ananke in the second half of *Eros and Civilization,* he turns to Schiller to reactivate forgotten historical possibilities. What goes unnoticed is why Marcuse does not make the historically intuitive move to follow or even substantially address Novalis' own extension of Schiller's aesthetic education into a theology of Eros. There are several reasons that can explain Marcuse's neglect here, and one of them rests in his misreading of Novalis' *Bildungsroman, Henry von Ofterdingen*, as apolitical, when Novalis himself called it "my *political novel*" (O'Brien 1995, p. 274). In this paper I have two aims: 1) to demonstrate the mistakenness of Marcuse's negative reading of Novalis in his dissertation on *The German Artist Novel*, and 2) to reconstruct how Marcuse's utopianism would benefit from something like Novalis' theory of Eros as divine. Because Novalis is tackling the Fichtean theory of the drives that animates the central letters of Schiller's *Aesthetic Education of Man*, and because Marcuse is dealing with a similar problematic in Freud's theory of the struggle between the death drive (Thanatos) and the life instincts (Eros), Novalis proves to be a useful figure for illuminating overlooked possibilities for the reconciliation of that problematic.

In essence, I will argue that Novalis puts forth a kind of "theology of Eros" that—as an elaboration of Schiller's idea that "energetic beauty" follows from the play drive—allows an organism to perpetually progress in desire toward an ideal without exhaustion. This in turn allows us to conceive of Eros as similarly keen and self-evolving without devolving into the restrictiveness of Marcuse's "dialectic of domination." In other words, it gives us another way to conceive of Marcuse's metaphysics, whose residually Heideggerian focus on mortality undercuts his politics of life-affirming Eros. I will be assuming a fair degree of familiarity with Schiller and Novalis, and therefore I will direct the majority of my exegetical attention to Marcuse.

1

Let's begin with an overview of Marcuse's attempt to rethink the traditional subordination of sensuality to rationality. Marcuse raises characters from Freudian depth psychology—the pleasure principle (*Eros*) and the reality principle (Ananke)—to retell Freud's tale of human history with a Marxist voice. Civilization is marked by a "dialectic of domination" (Marcuse 1970, p. 37), an ongoing cycle of ever-mounting expectations of productivity in tandem with nebulous fears of scarcity and chaos that are increasingly irrational to the extent that technological progress develops easier and faster ways of meeting our genuine biological needs. However, because what drives this progress is a pre-rational mistrust of relaxation and enjoyment—an internalisation of the primal father's aggression in ever more subtle individual and social forms (Marcuse 1970, p. 37– 38)—we are also driven to seek out pseudo-justifications for more stringent order and toil, equating the hardness of our labour with our worth as persons (EC, p. 221).

This is why we can frequently say things like, "You need to earn a living," without thinking twice about why exactly it is that life is something you have to earn, as though you perpetually deserve death unless you "keep up the good work." It strikes us as perfectly rational to say, even though it has no real rationale behind it. More than that, suggestions that we spend most of our free time in play instantly appear irrational, or even threatening to all morality and possibility of social cooperation (EC, p. 111). The twisted criterion that equates rationality with sacrifice—the subsumption of desires and wishes to "brutal honesty," "the hard truth," or "the facts of life," as we might say—is what Marcuse terms "the Logos of domination" (EC, p. 118). It is, in other words, the flat (and flattening) equivalence of self-denial with reason itself.

The irony is that this Logos of domination undermines the possibility of genuine cooperation precisely by undermining the legitimacy of free play. When our basic way of experiencing reality is to regard the desires of ourselves and of others as threatening, then we categorically reject even the mere act of *imagining* a better world as foolish, as self-absorbed, as childish, as artsy, as utopian (EC, p. 143–144)—in a word, as *romantic*. Given the iron grip the Logos of domination has over our sense of what is rational, such that we equate rationality with an iron fist, to overcome this deadlock in our lack of political imagination, we need to teach ourselves how to *feel* in a new way, how to feel that widespread joy and playfulness are not only permissible but necessary features of a progressive society (Marcuse 1970, p. 39–42). This new way of feeling would change everything:

> The new sensibility, which expresses the ascent of the life instincts over aggressiveness and guilt, would foster, on a social scale, the vital need for the abolition of injustice and misery and would shape the further evolution of the "standard of living." The life instincts would find rational expression (sublimation) in planning the distribution of the socially necessary labor time within and among the various branches of production, thus setting priorities of goals and choices: not only what to produce but also the "form" of the product. The liberated consciousness would promote the development of a science and technology free to discover and realize the possibilities of things and men in the protection and gratification of life, playing with the potentialities of form and matter for the attainment of this goal. Technique would then tend to become art, and art would tend to form reality: the opposition between imagination and reason, higher and lower faculties, poetic and scientific thought, would be invalidated. Emergence of a new Reality Principle: under which a new sensibility and desublimated scientific intelligence would combine in the creation of an *aesthetic ethos*. (Marcuse 1969, p. 23–24).

2

Under the Logos of domination, we have been mis-educated into mistaking misery for mirth, miserliness for morality. We need a new pedagogy in accordance with the new sensibility that allows individual needs to come into accord. This pedagogy would need to integrate rationality with sensibility, a new reality principle that incorporates the pleasure principle. The properly humane education that would pull up the downtrodden so that all can live according to "an *aesthetic ethos*" is not only Marcuse's project, but the project of Friedrich Schiller as well. Inspired by Kant's idea in §59 of the Third Critique that "beauty is the symbol of morality" (Kant 2000, p. 225), Schiller posits that the heretofore opposed drives or impulses within human beings can be reconciled and satisfied through "the playful impulse," the desire to freely reshape and appreciate reality's infinite potential for shapeliness. Schiller argues that "[...] man plays only when he is a man in the full sense of the word, and *he is only a complete man when he plays.*" (AE, p. 56–57). According to Schiller, the play drive is the synthesis of the "material drive" (*Sinntrieb*, also translatable as "sense drive") for immersing ourselves in sensuous particulars (roughly analogous to the pleasure principle) and the "formal drive" (*Formtrieb*) for structure and intelligibility (roughly analogous to the reality principle) (AE, pp. 41–43; EC, pp. 181–182).

The relative simplicity of the archaic world's structures for material and intellectual production meant a society dominated by the sense drive. This gave way to the very different society in which we live, a highly structured society where abstract rules and impersonal methods predominate, which Schiller calls "barbarism" (AE, p. 12). Barbarism is defined by an excess of the formal drive, at the expense of the sense drive—quite similar to Marcuse's notion of the dialectic of domination that endures throughout modern life. According to Schiller, we have yet to see the realisation of the authentically free and humane society the French Revolution failed to bring about. Schiller thinks a better world is indeed possible despite this ostensible failure, the world of culture (AE, p. 45–46), which can only come about through a very different kind of revolution, a revolution that does not fall prey to what Marcuse once called "*psychic Thermidor*" (Marcuse 1970, p. 38): the self-implosion of the revolutionary into the reactionary (EC, pp. 90–91). Only a culture built around the holistic self-determination of the play drive—the capacity of Eros to self-sublimate as a kind of foreplay, as Marcuse might put it (EC, p. 204–205)—can complete the revolution because only a state with an aesthetic ethos can "give freedom by means of freedom" (AE, p. 110), instead of the recurring mistake of dictating freedom through a vanguard party.

3

We see a similar development in Novalis' theory of symbolic monarchy in his *Faith and Love*. As this is a deliberately cryptic text, one that could take one or more separate papers to thoroughly stake out an interpretation and defend it against alternate ones, my analysis must build upon others. I mostly follow William Arctander O'Brien's interpretation that Novalis articulates a politics of "crowned anarchy" (to use Artaud's phrase), and uses the king as a symbol for the well-rounded and autonomous human being (O'Brien 1995, pp. 184–185). This king's function is not to give orders but to exemplify to everyone in a democratic republic how they can rule themselves (FL §16, pp. 38–39). Like Schiller and Marcuse, Novalis is sceptical of the binary of ruler and ruled, as he thinks it keeps emancipatory politics ruled by a hollow spirit of self-interest, and the French Revolution failed because it was carried out by "miserable philistines, empty in spirit and poor in heart [...]." (FL §23, p. 41). Democratic experiments fail not because there is a flaw inherent in democracy or autonomy itself, but because we are starting out from an immoral spirit of barbarism, or as Novalis calls it, *philistinism*.

The philistine is like the well-adjusted citizen of Marcuse's repressive society, a "Happy Consciousness" (Marcuse 1964, p. 84) smoothly integrated with what Shelly Johnson calls "the instrumentalising sensibility" (Johnson 2016). As Novalis puts it, "The chief means appears to be their only end" (PL §77, p. 24). Philistines like their boundaries and want their wants to stay fixed, static, frozen—because then they are assured the success of reaching their goals. Hence "even their pleasures are worked through like everything else, laboriously and formally" (PL §77, p. 25). The philistine confuses tranquillity with tranquilisation. His hedonism is not for the sake of making real connections with other people or in his mind, but instead his goal is to disconnect, to numb himself. His religion is not a *"religion of the senses"* (Anonymous 2005, p. 5), but an "opiate: stimulative yet numbing" (PL §77, p. 25). The philistine is caught up in workaday ("daily") life, and mechanically goes through socially expected routines (PL §77, p. 24). He can't imagine it getting much better than this; he lacks the spiritedness to imagine and work toward a better world. Even when he is at "play" it is a kind of work.

Philistines think the key to peace is to abandon transcendence, to never be passionate or carried away by anything, to administer everything through bureaucracy (which can multiply nodes of oppression), but this is a subtle disdain for diversity, unlike the manifold richness of kingly life (FL §§38–39, p. 47–48). What makes the king kingly is his absolute love for the queen, and without that kind of selflessness, democracy has no hope of becoming truly realised (FL §24, p. 42). Novalis wants a symbolic monarchy in place to model the organic and personal commitment we could have with each other; instead of the glue of society being the "stale paste" of self-interest, "[a]ll humanity will melt together like a pair of lovers" (FL §16, pp. 38–39). Novalis thinks that a virtuous king's loving marriage with a virtuous queen could inspire us to reflect their lifestyle, and indeed, he wants a society where everybody can live like a king (FL §18, pp. 39–40). This unforced inspiration is what makes this monarchy compatible with his anarchism.

Novalis thinks the key to realising Schiller's "aesthetic state" is this spirit that is inspired by love's mystical significance. He wants each person to be able to have a kingly lifestyle of sensual and educational enrichment. What keeps this from being the despotism of a "sultan" who is enslaved to his own desires (PA §50, p. 50) is that the king's love for something outside himself (the queen) is higher than any finite stimulation earthly goods could bring (FL §24, p. 42; PA §§51, 53, and 56, p. 54). A true king would not cling to his status (PA §51, p. 54). This is because he "tune[s] his harp" to his muse, the queen, and out of that he spends his reign creating opportunities for everybody to be artistic (FL §39, p. 48). The key here is that to truly enact the ethics of autonomy—self-rule—we need to be inspired by something outside of ourselves, somebody who functions as a "mediator" for the absolute value of freedom: "True religion is what regards the mediator as a mediator, what sees it as the organ of divinity, as its sensible appearance" (PL §74, p. 23). Novalis therefore puts forth what the *Systemprogramm* calls a "religion of the senses" (Anonymous 2005, p. 5), oriented around the "absolute stimulus" of "absolute love," which functions as the anchor point for all "finite stimuli" to fall into unplanned yet non-coercive order (PA §§52–53, p. 54). The playful impulse of Schiller's aesthetic state is realisable through a religion of love, in which all are freed from the false and deadening relations of philistine self-interest.

4

We see this richly symbolised at the end of Klingsohr's fairytale in *Henry von Ofterdingen*. The characters of Love and Peace (who are literally named Eros and Freya) revitalise the natural world from the wedding bed that is their throne, while all their "subjects" receive crowns of self-determination from this sexual consummation (HO, pp. 147–148). This comes after a period of time in which an army of skeletons overtakes the realm and attacks Life (HO, p. 130), but later all war is banished to the chessboard, sublimated into a game (HO, p. 147). One would think that this ascendency of Eros and life-instincts over the forces of Death would draw Marcuse's approval, yet Marcuse's dissertation on *The German Artist Novel* interprets this fairytale to be a symbolic substitution for real, material social change. In taking the transcendental world to be the real world, the poet Klingsohr fails to transform the real (Marcuse 1978, p. 119). "Reality is overcome, but a new world—the idea—has become reality" (Marcuse 1978, p. 108).[1] Thus however much Novalis conceived his novel to be the antithesis of Goethe's *Wilhelm Meister*—Novalis came to detest as philistine the message that the artist's *Bildung* consists in adjusting to bourgeois society—Marcuse

---

[1] Translation mine. The original text reads: "Die Wirklichkeit ist überwunden, aber eine neue Welt—die Idee—ist Wirklichkeit geworden."

thinks that "overcoming" the world is just as inconsequential as "winning" it on its terms (Marcuse 1978, p. 120).

Here Marcuse is largely replicating the basic position worked out in Georg Lukács' *Theory of the Novel*, published in 1920, two years previous to Marcuse's dissertation (1922). We know Marcuse was familiar with Lukács' analysis, as he cites this work directly albeit momentarily (Marcuse 1978, p. 10). According to Lukács, the novel is a literary form that represents a distinctively modern sense of disconnection between things as they are and things as they ought to be, over against the more naïve unity of "life" (what is) and "essence" (what ought to be) in ancient epic poetry (Lukács 1971, p. 3). This sense of disconnect is a reflection in fiction of the factual alienation of modern life; the lack of integration in civilization gives rise to literary forms that thematise how our lives fall short of "totality" (wholeness), but even a Romantic's self-aware thematisation of reality's inadequacies is nonetheless bound to replicate this diremption, as the artist can never fully excogitate their way beyond the limits of their society. Lukács therefore thinks Klingsohr's fairytale fails to transcend bourgeois life even more than Goethe's *Wilhelm Meister* "because it stems too directly from the philosophico-postulative sphere of pure abstraction, that the two are unable to unite in a living totality. And so the artistic fault which Novalis so penetratingly detected in Goethe is even great—is irreparable—in his own work" (Lukács 1971, pp. 139–140). To Lukács' mind, Novalis' quasi-surrealism is inferior to Goethe's more grounded realism, and Marcuse's own castigation of Novalis for blending "art" and "life" in ideality rather than reality largely follows Lukács critique (Marcuse 1978, p. 119). Yet in following Lukács so closely, Marcuse's dissertation is ironically too beholden to literary realism by the standards of Marcuse's own later position on the importance of surrealist art to provide and cultivate the imagination of alternative forms of life that revolutionary praxis can materialise. Marcuse subverts his own utopianism when he follows Lukács in faulting Novalis for not being "realistic."

Thus we should be wary of taking the analysis of the young Marcuse, which so closely follows Lukács' project (with its own background aims and presuppositions), to be a definitive statement about the profound sympathies between Marcuse and Novalis. Simply put, Marcuse fails to take consideration of Novalis' politics of anarchist mysticism we just finished sketching, so it is no wonder he fails to see the resonance of Klingsohr's fairytale with the "aesthetic state" of Schiller that Marcuse will lionise in his mature writings. Marcuse is hardly alone in taking Novalis' mysticism to imply a lack of political vision, a mistake made by O'Brien as well (O'Brien 1995, p. 22 and pp. 238–240). Novalis very much was a mystic, but for him mysticism both presupposes and completes revolutionary subjectivity. According to Novalis' *Christianity or Europe*, "True anarchy is the creative element of religion" (CE, p. 72). That is, free play culminates in amazement about the infinity of the possibilities that make our play eternally evolvable. It follows that the new religion of Novalis' romanticism is one that does not demand conformity to a pre-given story about what the divine is and does, and instead allows this story to organically unfold according to the unique perspective each person has (cp. Kleingeld 2008, pp. 277–278). Novalis thinks that we live in the preliminary stages of a new epoch in history, when the messianic promises of Christianity go hand in hand with "the holy revolution," in which "the plural messiah" will show himself or herself in a manner that is different for each person.[2]

> Woken from the morning dream of helpless childhood, one part of the human race exercises its powers on the vipers that encircle its cradle and attempt to deprive it of the use of its limbs. These are still intimations, unconnected and crude, but they betray to the historical eye a universal individuality, a new history, a new humanity, the sweetest embrace of a young surprised church and a loving god, not to mention the inner reception of a new messiah in all his thousand forms. Who does not feel hope with sweet shame? The new born will be the image of its father, a new golden age with dark infinite eyes, a prophetic, miraculous, healing, consoling time that generates eternal life. It will be a great age of reconciliation, of a redeemer who, like a true genius, will be at home with men, believed but not seen. He will be visible to the believer in countless forms: consumed as bread and wine, embraced as a lover, breathed as air, heard as word and song, and as death received into the heart of the departing body with heavenly joy and the highest pains of love. (CE, p. 74).
>
> (Aus dem Morgentraum der unbehülflichen Kindheit erwacht, übt ein Teil des Geschlechts seine ersten Kräfte an Schlangen, die seine Wiege umschlingen und den Gebrauch seiner Gliedmaßen ihm benehmen wollen. Noch sind alles nur Andeutungen, unzusammenhängend und roh, aber sie verraten dem historischen Auge eine universelle Individualität, eine neue Geschichte, eine neue Menschheit, die süßeste Umarmung einer jungen überraschten Kirche und eines liebenden Gottes und das innige Empfängnis eines neuen Messias in ihren tausend Gliedern zugleich. Wer fühlt sich nicht mit süßer Scham guter Hoffnung? Das Neugeborne wird das Abbild seines Vaters, eine neue goldne Zeit mit dunkeln, unendlichen Augen, eine prophetische, wundertätige und wundenheilende, tröstende und ewiges Leben entzündende Zeit sein – eine große Versöhnungszeit, ein Heiland, der wie ein echter Genius unter den Menschen einheimisch, nur geglaubt, nicht gesehen werden, und unter zahllosen Gestalten den Gläubigen sichtbar, als Brot und Wein verzehrt, als Geliebte umarmt, als Luft geatmet, als Wort und Gesang vernommen und mit himm-

---

[2] See Novalis' letter to Friedrich Schlegel regarding *Lucinde:* "You [F. Schlegel] will be the Paul of the new religion, which is everywhere breaking forth—one of the first-born of the new age—of the religious age. A new world history is beginning with this religion. You understand the secrets of the time—The Revolution has worked upon you, what it should work; or rather, you are an invisible member of the holy revolution, the plural messiah, which has appeared on earth" (quoted in O'Brien 1995, p. 226).

lischer Wollust als Tod unter den höchsten Schmerzen der Liebe in das Innre des verbrausenden Leibes aufgenommen wird.) (NS, p. 38–39).

Novalis' messianic hope is pluralistic. His hope for the future golden age is one where the polymorphous capacities for joy and play are celebrated in spite of their current rejection as being "perverse" (cp. EC, p. 49). Novalis explicitly indicates that amidst his many forms of presence the plural Messiah will be "embraced as lover," and the word translated as "embraced" is *umarmt* (CE, p. 74). In Novalis' day this word had decidedly explicit connotations of sexual congress, indicating his positive attitude toward sexuality as a revelation of the divine (Daub 2012, p. 117). The lush joy of communion with the plural Messiah is therefore not merely permissible upon the condition that the union of Christ with his bride be so metaphorically rendered that it lacks all eroticism. Instead, Novalis embraces the eroticism of a religion that identifies God as Love, as Eros. For Novalis, "the creative element of religion [is] the joy in all religion." (CE, p. 78). Now we can easily see why Novalis says "Every loved object is the center of a paradise" (PL §51, p. 18).

§5. It is significant that it is shortly after mentioning Novalis that Marcuse begins resurrecting the myth of Orpheus as a liberator-poet of a future culture whose values appear to our one-dimensional age as ridiculous: "the redemption of pleasure, the halt of time, the absorption of death; silence, sleep, night, paradise—the Nirvana principle not as death but as life" (EC, p. 164).[3] By reflecting on Schiller's notion of what is necessary to synthesise the formal and material impulses into the playful impulse, we can further develop how Novalis' identification of Eros as divine fits within Marcuse's project to attain a messianic peace—Nirvana—through Eros rather than Thanatos (cp. Edwards 2013). Schiller illustrates that we can harmonise the material and formal impulses either by mollifying the effects of the one in excess, which is "liquefying" or "relaxing" beauty. More in keeping with the *Aufhebung* of the drives is the tricky intensification of both that elevates both without negating what makes either special. "When its pans are empty, a scale balances; but it also balances if the pans contain equal weights" (AE, p. 74). This form of the play is "energetic beauty" (AE, pp. 58–59), and though it can never be fully realised, the idea of it is synonymous with divinity, and we see a glimpse of it in the grace and dignity of Juno Ludovisi:

> The entire form reposes within itself, as if she were beyond space, unyielding, unresisting; there is no force here that fights other powers, no weak spot where temporality might break

---

[3] Marcuse praises Novalis' validation of imagination on EC, pp. 160–161.

in. Irresistibly drawn in by the first, while kept at a distance by the second, we find ourselves at once in a state of complete rest and complete movement, and that wonderful arousal develops for which intellect has no concept, and language no name. (AE, p. 57).

(In sich selbst ruhet und wohnt die ganze Gestalt, eine völlig geschlossene Schöpfung, und als wenn sie jenseits des Raumes wäre, ohne Nachgeben, ohne Widerstand; da ist keine Kraft, die mit Kräften kämpfte, keine Blöße, wo die Zeitlichkeit einbrechen könnte. Durch jenes unwiderstehlich ergriffen und angezogen, durch dieses in der Ferne gehalten, befinden wir uns zugleich in dem Zustand der höchsten Ruhe und der höchsten Bewegung, und es entsteht jene wunderbare Rührung, für welche der Verstand keinen Begriff und die Sprache keinen Namen hat.) (SW, p. 618–619).

This desire that escalates without exhausting, which synthesises rationality and sensuality, contains a spontaneous self-ordering *and* a cooperative creativity or play with others.

It is precisely this synthesis that Eros represents in Marcuse's metaphysical critiques of Heidegger's ideology of death: despite the Logos of domination treating sensuality and rationality as though they are mutually exclusive, they can find fulfilment in a synthesis of liveliness so heightened it is theologically inflected (cp. EC, p. 234–236). In *Beyond the Pleasure Principle*, Freud says that each organism has a tension inherent in it, where it simultaneously is excited by stimuli but also capable of being overtaxed by stimuli. There are two ways of resolving this tension: either by seeking to quiet down the stimuli and return to a state of inertness (i.e., death, Thanatos), or to team up with other organisms and, through engagement with them, amplify our ability to handle the stimuli (i.e., "ever-greater unities of life," Eros) (Freud 1961, p. 60–61). Marcuse maintains that whereas it is impossible to do away with Ananke—we will always come up against limits as finite beings—Thanatos is a strategy of seeking peace through war that is only of contingent and historical utility, one that becomes dispensable given the technological means to make life less of a burden and more of a delight (EC, pp. 234–235). We have seen how Novalis' polymorphous theology of Eros revolves around this very same "absolute stimulus" of "absolute love," which allows finite stimuli to take on peaceful order. It is the energetic beauty that adds weight while maintaining balance in Schiller's scales, which Schiller considered divine.

Instead of doing away with life to reduce the tension inherent in life (the philistine pseudo-solution of Thanatos), sexuality could be integrated with rational order to form Eros in the most proper sense of the term, and life's stimulation would be felt as joy because it would be creatively and cooperatively shared: "The culture-building power of Eros *is* non-repressive sublimation: sexuality is neither deflected from nor blocked in its objective; rather, in attaining its objective, it transcends it to others, searching for fuller gratification" (EC,

p. 211). Being-toward-death would no longer be definitive for human existence, and we could flourish as individuals and as a civilization without death; indeed, we could desire immortality not to *escape* the world, but as a way to *engage* the world, to play in it (EC, p. 158). This would be the highest *amor mundi:* to live a life with others that sees each as worth spending an eternity with, each feeling through this mediation the plural messiah, Eros.

Bibliography

Anonymous (2005): "The Oldest Systematic Program of German Idealism." In: *The Early Political Writings of the German Romantics.* Ed. and trans. Beiser, Frederick C. Bloomington, Indiana: Cambridge University Press.

Daub, Adrian (2012): *Uncivil Unions: The Metaphysics of Marriage in German Idealism and Romanticism.* Chicago / London: University of Chicago Press.

Edwards, Caroline (2013): "From Eros to Eschaton: Herbert Marcuse's Liberation of Time." In: *Telos* 165, p. 91–114.

Freud, Sigmund (1961): *Beyond the Pleasure Principle.* Trans. Strachey, James. New York, New York: W.W. Norton & Company, Inc.

Johnson, Shelly (2016): "Compassion and the New Sensibility: A Marcusean and Buddhist Approach to Environmental Degradation." In: *21st-Century Socialism: Concepts and Visions.* Radical Philosophy Association (Ed.). Lexington: University of Kentucky.

Kant, Immanuel (2000): *Critique of the Power of Judgment.* Trans. Guyer, Paul / Matthews, Eric. New York, New York: Cambridge University Press.

Kleingeld, Pauline (2008): "Romantic Cosmopolitanism: Novalis's 'Christianity or Europe.'" In: *Journal for the History of Philosophy* 46:2, p. 269–284.

Lukács, Georg (1971): *The Theory of the Novel: A Historico-Philosophical Essay on the Forms of Great Epic Literature.* Trans. Bostock, Anna. Cambridge, Massachusetts: MIT Press.

Marcuse, Herbert (1964): *One-Dimensional Man: Studies in the Ideology of Advanced Industrial Society.* Boston, Massachusetts: Beacon Press.

Marcuse, Herbert (1966): *Eros and Civilization: A Philosophical Inquiry into Freud.* Boston, Massachusetts: Beacon Press.

Marcuse, Herbert (1969): *An Essay on Liberation.* Boston, Massachusetts: Beacon Press.

Marcuse, Herbert (1970): "Progress and Freud's Theory of Instincts." In: *Five Lectures: Psychoanalysis, Politics, and Utopia.* Trans. Shapiro, Jeremy J. / Weber, Shierry M. Boston, Massachusetts: Beacon Press.

Marcuse, Herbert (1978): "Der deutsche Künstlerroman." In: *Herbert Marcuse Schriften,* Vol. 1. Frankfurt a. M.: Suhrkamp Verlag.

Novalis (1907): *Novalis Schriften,* Vol. 2. Jena: Eugen Diederichs.

Novalis (1992): *Henry von Ofterdingen.* Trans. Hilty, Palmer. Prospect Heights, Illinois: Waveland Press.

Novalis (2005a): "Faith and Love." In: *The Early Political Writings of the German Romantics.* Ed. and trans. Beiser, Frederick C. Bloomington, Indiana: Cambridge University Press.

Novalis (2005b): "Christianity or Europe." In: *The Early Political Writings of the German Romantics*. Ed. and trans. Beiser, Frederick C. Bloomington, Indiana: Cambridge University Press.
Novalis (2005c): "Political Aphorisms." In: *The Early Political Writings of the German Romantics*. Ed. and trans. Beiser, Frederick C. Bloomington, Indiana: Cambridge University Press.
Novalis (2005d): "Pollen." In: *The Early Political Writings of the German Romantics*. Ed. and trans. Beiser, Frederick C. Bloomington, Indiana: Cambridge University Press.
O'Brien, William Arctander (1995): *Novalis: Signs of Revolution*. Durham and London: Duke University Press.
Schiller, Friedrich (1975): *Sämtliche Werke*, Vol. 5. München: Carl Hanser Verlag.
Schiller, Friedrich (2016): *On the Aesthetic Education of Man*. Trans. Tribe, Keith. London a. o.: Penguin Books.

Abbreviations

AE = Schiller, Friedrich (2016): *On the Aesthetic Education of Man*. Trans. Tribe, Keith. London a.o.: Penguin Books.
CE = Novalis (2005b): "Christianity or Europe." In: *The Early Political Writings of the German Romantics*. Ed. and trans. Beiser, Frederick C. Bloomington, Indiana: Cambridge University Press.
EC = Marcuse, Herbert (1966): *Eros and Civilization: A Philosophical Inquiry into Freud*. Boston, Massachusetts: Beacon Press.
FL = Novalis (2005a): "Faith and Love." In: *The Early Political Writings of the German Romantics*. Ed. and trans. Beiser, Frederick C. Bloomington, Indiana: Cambridge University Press.
HO = Novalis (1992): *Henry von Ofterdingen*. Trans. Hilty, Palmer. Prospect Heights, Illinois: Waveland Press.
NS = Novalis (1907): *Novalis Schriften*, Vol. 2. Jena: Eugen Diederichs.
PA = Novalis (2005c): "Political Aphorisms." In: *The Early Political Writings of the German Romantics*. Ed. and trans. Beiser, Frederick C. Bloomington, Indiana: Cambridge University Press.
PL = Novalis (2005d): "Pollen." In: *The Early Political Writings of the German Romantics*. Ed. and trans. Beiser, Frederick C. Bloomington, Indiana: Cambridge University Press.
SW = Schiller, Friedrich (1975): *Sämtliche Werke*, Vol. 5. München: Carl Hanser Verlag.

Hölderlin and Nietzsche: The Ecological Complication of Idealist Aesthetics

Gert Hofmann
Hölderlin's Poetics of *Zärtlichkeit:* The Corporeal Turn of Transcendental Idealism

Abstract: In 1796, having just returned to Nürtingen from a yearlong sojourn in Jena under the auspices of his intellectual benefactor Schiller, Hölderlin reveals in a letter to his friend Immanuel Niethammer his plan of writing "Neue Briefe über die ästhetische Erziehung" ("New Letters on the Aesthetic Education"). The title is an overtly impudent affront to Schiller, whose "Briefe über die ästhetische Erziehung des Menschen" ("Letters on the Aesthetic Education of Man") dominate at the time the discourse on aesthetics and philosophical anthropology (published in Schiller's own journal *Horen* in 1795). Staging his argument in radical opposition to Schiller, he emphasises that he wants to "make disappear" the antagonism between "our Self and the world" in a *theoretical* approach, i.e. as an immediate "intellectual intuition, without practical reason having to come to our aid." Criticising Schiller's *Spieltheorie*, Hölderlin aims to develop human "aesthetic sense" as an intellectual capacity in its own right, and as a genuine way to undercut the Kantian aporia between intelligible freedom and empirical necessity, without degrading the aesthetic sense of art and poetry to a playground of propaedeutic exercise for the advancement of practical reason.

Even though Hölderlin never realised this project of "Neue Briefe," in some of his latest writings before his final mental breakdown, he seems to have undertaken a radical attempt to formulate some of the principles of a post-idealist poetic which propagates a sovereign aesthetic sense of *Zärtlichkeit* (tenderness) and suggests an intellectual experience (rather than intuition) of the ultimately groundless shape of human life in an aesthetic of "tenderness" which appears to be subject to the corporeal conditions of human existence before being manifested in the transcendental realm of human consciousness.

In the last productive phase of Hölderlin's life (since 1802), he wrote a series of texts, in which he developed the basic ideas of a fundamentally new kind of poetological thought (particularly in his letters to Casimir Ulrich Böhlendorff and his commentaries on Sophocles). These ideas focused on art's and poetry's capacity for a form of genuine corporeal-aesthetic reflection, rather than the transcendental-intellectual reflection of the philosophical tradition. I will be primarily concentrating on the poetological content of the two letters to Böhlendorff and on the central role played by the concept of "Zärtlichkeit" or "tenderness," which he develops in those letters. When writing to Böhlendorff, Hölderlin was on the cusp of a period of descending into silence, which preceded his final mental breakdown in 1806. The letters he wrote are a condensed demonstration of the immense intellectual intensity of his literary and philosophical pursuits at that time, during which he also produced his great "patriotic" hymns, as well as multiple poetic experiments and his Sophocles translations and commentaries.

The letters have two main, significant features; the first is that they resonate with the refined skill of a sophisticated literary culture of letter writing and the idealised enthusiasm of a cult of platonic, philosophical friendship, emphasizing that to artists "the spirit among friends, the evocation of thought in conversation and letters is necessary."

The second is that the letters are also a stark expression of existential sorrow and a fear of impending isolation, which continuously discourages the idealistic gestures of brotherly love.

Both of these elements, the philosophical idea of love along with the personal, basic sorrow, influence poetological discourse in the letters.

The first letter, written on 4th December, 1801, is mainly about the differences between the "national" characteristics of Greek and German poetry, comparing the "beautiful passion" of the Greeks with the "junoesque austerity" of the Germans and noting that these opposing ideas complement each other almost erotically. These reflections lead to the following observations:

> I have laboured long over this and know by now that, with the exception of what must be the highest for the Greeks and for us—namely, the living relationship and destiny—we must not share anything identical with them. (Pfau 1988, p. 150).

> (Ich habe lange daran laborirt und weiß nun dass außer dem, was bei den Griechen und uns das höchste seyn muß, nemlich dem lebendigen Verhältniß und Geschik, wir nicht wohl etwas gleich mit ihnen haben dürfen.) (StA 6,1, p. 425 f., Brief Nr. 236, Z. 32–39).

The second letter, which was probably written in November 1802, continues this discussion on the idea of the "national" (= German "nationell" as opposed to "national"), however, this time with a new twist and an expanded spectrum of meaning, Hölderlin is not only using "national" in the sense of "patriotic," but also in the sense of "original," based on the etymological connotations of the Latin root, *nasci*, a verb which means 'to be born'. In the second last paragraph, he clearly expresses his hope that German poetry might have a new "beginning" based on its own "national" characteristics; here, this reference to the first letter is associated with a very concrete, corporeal perception of 'birth' and 'child-bearing', which in turn accounts for the sensuously emphasised ideas elaborated throughout the letter, on a body-centred, rather than mind-centred form of awareness. In the "athleticism of the southern peoples," in the exposed nature of their "bodies" and the "virtuosity" of a "sense of death" produced by the body, Hölderlin means to identify the "real essence" of the Greeks, that is, their national characteristics, and their artistic "popularity" (indicating here a national character rather than a state of popular/common appreciation). It is this virtuosity, stemming from an embodied form of perception, which is the source of their "power of reflection," namely, their particular ability to "attract alien natures and impart something of themselves to them":

> And this gave them their peculiar individuality, which is manifest in live insofar as the highest understanding, for the Greeks, was power of reflection and we can grasp this when we understand the heroic body of the Greeks. Their power of reflection is tenderness like our popularity. (Hölderlin 1996, p. 224f.).
>
> (Darum haben sie ihr Eigentümlichindividuelles, das lebendig erscheint, so fern der höchste Verstand im griechischen Sinne Reflexionskraft ist, und diß wird uns begreiflich, wenn wir den heroischen Körper der Griechen begreifen; sie ist Zärtlichkeit, wie unsere Popularität.) (StA 6,1, p. 432, Brief Nr. 240, Z. 23–27).

In this way, the concept which Hölderlin had identified as the "peculiar individuality" of Greek "rationality" (*Verstand*), that is, a body-centred power of reflection which expresses itself corporeally rather than intellectually, is now associated with the German "popularity": the two concepts are linked though by the "tenderness" of their power of reflection. This is surprising at first, but within the next paragraph it becomes clear that insofar as the "tenderly" erotic power of reflection does not just define but also simultaneously transcend the corporeality of the Greek understanding, it contains recognisable elements of that which is "highest in art," and which does therefore not appear to be restricted to any "national" characteristic.

Tenderness is a form of communication and reflection that is dominated by the sensuous-erotic; it does not take place between the subject and object in the intelligible mode of cognitive appropriation, but rather undermines the cognitive dichotomy of subject and object, self and the other, by way of a tactile, bodily convergence. It conveys a presence of the Other, qua Eros, that is paradox, as a presence that is essentially *not* at our intellectual disposal, neither epistemologically nor ontologically, but at the same time heightens our corporeal awareness.[1]

---

[1] Cf. Emmanuel Levinas on the philosophical discourse of the erotic since Plato, and on the phenomenology of Eros as a form of communication with the Other in its Otherness, prior to

The paradoxality of the phenomenology of the Other (with *otherness* being precisely that which fails to manifest itself to the subject of the phenomenological reflection) thus converges with the categorical impossibility of a phenomenology of the body (as a presence that ultimately escapes intelligible conceptualisation). Both become real though in the experience of *touch*, instigating an awareness of tender communion with the other.

"Tenderness" as a fundamentally aesthetic form of reflection is Hölderlin's answer to both of these trans-intelligible paradoxes. Tenderness is realised in acts of mere *touch*, generating, in Jean-Luc Nancy's approach to "Hyperion's Joy," a sense of "ipseity" which only "consists in *not possessing* the Self of subjectivity, and in *not being* the sign of its own sense" but in "the very ex-position of this body. This joy is birth, is coming into presence, outside of sense, in the place of sense, taking the place of sense, and making a place for sense" (Nancy 1993, pp. 203–204; emphases mine).

This suggests that the transcendental intentionality of art, in its most idealistic sense, is completely reversed for Hölderlin: its aim is no longer to idealise an unstable phenomenon so as to produce the fixed form of a conceptually recognisable idea, but rather conversely to "phenomenonalise" all transcendental forms, concepts and ideas, making them into their own fully sovereign, aesthetic "sign" language, produced by and articulated through the body as the agent of writing.

This language of art is capable of expressing "alles Ernstlichgemeinte"[2] (not just rational concepts) in a still and self-contained way,[3] without needing to refer to transcendentally preconfigured (metaphysical) forms of meaning. It is only in

---

all intelligible acts of self-appropriation. See Levinas 1989, pp. 59–60; also Levinas 1963. Jennifer Gosetti-Ferencei has noted the "downfall of the subject" in Hölderlin's late poetological writings: "For Hölderlin, poetic language admits the radical interdependence of self upon its other that grounds all language. Poetry, rather than suppressing this dependence, brings it into language in form. [...] The problem of opposition between self and other, subject and object, is treated in tragedy, wherein Hölderlin finds that the hubris of identification with the "other" in the realm of language provokes the downfall of the subject" (Gosetti-Ferencei 2004, p. 221). Cp. also James Luchte, who considers Hölderlin as "credited with the critical philosophical move that gave rise to the possibility of an Absolute that did *not* reside in the subject, as with Fichte, nor in the object, as with the Platonic rationalists, but as an Absolute, in which are immersed 'subject' and 'object'." (Luchte 2016, p. 10). Apparently, Luchte's "Absolute" is precisely what escapes philosophical categorisation and provokes poetic figuration.

2 "all that is meant seriously." All translations without bibliographical reference are by Máiréad Jones.

3 "[...] die auch in der höchsten Bewegung und Phänomenalisierung der Begriffe und alles Ernstlichgemeinten dennoch alles stehend und für sich selbst erhält" (StA 6,1, pp. 432–433, Brief Nr. 240, Z. 30–32).

this sense that art and poetry can be understood as "the highest kind of sign" ("die höchste Art des Zeichens") (StA 6,1, p. 433, Brief Nr. 240, Z. 32).

There is a line in the manuscript of the hymn *Mnemosyne* which can be read as an explanation of this part of the letter: "A sign are we, without meaning [...] and have nearly lost our language in foreign lands." (Hölderlin 1984, p. 117) ("Ein Zeichen sind wir, deutungslos [...] und haben fast / Die Sprache in der Fremde verloren.") (StA 2,1, p. 195). The hymn mourns the death of Mnemosyne, the mythical goddess of memory, but not the total loss of language, which, as a poetic "sign," can apparently withstand the loss of all possible meaning while re-enacting its own intrinsic power of signification from its deserted remains.[4] A corresponding thought we find in the latest drafts for the hymn *Der Einzige*, written at about the same time (1803). Here it is merely "a trace though of a word" ("eine Spur doch eines Wortes") which remains as the sole source of inspiration for the writing of the poet in a world deserted of humane meaning:

> Always, indeed, the world jubilates to escape
> From this earth, in order to
> Expose her—where humanity does not contain her. But always remains a trace
> Though of a word—captured by man. The place, however, was
> The desert. (Translation mine).
>
> (Nemlich immer jauchzet die Welt
> Hinweg von dieser Erde, daß sie die
> Entblößet; wo das Menschliche sie nicht hält. Es bleibet aber eine Spur
> Doch eines Wortes; die ein Mann erhaschet. Der Ort war aber
> Die Wüste.) (StA 2,1, p. 163, Z. 71–75).

We can read this note about "a trace though of a word" ("Spur doch eines Wortes") as an elaboration on the poetological statement in *Mnemosyne:* "A sign are we, without meaning" ("Ein Zeichen sind wir, deutungslos")—as the condition of an *almost* lost linguistic capability. What remains is just a *trace* of language, a mere semiotic sediment, a sign without given reference that nevertheless suggests a human presence initiating a new semiotic process of signification, and a new life, a new lived world of existential (rather than transcendental) meaning which emerges from the desertification of the old one—without depending on a system or realm of philosophically, transcendentally or mythically authorised significates.

This inversion of the transcendental argument where a system of trans-empirical concepts motivates and critically informs the linguistic discourse (be it

---

4 Cf. author's interpretation of the hymn in Hofmann 1996, pp. 231–255.

philosophical or aesthetic) into a poetic statement where a singular and rudimentary semiotic entity ("trace though of a word") becomes the source of a world of existential meaning points at what Walter Benjamin called in his essay on *The Task of the Translator* the core of "pure language:"

> And that which seeks to represent, indeed to produce, itself in the evolving of languages is that very nucleus of the pure language. (Benjamin 1996, p. 261).

> (Und was im Werden der Sprachen sich darzustellen, ja herzustellen sucht, das ist jener Kern der reinen Sprache selbst.) (Benjamin s. a., par. 12).

To free this core of pure language from the alienating effects of all trans-linguistically imposed significates is for Benjamin the true task of the translator—and it does not surprise us that he suggests Hölderlin's *Sophokles*-translations as a model for this radicalised translation process which is meant to establish a language, beyond regular communication ("Mitteilung") and representation ("Ausdruck") functions, that brings to bearing solely its own originally signifying potencies:

> [...] to turn the symbolizing into the symbolized itself, to regain pure language fully formed from the linguistic flux, is the tremendous and only capacity of translation. In this pure language—which no longer means or expresses anything but is, as expressionless and creative Word, that which is meant in all languages—all information, all sense, and all intention finally encounter a stratum in which they are destined to be extinguished. (Benjamin 1996, p. 261).

> ([...] das Symbolisierende zum Symbolisierten selbst zu machen, die reine Sprache gestaltet der Sprachbewegung zurückzugewinnen, ist das gewaltige und einzige Vermögen der Übersetzung. In dieser reinen Sprache, die nichts mehr meint und nichts mehr ausdrückt, sondern als ausdrucksloses und schöpferisches Wort das in allen Sprachen Gemeinte ist, trifft endlich alle Mitteilung, aller Sinn und alle Intention auf eine Schicht, in der sie zu erlöschen bestimmt sind.) (Benjamin s. a., par. 12).

Hölderlin's language, the language of the translator as of the poet of "pure language," suggests a poetology which pays tribute to the abysmal, fragile nature of all assumed meaning that is not language-immanent:

> Hölderlin's translations are prototypes of their form; they are to even the most perfect renderings of their texts as a prototype is to a model [...] Hölderlin's translations from Sophocles were his last work; in them meaning plunges from abyss to abyss until it threatens to become lost in the bottomless depths of language. There is, however, a stop. It is vouchsafed in Holy Writ alone, in which meaning has ceased to be the watershed for the flow of language and the flow of revelation. Where the literal quality of the text takes part directly, without any mediating sense, in true language, [...] this text is unconditionally translatable. (Benjamin 1996, p. 262).

> (Hölderlins Übersetzungen sind Urbilder ihrer Form; sie verhalten sich auch zu den vollkommensten Übertragungen ihrer Texte als das Urbild zum Vorbild [...] Die Sophokles-Übersetzungen waren Hölderlins letztes Werk. In ihnen stürzt der Sinn von Abgrund zu Abgrund, bis er droht in bodenlosen Sprachtiefen sich zu verlieren. Aber es gibt ein Halten. Es gewährt es jedoch kein Text außer dem heiligen, in dem der Sinn aufgehört hat, die Wasserscheide für die strömende Sprache und die strömende Offenbarung zu sein. Wo der Text unmittelbar, ohne vermittelnden Sinn, in seiner Wörtlichkeit der wahren Sprache [...] angehört, ist er übersetzbar schlechthin.) (Benjamin s. a. par., 13).

These poetological traces become more legible in Hölderlin's Böhlendorff-letters by the interplay between two factors, the philosophically erotic enthusiasm, or rather the intensely felt corporeality of aesthetic reflection and the residual language, stripped of all meaning, which, through the virtuosity of the poetic sign, is able to draw near to the invasion of meaninglessness and loss of the world that Hölderlin calls the "sense of death."

It appears to me that the aesthetic course which Hölderlin is following here runs more radically than "overcoming classicism," as argued by Peter Szondi (Szondi 1970). The ultimate end of this course is not merely to overcome the archetypical, classicist strictness of form, but rather to overcome the idealistic conception of humanity as such in a fundamental way,[5] and then to turn it upside down, not as Karl Marx would have, on the material basis of social economics, but in the materiality of the limited, fragile, mortal body—in the human condition of an elemental sense of life or even of death. Such sense of life and death can only be properly represented or reflected upon from an *aesthetic* perspective, not through an ethical recourse to the metaphysical forms of transcendental subjectivity.

It is very tempting to interpret Hölderlin's correspondence with Böhlendorff as a belated approach to actualise his project of "philosophical letters," which he had initially planned in 1796 after his stay in Jena, but never really carried out. The long-term consequences of the sense of alienation and philosophical radicalisation which was taking hold of him at that time, are almost never taken into consideration. In a letter to his fellow Swabian and Tübingen alumnus, Immanuel Niethammer, who was a philosophy lecturer in Jena at the time, Hölderlin sets out the goal of the project as follows:

> I want to use the philosophical letters to find the principle, which will explain to me the separations in which we think and exist, but which is also capable of eliminating this conflict [...] between the subject and the object, between our Self and the world, even between

---

5 Regarding Hölderlin's position within the discourse of idealism cf. the comprehensive analyses, documents and commentaries by Jamme und Völkel 2003.

reason and revelation—theoretically, from an intellectual point of view, without needing to resort to our practical reason. (Trans. Mairéad Jones).

(In den philosophischen Briefen will ich das Prinzip finden, das mir die Trennungen, in denen wir denken und existiren, erklärt, das aber auch vermögend ist, den Widerstreit verschwinden zu machen [...] zwischen dem Subject und dem Object, zwischen unserem Selbst und der Welt, ja auch zwischen Vernunft und Offenbarung – theoretisch, in intellectualer Anschauung, ohne daß unsere praktische Vernunft zu Hilfe kommen müßte.) (StA 6,1, p. 203, Brief Nr. 117, Z. 29–35).

The primacy which Hölderlin here confers to theoretical reason over practical reason might be astonishing at first, as it contradicts both the structures of Kantian philosophy, and his own subsequent corporeal turn towards "tenderness" as the supreme form of artistic reflection. However, Hölderlin clears up this confusion in the very next sentence, in which he explains that, just like Schiller, he is focusing on the "aesthetic sense" in its immanent logic, in order to overcome the aporetic state of human nature between subjective freedom and objective necessity—however, he does so much more emphatically than Schiller, whose theory of play ensues the degrading of the aesthetic essence of art for its playfulness and illusory nature, "as though no one took it seriously" (StA 6,1, p. 305, Brief Nr. 172, Z. 124) until in the end, it is viewed as being a mere servant of morality.[6] Consequently, Hölderlin establishes the primacy of theoretical reason, because, through its sensuous perceptivity and embeddedness in corporeal empiricism, theoretical reason gives the "aesthetic sense" of art, which should be taken "seriously," for the first time full admittance into the world of sensuously lived, tangible experience. With Hölderlin's interpretation of an independent "aesthetic sense" as *reason of art*, Kant's thought (in his *Critique of Judgement*) about the possibility of "aesthetic ideas"[7] acquires a new and radically aestheticised philosophical virulence. In comparison, the discourse of *practical reason*, as a purely

---

[6] In the letter to his brother from 1. Januar 1799 his complaints about Schiller's aesthetic theory are most explicit and without restraint: "[...] und es wäre zu wünschen, dass der gränzenlose Misverstand einmal aufhörte, womit womit die Kunst, und besonders die Poësie [...] herabgewürdigt wird. Man hat schon so viel gesagt über den Einfluß der schönen Künste auf die Bildung des Menschen, aber es kam immer heraus, als wär' es keinem Ernst damit [...]; man nahm sie für Spiel, weil sie in der bescheidenen Gestalt des Spiels erscheint, und so konnte sich auch vernünftiger weise keine andere Wirkung von ihr ergeben, als die des Spiels, nemlich Zerstreuung, beinahe das Gegenteil von dem, was sie wirket, wo sie in ihrer wahren Natur vorhanden ist." (StA 6,1, p. 305, Brief Nr. 172, Z. 119–133).

[7] Cp. Chaouli 2011.

intellectual possibility of ideas, seems like a mere abstraction.[8] When Hölderlin finally admits in his letter to Niethammer, that he would like to call his philosophical letters, "New letters on the aesthetic education of man" ("Neue Briefe über die ästhetische Erziehung des Menschen") (StA 6,1, p. 203, Brief Nr. 117, Z. 37), it becomes entirely clear who the real opponent is: Schiller, the philosopher on whose theories Hölderlin had been doggedly working since his youth, the intellectual father figure who inspired and encouraged Hölderlin and from whom he was now emancipating himself. Yet where did this emancipation lead?

Unlike Schiller, Hölderlin could not simply view art as a means for transforming human education from a state of physical necessity to a state of moral freedom. However, neither did he pursue the dialectical route of his fellow student at Tübingen, Hegel, who based his theories on the notion of synthesis (of ideas and experiences in the historicity of the "Geist"), that is, on the principal of the sublation of all opposing ideas of freedom and sensuous conditions in the historical sequence of artistic phenomena. Hölderlin's reflections were in no way congruent with the metaphysical regime of a practical idea, which dictates the final historical or philosophical purpose of sensuous art—neither did he attempt an intellectual synthesis of sensuousness and morality. He does not *synthesise*, but rather further accentuates the Kantian antinomies by reversing their order. He directs his thought to the reflexive dynamic of the emergence of living art as something more ephemeral in the corporeality of artistic life itself—in the mode of "tenderness"—rather than the authorisation of living art through a lasting idea. The philosophical hierarchies of the idealistic conception of humanity reverse themselves in the name of an aesthetically emancipated art and poetry: the intellectual no longer takes precedence over the sensuous, and the logical apriority of the transcendental idea over the empirical, individual instance becomes invalid. The principle upon which this reversal is based is captured in a tiny snippet of philosophical thought which Hölderlin wrote at around the same time as the second letter to Böhlendorff in the so-called Homburg Folio, almost as though it were a caption for the hymn fragment that follows: "The apriority of the individual over the whole" ("Die Apriorität des Individuellen über das Ganze") (Uffhausen 1989, p. 146).[9]

Immediately below this note is a hymn fragment whose opening verses have been reconstructed as follows by Friedrich Beißner:

---

[8] Michel Chaouli parallels practical (philosophical) and aesthetic (artistic) ideas in an equation of "inadequacy": "In the one, reason generates representations – God, immortality – with which the imagination fails to keep up; in the other, the imagination generates representations that outstrip concepts." (Chaouli 2011, p. 57).
[9] Cf. the analysis of Burdorf 1993.

> We set out from the abyss / And proceeded like the lion, / Vexed with doubt, / Since men sense more / In the scorch / Of deserts, / Drunk with light, and the spirit of animals / Rests with them. But soon, like a dog in hot weather, / My voice shall amble through alleys of gardens / In which people live / In France. / The Creator. / But Frankfurt, to speak of man / By nature's stamp upon / The human shape, is the navel / Of this earth, [...]. (Hölderlin 1984, p. 199)

> (Vom Abgrund nemlich haben
> Wir angefangen und gegangen
> Dem Leuen gleich, in Zweifel und Ärgerniß,
> Denn sinnlicher sind Menschen
> In dem Brand
> Der Wüste
> Lichttrunken und der Thiergeist ruhet
> Mit ihnen. Bald aber wird, wie ein Hund, umgehn
> In der Hizze meine Stimme auf den Gassen der Gärten
> In denen wohnen Menschen
> In Frankreich
> Der Schöpfer
> Frankfurt aber, nach der Gestalt, die
> Abdruk ist der Natur zu reden
> Des Menschen nemlich, ist der Nabel
> Dieser Erde, [...]) (StA 2,1, p. 250).

I want to point out here, that in this fragment, which Hölderlin later gave the caption, "the apriority of the individual over the whole," the same themes and conceptualisations are in question as in the letters to Böhlendorff (and in his other poetological writings of the time, for example, his commentaries on Sophocles): the *Abgründigkeit*, hardship and necessity of "beginning" for a new kind of poetry, the meaning that the "national" held for the "voice" of the poet in this context (both in the sense of the 'patriotic' as well as the 'original'), the "spirit of animals" as the paragon of all sensuous-corporeal faculties of the soul and thus also the embodiedness of this voice (and its national character; here language qua voice means the *resonance effect of the body* which follows the closeness of touch rather than the *inscription in the body* which represents an act of surrender and appropriation), as well as the sensuousness of the southern sunlight, the bodily sensation of heat in which the voice moves and the variety of nature's national characteristics (in Germany and southern France) which affect the bodily aspects of the voice (where bodies are the resonance chamber of the landscape). Lastly, there is also a reference to Susette Gontard, that "figure" who, for Hölderlin, represents "nature's stamp upon the human shape." She lived in Frankfurt, the "navel of this earth," and she almost appears to be the source of that tenderness which is the focus of Hölderlin's aesthetic reflection in the letters to Böhlendorff: this tenderness, we remember, is a primary characteristic of "that which is highest in art" and a trait which is shared by the Greeks and the Germans.

This seems to prove that towards the end of Hölderlin's poetological work, he was ready to take a radical step and begin the search for the conditions of possibility for aesthetic reflection and artistic production in the most radical sense, not in the transcendental condition of an intelligible consciousness, but rather in the sensory or even physiological conditions of individual corporeality as a source of artistic originality. He wished to explore the limitations of the human condition, including its mortality and the perceived recognition of that mortality and the fragility of the body, that is, the real need for an experience of being. So, the corporeality of Hölderlin's poetic drive, his "tenderness," does not lead to a synthesis of true ideas and absolute knowledge, but to the contingency of an, as it were, touch-based perception, and to the topographic togetherness of the different forms of the "national" at the site of the poetic, creating a sense of the "human" as a fragile, scintillating whole without identity.

The second letter to Böhlendorff relates to this togetherness somewhat enigmatically as "the gathering of different characteristics of Nature in one location, so that all sacred places of the earth are together around one place, [...]" (Trans. Michael Shields) ("das Zusammentreffen in einer Gegend von verschiedenen Charakteren der Natur, daß alle heiligen Orte der Erde zusammen sind um einen Ort, [...]") (StA 6,1, p. 433, Z. 42 ff.).

This place is the topography of the poem. The previously quoted hymn fragment, *Vom Abgrund nemlich*, makes this point with even greater emphasis:

Here I am everything / At once. (Hölderlin 1984, p. 199).

(Allda bin ich / Alles miteinander.) (StA 2,1, p. 250).

As a symptom of the human condition in all its individuality, fragility and mortality, exposed to nature and history, the body in its capacity of "tenderness" becomes the sensorium, the subject and the agent of aesthetic reflection, which presents society with a, so to speak, poetic "myth" as a basis for linguistic survival (but not as an interpretative meta-narrative). In poetological terms, this marks the end of the epoch of idealism and the beginning of the period previously described by Gisela Dischner as the "Hölderlin-Linie der Moderne," which has lasted to this day, from Nietzsche to Rilke, Celan, Bachmann and beyond.

Bibliography

Benjamin, Walter (s. a.): "Illuminationen." In: *Ausgewählte Schriften 1 (1920–1940)*. Textlog.de; Historische Texte & Wörterbücher. http://www.textlog.de/benjamin-illumina tionen.html; 01/01/2018.
Benjamin, Walter (1996): *Selected Writings*. Vol. 1. Eds. Bullock, Marcus Paul / Smith, Gary. Cambridge, MA: Harvard University Press.
Burdorf, Dieter (1993): *Hölderlins späte Gedichtfragmente: "Unendlicher Deutung voll."* Stuttgart Weimar: J. B. Metzler.
Chaouli, Michel (2011): "A Surfeit in Thinking. Kant's aesthetic ideas." In: *The Yearbook of Comparative Literature 57: Poetic Thinking*, pp. 55–77.
Dischner, Gisela (1995): *… bald sind wir aber Gesang: Zur Hölderlin-Linie der Moderne.* Bielefeld: Aisthesis.
Gosetti-Ferencei, Jennifer Anna (2004): *Heidegger, Hölderlin, and the Subject of Poetic Language: Toward a New Poetics of Dasein*. New York, NY: Fordham University Press.
Hölderlin, Friedrich (1943–1985): *Sämtliche Werke*. 15 Bde. [Große Stuttgarter Ausgabe]. Ed. Beißner, Friedrich. Stuttgart: W. Kohlhammer Verlag.
Hölderlin, Friedrich (1984): *Hymns and Fragments*. Trans. and introduced by Sieburth, Richard. Princeton, NJ: Princeton University Press.
Hölderlin, Friedrich (1996): "Letter to Bohlendorff." In: Benjamin, Walter: *Selected Writings*. Vol. 3. Trans. Eiland, Howard. Eds. Bullock, Marcus Paul / Jennings, Michael William / Eiland, Howard / Smith, Gary. Cambridge, MA: Harvard University Press.
Hofmann, Gert (1996): *Dionysos Archemythos. Hölderlins transzendentale Poiesis*. Tübingen and Basel: A. Francke Verlag.
Jamme, Christoph / Völkel, Frank (2003): *Hölderlin und der deutsche Idealismus*. 4 vols. Stuttgart / Bad Cannstatt: Frommann-Holzboog Verlag.
Levinas, Emmanuel (1963): *Die Spur des Anderen*. Freiburg, Br.: Alber.
Levinas, Emmanuel (1989): *Die Zeit und der Andere*. 2nd ed. Hamburg: Meiner.
Luchte, James (2016): *Mortal Thought. Hölderlin and Philosophy*. London, Oxford, New York: Bloomsbury.
Nancy, Jean-Luc (1993): *The Birth to Presence*. Trans. Holmes, Brian et al. Redwood City, CA: Stanford University Press.
Pfau, Thomas (Ed.) (1988): *Friedrich Hölderlin: Essays and Letters on Theory*. New York, NY: SUNY Press.
Szondi, Peter (1970): "Überwindung des Klassizismus. Der Brief an Böhlendorff vom 4. Dezember 1801." In: *Hölderlin-Studien. Mit einem Traktat über philologische Erkenntnis*. Frankfurt a. M.: Suhrkamp, pp. 95–118.
Uffhausen, Dietrich (1989) (Ed.): *Friedrich Hölderlin: "Bevestigter Gesang." Die neu zu entdeckende hymnische Spätdichtung bis 1806*. Stuttgart: J. B. Metzler.

Abbreviations

StA = Hölderlin, Friedrich (1943–1985): *Sämtliche Werke*. 15 Bde. [Große Stuttgarter Ausgabe]. Ed. Beißner, Friedrich. Stuttgart: W. Kohlhammer Verlag.

Ansgar Mohnkern
Grund/Abgrund.
On Kant and Hölderlin

Abstract: German Idealism started, surprisingly, not with the search for ideas. Rather, it began with the search for ground. Kant's *Kritik der reinen Vernunft* (1781/87), while announcing the program of establishing a philosophy based on "the secure course of a science," was literally entangled in a metaphorical field around "well-groundedness" on which such course would have to be established. Kant himself, notably a philosopher of "Grundlegung," "Grundsätze," and "Anfangsgründe" and other derivatives of "ground" (*Grund*), found it necessary to mark the use of a philosophical terminology built around "ground" explicitly as "symbolic" (*Kritik der Urteilskraft*), but did not entirely resolve the remaining problems around such a "ground" established through a metaphorical operation.

The rhetoric of "groundedness" however will take new forms in Kant's aftermath. Most notably, in Hölderlin's poetry, the language of "ground" silently retreats, even though particularly Hölderlin's late poetry often revolves around aspects that could be brought together with what Kant called "the secure course": wandering, moving, or—in Hölderlin's language—dwelling ("wandeln"). The following article, apart from offering a reading of Hölderlin's elegy *Menons Klagen um Diotima* (1802/03), examines Hölderlin's poetic version of breaking a fundamental promise of German Idealism, the establishment of a fundament itself, by turning from a language of "ground" (Grund) towards a language of abyss and "chasm" (Abgrund).

1

It can perhaps be considered one of the subtle ironies about what used to be called "German Idealism" that those very "twenty-five years of philosophy" (Förster 2012) after the publication of the first edition of Kant's *Kritik der reinen Vernunft* (1781) did not, in fact, begin with the search for ideas. For, if the *Kritik der reinen Vernunft* is to be considered the inauguration of a constellation of thinking traditionally reconstructed within the framework of a narrative "From Kant to Hegel," it is nonetheless already surprisingly apparent from the preface of the second edition of Kant's first *Kritik* (1787) that at least Kant's version of so-called Idealism identifies its very beginning in stunningly material fashion. Rather than

https://doi.org/10.1515/9783110586602-014

proclaiming an idealist foundation, its initial gesture lies in establishing a philosophy that is based on what Kant famously calls "the secure course of a science" (Kant 1998, p. 106): "der sichere Gang einer Wissenschaft." The particular diction is worth noting. It is well-known by now that it is not only the conceptual reconstruction of Kant's philosophy as a system of thought that leads to fertile ground in the attempt to understand the dimension of his intervention in what might be called the history of ideas, but also the (at least) symptomatic effects of Kant's language.[1] This said, such "sicherer Gang einer Wissenschaft" has often become a key metaphor with which many introductions to the work of Kant have attempted to illustrate Kant's transcendental project of distinguishing legitimate knowledge, within the boundaries of a critique of reason, from all other temptations of reason and its desire to produce knowledge beyond the capacities of human understanding; it remains a mystery why a literal reading of the metaphorical order of Kant's language has yet to be expounded. For, if philosophical metaphysics, as promised in the very preface of the second edition, is to be liberated from "merely groping about" ("bloßes Herumtappen") (Kant 1998, p. 106) in a realm of what Kant names "speculation" (Kant 1998, p. 118), then the literal implications of Kant's language suggest that such a "Gang" not only corresponds to someone who walks in it but also, speaking in legal terminology, serves as a *locus delicti* where it could literally take place. With regard to the "secure course of a science," Kant, in his second preface from 1787, therefore elaborates further:

> Thus even if it cannot be all that difficult to leave to posterity the legacy of a systemic metaphysics, constructed according to the critique of pure reason, this is still a gift deserving of no small respect; to see this, we need merely to compare the culture of reason that is set on the course of a secure science with reason's unfounded groping and frivolous wandering about without critique (grundloses Tappen und leichtsinniges Herumstreifen [...] ohne Kritik), or to consider how much better young people hungry for knowledge might spend their time than in the usual dogmatism that gives so early and so much encouragement to their complacent quibbling (bequem vernünfteln) about things they do not understand, and things into which neither they nor anyone else in the world will ever have any insight, or even encourages them to launch on the invention of new thoughts and opinions, and thus to neglect to learn the well-grounded sciences (gründliche Wissenschaft). (Kant 1998, p. 117).

The danger of "groping about" ("Tappen") is its groundless ("grundlos") nature, and *ex negativo* it becomes apparent that a crucial aspect of its opposite, the "secure course," is thus to be found in the fact that it takes place on *Grund*, i.e. on the foundation of a supposedly stable ground. As often in the realm of meta-

---

[1] Particularly noteworthy for illustrating the nuances of Kant's language is Goetschel 1990.

phors, the metaphorical domain itself—in this case a field being opened by Kant's euphoric understanding of "sicherer Gang"—here too proliferates. And if metaphors have, as famously pointed out by Hans Blumenberg, the potential of becoming "foundational elements (Grundbestände) of philosophical language" (Blumenberg 2010, p. 3) themselves, then it appears that they do so in the case of a "secure course" in its most literal way. Doubtlessly, more is at stake for Kant than simply moving smoothly through the field of metaphysics. For, if this "Gang" is posited as an answer to the question of whether or not such *Grund* can be found as a foundation for the discipline of philosophical metaphysics, then on such *Grund* hinges not only the decisive proposition asserting whether or not knowledge about—most generally speaking—the world can be established, but also whether or not this proposition can literally be established on legitimate grounds.

This, then, also hints at an answer to the question of why only "as a fundamental science (Grundwissenschaft), metaphysics is also bound to achieve this completeness" (Kant 1998, p. 114), a completeness that it desperately needs as a discipline in order to fulfil the criteria for being legitimate. For metaphysics must function as a "fundamental science" in a two-fold manner: on the one hand, the discipline forms, as *prima philosophia*, a base, a ground, and a foundation for all other possible "Wissenschaften," while on the other hand such metaphysics is a "Wissenschaft" about the formation of this very ground itself. Its critique is therefore to be thought of as a critique of "principles (Prinzipien)" (Kant 1998, p. 114) which are needed to safeguard the status of philosophy as a system based on general principles, while faced with specific "limitations" (Kant 1998, p. 114) forcing metaphysics to take on a continuous struggle to justify the very principles that it hopes to establish. Analogous to the fate of a "secure course," then, these principles must arrive as precisely "secure principles" (Kant 1998, p. 119) if they are to be used legitimately.

However, the philosophical nomenclature of "principles" also latently indicates a fate in which, *in nuce*, might be contained not only the fate of philosophical language, but also the project of turning metaphysics into a legitimate "Wissenschaft" itself. Already foreshadowing the hegemony of the modern paradigm according to which all knowledge can only be legitimate insofar as it carries the nature of being a "science," the secureness of metaphysical principles must be identified with the secureness of their foundation, i.e. of *Grund*. However, inasmuch as those "Prinzipien" also echo, in their essence, the Latin *principia*, which, in philosophical language until the 18th century, indicated nothing else but what in German philosophy was from then on to be called a *Grundsatz* or even a *Grund* itself, Kant's language of "principles" implicitly reflects a far-reaching dilemma. This dilemma—perhaps the dilemma of all modern philosophy in general—is distilled in the question: How can a principle be "secure" if it can only be secured on the foundation of a *Grund*, while at the same time—as a *Grund* itself—it is in need of being "secure"? In other words, this constellation leads to the question: How can a ground 'ground' itself?

While engaged in a literal search for groundedness, Kant's language now washes several derivatives of such *Grund* ashore. There are, as shown, "Grund" and "Gründe" themselves, but also "Grundsätze" as well as a famous *Grundlegung zur Metaphysik der Sitten*, which demonstrates the relevance of thinking and writing within a framework drawn from a nomenclature of "Grund." As for the *Kritik der reinen Vernunft*, the system as a whole is built within a narrative framework that deliberately starts out with a reference to experience ("Erfahrung")[2] and objects ("Gegenstände"), which are themselves referred to in the language of "foundational material" ("Grundstoffe") (Kant 1998, p. 136). It is this very relation to the experienced object as a "Grundstoff" that thus remains, throughout the whole argumentation of the *Kritik der reinen Vernunft*, the critical touchstone dividing the objects about which legitimate knowledge can be acquired from those three famous transcendental "ideas" which Kant describes;[3] each of them is a "concept made up of notions, which goes beyond the possibility of experience" (Kant 1998, p. 399). These are the immortality of the soul, freedom, and finally God as the "ideal of pure reason" (Kant 1998, p. 551) itself.

Written thus in the "spirit of well-groundedness" ("Geist der Gründlichkeit") (Kant 1998, p. 123), Kant's *Kritik der reinen Vernunft* implicitly contributes to a discourse of legitimacy that can only be debated metaphorically, while essentially attempting to carve out the limitations of human cognition as a whole. No matter whether such legitimacy is a legitimacy of knowledge (such as in the *Kritik der reinen Vernunft*) or a legitimacy of ethics or even of law (such as in the *Grundlegung zur Metaphysik der Sitten*), the language of *Grund* refers, in its broadest sense, to the idea of a beginning, of an origin, of something that comes "first" in a chain of causalities as much as in a chain of arguments. Its status as such appears, however, ambiguously labile when its rhetorical status is taken into account: that is, as a "ground" on which a coherent system of cognition can be built or, more precisely, performed as a "secure course" only under the condition of becoming a metaphor. Some years after the *Kritik der reinen Vernunft*, Kant will therefore feel forced to acknowledge what could, consider-

---

[2] The first sentence of the introduction to the second edition reads famously: "There is no doubt whatever that all our cognition begins with experience […]." ("Daß alle unsere Erkenntnis mit der Erfahrung anfange, daran ist gar kein Zweifel.") (Kant 1998, p. 136).
[3] See the second part of the *Kritik*, the "transcendental dialectic."

ing the unstable nature of metaphors themselves, certainly be seen as an (if not *the*) Achilles' heel with regard to the problem of legitimacy in Kant's transcendental philosophy as a whole. In a well-known passage in §59 of the *Kritik der Urteilskraft* (1790) Kant eventually reflects on what he calls "symbolic hypotyposis" (Kant 2000, p. 226) by which is meant nothing other than metaphors. In order to illustrate what "is represented [...] symbolically" (Kant 2000, p. 222), Kant remarks:

> Examples are the words *ground* (Grund) (support, basis), *depend* (to be held from above), from which *flow* (instead of follow) *substance* (as Locke expresses it: the bearer of accidents), and innumerable other nonschematic but symbolic hypotyposes and expressions for concepts not by means of a direct intuition, but only in accordance with an analogy with it, i.e., the transportation of the reflection on one object of intuition to another, quite different concept (Übertragung der Reflexion über einen Gegenstand der Anschauung auf einen ganz andern Begriff), to which perhaps no intuition can ever directly correspond. (Kant 2000, p. 226–227).

In his *Poetics*, Aristotle has already constructed his definition of metaphor on the principle of just such an analogy. But what in the case of Aristotle was conceived as a replacement of one word by another "word that belongs to another thing" ("*onomatos allotriou epiphora*") (Aristotle 1995, p. 105), was for Kant rather thought as an operation wherein such a word becomes an "object of intuition" itself, and thus an essential part of that very experience on which all cognition and knowledge is literally grounded. In other words: speaking the language of *Grund* and *Gründlichkeit* invokes a concept "not by means of a direct intuition," i.e. by a substituting "concept, to which perhaps no intuition can ever directly correspond." If, then as in the case of *Grund*, this very *Grund* is to be defined as stable and solid, i.e. as something that, according to the systemic approach, itself necessitates a proper, direct intuition on which it can be founded, then the premise of §59 of the *Kritik der Urteilskraft* contests precisely that this "Grund" on which all "secure course of a science" must potentially take place is in fact no *Grund* at all. Thus the system must paradoxically reject the fundamental premise on which it is founded. It is only the "Übertragung," the "transportation of the reflection," but not the very "basis," not the foundation itself. For "Grund" turns out to be only a metaphorical placeholder for such a foundation of which the system finds itself so desperately in need: that is, if it wants to be legitimate on its own terms. Therefore "Grund," inasmuch as it has to be an object of direct intuition in order to guarantee solidity, fails to be such an object, and instead takes on qualities of those very speculative ideas of reason which Kant essentially dismissed of ever becoming objects of direct intuition and therefore of any possible cognition.

According to Habermas, Kant's achievement for modern philosophy was, among other things, the separation of the "spheres of knowing" from the "spheres of belief" (Habermas 1987, p. 19). It seems somewhat ironic, then, that an element of "faith" creeps into the foundation of Kant's "spheres of knowing;" for the essence of faith also contains an element of imagination, corresponding with an act of "taking something to be true" ("Fürwahrhalten") (Kant 1998, p. 684) which itself cannot be proven as true. The operative use of *Grund* as metaphor is precisely such an imaginative act.[4] Perhaps in no other case does such an imaginative constellation, hinting towards the sphere of "Einbildung," become as problematically obvious as in the case of Kant's discussion of "Vernunftglauben" as the only possible version of belief after all attempts at proving the existence of God have been shown to fail in the *Kritik der reinen Vernunft*. Perhaps no other piece of Kant's writing makes the intimate relationship between the idea of "Vernunftglauben" and an imaginative speech of "einbilden" more apparent than his short contribution to the so-called pantheisms controversy, his essay *Was heißt: sich im Denken orientieren?* (1786). Here, Kant defends Moses Mendelssohn's (and Lessing's) position against Jacobi's accusation that they were working essentially towards a form of atheism, a charge Jacobi makes by introducing Spinoza's thinking into the philosophical debate about the essence of God. Through the dilemma of having to safeguard the idea of a belief without the ability to prove that belief, in this case the existence of God, Kant develops, in accordance with the principles of the *Kritik der reinen Vernunft*, the idea of a "rational faith" ("Vernunftglauben") as a "holding true which is subjectively sufficient, but consciously regarded as objectively insufficient" (Kant 1996, p. 13). Considering the absence of such objective sufficiency, by which belief is carefully separated from the realm of knowledge, Kant must again search for a substitutive order which, in anticipation of the formulation in §59 of the *Kritik der Urteilskraft*, is found in a version of metaphorical order. Thus the essay opens programmatically with a reference to "bildliche Vorstellungen" ("image representations"):

---

4 In the chapter "on having opinions, knowing, and believing," the *Kritik der reinen Vernunft* states: "Since, however, even though we might not be able to undertake anything in relation to an object, and taking something to be true is therefore merely theoretical, in many cases we can still conceive (in Gedanken fassen) and imagine (einbilden) an undertaking for which we would suppose ourselves to have sufficient grounds (hinreichende Gründe) if there were a means for arriving at certainty about the matter; thus there is in merely theoretical judgments an *analogue* (Analogie) of practical judgments, where taking them to be true is aptly described by the word *belief* (Glauben), and which we can call *doctrinal beliefs*." (Kant 1998, p. 687).

> However exalted the application of our concepts, and however far up from sensibility we may abstract them, still they will always be appended to *image* representations (bildliche Vorstellungen), whose proper function is to make concepts, which are not otherwise derived from experience, serviceable for experiential use. (Kant 1996, p. 7).

As the essay explores what in the *Kritik der reinen Vernunft* was named "speculation," Kant makes apparent the way in which a metaphorical order of such "*image* representations" serves as a prosthetic in order to provide quasi-intuition where no actual intuition can be found as a base of epistemological proof. This approach was already indicated in the first *Kritik* when Kant spoke of God as the "transcendental ideal," understood as "the ground of the thorough-going determination that is necessarily encountered in everything existing" (Kant 1998, p. 556), but lacking the status of an object accessible to the apparatus of cognition. Such a transcendental ideal is thus also named an "original image (Urbild) (protoypon) of all things" (Kant 1998, p. 557). The metaphor now employed to serve as a guideline through the discussion of a "rational belief" is, in the essay from 1786, the metaphor of orientation, which Kant breaks down to its very literal meaning. This ironically happens in order to speak within the metaphorical order of the language of *Eigentlichkeit* (authenticity), for

> in the proper meaning (in der eigentlichen Bedeutung) of the word, to *orient* oneself means to use a given direction (*eine gegebene Weltgegend*) (when we divide the horizon into four of them) in order to find the others—literally, to find the *sunrise*. (Kant 1999, p. 8).

Opening the essay with a gesture that admits to speaking in the language of images, and thus indirect intuitions, therefore becomes somewhat ironically broken in the light of speaking within this very "symbolic" order a language of literalness, i.e. a language of "proper meaning," of "eigentliche Bedeutung." However, as soon as such literalness is supposedly established, Kant falls back onto the language that, a year later, in his preface to the second edition of the *Kritik der reinen Vernunft*, will serve as an explicit criterion for distinguishing legitimate knowledge from the illegitimate desire of reason to produce a literally groundless knowledge about ideas without proper intuition: the benchmark of *Grund*. In *Was heißt: sich im Denken orientieren?* Kant continues: "Thus even with all the objective data of the sky, I orient myself *geographically* only through a *subjective* ground of differentiation (durch einen *subjektiven* Unterscheidungsgrund)." (Kant 1999, p. 9). If, then, orientation serves as a metaphorical placeholder in order to speak about the issue of a "rational faith" ("Vernunftglauben"), then even within the context of such "rational faith" the matter of ground appears at the critical moment of defining an element on which the system of faith can be legitimately founded. Here, however, objective ground can be neither given nor found. So, Kant turns, in the embarrassment of potential groundlessness, to a subjective order of ground. In other words: ground fails to be ground in the sense of an objective, material foundation, and instead is transformed into an inner ground which, again, can only be spoken of in a symbolic, metaphorical manner. Such such symbolic formation corresponds now to a faith that, failing to prove its object intuitively, can only be thought of as faith built on what Kant calls "presupposing" ("Annehmung") (Kant 1996, p. 11). With reference to its non-objective object, the idea of a "first *original being*" ("Urwesen") (Kant 1996, p. 11), Kant thus writes:

> [...] not only does our reason already feel a need to take the *concept* of the unlimited as the ground of the concepts of all limited beings—hence of all other things –, but this need even goes as far as the presupposition (Voraussetzung) of its *existence*, without which one can provide no satisfactory ground at all for the contingency of the existence of things in the world, let alone for the *purposiveness* (*Zweckmäßigkeit*) and order which is encountered everywhere [...]. Without assuming an intelligent author (Ohne einen verständigen Urheber anzunehmen) we cannot give any *intelligible ground* (*verständiger Grund*) of it without falling into plain absurdities; and although we cannot *prove* the impossibility of such a purposiveness apart from an *intelligent cause* [...], given our lack of insight there yet remains a sufficient ground for *assuming* such a cause in reason's need to presuppose something intelligible in order to explain this given appearance, since nothing else with which reason can combine any concept provides a remedy for this need. (Kant 1999, p. 11–12).

As so often in Kant, reason appears to be peculiarly needy: certainly far needier than a vulgar understanding of reason as a rational, logical faculty may ever suggest. And the multiplicity of grounds indicates that in such a state of need, if not despair, it is reason itself that gives itself over to the language of ground; for, in its very metaphorical nature, this language replicates on a rhetorical level what Kant's model of faith implicates structurally: faith is a mode of presupposition, of "Annahme," of taking something as given which in fact is not given at all. For what is presupposed is not present and can through no mode of intuition be an object of experience, and much less as an object of knowledge in general. In order to be made present, however, it turns for assistance to what might—in its broadest sense—be called a symbolic order of purposiveness, of "Zweckmäßigkeit." The *Kritik der Urteilskraft* will eventually evince the inner link binding such a "purposiveness that is not grounded in a purpose" (Kant 2000, p. 236) to the realm of aesthetic experience. As the experience of the beautiful (such as in the shape of art), it is doubtlessly intimately linked to symbolic orders in general.[5]

---

5 About the judgment of taste, the *Kritik der Urteilskraft* notes: "Thus nothing other than the

What becomes apparent for the matter of ground itself, however, is that it only seems possible insofar as it is literally invented by the subject itself. Thus, not only is, with Habermas "modernity [...] to ground itself" (Habermas 1987, p. 21), but, in Kant, it even has to ground that very ground on which it must then ground itself. However, according to the laws of a system that is to define the limits of knowledge in general, as much as the limits of ground, there is ironically no ground to be found that could itself legitimately serve the "spirit of well-groundedness" as precisely a source of legitimacy. Returning to the preface of the second edition of the *Kritik der reinen Vernunft*, any "secure course" in need of a stable ground can only be taken by those who establish ground themselves in a non-objective, but assumed, i.e. presupposed manner. Not only can such implicitly illegitimate establishment of ground not happen in a "spirit of well-groundedness," but this very idea of well-groundedness itself becomes, in the most literal sense, a spirit, a "Geist" i.e. ghostly spectre haunting Kant's struggle for legitimacy itself; and perhaps not only haunting it, but causing it to inherently fail in the very moment it attempts to secure itself against such failure. For Kant's grounds remain groundless.

2

To those who, from the literary world around 1800, are best-know for their intense reception of, and reaction to, the problems which Kant's philosophy raised, certainly belongs, next to names like Schiller and Kleist, Friedrich Hölderlin. It may or may not be mere coincidence that, in one of the most detailed contributions to the understanding not only of Hölderlin's poetry, but also of his philosophical position, Dieter Henrich applied the language of *Grund* to demonstrate Hölderlin's alleged desire to define, (at least early on) the systemic foundation of that position as a ground in consciousness, a "Grund im Bewußtsein" (Henrich 2004). In its broadest sense, such a reading of Hölderlin almost inevitably leads to an attempt to understand particularly his theoretical writings in light of what has already been noted as a problem of legitimacy. This problem includes, however generally, questions about the status of first things, as the

---

subjective purposiveness [subjektive Zweckmäßigkeit] in the representation of an object without any end (objective or subjective), consequently the mere form of purposiveness in the representation (in der Vorstellung) through which an object is given to us, insofar as we are conscious of it, can constitute the satisfaction that we judge, without a concept, to be universally communicable, and hence the determining ground (Bestimmungsgrund) of the judgment of taste." (Kant 2000, p. 106).

matter of legitimacy is, directly or indirectly, linked to the very idea of a first source thereof, or—speaking with Aristotle—to the idea of a *primum mobile*. Henrich's language of *Grund* with regard to Hölderlin appears relevant for his theoretical approaches in which, particularly in his 1795 fragment *Urtheil und Seyn*, he attempts to define first and original identity as "the connection of subject and object" ("Verbindung des Subjects und Objects") (Hölderlin 2009, p. 231, StA 4,1, p. 216). Ironically, however, "primal" (Hölderlin 2009, p. 231) in the sense of "ursprünglich" (StA 4,1, p. 216) is, in *Urtheil und Seyn*, not such an identity, such a "Seyn," but rather the very moment that leads to the dissolution of such identity. For Hölderlin writes about the act of "judgment" ("Urtheil" famously (and etymologically incorrect) as "Ur-Theilung" (StA 4,1, p. 216), by which he refers to "the primal separation of the object and the subject" (Hölderlin 2009, p. 231). It thus becomes apparent that Hölderlin's thinking on origins may perhaps be less concerned with what actually *was* first, but with what already *is*. For only that which already dissolves the "original" "Seyn," the "separation," is being named as "ursprünglich."

There can be no doubt that Hölderlin's thinking closely relates to the problems and questions raised in Kant's philosophy. But, as with his friends Schelling and certainly Hegel, Hölderlin soon finds the somewhat static system, such as it is sketched out by Kant's critical philosophy, implacably dynamic. For the initial *Kritik* of reason, as it was designed by Kant, takes on a historical dimension, a perspective under which "Vernunft" turns eventually into the idea of an all-encompassing "Geist" that unfolds, moves, develops, and thus literally sets into motion what Kant wanted to be spoken of, however metaphorically, only as the "secure course." Such a "secure course of a science" originally had not been thought of as a course with a direction or with an implicit teleology, and it was precisely Kant's intention to give it such a stable and lasting ground. While Schelling, in his *System des transzendentalen Idealismus* (1800), works towards a philosophy of identity by employing the idea of "a progressive history of self-consciousness" and representing its "individual stages" ("Epochen") (Schelling 1978, p. 2), Hegel eventually turns philosophy itself into a *Philosophie der Geschichte* (1822/23), after having marked the work of the "Weltgeist" as the "enormous labour of world-history" ("ungeheure Arbeit der Weltgeschichte") (Hegel 1977, p. 17) in his *Phänomenologie des Geistes* (1807).

Such programmatic mobilisation of thinking, as it characterises the situation of German philosophy after Kant, finds elements of correspondence also in Hölderlin's writing. Not only will the Kantian "Gang" latently be associated with a direction, but even the very *Grund* itself is literally set into motion. The well-known reference to an "exzentrische Bahn" (StA 3, p. 236) in the preface to an unfinished version of *Hyperion* from 1795 is only one example of such mobilisation. Some of Hölderlin's best-known poems also carry titles such as *Der Wanderer* (1796), *Lebenslauf* (1797), *Heimkunft* (1801), or *Die Wanderung* (1802), and all of them are literally invested in acts and schemes of mobilisation. And while the beginning of the hymn *Wie wenn am Feiertage* (1800) famously reads "As on a Holiday, to see the field / A countryman goes out [...]" (Hölderlin 1994, p. 172), it is particularly the language of "paths," of a "Pfad, worauf ich wandle" (StA 4,1, p. 24) that recurs in Hölderlin's repertoire of poetic language, indicating that his poetry can perhaps be literally called a 'poetry on the move.'

Such descriptive tools could certainly also be applied to one of the long pentametric elegies Hölderlin wrote around the turn of the century, the poem *Menons Klagen um Diotima* (1800/1801). In the spirit of mobilisation, the opening lines read as follows:

> Daily I search, now here, now there my wandering takes me
> Countless times I have probed every highway and path;
> coolness I seek on those hilltops, all the shades I revisit,
> Then the well-springs again; up my mind roves and down
> Begging for rest; so I wounded deer will flee to the forests [...].
> (Hölderlin 1994, p. 127).
>
> (Täglich geh' ich heraus, und such' ein Anderes immer,
> Habe längst sie befragt alle die Pfade des Lands;
> Droben die kühlenden Höhn, die Schatten alle besuch' ich,
> Und die Quellen; hinauf irret der Geist und hinab,
> Ruh' erbittend; so flieht das getroffene Wild in die Wälder [...].) (StA 2,1, p. 75).

The poem, in its first version simply named *Elegie*, speaks from the perspective of remembering a past love that is irretrievably mourned in the spirit of lamentation. Hölderlin's poetic practice thus follows quite accurately the tradition he inherited, particularly from Klopstock, who called his own *Elegie* (1751) a tibullic song, "ein tibullisches Lied" (Klopstock 1962, p. 24). What in the gesture of the poem is remembered, the love for the figure of Diotima, can on first glance certainly be brought together with Hölderlin's relationship to Susette Gontard which is known to have ended around the time the first version of the poem was written. In the poem, however, the remembered peculiarly lacks substance, as the memory is merely referred to as an "all-saddening dream" (Hölderlin 1994, p. 129). And instead of addressing the missed directly, the poem, as often happens in Hölderlin, shifts towards a language in which conceptual elements ("hinauf irret der Geist und hinab") merge with a voice speaking the language of comparisons: "so flieht das getroffene Wild in die Wälder [...]." However, this comparison of the fleeing deer is already embedded in an overall metaphorical order, as the setting evoked in the beginning of the poem is situated in a world of wandering where a lane has been established through a "Land" that, developed by both "Pfad" and poem itself, appears on the threshold of having already been cultivated. In the light of such cultivation, the state of "Seyn" has already been abolished and instead the search of the "ich" for what is conceptually marked as "ein Anderes" has replaced it. Thus, it becomes apparent how the elegiac constellation of remembrance is transformed into a ground wherein such remembrance conflates with the philosophical problem of bridging the "primal separation of the subject and the object," such as brought up in *Urtheil und Seyn*. Such a search is carried out in the movement of "geh[en]," and thus introduces the aspect of mobilisation into the operations of both remembrance and bridging the subject-object-separation. If the first stanza of the elegy is to be considered a poetic formalisation of the situation not so much of Hölderlin's own mourning of the loss of Susette Gontard, but perhaps rather of the situation of philosophy around 1800 in general as a coming-to-consciousness of both its historical position and its position in history, then, speaking with Freud, it appears to revolve around the problem of *Nachträglichkeit* with relation to the "all-saddening dream." In this sense, the wandering movement as the inner mode of relating to such *Nachträglichkeit* reflects the moment of "primal separation" and thus makes the elegy readable from the perspective of a 'coming too late' in the attempt to bridge the gap, the "primal separation" between "ich" and "ein Anderes."

Such movement, however, is paired with a peculiar form of temporalisation that is at work throughout the whole poem. For what is memorialised carries the trace of "radiant visions recalled" (Hölderlin 1994, p. 129), which in the original reads as "Bilder aus hellerer Zeit" (StA 2,1, p. 76). These "visions" are visions only insofar as they are poetically transformed images speaking literally from the perspective of things having lost their full light, thus becoming darkened, if not blurred or distorted. This explicitly temporal dimension in which a historical consciousness is introduced as the latent consciousness of decline or corruption of an original state governs the poem on a conceptual level, but is carried out within the framework of a poetic and thus metaphorical order in its broadest sense. This conflation of structure and imagery, of conceptual and non-conceptual elements, reads in the third stanza eventually as follows:

> Springs, it is true, go by, one year still supplanting the other,
> Changing and warring, so Time over us mortal men's heads
> Rushes past up above [...]. (Hölderlin 1994, p. 129–131).

(Wohl gehn Frühlinge fort, ein Jahr verdränget das andre,
Wechselnd und streitend, so tost droben vorüber die Zeit
Über sterblichem Haupt [...].) (StA 2,1, p. 76).

Time, which may well be understood as a conceptual element *per se*, is of a "warring" nature. It "rushes" ("tost") and thus indicates violent and uncultivated elements standing in the background of the poemic setting. While for Kant time was, as a necessary *a priori* element of cognition, the "form of inner sense" (Kant 1998, p. 180), such time now appears in Hölderlin as the prior force which abandons its merely inner nature and becomes the form in which not only the poem, but also the struggling search of an "ich" for "ein Anderes" becomes apparent as movement itself. Its elements, here "springs," literally "go by" and thus correspond with the movements of the elegiac search itself. In this "warring" of time, temporal orientation is difficult, perhaps impossible. If any orientation can be established as coordinate between "ich" and "ein Anderes," and thus between subject and object, it can only be granted by spatial elements, by "pleasant gardens" (Hölderlin 1994, p. 129) and "mountains tinged with crimson at sunset" (Hölderlin 1994, p. 129). But even these points of geographical reference cannot avoid the theme of a movement corresponding latently with the idea of having no firm place, a lyrical variation of "transcendental homelessness" (Lukács 1971, p. 41), the proper expression of which, Lukács once claimed, was the novel. For, only the "murmurless path[s] of the grove [schweigende Pfade des Hains]" (Hölderlin 1994, p. 129, StA 2,1, p. 76) serve as "witness[es] to heavenly joy" (Hölderlin 1994, p. 129), as "Zeugen himmlischen Glüks" (StA 2,1, p. 76), bringing the search back to "highway and path" whence it initially started. These paths serve as signposts of memorialising a past, but as this past remains irretrievable they do so only insufficiently. Instead, only the initial state of "irren" is repeated once more in "That is why, astray [darum irr' ich umher], like wandering phantoms I love now." (Hölderlin 1994, p. 131, StA 2,1, p. 76).

Such pathing also opens a system in which those who are involved, various subject positions of the "ich" as much as the "Anderes," are literally floating rather than becoming stable markers of defined references themselves, no matter whether they appear in the form of a "wir," an "ihr," or even of a "dich" (StA 2,1, p. 76–77). These subject positions never find firm identity and are instead entangled in a constant stream-like movement, shifting, and changing form and places. This is all to be understood under the condition of that very "Zeit" which—with such violence, certainly echoing many other tempests and storms in Hölderlin's work—"tost." Eventually, such unstable conditions go together with the remembered moment of love itself, and the fourth stanza of the poems reads:

> Meanwhile we—like the mated swans in their summer contentment
> When by the lake they rest or on the waves, lightly rocked,
> Down they look, at the water, and silvery clouds through that mirror
> Drift, and ethereal blue flows where the voyagers pass—
> Moved and dwelled on this earth. (Hölderlin 1994, p. 131).
>
> (Aber wir, zufrieden gesellt, wie die liebenden Schwäne,
> Wenn sie ruhen am See, oder, auf Wellen gewiegt,
> Niedersehn in die Wasser, wo silberne Wolken sich spiegeln,
> Und ätherisches Blau unter den Schiffenden wallt,
> So auf Erden wandelten wir.) (StA 2,1, p. 76).

Again, the poem moves towards a language of comparison, distorting, if not hiding the preciously memorialised moment of community in the embarrassment of having failed to find a proper mode of representation. And as such a mode of representation, the comparison itself introduces—in anticipation of the famous "loving swans" ("holden Schwäne") (Hölderlin 1994, p. 170, StA 2,1, p. 117) from *Hälfte des Lebens* (1803)—a state of highest fragility, fluidity, instability. As subject positions literally caught between "the lake" and "silvery clouds," the "we" here is one of hovering, floating nature rather than a "we" on stable ground.

Here, the poem introduces a word belonging to the key repertoire of Hölderlin's poetic language: "wandeln." The meaning of "wandeln" oscillates between both its literal and metaphorical connotations of walking and living, of—as Michael Hamburger translates—moving and dwelling.[6] As unstable as such oscillation appears is also the foundation on which "wandeln" happens, for what in the form of "auf Erden wandelten wir" carries a trait of solidity, of earthliness, becomes, in light of the chosen comparison of floating on water, decidedly destabilised itself. As Paul Celan once, with reference to Büchner's *Lenz*, spoke of heaven as an abyss underneath, as "Himmel als Abgrund unter sich" (Celan 1983, p. 195), so does this very "Abgrund" here take the shape of an earth which Hölderlin can only characterise as "water" and "ethereal blue." Thus, it seems that the comparison reveals what literal language hides: earth is a fluid element, and those who "move and dwell" on it are swans, swimming birds, moving between flying and drowning.[7] The comparison with the swans under

---

[6] Grimm's *Deutsches Wörterbuch* refers explicitly to the instability of reference, giving both literal and metaphorical meanings when speaking with reference to "wandeln" of a "Bedeutung 'hin und her ziehen, reisen, gehen,' übertragen 'leben sein leben führen'." (Grimm 1999, XXVII, colm. 1587).

[7] The third stanza of the first version of *Dichtermuth* (1800) posits a comparable configuration: "For, as quite near shores, or in silvery / Flood resounding afar, or over silent deep / Water trav-

which an abysmal and unfathomable blue depth "flows" thus indicates that Hölderlin's "wandeln" is to be understood as literally bottomless; it lacks firm foundation, or, speaking once more the language of Kant, it lacks the nature of ground.

Most often, the practice of reading takes into consideration only what is actually to be found in literature. What, however, is easily forgotten in such a practice is to acknowledge what actually *cannot* be found. And while *Menons Klage um Diotima*, as much as other poetry of Hölderlin, works through material which may at any moment make the reader expect to eventually hit a ground, the poem itself disdains to speak of any *Grund*. This seems to be the case not only in the elegy itself, but in Hölderlin's literature in general. While regularly making reference to "Boden," to "Erde," and to "Pfad," any mentioning of *Grund* is surprisingly rare. And what makes Hölderlin's subtle avoidance of it even more apparent is that those sparse cases in which Hölderlin speaks of a "Grund" often refer, implicitly or explicitly, to its peculiar instability, if not even to its total disappearance. Such instances of instability evince an almost Heraclitian prioritisation of water as the element about which poetry speaks. This is well documented throughout Hölderlin's works, from the so-called *Schicksalslied* in *Hyperion* (1797) until his late hymn *Der Rhein* (1801). In *Heimkunft* (1801), one such liquefaction reads as follows:

> Growth it foreknows, for already ancient torrents like lightning
> Crash, and the ground below steams with the spray of their fall [...].
> (Hölderlin 1994, p. 161).
>
> (Wachstum ahnend, denn schon, wie Blize, fallen die alten
> Wasserquellen, der Grund unter den Stürzenden dampft [...].) (StA 2,1, p. 96).

"Ground" here takes on the qualities of its very opposite. For rather than forming a substance of firm foundation it "steams," evaporates, and thus literally dissolves before the witnessing eyes. When the *Communist Manifesto* (1847/8), some decades after Hölderlin, mentions in its polemic analysis of modern bourgeois societies that "all that is solid melts into air" (Marx/Engels 1978, p. 476), this steaming ground of Hölderlin's may come again to hover before the mind's eye with renewed intensity, inviting a reading wherein it is the brave poetic anticipation of this disintegrating solidity and hinting at the same time at what has been called "the experience of modernity" (Berman 1982) in general.

---

els the flimsy / Swimmer, likewise we love to be." ("Denn, wie still am Gestad, oder in silberner / Fernhintönender Fluth, oder auf schweigenden / Wassertiefen der leichte / Schwimmer wandelt, so sind auch wir.") (Hölderlin 1994, p. 101, StA 2,1, p. 62).

This disintegration, however, also indicates an implicit, though radical, shift away from the Kantian obsession with saving the idea of a groundedness, which had failed to secure both the ground for such groundedness itself and—speaking in metaphors—its proper medium. Hölderlin, "the early modern" (George 1972), avoids the consequences of such dilemmatic groundlessness, in which any attempt to ground finds itself more and more deeply entangled the more it strives toward what it searches for. Therefore, Hölderlin also avoids, in the context of grounds, both letting such ground be established by an emphatic version of subjectivity and letting this subjectivity establish ground itself. Instead, in utter dismay about the state of "the soul of that mortal," the seventh and central stanza of *Mein Eigentum* (1799) reads:

> For like the plant that fails to take root within
> Its native ground, the soul of that mortal wilts
> Who with the daylight only roams, a
> Pauper astray on our Earth, the hallowed. (Hölderlin 1994, p. 39).
>
> (Denn, wie die Pflanze, wurzelt auf eignem Grund
> Sie nicht, verglüht die Seele des Sterblichen,
> Der mit dem Tageslichte nur, ein
> Armer, auf heiliger Erde wandelt.) (StA 1,1, p. 307).

Thus, what in *Menons Klage um Diotima* is only latent was apparent already in the earlier *Mein Eigentum:* "wandeln," no matter whether it happens as such or "auf heiliger Erde," is defined as the mode of being without "Grund," being rootless, of having no firm or binding place. And while the matter of "Erde" serves as a surface for such "wandeln," it fails to serve as a ground. Unlike with Goethe, for example, earth for Hölderlin never reaches the status of a geological category, but rather remains a highly symbolic place on which "wandeln" happens. This said, "wandeln" takes place as a conceptually groundless mode of moving, of—speaking with Kant—a course that fails to be secure on its own and that can only be kept in motion "with his golden / Leading-strings" ("an goldnen / Gängelbanden") (Hölderlin 1994, p. 103, StA 2,1, p. 66), as mentioned in *Blödigkeit* (1803).

In *Menons Klagen um Diotima*, this now seems to be the case for the "So auf Erden wandelten wir" as much as for "to walk anew the soil that is sprouting new verdure" ("neu auf grünendem Boden zu wandeln") (Hölderlin 1994, p. 133, StA 2,1, p. 77), an image in which the poem repeats the elegiac past only under the condition of "a miracle's power" ("eines Wunders Gewalt") (Hölderlin 1994, p. 133, StA 2,1, p. 77), carefully excluding any terminology of *Grund*. In the climactic moment of the triadic poem, the ninth stanza, both the mourning voice and the mourned Diotima eventually find a "communal ground"

(Hölderlin 1994, p. 135) which, however, does not happen in the name of a *Grund*, but again only of "gemeinsamem Boden" (StA 2,1, p. 79). In fact, even such "Boden"—Hamburger translates it erringly as "ground"—only arrives through the imagining of a future moment, framed as an address to those "up in heaven" ("Himmlischen") (Hölderlin 1994, p. 135, StA 2,1, p. 79):

> Stay with us two until on communal ground, reunited
> Where, when their coming is due, all the blessed souls will return,
> Where the eagles are, the planets, the Father's own heralds,
> Where the Muses are still, heroes and lovers began,
> There shall we meet again, or here, on a dew-covered island
> Where what is ours for once, blooms that a garden conjoins,
> All our poems are true and springs remain beautiful longer
> And another, a new year of our souls can begin. (Hölderlin 1994, p. 135).

> (Bleibt so lange mit uns, bis wir auf gemeinsamem Boden
> Dort, wo die Seeligen all niederzukehren bereit,
> Dort, wo die Adler sind, die Gestirne, die Boten des Vaters,
> Dort, wo die Musen, woher Helden und Liebende sind.
> Dort uns, oder auch hier, auf thauender Insel begegnen,
> Wo die Unsrigen erst, blühend in Gärten gesellt,
> Wo die Gesänge wahr, und länger die Frühlinge schön sind,
> Und von neuem ein Jahr unserer Seele beginnt.) (StA 2,1, p. 79).

The emphasis on staying, in this final gesture of acclaiming to the "Himmlischen," brings back the crucial element of time. For if only that which *is* can "stay," then it is surprising that this injunction is directed towards the anticipation of a future moment, a moment in which staying becomes obsolete, as signified in the original by the "bis wir." Such a future, however, is not to be understood as a singular moment alone. Its very nature is rather that of repetition. For it is structured by the fourfold calling of a "dort," anticipating the expansion of time itself into what is first identified as a mode of being wherein "springs remain beautiful longer," before revealing its cyclicality in the very last line: "And another, a new year of our souls can begin." What appears first in the form of a "communal ground" ("Boden") turns not only into longer springs, nor into years, but rather into the exposition of time itself. For above every singular "dort," and even beyond "all our poems," the poem closes with a version of the earlier "tosen" that now loses its violent dimension, revealing its eidetic form. In what could perhaps be seen as a grand ironic gesture, the poem ends with the word "beginnt." As it happens, however, such a beginning has already occurred before, and can only come, as with the years in their almost planetary cyclicality, in a gesture of potentially endless repetitions ("von neuem").

In light of such a repetitive version of temporal infinity, it might now perhaps be possible to answer the question of why Hölderlin's language distinctly avoids so carefully the mentioning of any *Grund*. For if there was any *Grund* to speak of (remembering that in 18th century German this word still oscillates between connotations of *ratio, causa,* and *fundus*), then it would unavoidably lead to questions about aspects of foundation and of legitimacy, for which a foundation is necessary as something which comes first and before all other things. Hölderlin's poetics thus carefully avoid what in Kant led to an insoluble problem of grounding a ground. Instead, the return to the prioritisation of time itself must, in this context, be understood as a programmatic step perhaps deliberately avoiding a tradition of not only German, but occidental thinking in general. For his gesture goes back behind what in Aristotle appears as the idea of the *primum mobile* and what later in Christian theology became the blueprint for thinking about God as the first mover, as well as the stable, unmovable foundation (if not ground) on which all earthly matters exist. In constructing his elegy according to the laws of circularity, Hölderlin, in fact, reverts to a model he finds in Plato, specifically in Plato's *Timaeus*, in which time is literally celebrated as what comes before all life and matter as well as before all possible distinctions and differentiations between, for example, "both 'above' and 'below,' according as he [a solid body, A.M.] stood now at one pole, now at the opposite" (Plato 1929, p. 159). For the understanding of time culminates, in Plato, in the idea of "an eternal image, moving according to number" (Plato 1929, p. 77), specifically representing an eternity into a two-fold direction. Troubling to most traditions of Christian theology, such an eternity has neither beginning *nor* end. It is an eternity in which—such as in Hölderlin—the end rather falls together with the beginning, for the end is what literally "beginnt." It may certainly be argued that, precisely in this idea of an all-encompassing time which "tost," a link can be found in Hölderlin's emphatic notion of a numeric and calculable order,[8] such as was famously documented in *Brod und Wein* (1803):

> And the watchman calls out, mindful, no less, of the hour. (Hölderlin 1994, p. 151).
>
> (Und der Stunden gedenk rufet ein Wächter die Zahl.) (StA 2,1, p. 90).

Meanwhile, Plato's *Timaeus* reads as follows:

> For we say that it "is" or "was" or "will be," whereas, in truth of speech, "is" alone is the appropriate term; "was" and "will be," on the other hand, are terms properly applicable to

---

[8] The element of calculability as a crucial poetic strategy has correctly been emphasised by Rainer Nägele in his reading of Hölderlin's *Der Rhein*. See Nägele 2005, pp. 29–71.

the Becoming which proceeds in Time, since both of these are motions; but it belongs not to that which is ever changeless in its uniformity to become either older or younger through time, nor ever to have become so, nor to be so now, nor to be about to be so hereafter, nor in general to be subject to any of the conditions which Becoming has attached to the things which move in the world of Sense, these being generated forms of Time, which imitates Eternity and circles round according to number. (Plato 1929, p. 77).

This imitation of eternity thus stands in the centre of the project to which Hölderlin's poetics return. However, such eternity must necessarily abandon any idea of a *Grund*, as it literally has no ground and is, in its circularity, in no need of one. Time, in this sense, does not know a direction; it knows only "Hours of Communion" ("Weihestunden") (Hölderlin 1994, p. 135, StA 2,1, p. 79), insofar as each singular unit of time—no matter whether "hour," "spring," or "year"— represents the entirety of time in its eternal, circular dimension.

The elegiac structuring of remembrance works likewise according to such a Platonic concept of time. After all, *Meno*, to which one encounters the reference in the elegy's title, is the dialogue of *anamnesis:* the faculty to recollect memories of "the truth of all things that are" which "is always in our soul" (Plato 1924, p. 321). Plato's *anamnesis* thus carries a trace of the repetition that, in Hölderlin's *Menons Klage um Diotima*, resurfaces in the shape of a four-fold "dort." But instead of truly remembering a singular and distinctly definable moment in the past, the poem itself stands in a series of potentially endless repetitions from which, however, it seems impossible and perhaps structurally unnecessary to define the primal scene of a first and original experience at all. As in light of eternity that, in a Platonic sense, is also expressed in an immortal soul, there has been and will always be repetition. Moving, therefore, radically away from anything close to what at an earlier moment, in 18th century philosophy, was called the *fundus animae*, i.e. the ground of the soul as the place of *perceptiones obscurae* (Baumgarten 1963, p. 176), such repetition, again, allows for no beginning, no foundation, no *fundus*, no *Grund* of any shape. What instead remains is both "at peace," as the famous image of "the modest hearth" (Hölderlin 1994, p. 31) in the earlier ode *Abendphantasie* (1799), and disturbingly groundless at the same time. As a sort of revocation of *Grund*, the consequences are named in the second version of *Stimme des Volks* (1800): "that mysterious yearning toward the chasm" (Hölderlin 1994, p. 83). In German, such yearning reads far more abysmal than chasmic, revealing the dangers of enigma as much as the dangers of living literally groundless in "das wunderbare Sehnen dem Abgrund zu" (StA 2,1, p. 49).

Bibliography

Aristotle (1995): *Poetics*. Ed. and trans. Halliwell, Stephan. Cambridge: Harvard University Press [=Loeb Classical Library].
Baumgarten, Alexander Gottlieb (1963): *Metaphysica*. Hildesheim: Georg Olms [reprint of the edition Halle: Hemmerde 1776].
Berman, Marshall (1982): *All That Is Solid Melts Into Air: The Experience of Modernity*. London: Penguin.
Blumenberg, Hans (2010): *Paradigms for a Metaphorology*. Trans. Savage, Robert. Ithaka: Cornell University Press.
Celan, Paul (1983): "Der Meridian: Rede anläßlich der Verleihung des Georg-Büchner-Preises (1961)." *Gesammelte Werke*, vol 3. Eds. Allemann, Beda / Reichert, Stefan. Frankfurt a. M.: Suhrkamp, pp. 187–202.
Förster, Eckart (2012): *The Twenty-Five Years of Philosophy: A Systematic Reconstruction*. Cambridge: Harvard University Press.
George, Emery Edward (Ed.) (1972): *Friedrich Hölderlin, An Early Modern*. Ann Arbor: University of Michigan Press.
Goetschel, Willi (1990): *Kant als Schriftsteller*. Wien: Passagen Verlag.
Grimm, Jacob/Grimm, Wilhelm (1999): *Deutsches Wörterbuch*, 33 vols. München: Deutscher Taschenbuch Verlag.
Habermas, Jürgen (1987): *The Philosophical Discourse of Modernity. Twelve Lectures*. Trans. Lawrence, Frederick. Cambridge: Policy Press.
Hegel, Georg Wilhelm Friedrich (1977): *Phenomenology of Spirit*. Trans. Miller, Arnold Vincent. Oxford: Clarendon Press.
Henrich, Dieter (2004): *Der Grund im Bewußtsein: Untersuchungen zu Hölderlins Denken*. Stuttgart: Klett-Cotta.
Hölderlin, Friedrich (1943–1985), *Sämtliche Werke in 15 Bänden*. Ed. Beißner, Friedrich. Stuttgart: W. Kohlhammer Verlag [= Große Stuttgarter Ausgabe].
Hölderlin, Friedrich (1994): *Selected Poems and Fragments*. Trans. Hamburger, Michael, ed. Adler, Jeremy. London: Penguin.
Hölderlin, Friedrich (2009): *Essays and Letters*. Ed. and trans. Adler, Jeremy / Louth, Charlie. London: Penguin.
Kant, Immanuel (1996): *Religion and Rational Theology*. Ed. and trans. Wood, Allen W. / di Giovanni, George. Cambridge: Cambridge University Press.
Kant, Immanuel (1998): *Critique of Pure Reason*. Ed. and trans. Guyer, Paul / Matthews, Eric. Cambridge: Cambridge University Press.
Kant, Immanuel (2000): *Critique of the Power of Judgment*. Ed. and trans. Guyer, Paul / Matthews, Eric. Cambridge: Cambridge University Press.
Klopstock, Friedrich Gottlieb (1962): *Ausgewählte Werke*. Ed. Schleiden, Karl August. München: Hanser.
Lukács, Georg (1971): *The Theory of the Novel: A Historico-Philosophical Essay on the Forms of Great Epic Literature*. Trans. Bostock, Anna. London: Merlin Press.
Marx, Karl / Engels, Friedrich (1978): "Manifesto of the Communist Party." In: *The Marx-Engels Reader*, 2nd edition. Ed. Tucker, Robert C. New York / London: Norton, pp. 469–500.
Nägele, Rainer (2005): *Hölderlins Kritik der poetischen Vernunft*. Basel: Engeler.

Plato (1924): *Laches. Protagoras. Meno. Euthydemus.* Trans. Lamb, Walter Rangeley Maitland. Cambridge: Harvard University Press [=Loeb Classical Library].
Plato (1929): *Timaeus. Critias. Cleitophon. Menexenus. Epistles.* Trans. Bury, Robert Gregg. Cambridge: Harvard University Press [=Loeb Classical Library].
Schelling, Friedrich Wilhelm Joseph (1978): *System of Transcendental Idealism.* Trans. Heath, Peter. Charlottesville: University of Virginia Press.

Abbreviations

StA = Hölderlin, Friedrich (1943–1985), *Sämtliche Werke in 15 Bänden.* Ed. Friedrich Beißner. Stuttgart: W. Kohlhammer Verlag [=Große Stuttgarter Ausgabe].

Jennifer Anna Gosetti-Ferencei
Nietzsche and Cognitive Ecology

Abstract: Although the reception of Nietzsche's thought has complicated its relation to ecologically-oriented philosophy, a recent flurry of interpretations has demonstrated the ecological relevance of Nietzsche in a number of ways, attending to Nietzsche's interest in animal life, the importance of natural topography in his works, and his critique of anthropocentric views of nature. The present study traces Nietzsche's philosophy of immanence, his Zarathustra's exhortation to remain faithful to the earth, to his earlier view of language and its tendency toward an abstraction that supports idealist thinking and, according to Nietzsche, alienates human consciousness from its more aesthetic and vital origins. Nietzsche's greatest relevance to ecology, it is suggested here, is rooted not primarily in the description of nature in his works, in the sacred rendering of natural topographies, or even in his attempts to imagine animal perspectives, but rather in his critical cognitive ecology, by which I mean an ecocritical critique of human cognition itself. Nietzsche identifies epistemic habits and metaphysical fixations in human thought that must be overcome in order for humans to live vitally rather than destructively within the natural world. Nietzsche's cognitive critique remains relevant for ecocritical thinking—particularly for reimagining our possible relations to nature—even if Nietzsche underestimated the actual and potential environmental consequences of human alienation.

From Realism and Reverential Topography to Cognitive Ecology

Despite Dilthey's early recognition of the importance of vital nature in Nietzsche's thought, the ecocritical reception of Nietzsche has had to overcome the influence of a number of interpretations of Nietzsche over the last century (Dilthey 1985). Rejected by Heidegger as the last metaphysician, as distorting nature by the concept of the will-to-power, Nietzsche's thinking was excluded from the new beginning in the history of being, and from the vision of poetic dwelling on earth poetry was to cultivate, that Heidegger saw inaugurated with Hölderlin (Heidegger 1977, p. 275). This exclusion was reinforced by Walter Kaufmann's insistence on Nietzsche's refusal of any Romantic or nostalgic longing for nature, focused as Nietzsche's thought was on the primacy of the present, and again later by Theodore Roszak, who in his *Ecopsychology* counted Nietzsche among those alienated modernists concerned more with the *Eigenwelt* than the *Umwelt* (Kaufmann 1975, pp. 321–22; Roszak 1993, p. 66). It is quite apart from the sentiments of a Heideggerian inspired deep ecology, and the idea of poetic dwelling promoted in Heidegger's readings of Hölderlin, then, that Nietzsche's ecological credentials, including his regard for animals, have been more recently examined by a number of scholars (Shapiro 2016, 2006; Storey 2016; Lemm 2009; del Caro 2004; Hallman 2001). What Deleuze and Guattari called Nietzsche's "geophilosophy" is now read with distinctly ecological implications (Deleuze and Guattari 1994; Günzel 2003). While some have pointed to the difficulties that would attend any Nietzschean environmentalism (Zimmerman 2008; Acampora 1994), Nietzsche has been recognised as "the West's first major diagnostician of ecological ignorance" (del Caro 2004, p. x). Nietzsche's philosophy of nature, it is argued, "qualifies him as one of the most powerful ecological thinkers of the modern age" (Parkes 1999, p. 167).

Of course, nature in Nietzsche's writings is less described in his works than mythologically or symbolically evoked, and the human access to nature is less celebrated than persistently questioned. To the natural topographies in Nietzsche's writings it would be difficult to assign any form of realism. In Nietzsche's novel *Also Sprach Zarathustra,* there is ample reference to trees, forests, rivers, the sun, stars, the sea, islands, mountains, birds, insects, and animals, and reference to the earth itself. Zarathustra often dwells, along with his animal companions, in open nature, and it has been argued that "the natural environment of mountain and sea, lake and forest, is the indispensable context for [the] self-unfolding" of Zarathustra (Parkes 1999, p. 171). Yet in his efforts to present nature outside the constrictions of mechanistic rationality, we find mythologisations in Nietzsche, just as we do in Hölderlin: both regard nature through the motives of classical Greek gods, among other motives. From *Die Geburt der Tragödie* onwards, Nietzsche associates nature with Dionysus and the Dionysian, and the sun, animals, mountains, and so forth, tend to take on symbolic rather than literal meaning in his novel. Despite a number of transformations, the Dionysus concept persists in Nietzsche's thinking (Sokel 2005, 503–17; del Caro 2004, 22–27; del Caro 1981), and this strategy allows nature to appear as divine, and preserves a cultural memory, or offers a productive retrieval, of a form of life for which nature was revered by means of the narration of its divine origins. Yet one could argue that anthropocentric thinking cannot be overcome in this way, if mythologisation primarily evokes nostalgia for but another human civilisation, albeit one ecologically preferable, and so precludes recognition of nature's pre- or extra-cultural value. One challenge of ecological thinking, at least according to deep ecologists, is to recognise both our deep interconnections with nature, and its value apart from human life.

If realist representations of nature are not to be found in Nietzsche, scholars look for ecological significance in his sense of place, his reverent rendering of particular topographies. In Nietzsche, we find real natural spaces relevant to his literary renderings. Nietzsche's contemplation of gardens in Genoa has been related to Zarathustra's awakening to an earth that, as his animals repeatedly proclaim to him, await him as a garden (see Shapiro 2013, pp. 70–71). Nietzsche has described Lake Silvaplana in Switzerland where he came to understand the idea of eternal recurrence, and designated "the question of place and climate" as among the conditions of thinking. It has been argued thus that Nietzsche's thinking is "embedded in his surroundings and dependent upon them." (Malpas 2014, p. 203). Yet the topography of *Zarathustra*, the text in which Nietzsche's titular figure urges us to be faithful to the earth, is more symbolic than concrete. While Zarathustra himself in "A Thousand and One Goals" is said to have travelled widely—he is described as having seen many lands and many peoples—Nietzsche could not by virtue of ill health visit all the places that his topographical imagination would have taken him. One result is that "Nietzsche's descriptions of landscapes consist in more or less stereotypical literary descriptions," and it has been argued that while topographical metaphor is crucial for Nietzsche's geophilosophy, actual places are of little relevance, based as they are on only a "virtual geography" (Günzel 2003, p. 79, p. 87; c.f. Malpas 2014). This may not be entirely so, if, as Ernst Bertram convincingly showed, the landscapes of Engadin in Switzerland and Rapallo in Italy inspire both concrete scenes and topographical ideas in *Zarathustra*. Yet Bertram admitted that these gain "the highest degree of reality and forcefulness" for Nietzsche precisely in becoming in his text "allegorical, symbolic, decipherably ambiguous" (Bertram 2009, p. 231). This confounding of the literal and the symbolic in Nietzsche's topographies was examined by J. Hillis Miller as a trope of parable, such that the reader of *Zarathustra* "is given the figurative without the literal," so that the "mountains, night sky, and sea have become vehicles for expressing something else [...] in terms exclusively drawn from the landscape" (Miller 1995, p. 182, p. 184). While these difficulties may be specific to Nietzsche, a challenge to topographical ecocriticism more generally may be that any local rootedness does not necessarily nurture environmental responsibility, and that ecological threats are now global in genesis, as in the causes of climate change (Heise 2008). A contemporary ecology, it has been argued, "can be no simple return to local belonging and the caring that allegedly follows from it: sense of place must be complemented by 'sense of planet' and local belonging subordinated to global identification" (Goodbody 2011, p. 56).

We can then turn to the further question of human access to nature, what cognitive divisions may pertain, how human consciousness, reason, and knowledge connect us to, or divide us from, the earth. While Goethe's scientific approach to nature, for example, remains untroubled by the Kantian critical paradigm that designates the in-itself as withheld from our direct grasp, a mere regulative ideal, Nietzsche responds to the problem in a wholly different way. In sharp contrast to any epistemic optimism, Nietzsche promotes the truth only of appearances in their multiplicity, potential illusoriness and contradiction, experienced in and through embodied life. Furthermore, Nietzsche illuminates the disasters, for the human species, of constructing an abstract ideal, a stable truth behind or beyond them. Indeed, Nietzsche's promotion of a new kind of human species in *Also sprach Zarathustra* may be read as the promotion of a new cognitive ecology, for in order to live differently upon the earth, we must think, feel, and experience differently.

This notion of a cognitive ecology draws from, among other sources, Gregory Bateson's foundational *Steps to an Ecology of Mind*, where mind is understood as a network of interacting elements within a closed system that responds to environmental changes. This definition offers mind not as a uniquely human intellect segregated from nature, but rather in continuity with other natural phenomena. Bateson highlights a kind of resemblance, for example, among such phenomena as the bilateral symmetry of an animal body, the arrangement of leaves in a plant, the nature of play, the grammar of a sentence, and so forth. Within an ecology of mind, our own human thought systems, our aggregates of ideas, can be seen not only as knowledge or thinking *about* the natural world, but as part of, and integrated with it—an integration Bateson also considered under the notion of the sacred. In this way, we can describe a given manifestation of mind as healthy or unhealthy, as flourishing or not, in an ecological sense. More recently, cognitive studies of literature, which recognise in the latter manifestations of mind as embodied, enactive, and interwoven with its environment, have relied upon the notion of a cognitive ecology (Cave 2016). The emerging field of cognitive literary studies has focused on the distributed nature of the human mind and its reflection in literary texts, having yet to explicitly connect with the wider environmental concerns of literary ecocriticism. Yet since literature in this context is read for its evidence of the origins in embodied and material life of our cognitive and linguistic facilities, such cognitive approaches to literature ought to be helpful in addressing, as Bateson argued was central to his own notion of ecology of mind, "contemporary crises in the human relation to the environment." (Bateson 1972, p. xv). Nietzsche recognised both the physiology of the human mind, and our connection, through embodiment, with the earth as the ground of all human action and thought.

Earth, Physiology, and Human Cognition

Nearing the end of the century which Hölderlin, in "Brod und Wein" (1801), inaugurated as a modernity threatened by the loss of the divine, Nietzsche's protagonist of *Also sprach Zarathustra* (1883) implores his listeners to remain "true to the earth" ("der Erde treu"), and promotes the idea of a future manifestation of human life as the "meaning of the earth (Sinn der Erde)" (HW/III, p. 9). Intervening between Hölderlin's poetry and the composition of Nietzsche's novel is of course Darwin's *On the Origin of Species* (1859), which Nietzsche recognised as toppling traditional values with its natural, atheological explanation of human origins. It is consistent with Nietzsche's critique of Darwin's theory—"that it places an over-intellectualized view of life—an over-Apollonian view of life— [...] at the foundation of biology"—that Zarathustra renders the human being as having evolved from apes, but not entirely successfully (Pence 2011, p. 167). "Once you were apes, and yet the human being is even now still more ape than any ape (Einst ward ihr Affen, und auch jetzt noch ist der Mensch mehr Affe, als irgend ein Affe)" (HW/III, p. 8), he declares. This view is echoed elsewhere in Nietzsche, where it is hypothesised, somewhat more comically, that the human being may be considered but a limited phase in the evolution of the ape, "such that the human being arose from the ape and will again become ape (so dass der Mensch aus dem Affen geworden ist und wieder zum Affen wird)" (KSA/2, p. 205). Yet if all of nature is dynamically evolving, the human being could go further, not just by struggling for existence and self-propagation, but by striving to become something better, striving for a more vital existence. Zarathustra's naturalistic identification of human and ape is followed by a potentially more promising, if metaphoric identification: "The human being is a rope, strung between animal and the overman—a rope across an abyss. (Der Mensch ist ein Seil, geknüpft zwischen Tier und Übermensch,—ein Seil über einen Abgrunde)." (KSA/4, p. 16; HW/III, 11). If the human being is, as Nietzsche declares in *Jenseits von Gut und Böse*, "the not yet determined animal, (das noch nicht festgestellte Thier)" (KSA/5, p. 81), Zarathustra's conviction seems to be that, through creative flourishing, the human could become "virtually a new species" (Pippin 2006, p. x). This conviction, and the doctrine of eternal return which would enable such transformation, comprise Zarathustra's central teachings, which develop as Zarathustra descends like the sun from his mountaintop, to traverse town, forest, sea, and islands, in order to promote the earthly roots of human thinking, feeling, and being.

Condemning those that seek their highest values "beyond the stars (hinter den Sternen)," Zarathustra applauds those "who sacrifice themselves to the earth (die sich der Erde opfern)" (HW/III, p. 11). The phrase invokes Empedocles, about whom Nietzsche, undoubtedly influenced by Hölderlin, attempted to compose his own drama in 1871 (Söring 1990). Yet the nature of such sacrifice can be understood only when we consider how Nietzsche's sense of ecology includes the human intellect. The modern manifestation of human intellect is unhealthy, Nietzsche suggests, a compensation for us as a weaker species, "as those to whom it is denied to wage the battle for existence with the horns or the sharp teeth of predators (als welchen einen Kampf um die Existenz mit Hörnern oder scharfem Raubtier-Gebiß zu führen versagt ist)" (KSA/1, p. 876). This assessment of the human as a weak specimen was expressed a decade before *Zarathustra*, in the essay "Über Wahrheit und Lüge im außermoralischen Sinne" (1873). That essay begins with an ironic fairy tale meant to expose the delusions of anthropocentrism.

> In some or other remote corner of that universe which is dispersed into innumerable twinkling solar systems, there was once a star upon which clever beasts invented knowing. [...] After nature had drawn a few breaths, the star congealed, and the clever beasts had to die. One might invent such a fable, and yet he still would not have adequately illustrated how miserable, how shadowy and fleeting, how aimless and random the human intellect stands out within nature. There were eternities during which it did not exist. [...][1]

> (In irgend einem abgelegenen Winkel des in zahllosen Sonnensystemen flimmernd ausgegossenen Weltalls gab es einmal ein Gestirn, auf dem kluge Tiere das Erkennen erfanden. [...] Nach wenigen Atemzügen der Natur erstarrte das Gestirn, und die klugen Tiere mußten sterben.—So könnte jemand eine Fabel erfinden und würde doch nicht genügend illustriert haben, wie kläglich, wie schattenhaft und flüchtig, wie zwecklos und beliebig sich der menschliche Intellekt innerhalb der Natur ausnimmt. Es gab Ewigkeiten, in denen er nicht war. [...]) (KSA/1, p. 874).

Displacing the human perspective as the epistemic centre of the universe, Nietzsche imagines a cosmological vantage point, introducing an image of our planet among numberless solar systems and on a temporal scale that dwarfs not only the individual human lifespan, but that of the existence of all living species. From this cosmic image, Nietzsche shifts to the perspective of the smallest animals—a shift from macrocosm to microcosm that recalls Pascal's imaginative efforts to expose the limits of human knowledge. But while Pascal aimed to illustrate what may exceed human cognition by virtue of its incalculable vastness or minuteness, Nietzsche exposes the specificity, and thus limitedness, of human cognition on physiological grounds, by contrasting it with that of other animals.

---

[1] For "On Truth and Lies in an Extra-Moral Sense," I have drawn from, but sometimes altered, translations by Daniel Breazele (Nietzsche 1979), and Walter Kaufmann (Nietzsche 1976).

It even costs much effort for [the human being] to admit to himself that the insect or the bird perceives an entirely different world from the human, and that the question, which of these world-perceptions is the more correct, is an entirely meaningless one, for this would have to have been measured previously in accordance with the criterion of the correct perception, which means, in accordance with a criterion which is not available.

(Schon dies kostet ihm Mühe, sich einzugestehen, wie das Insekt oder der Vogel eine ganz andere Welt perzipieren als der Mensch, und daß die Frage, welche von beiden Weltperzeptionen richtiger ist, eine ganz sinnlose ist, da hierzu bereits mit dem Maßstabe der richtigen Perzeption, das heißt mit einem nicht vorhandenen Maßstabe gemessen werden müßte.) (KSA/1, p. 884).

Nietzsche argues that there is no ultimate criterion of objectivity, no "richtige Perzeption," which could decide whether the perspective of human, insect, or bird is truer. In explaining this Nietzsche exploits the Kantian insight that so preoccupied Hölderlin—that direct knowledge of the in-itself is not possible:

But in any case, it seems to me that the correct perception—which would mean the adequate expression of an object in the subject—is a contradictory impossibility. For between two absolutely different spheres, as between subject and object, there is no causality, no correctness, no expression, rather at most an aesthetic relation, I mean a suggestive transference, a stammering translation into a completely foreign tongue—for which there is required, in any case, a freely poetizing and freely inventive intermediate sphere and mediating power.

(Überhaupt aber scheint mir "die richtige Perzeption" – das würde heißen: der adäquate Ausdruck eines Objekts im Subjekt—ein widerspruchsvolles Unding: denn zwischen zwei absolut verschiednen Sphären, wie zwischen Subjekt und Objekt, gibt es keine Kausalität, keine Richtigkeit, keinen Ausdruck, sondern höchstens ein ästhetisches Verhalten, ich meine eine andeutende Übertragung, eine nachstammelnde Übersetzung in eine ganz fremde Sprache: wozu es aber jedenfalls einer frei dichtenden und frei erfindenden Mittelsphäre und Mittelkraft bedarf.) (KSA/1, p. 884).

Nietzsche's claim here that the adequate expression of an object in the subject is a contradictory impossibility ("ein widerspruchsvolles Unding") echoes Hölderlin's critique of subjective idealism. While Hölderlin rejected a grounding of knowledge of being in a transcendental, originary I, because any judgment is preceded by division, Nietzsche will reject any transcendentally grounding ego at some metaphysical remove from the material world and our direct experience of it. Rather, subjectivity itself is conditioned by the physiology of our species, thus Nietzsche refers in this context to the "starting point of the body and physiology (Ausgangspunkt vom Leibe und der Physiologie)" (KSA 11, p. 638). Like Hölderlin, Nietzsche recognises an aesthetic possibility of intimate, but indirect, recovery of the object. Where Hölderlin describes in *Hyperion* an eccentric path, an infinite approximation, and elsewhere refers to tragedy as the metaphor of an intellectual intuition, Nietzsche here refers to "a stammering translation into a completely foreign tongue (eine nachstammelnde Übersetzung in eine ganz fremde Sprache)." This approximating and indirect approach would make use of "a freely poetizing, freely inventive mediating force ("einer frei dichtenden und frei erfindenden Mittelsphäre und Mittelkraft"). Reference to *Die Geburt der Tragödie,* appearing the year before the composition of this essay, would support the conclusion that Nietzsche envisions such mediation in the form of art. Nietzsche writes in this essay, too, of pre-intellectual experience in artistic terms.

In the decade between these works and *Zarathustra,* Nietzsche abandons any question of the true grasp of object, launching a critique of the will to truth and an affirmation of appearances. By 1886, in the preface to the second edition of *Die fröhliche Wissenschaft,* Nietzsche praises the necessity "to stop courageously at the surface, the fold, the skin, to adore the appearance, to believe in forms, tones, words, in the whole Olympus of appearances[2] (tapfer bei der Oberfläche, der Falte, der Haut stehen zu bleiben, den Schein anzubeten, an Formen, an Töne, an Worte, an den ganzen Olymp des Scheins zu glauben!)" (KGA/V, p. 20). Yet it is worth recalling Nietzsche's critique of intellect in the earlier essay as alienating human beings from the very nature we aim to grasp. Just as Hölderlin's *Hyperion* targeted "Wissenschaft" as distancing the human subject from what would be an intimately enveloping nature, Nietzsche aims to expose the role of language and concepts in "disparaging the earth" through the erection and validation of our own abstractions over and against it (del Caro 2004, p. 75). Language, Nietzsche suggests, only provides the illusion of a true grasp of things:

> We believe that we know something about the things themselves when we speak of trees, colours, snow, and flowers, and yet we possess nothing but metaphors for things—metaphors which correspond in no way to the original entities.
>
> (Wir glauben etwas von den Dingen selbst zu wissen, wenn wir von Bäumen, Farben, Schnee und Blumen reden, und besitzen doch nichts als Metaphern der Dinge, die den ursprünglichen Wesenheiten ganz und gar nicht entsprechen.) (KSA/1, p. 879).

This illusion will have consequences, for language enables us to overlook our more original experiences of nature.

In Nietzsche's account in "Über Wahrheit und Lüge," language operates through a series of metaphorical transfers. A nerve stimulus from the perceptual world (his example is a leaf) triggers in the mind a certain image. At this level,

---

[2] For translations of *The Gay Science* I have relied upon Walter Kaufmann's translation (Nietzsche 1974).

the drive toward language is artistic, generating images. The stimulus is repeatedly identified with the image (of a leaf); and the latter comes to be articulated through the word-sound ("leaf"). Repetition of this procedure through stimulus, image, and sound, endows a concept, a universal idea (the definitional leaf, or the essence of leaf) that comes to subsume all instances. At the conceptual level language demands conventional fixation. The linguistic process renders "each displacement further from the unknowable thing in itself: from nerve excitation to subjective image to word-sound" (Miller 1995, p. 190). Concepts are thus generated from a series of cognitive-metaphorical abstractions. But the origin of the concept in the metaphoric transfer from perceptions—from what Nietzsche regards as nerve stimuli, or workings of the material world upon, and strictly speaking, within the body—is forgotten, along with the images to which they first give rise and the diversity within these more original strata of experience. The original linguistic instinct toward the creation of metaphors, a creative, artistic drive, becomes fixed in convention, "enabled by the very forgetting of the original unconscious process of their formation" (Crawford 1988, p. 202).

Literary or artistic metaphor has of course been celebrated, in more recent treatments, for its relation to productive imagination. Not merely extracting and combining likeness, metaphor, Paul Ricoeur argues, creates new meaning in and through difference between terms, such that "the tension between identity and difference in the predicative operation set in motion by semantic innovation" has the power to "redescribe reality" (Ricoeur 1977, p. 4, p. 291). Metaphor's generation of meaning arises not only from synthesis, but also through the tensions it keeps in play: between the primary and secondary subjects of the comparison, between literal and metaphorical interpretations of statements, and between identity and difference in the jointure of two terms (Riceour 1977, p. 292). Echoing Nietzsche, Ricoeur conceives metaphor in biological terms—at least, as animate—in its limitless potential for the generation of meaning. Other theorists more directly ground metaphor in human embodiment. Gaston Bachelard recognised the metaphors of poetic language as originating from the physiological habits of embodied experience, such as that of the body finding shelter and refuge or wandering and exposed. The experience of physical objects—such as the feel of the latch of a door in a house where we once lived—seems to remain within us and gives rise to poetic imagery and its power to resonate within the consciousness of readers (Bachelard 1958). More recently, cognitive linguists have argued for the origins of conceptual thought in metaphor, and for the origins of foundational metaphors—containment, balance, weight, direction, and so forth—in embodied experience (Lakoff / Johnson 1980, 1999).

Nietzsche's concern in "Über Wahrheit und Lüge" centres on the de-vivification and reduction of experience, and a falsification in our corresponding understanding of reality, whenever metaphoric transfers become rigid concepts. While such a process may be necessary for higher, and certainly for philosophical cognition, the generalisation involved, complains Nietzsche, eliminates the individuality and diversity of pre-conceptual experience.

> Every word immediately becomes a concept, inasmuch as it is not intended to serve as a reminder of the unique and wholly individualized original experience to which it owes its birth, but must at the same time fit innumerable, more or less similar cases—which means, strictly speaking, never equal—in other words, a lot of unequal cases. Every concept originates through our equating what is unequal.
>
> (Jedes Wort wird sofort dadurch Begriff, daß es eben nicht für das einmalige ganz und gar individualisierte Urerlebnis, dem es sein Entstehen verdankt, etwa als Erinnerung dienen soll, sondern zugleich für zahllose, mehr oder weniger ähnliche, daß heißt streng genommen niemals gleiche, also auf lauter ungleiche Fälle passen muß. Jeder Begriff entsteht durch Gleichsetzen des Nichtgleichen.) (KSA/1, p. 879).

The perceptual and imagistic elements out of which concepts originate are diminished in the repeated circulation of words, just as edges may be worn from a stone or the imprint from an ancient coin. Nietzsche elsewhere contrasts words to music, claiming that compared with music, "all communication through words is shameless: words dilute and stultify [...] words make the uncommon common (Im Verhältnis zur Musik ist alle Mitteilung durch Worte von schamloser Art: das Wort verdünnt und verdummt [...] das Wort macht das Ungemeine gemein)" (WD/III, p. 610). Hardened by repetition into concepts, the metaphorical origins of linguistic designation are forgotten in rational thought, for the thinker forgets "the original perceptual metaphors *as* metaphors (die originalen Anschauungsmetaphern *als* Metaphern)" and takes them as the things themselves ("als die Dinge selbst") (KSA/1, p. 883).

Such cognitive erasure, or the forgetting of what Nietzsche calls the unique "Urerlebnis," enables idealist thought. For this abstracting process promotes the projection of an ideal "leaf," the presumed "Urform" from which, in a conceptual reversal, any actual leaf would seem to be derived. It is for such a primal model which Goethe on his Italian journey expressed desire to empirically seek in nature, the irony of which Nietzsche would not have overlooked (see Allison 2001, p. 266, n. 14). The irregularity of the presumed derivative is regarded as an imperfection, a lack.

> Just as it is certain that one leaf is never entirely identical to another, so it is certain that the concept "leaf" is formed by arbitrarily discarding these individual differences and by forgetting the distinguishing aspects, and it awakens the idea that, in addition to the leaves, there exists in nature the "leaf": the original model according to which all the leaves were

perhaps woven, sketched, measured, coloured, curled, and painted—but by incompetent hands, so that no specimen has turned out to be a correct, reliable, and faithful likeness of the original model.

(So gewiß nie ein Blatt einem andern ganz gleich ist, so gewiß ist der Begriff Blatt durch beliebiges Fallenlassen dieser individuellen Verschiedenheiten, durch ein Vergessen des Unterscheidenden gebildet und erweckt nun die Vorstellung, als ob es in der Natur außer den Blättern etwas gäbe, das "Blatt" wäre, etwa eine Urform, nach der alle Blätter gewebt, gezeichnet, abgezirkelt, gefärbt, gekräuselt, bemalt wären, aber von ungeschickten Händen, so daß kein Exemplar korrekt und zuverlässig als treues Abbild der Urform ausgefallen wäre.) (KSA/1, p. 880).

Abstracted from the experiences which give rise to them, such projected originals emerge with greater metaphysical status—in essentialist thought, a greater claim on being, or claim to reality—than the actual originals of immediate embodied experience. Truth becomes but a metaphysical edifice, the intellectual world Hölderlin's Hyperion claims we erect in place of nature. Once again Nietzsche critically contrasts the human being to an animal, in this case, the bee. The latter constructs its hive with wax produced from real material, directly from nature, whereas humans merely fabricate "from far more delicate conceptual material, which the human first must fabricate from himself (aus dem weit zarteren Stoffe der Begriffe, die er erst aus sich fabrizieren muß)" (KSA/1, p. 883). The inevitable result of this conceptual fabrication, Nietzsche charges, is cognitive anthropomorphism: the human being transforms the world into ideas peculiar to human cognition itself.

Ecological Crisis, Aesthetic Response

This betrayal of the origins of our experience has been linked not only to the neglect of the well-being of the planet, but to "spiritualized and organized aggression" against the earth (Lampert 1993, p. 585), aggression "goaded by the Platonic lie" of its "defective or fallen character" (del Caro 2004, p. 62). While in the "Über Wahrheit und Lüge" essay and in *Zarathustra* Nietzsche's diagnoses are primarily spiritual, in *Genealogie der Moral* Nietzsche connects human hubris to actual violation of nature: "Hubris is today our entire position on nature, our violation of nature with the help of machines and the ever so thoughtless ingenuity of technicians and engineers (Hybris ist heute unsre ganze Stellung zur Natur, unsre Natur-Vergewaltigung mit Hilfe der Maschinen und der so unbedenklichen Techniker- und Ingenieur-Erfindsamkeit)." (KSA/5, pp. 356–57). If Empedoclean hubris—properly tragic hubris—leads to the sacrifice of the knowing subject that restores equilibrium among the divine, nature, and human, this modern hubris will find no such resolution, unless the human being can dramatically transform itself as a species.

While criticizing human hubris, however, Nietzsche repeatedly underscores the weakness and ineffectuality of modern humanity, and thus fails to anticipate anything like the actual ecological disasters that will unfold in the coming century as a result of human activity. From the cosmic scale in which Nietzsche's image of the earth is often placed, the activities of human beings appear to be inconsequential. Nietzsche even dismisses concern about the exhaustion of the earth's finite resources and human overpopulation:

> That which in senile short-sightedness you call the overpopulation of the earth is precisely what offers the more hopeful their greatest task: mankind shall one day become a tree that overshadows the whole earth bearing many billions of blossoms that shall all become fruit alongside one another, and the earth itself shall be prepared for the nourishment of this tree.³
>
> Das, was ihr als Übervölkerung der Erde in greisenhafter Kurzsichtigkeit fürchtet, gibt dem Hoffnungsvolleren eben die grosse Aufgabe in die Hand: die Menschheit soll einmal ein Baum werden, der die ganze Erde überschattet, mit vielen Milliarden von Blüten, die alle nebeneinander Früchte werden sollen, und die Erde selbst soll zur Ernährung dieses Baumes vorbereitet werden. (KSA/2, *Menschliches* Allzumenschliches II, par. 189).

Rather than like ants on an ant-hill, left to instinct, Nietzsche hopes for the deliberate promotion of this expansive growth of humanity. In contrast, in *Zarathustra* Nietzsche refers to the human population as constituting a disease on the surface or skin of the earth, yet even there suggests that its heart remains of gold, suggesting, Gary Shapiro argues, "an unsupported faith in earth's potential for self-renewal" (Shapiro 2013, pp. 82–83). This faith cannot be dismissed as mere historical naiveté, for others of Nietzsche's time took a more urgent view of the effects of human activity on earth and predicted coming ecological crises. John Ruskin condemned the effects of unconstrained industrialism on the natural world in *Unto This Last*, first published as an essay in 1860. Just a few years after Nietzsche's death, Max Weber attacked the industrial capitalist compulsion to exploit the earth "until the last ton of fossil fuel has burnt to ashes" (Weber 1958, p. 181). The idea that the earth is, other than superficially, immune to the unhealthy activities of humanity, may be implicitly supported not only by Nietzsche's tendency toward a cosmic perspective, but also by the specific doctrine of eternal return. In the cosmic affirmation of endless repetition, nature itself seems to be affirmed as infinitely cyclical and regenerating. Such a view

---

3 This translation, altered here, is drawn from R.J. Hollingdale (Nietzsche 1996, p. 356).

would obviate any reckoning with the fragility of the earth—or at least of life on earth—and obstruct a grasp of the pressure on its resources.

Nietzsche's dismissal of the impending ecological crisis notwithstanding, there are hints elsewhere in Nietzsche of a more urgent ecological recognition. Zarathustra, albeit figuratively, presents a devastating picture of the potential consequences of human hubris. For Zarathustra is haunted by the soothsayer's description of a wrecked and wretched earth on which humanity stands as on a graveyard:

> We harvested well, but why did all our fruits turn foul and brown?
> What fell down from the evil moon last night?
> All work was for naught, our wine has become poison, the evil eye
> seared yellow our fields and hearts.
> All of us became dry, and if fire were to touch us, then we would turn
> to dust like ashes – yes, fire itself we have made weary.
> All our wells dried up, even the sea retreated. All firm ground wants to
> crack, but the depths do not want to devour!
> 'Oh where is there still a sea in which one could drown?'—thus rings
> our lament – out across the shallow swamps.
> Indeed, we have already become too weary to die; now we continue to
> wake and we live on—in burial chambers!" (Nietzsche 2006, p. 106).
>
> (Wohl haben wir geerntet: aber warum wurden alle Früchte uns faul und braun? Was fiel vom bösen Monde bei der letzten Nacht hernieder?
> Umsonst war alle Arbeit, Gift ist unser Wein geworden, böser Blick sengte unsre Felder und Herzen gelb.
> Trocken wurden wir Alle; und fällt Feuer auf uns, so stäuben wir der
> Asche gleich: – ja das Feuer selber machten wir müde.
> Alle Brunnen versiegten uns, auch das Meer wich zurück. Aller Grund will reissen, aber die Tiefe will nicht schlingen!
> 'Ach, wo ist noch ein Meer, in dem man ertrinken könnte': so klingt unsre Klage – hinweg über flache Sümpfe.
> Wahrlich, zum Sterben wurden wir schon zu müde; nun wachen wir noch und leben fort –
> in Grabkammern!) (HW/III, p. 146).

Affected profoundly by this vision, Zarathustra must overcome his nausea in the thought of eternal recurrence, having to countenance that the human being's sickly, earth-alienated existence would be repeated in perpetuity. In his dream, Zarathustra tells his animals, "the human earth transformed into a cave, its chest caved in; everything living became human mould and bones and crumbling past. (Zur Höhle wandelte sich mir die Menschen-Erde, ihre Brust sank hinein, alles Lebendige ward mir Menschen-Moder und Knochen und morsche Vergangenheit.)" (HW/III, p. 243).

From "Über Wahrheit und Lüge" to *Zarathustra* we find a devastating critique of our cognitive habits, with distinctly ecological implications. Nietzsche's deconstruction of metaphysics, his critique of the ecological implications of idealism, has been interpreted "as a conservational, restorative act," an effort to recover earth as the ground of our being and thinking (del Caro 2004, p. 9). Yet in referring to a stammering language that arises from the "primal faculty of human imagination (aus dem Urvermögen menschlicher Phantasie)" (KSA/1, p. 883), Nietzsche holds out the possibility that novel and creative forms of expression, in breaking with ordinary modes of conceptualisation, may help us to appreciate other, more primal connections we may have to our earthly origins. Such would be the contribution of the artist or poet, promoting restoration of a more primal and original, and indeed healthier, form of cognition. This would involve, according to Nietzsche's reflection on his novel, "the return of language to the nature of imagery (diese Rückkehr der Sprache zur Natur der Bildlichkeit)," or a recovery of experiential imagination in its interconnections with biological and earthly life (KSA/6, p. 344). Here Zarathustra's future-directed vision of human ecology may be productively inspired by something like Hölderlin's *Andenken*, the task of founding what remains through poetical remembrance. Accordingly, the ecological task of poet and artist would not be to merely represent nature in realist description, or primarily to sustain in memory reverence for particular topographies—though these may be valuable in themselves—but to regenerate, in futurally-directed recollection, possibilities for earth-oriented cognition.

Conclusion

A number of questions remain in considering the contributions of Nietzsche to a cognitive ecology, or to an ecologically-minded approach to human cognition, only two of which I will mention in conclusion. One question may be whether it is at all effectual to promote artistic and poetic activity as any kind of solution to a contemporary environmental crisis that threatens, after all, to realise the soothsayer's nightmare of a poisoned harvest on a dried-up, ashen planet. While countering idealism, the ecological thinking such as fostered by these considerations in Nietzsche's philosophy offers neither a practical itinerary, nor a particularly pragmatic ethos. Yet literary ecocritics have long insisted that in order to change our comportment toward the planet, we need other, more reverent or respectful modes of living with nature, modes literary and artistic descriptions may preserve and sustain—whether this is accomplished primarily through realist renderings, or nostalgic sacralisations of local topographies. I have tried to suggest here the value of Nietzsche's excavation of the cognitive—that is, epistemic, linguistic, conceptual—operations that underlie human relationships to nature. It is by now fairly well recognised that coping with the ecological crisis requires, among other things, an evolution in our self-understanding, that we invent new ways of being human. That some of these new ways may turn out to be retrievals of more "primal" or original experiences need not be dismissed as aestheticizing nostalgia, but can be productive and imaginative ways of retrieving inspiration for thought, feeling, and action within our embodied connections to the earth.

Related to this question is that of the place of ecological science in a Nietzschean critique of cognition. Despite his critique of abstract thinking, Nietzsche expressed considerable respect for science in "endeavouring to help us see what is there, help us to avoid the errors of beyond-looking [...] that plague us as a species" (del Caro 2004, p. 17). But contemporary science can be informed by a broader experiential sensibility than its disciplinary modes of verification afford, and it is highly probable that the efforts of its practitioners are motivated by values—such as the desirability of preserving life on the planet—that are not themselves, strictly speaking, candidates for conventional scientific proof. Nietzsche's own vision of science, it has been argued, "attempts to train the heart to delight in the earth as illuminated by intellect, to be loyal to the earth as a haven of life that has appeared and will perish with the deep and mysterious immensities of space and time" (Lampert 1993, pp. 6–7). Just as medicine devoted to healing the human body may involve an art wholly rooted in science, so too the attendance to our ailing planet through scientific study and technological intervention must be enabled by our most creative modes of thinking—above all about the kind of animals we are, wish and are able to become.

Bibliography

Acampora, Ralph R. (1994): "Using and Abusing Nietzsche for Environmental Ethics." In: *Environmental Ethics* 16: 2, pp. 187–194.
Allison, David B. (2001): *Reading the New Nietzsche*. Lanham, MD: Rowman and Littlefield.
Bachelard, Gaston (1958): *La Poétique de l'espace*. Paris: Presses Universitaires de France.
Bateson, Gregory (1972): *Steps to an Ecology of Mind*. Chicago: University of Chicago Press.
Bertram, Ernst (2009): *Nietzsche: Attempt at a Mythology* [1918]. Trans. Norton, Robert E. Urbana / Chicago: University of Illinois Press.
Cave, Terence (2016): *Thinking With Literature: Towards a Cognitve Criticism*. Oxford: Oxford University Press.
Crawford, Claudia (1988): *The Beginnings of Nietzsche's Theory of Language*. Berlin / New York: De Gruyter.

Del Caro, Adrian (1981): *Dionysian Aesthetics: the Role of Destruction in Creation as Reflected in the Life and Works of Friedrich Nietzsche.* Frankfurt am Main: Peter Lang.
Del Caro, Adrian (2004): *Grounding the Nietzsche Rhetoric of Earth.* Berlin: Walter de Gruyter.
Deleuze, Gilles / Guattari, Felix (1994): *What is Philosophy?* Trans. Birchill, Graham / Tomlinson, Hugh. New York: Columbia University Press.
Dilthey, Wilhelm (1985): *Selected Works, vol. V, Poetry and Experience.* Eds. Makkreel, Rudolph A. / Rodi, Frithjof. Princeton NJ: Princeton University Press.
Goodbody, Axel (2011): "Sense of Place and Lieu de Memoire." In: Goodbody, Axel / Rigby, Kate (Eds.): *Ecocritical Theory: New European Approaches.* Charlottesville, VA: University of Virginia Press, pp. 55–68.
Günzel, Stephan (2003): "Nietzsche's Geophilosophie." In: *Journal of Nietzsche Studies* 25, pp. 103–116.
Hallman, Max O. (1991): "Nietzsche's Environmental Ethics." In: *Environmental Ethics* 13, pp. 99–125.
Heidegger, Martin (1977): *Holzwege* (Gesamtausgabe, Bd. 5). Frankfurt a. M.: Vittorio Klostermann.
Heise, Ursula (2008): *Sense of Place and Sense of Planet: The Environmental Imagination of the Global.* Oxford / New York: Oxford University Press.
Kaufmann, Walter (1975): *Nietzsche: Philosopher, Psychologist, Antichrist.* 4th edition. Princeton: Princeton University Press.
Lakoff, George / Johnson, Mark (1980): *Metaphors We Live By.* Chicago: University of Chicago Press.
Lakoff, George / Johnson, Mark (1999): *Philosophy in the Flesh: The Embodied Mind and Its Challenge to Western Thought.* New York: Basic Books.
Lampert, Lawrence (1993): *Nietzsche and Modern Times: A Study of Bacon, Descartes, and Nietzsche.* New Haven: Yale University Press.
Lemm, Vanessa (2009): *Nietzsche's Animal Philosophy: Culture, Politics, and the Animality of the Human Being.* New York: Fordham University Press.
Malpas, Jeff (2014): "We Hyperboreans: Naturalism, Nietzsche, and Topography." In: Young, Julian (Ed.): *Individual and Community in Nietzsche's Philosophy.* Cambridge: Cambridge University Press, pp. 195–213.
Miller, J. Hillis (1995): *Topographies.* Stanford, CA: Stanford University Press.
Nietzsche, Friedrich (1954 ff.): *Werke in drei Bänden.* Ed. Schlechta, Karl. Munich: Hanser.
Nietzsche, Friedrich (1967 ff): *Werke. Kritische Gesamtausgabe,* Eds. Colli, Giorgio / Montinari, Mazzino. Berlin / New York: Walter de Gruyter.
Nietzsche, Friedrich (1974): *The Gay Science.* Trans. Kaufmann, Walter. New York: Viking Press.
Nietzsche, Friedrich (1976): *The Portable Nietzsche.* Ed. and trans. Kaufmann, Walter. New York: Viking Press.
Nietzsche, Friedrich (1979): *Nietzsche, Philosophy, and Truth: Selections from Nietzsche's Notebooks of the 1870's.* Ed. and Trans. Breazele, Daniel. Atlantic Highlands, NJ: Humanities Press.
Nietzsche, Friedrich (1980): *Sämtliche Werke. Kritische Studienausgabe in 15 Bänden.* Eds. Colli, Giorgio / Montinari, Mazzino. Berlin / New York: Walter de Gruyter and dtv.
Nietzsche, Friedrich (1990): *Das Hauptwerk.* Munich: Nymphenburger Verlagsanstalt.

Nietzsche, Friedrich (1996): *Human, All-Too-Human: A Book for Free Spirits*. Trans. Hollingdale, R. J. Cambridge: Cambridge University Press.
Nietzsche, Friedrich (2006): *Thus Spoke Zarathustra*. Ed. Pippin, Robert, trans. del Caro, Adrian. Cambridge: Cambridge University Press.
Parkes, Graham (1999): "Staying Loyal to the Earth: Nietzsche as Ecological Thinker." In: Lippit, John (Ed.): *Nietzsche's Futures*. NY: St. Martin's Press, pp. 167–188.
Pence, Charles H. (2011): "Nietzsche's Aesthetic Critique of Darwin." In: *Hist. Phil. Life Sci.* 33, pp. 165–190.
Pippin, Robert (2006): "Introduction." In: Nietzsche, Friedrich. *Thus Spoke Zarathustra*. Ed. del Caro, Adrian / Pippin, Robert. Trans. del Caro, Adrian. Cambridge: Cambridge University Press.
Ricoeur, Paul (1977): *The Rule of Metaphor: The Creation of Meaning in Language*. Trans. Czernyi, Robert. Toronto: University of Toronto Press.
Roszak, Theodore (1993): *The Voice of the Earth: An Exploration of Ecopsychology*. New York: Simon and Schuster.
Shapiro, Gary (2006): "Nietzsche on Geophilosophy and Geoaesthetics." In: Pearson, Keith Ansell (Ed.): *A Companion to Nietzsche*. New York: Blackwell, pp. 477–494.
Shapiro, Gary (2013): "Earth's Garden-Happiness: Nietzsche's Geoaesthetics of the Anthropocene." In: *Nietzsche-Studien* 42:1, pp. 67–84.
Shapiro, Gary (2016): *Nietzsche's Earth: Great Events, Great Politics*. Chicago: University of Chicago Press.
Sokel, Walter H. (2005): "On the Dionysian in Nietzsche." In: *New Literary History* 36, pp. 501–520.
Söring, Jürgen (1990): "Nietzsches Empedokles-Plan." In: *Nietzsche-Studien* 19, pp. 176–211.
Storey, David E. (2016): "Nietzsche and Ecology Revisited: The Biological Basis of Value." In: *Environmental Ethics* 38, pp. 19–45.
Weber, Max (1958): *The Protestant Ethic and the Spirit of Capitalism* [1904–05]. Trans. Parsons, Talcott. New York: Allen&Unwin.
Zimmerman, Michael E. (2008): "Nietzsche and Ecology: A Critical Inquiry." In: Hicks, Steven V. / Rosenberg, Alan (Eds.): *Reading Nietzsche at the Margins*. West Lafayette, IN: Purdue University Press, pp. 165–186.

Abbreviations

HW = Nietzsche, Friedrich (1990): *Das Hauptwerk*. Munich: Nymphenburger.
KGW = Nietzsche, Friedrich (1967 ff.): *Werke. Kritische Gesamtausgabe*. Eds. Colli, Giorgio / Montinari, Mazzino. Berlin / New York: Walter de Gruyter.
KSA = Nietzsche, Friedrich (1980): *Sämtliche Werke. Kritische Studienausgabe in 15 Bänden*. Eds. Colli, Giorgio / Montinari, Mazzino. Berlin / New York: Walter de Gruyter and dtv.
WD = Nietzsche, Friedrich (1954 ff.): *Werke in drei Bänden*. Ed. Schlecta, Karl. Munich: Hanser.

Annamaria Lossi
Overturning Philosophy:

Classic and (Anti)-Classic Considerations on Nietzsche's *Ecce Homo*[1]

> "Life is possible only when we create stability in a constantly changing world" (Winchester 1994, p. 3)

Abstract: "Classic" can be said in many ways. In general, it defines that which conforms to Greek and Roman models in literature or arts; or, as the first meaning of the Oxford Dictionary suggests, 'classic' is "judged over a period of time to be of the highest quality and outstanding of its kind."[2] In this sense, in philosophy, "classical" is the adjective that outlines a philosophical period or a thinker who lived during antiquity, or the time after antiquity, revealing a model either for the present or for the time to come. This specification shows the hermeneutical connotation of a method through which the scientific approach towards ages and thinkers can be understood. Western thought in its all is believed to be a long story of spiritual and cultural development which departs from one golden and past moment—the classical period, when the first philosophical questions arose.[3] And it proceeds with other transformations whose value is measured up.

The aim of this article is to show some aspects of Nietzsche's way of writing and conceiving philosophy as a (self)description, to contribute to Nietzsche's rediscovery as an 'anticlassic' and—in this—as a 'classic' *sui generis*. The article explores how Nietzsche became a classic and which aesthetic features outline his philosophy as intimal net of thinking and poetics.

---

[1] The first version of this paper was presented at the workshop "*(Anti)classicism and (Anti)idealism* at the German Department, University of Cork, the 8th and 9th June 2017. I am very grateful to Gert Hofmann and Juliana de Albuquerque for the opportunity they gave me to discuss the paper with all the participants in Cork. A special thanks goes to Bethany Parsons for the stimulating comments and the linguistic review.
[2] See Oxford Dictionary at: https://en.oxforddictionaries.com.
[3] As Alfred North Whitehead noted "The safest general characterisation of the European philosophical tradition is that it consists of a series of footnotes to Plato. [...]. I allude to the wealth of the general ideas scattered thorough them [Plato's writings]." (Whitehead 1978, p. 39).

1

Observing the changes that have occurred in every historical period, it might be correct to say that every period has got its own classics. Throughout the centuries models and thoughts have changed, have constantly undergone transformation. So, when 'classic' is used to describe a doctrine or a "school" of thinking in modern times, it means that it has become a paradigm, something that everything is measured up to. In the case of philosophy, 'classic' has to be understood as an unifying and coherent reasoning with strong logical basis and an excellent constellation of deductions which finally become—or are believed to become—a model for "truth." In this sense, scholars have always considered Greek and Latin philosophy as 'classic', and the Renaissance as rebirth of the classics, which is strictly linked to the rediscovery of the writings of the Ancient time; but, in addition to these is German philosophy of 19th century, including the Idealism originating from Kant's philosophy and Goethe's poetry. This age has become particularly important as a new paradigm for Modern thinking: the height of philosophy in the sense of a systematic approach and theoretical accomplishment.

Things become more complicated when the name of Friedrich Nietzsche is mentioned. The philosopher, who died prophetically in 1900, closed a classical age in Germany and in Europe, and at the same time announced radical change for the cultural age to come. Today, in the 21st century, only a few would dare to deny that Nietzsche represents the greatest philosopher of Modernity, becoming herewith a "classic." Yet Nietzsche is classical in a quite unusual way: he broke the boundaries of systems and conventions, revealing to be not only the muse of the most important philosophers after him, like Georges Bataille, Michel Foucault or Gilles Deleuze as well as Oswald Spengler und Theodor Adorno, Emanuele Severino und Gianni Vattimo or José Ortega y Gasset, to quote only a few of them; but Nietzsche influenced profoundly also literature and art with his way of writing and combining metaphorically new images. Thomas Mann, Rainer Maria Rilke, Gabriele D'Annunzio or Milan Kundera would not have written as they did without Nietzsche. Paradoxically, it is his anti-classic philosophy, his hard critiques to traditional concepts and ideas such as God, I, and Truth that developed a new rhapsodic and asystematic thinking. This attitude towards philosophy let him become the master of complexity and the analyst of language, becoming the classical thinker for postmodern philosophy.

Nietzsche's history of effects represents a paradigmatic example of how the way to become a classic can be seen as an interlace of interpretations and misunderstandings. The 20th century has shown how the impact of Nietzsche's writings and notes started with a profound misreading of his thoughts, which were merely rejected and branded as disseminated provocative statements without solid philosophical frames, nor logical basis, appearing rather as the brainstorm of a mad man, or depicting him as an antisemitic agitator, according to his sister's editing work.[4]

One of the first interesting philosophical interpretations of Nietzsche was delivered by Martin Heidegger.[5] The German philosopher aimed at creating a synergy between his own antimetaphysical and ontological thinking, concerned in the uncovering of the Being, and Nietzsche's fragments. In Heidegger's hermenutical framework Nietzsche appeared as the last metaphysician of the history of philosophy. In other words, Nietzsche's work was believed to be the end of a certain period of the history of philosophy, which forgot being in this way from Athens (Plato) to Freiburg (Heidegger) passing by Naumburg (Nietzsche). According to Heidegger, Nietzsche exhausted all the possibilities of metaphysics, which had its origins during the Greek Classics with Plato, and in this reached its highest accomplishment.[6] The greatest merit of Heidegger's attempt to give an account of the arc from Plato to Nietzsche, believing the latter to be the *last* metaphysician, seems to be that of considering Nietzsche a philosopher, despite the fact that Nietzsche had not received any real academic valorisation til that moment. However, in offering a hermenutical view in which Nietzsche is believed to be a philosopher, the results of Heidegger's interpretation are insufficient and inadequate, unable as they are to give account of Nietzsche's corpus of writings. Moreover, his Freiburg lectures were built on the interpretation of Nietzsche's scattered fragments, which were not taken in a philological order as per Nietzsche's own thoretical development, but were given a conceptual structure per Heidegger's ontological view, oblivious to the issues of imposing this structure.

A new reading of Nietzsche's writings started thanks to the work of two Italian scholars, Giorgio Colli and Mazzino Montinari, who, during the Sixties, recontructed philologically the birth of Nietzsche's published works according to the unpublished fragments and notes as well as Nietzsche's lectures during his ten years at the university and at the Pädagogium of Basel. We can now

---

4 Alfred Baeumler used Nietzsche to legitimise Nazism in his book *Nietzsche der Philosoph und Politiker* of 1931.
5 The German philosopher held lectures from 1936 to 1940 at the University of Freiburg on Nietzsche's posthoumos fragments around the "concept" of will to power. These lectures were subsequently published by Heidegger himself 1961 in the two volumes of his *Nietzsche* by the German publisher Neske in Pfullingen.
6 On this point, more intensively, see Lossi 2006.

say that Nietzsche's way to becoming a 'classic' in history of philosophy was inaugurated by his rehabilitation as philosopher thanks to the philological reconstruction of his works. As a matter of fact, from that point on, interpreters started to consider Nietzsche as a thinker, to such an extent that the major thinkers of the 20th century had to contend with him. His style of philosophising has become prophetic for the so-called postmodern philosophy, and a new connotation of Modern thoughts studies, in the wider sense, started to be considered. The Nietzsche-Studien, the international review for the Nietzsche-Forschung, is dedicated to the reception of Nietzsche not only in philosophy, but also in other disciplines such as classical studies, literary studies or theology.[7]

On the changes of style, literature, and arts and their new tendencies, Nietzsche's way of reasoning and writing has a particular role. Nevertheless his works have been seldom read as literary masterpieces: Nietzsche became the (post)modern thinker par excellence, not the writer. His *Dichten und Denken* is not easy to grasp in a systematic interpretation nor in a narrative description because Nietzsche's narratology is not opposed to his philosophy, but intimately connected. Only in the last decades has Nietzsche's narrative significance *as* a writer come into light.[8]

2

New aesthetic and philosophical understandings occur by changing the way of writing and expressing philosophy. Even if philosophy and literature are largely considered as two different strategies of narrative schemes, and only rarely has philosophy been regarded as a literary genre,[9] they are in fact strictly related. A very good example of this connection is Nietzsche's understanding of philosophy. Among his many and different works, from his lectures to his fragments

---

[7] As we can read in the presentation of the Aims and Scopes of The *Nietzsche-Studien*, the Yearbook "serves not just the ideas of any one school or direction, but rather introduce various different approaches to interpreting Nietzsche." And, furthermore, each volume is completed by a section dedicated to the discovers and to the research of Nietzsche's sources—the socalled *Quellenforschung*—which aims at presenting every time new foundings in Nietzsche's numerous readings and influences. Last but not laest, the enourmos history of effects—*Wirkungsgeschichte*—Nietzsche's thought and works have, is documented by the lively Nietzsche-community of the last decades.

[8] In the contemporary German Nietzsche-Forschung Groddeck 1991, Benne 2005 and Zittel 2011 considered the representative forms of Nietzsche's thinking following the traditional Italian reasearch and increasing it in the direction of the literary significance of his works.

[9] I would like to mention on the opposite constellation Gentili 2003.

and the different styles of published texts the posthumous notes, which have been challenging scholars for more than a century, the work intitled *Ecco Homo* (EH) represents a good example to illustrate one of Nietzsche's self-descriptions in philosophy. Some of the aesthetical features of Nietzsche's writings come into light in this short work, composed roughly in 1888 and published posthumously in 1908, whose interpretation reveals a profound challenge to the usual philosophical and narratological considerations of Nietzsche's writing.

If 'anticlassic' means to break an established rule and the frame in which a concept or a thought has been acquired and taught, then Nietzsche opens up a completely different way of thinking about the philosophical subject and narration. This is the reason why EH cannot be considered an autobiographical work; *it* does not belong to any literary nor philosophical genre. Starting from the Table of contents, we can easily acquire what a reader can find in it: a short preface, three self-declaring chapters, followed by another self-describing section as conclusion of the entire book. What is herewith described? What expectations can a reader have of it?

Genre and style are certainly related to one another. In his—often considered intellectual autobiographical work—*Ecce Homo*, Nietzsche's style should be that of a literary work, that is: autobiographic and intellectual and fictional, to a certain point. At a first sight, EH's subtitle, *How one becomes what one is*, might confirm this opinion. Reading this late writing we are apparently in front of a historical description of personal and biographical impressions, or more precisely "small and, according to traditional judgment, quite insignificant things: [...] nutrition, locality, climate, recreation, the entire casuistry of selfishness" (EH, § 2, p. 23). The adjective "intellectual" would refer then to the collection of reflections coming from ten of Nietzsche's most meaningful past works which constitute the central part of the book. This retrospective reflection is not illogical, considering the work in the context of Nietzsche's late writings of 1888. Coming back to past works is not a new narrative strategy: in the Eighties, Nietzsche worked on new books, such as *Beyond Good and Evil*, but at the same time, on the reedition of his past works. *The Birth of Tragedy*, as well as *Human all too Human* (1886) and then *Daybreak* and the *Gay Science* (1887), all received new prefaces and this last work received the addition of a fifth book and a collection of poetic compositions. It seems to be an oversimplified explanation to regard this attitude towards his own past in terms of a pure critical reconsideration of Nietzsche's previous philosophy led by himself, which now in EH would represent just rough material for the account of his own life. This work would then be considered a classical literary work which might accord to the autobiographical pact, (cf. Lejeune 1975) the description of Nietzsche's intellectual life as philosopher and writer, how he developed and what he composed, written by himself, not even the story of embedded memories from the childhood of a great philosopher to his maturity. Rather than that, Nietzsche's EH opens up narrative and philosophical reflections on Nietzsche's own conception of self-knowledge and literature, which might also open the investigating perspective on narrative territories which have not yet been mapped. But Nietzsche's self-understanding in EH represents the goal, not the departing point of the book as traditional, even if fragmentary, autobiographies usually show. Taking EH for an autobiographical work would mean to reverse Nietzsche's goal, which is the philosophical self-definition through a self-description *a posteriori*. To understand this formulation, it must be argued how Nietzsche follows his reasoning, also taking into account other works, as well as fragments and thoughts, in a preliminary stage for their publication and belonging to the same period. Among them, the new prefaces to *The Birth of Tragedy* as well as to *Human all too Human* or to *Daybreak* and the *Gay Science* are all attempts at self-criticism; in the sense of a general reconsideration of his past thoughts in the light of the present. Here Nietzsche is responding to a will to self-interpretation which pushes him to face the past, but with the intention to write for the future. The will to self-interpretation emerges in the late prefaces, yet it is connected to Nietzsche's ideas on moral and natural instincts strictly linked to philosophy. According to Nietzsche, the instinct to philosophise a will to power, the instinctual need of something, is, for Nietzsche, strictly connected with the object of satisfaction itself—in this case, the need of affirming oneself, connected to the production of a philosophical thought[10]

A single notation cannot give account of such a complex concept. Many are the rhapsodic fragments, many are the changes in the elaboration of possible books beginnings with preliminary stages, uncompleted reflections among the years make Nietzsche's disclosure to our understanding difficult to grasp in one holistic and coherent hermenutic of his thought. In *Beyond of Good and Evil*, Nietzsche clearly connects this thinking with the need of philosophising, claiming that:

> I do not believe that a "drive for knowledge" is the father of philosophy, but rather that another drive, here as elsewhere, used knowledge (and mis-knowledge!) merely as a tool. But anyone who looks at people's basic drives, to see how far they may have played their little game right here as inspiring geniuses (or daemons or sprites –), will find that they all practiced philosophy at some point,—and that every single one of them would be only too

---

10 Nietzsche seems to give this interpretation when he writes in his Fragments of 1875: "Jeder Trieb ist ein Bedürfniß und enthält bereits die *Vorstellung von der Existenz eines Gegenstandes der Befriedigung*; so ist der Trieb ideenbildend." (NF Summer 1875, 9.1 in KSA 8, p. 131).

pleased to present itself as the ultimate purpose of existence and as rightful master of all the other drives. Because every drive craves mastery, and this leads it to try philosophizing.—Of course: with scholars, the truly scientific people, things might be different—"better" if you will—, with them, there might really be something like a drive for knowledge, some independent little clockwork mechanism that, once well wound, ticks bravely away without essentially involving the rest of the scholar's drives. For this reason, the scholar's real "interests" usually lie somewhere else entirely, with the family, or earning money, or in politics; in fact, it is almost a matter of indifference whether his little engine is put to work in this or that field of research, and whether the "promising" young worker turns himself into a good philologist or fungus expert or chemist:—it doesn't signify anything about him that he becomes one thing or the other. In contrast, there is absolutely nothing impersonal about the philosopher; and in particular his morals bear decided and decisive witness to who he is—which means, in what order of rank the innermost drives of his nature stand with respect to each other. (BGE, First Part, § 6, p. 20).

(Ich glaube demgemäss nicht, dass ein "Trieb zur Erkenntniss" der Vater der Philosophie ist, sondern dass sich ein andrer Trieb, hier wie sonst, der Erkenntniss (und der Verkenntniss!) nur wie eines Werkzeugs bedient hat. Wer aber die Grundtriebe des Menschen darauf hin ansieht, wie weit sie gerade hier als inspirirende Genien (oder Dämonen und Kobolde –) ihr Spiel getrieben haben mögen, wird finden, dass sie Alle schon einmal Philosophie getrieben haben, – und dass jeder Einzelne von ihnen gerade sich gar zu gerne als letzten Zweck des Daseins und als berechtigten Herrn aller übrigen Triebe darstellen möchte. Denn jeder Trieb ist herrschsüchtig: und als solcher versucht er zu philosophiren. – Freilich: bei den Gelehrten, den eigentlich wissenschaftlichen Menschen, mag es anders stehn – "besser", wenn man will –, da mag es wirklich so Etwas wie einen Erkenntnisstrieb geben, irgend ein kleines unabhängiges Uhrwerk, welches, gut aufgezogen, tapfer darauf los arbeitet, ohne dass die gesammten übrigen Triebe des Gelehrten wesentlich dabei betheiligt sind. Die eigentlichen "Interessen" des Gelehrten liegen deshalb gewöhnlich ganz wo anders, etwa in der Familie oder im Gelderwerb oder in der Politik; ja es ist beinahe gleichgültig, ob seine kleine Maschine an diese oder jene Stelle der Wissenschaft gestellt wird, und ob der "hoffnungsvolle" junge Arbeiter aus sich einen guten Philologen oder Pilzekenner oder Chemiker macht: – es bezeichnet ihn nicht, dass er dies oder jenes wird. Umgekehrt ist an dem Philosophen ganz und gar nichts Unpersönliches; und insbesondere giebt seine Moral ein entschiedenes und entscheidendes Zeugniss dafür ab, wer er ist – das heisst, in welcher Rangordnung die innersten Triebe seiner Natur zu einander gestellt sind. (KSA 5, Erstes Hauptstück, § 6, p. 20).

The first observation regards the reversing attitude Nietzsche has towards classical philosophy. Connecting the will to "mastery" and to philosophy, Nietzsche expresses an opposite idea to Cicero's conception, according to which freedom is believed to be the mastery of oneself and therefore the mastery of the drives themselves. Nietzsche reverses this Stoic view: the drives themselves are mastery of conscience and of rational leading instruments. If philosophising means to become master of something, or of ourselves, in as far as philosophy "always creates the world in its own image, it cannot do otherwise; philosophy is this tyrannical drive itself, the most spiritual will to power, to the 'creation of the world', to the causa prima" (BGE, § 9, p. 22) – then philosophising means to accomplish the most specific own personal need and not to respond to objectivity. The protagonist of philosophy is the "I" as the first subject of thoughts and plurality of interpretations.

This idea reaches its highest point when Nietzsche composed EH. The will of self-interpretation intensifies to such an extent in this work that it is carried out by a will of an unending self-creation in writing. In EH Nietzsche declared this future goal. The works of 1888, which EH belongs to, can be seen as a modified narrative realisation of Nietzsche's amibitious project of a transvaluation of all values, which Nietzsche planned, yet without a classic realisation. In 1888 this project is translated into a series of books Nietzsche wrote and published rapidly (except EH, which was published only 1908). The self-characterisation here is not shaped as a traditional philosophical system; it looks rather like a composition of notes with a future goal. The perspective in the age to come corresponds with Nietzsche's concerns about a future interpretation, in as far as Nietzsche considers himself being posthumous. The hyperbolic self-definition occuring in EH of being dynamite, that is, of having an explosive personality, reverses both: the classical thought according to which self-knowledge is the starting point of philosophy, and the autobiographical attitude which consders as narrative assumption a storytelling of the past. "Selbst-Kenntniss" is not even considerd a realistic goal, at least according to Nietzsche's claim in *Daybreak* (D), in the text entitled *Experience and Invention:*

> [...] far a man may go in self-knowledge [Selbstkenntniss], nothing however can be more incomplete than his image of the totality of his drives; their play and counterplay among one another and above all the laws of their nutriment remain entirely unknown to him. (D, II Book, § 119, p. 115).

> (Wie weit Einer seine Selbstkenntniss auch treiben mag, Nichts kann doch unvollständiger sein, als das Bild der gesammten *Triebe*, die sein Wesen constituiren. Kaum dass er die gröberen beim Namen nennen kann: ihre Zahl und Stärke, ihre Ebbe und Fluth, ihr Spiel und Widerspiel unter einander, und vor Allem die Gesetze ihrer *Ernährung* bleiben ihm ganz unbekannt.) (KSA 3, p. 111).

What does Nietzsche mean with this expression of being dynamite? How can it be interpreted to be posthumous ? Nietzsche's particular self-narration in EH occurs *sub specie futurae*, that is, in the light of his early conception of being untimely, as he claims in EH:

> I know my fate. One day my name will be associated with the memory of something tremendous—a crisis without equal on earth, the most profound collision of conscience, a decision

that was conjured up against everything that had been believed, demanded, hallowed so far. I am no man, I am dynamite. (EH Why I am a Destiny, § 1, p. 150).

(Ich kenne mein Loos. Es wird sich einmal an meinem Namen die Erinnerung an etwas Ungeheures anknüpfen, – an eine Krisis, wie es keine auf Erden gab, an die tiefste Gewissens-Collision, an eine Entscheidung heraufbeschworen *gegen* Alles, was bis dahin geglaubt, gefordert, geheiligt worden war. Ich bin kein Mensch, ich bin Dynamit.) (KSA 6, p. 365).

Nietzsche's specific attempt to give form to the dynamic and inexorable becoming challenges writing and language in an original philosophical-narrative process which involves the author as figure of a future interpretation. Nietzsche's transvaluating project aims at challenging the metaphysical and theoretical efforts of the past philosophically, by creating a new narrative context for it which challenges also the narrative genre. Parody is one of the means Nietzsche uses in EH for his purpose.[11]

Therefore, the main question in EH regards the representation of the own identity as philosopher in his works for a future interpretation as fulfillment of his own will of writing. The descriptions are based not on a real subject, but on the uninterrupted construction of "being a destiny," everyone's destiny, in as far as it is conceived to be a destiny for the entire humanity. Nietzsche reverses the idea of writing *about a past life* into the attempt of a *personal narrative and philosophical self-creation for the future.* Yet the self-characterisation transcends the philosophical based self-knowledge, that is: the understanding of the self passes through the interpretation of the other, the future reader, and not merely through the author's description. The challenge of this thought needs a more comprehensive aesthetic analysis of Nietzsche's conception of life.

3

EH has to be thought of as a work apart, which shows a will of being after the book itself. The metaphorical/parodistic intent deals with Nietzsche's conception of its own authoriality and future reception, which pleads for a different role of the aesthetic. The aesthetic issues of Nietzsche's thought constitute the main and most interesting question of Nietzsche's philosophy. As a matter of fact, differ-

---

11 As Bernd Magnus pointed out: "Parody is inherent in the persistent 'pas au dela' or step beyond of hyperbole/litote. Each of Nietzsche's major hyperboles, the stones he casts at the edifice of metaphysics, derives considerable impact as a deep parody of current attitudes, ways of comprehending and self-descriptions. [...] Self-representation can only be self-parody." (Magnus 1993, pp. 252–253).

ently from Kant, who thought the aesthetic to be a bridge between the cognitive-scientific sphere and the moral-ethical reason, aesthetic is for Nietzsche the only way to represent life as it is. Art, as it is written in the *Birth of Tragedy*, is the only justification of life, as art made life possible and worth living for the Greeks. Life has to do with change: the dynamical aspect does not match with the views of previous philosophers which tried to summarise the concept of life in theoretical systems or in a theory of knowledge, as Nietzsche states in *Beyond Good and Evil*. Differently from the Kantian and Idealistic philosophers Nietzsche's own perspective tries to match his own existence as writer and philosopher with his art of writing. Rather than opposing values between them such as good to evil, moral to immoral, or philosophy to art and poetry, Nietzsche's narrative attempt goes beyond these traditional metaphysical oppositions in as far as it aims at elaborating a style which collides with the usual formulations. Nietzsche's effort tries to give form to life, however neither describing it as a mere literary work (such as a biographical work), nor formulating a theory of (self-)knowledge which could not show the essential relation between life and philosophy as this latter is not the result of knowledge, but the path to a future self-understanding.[12]

The hermeneutic role of art in this contest is extremely relevant. Art can give affirmation through its tragic significance, representing life on a stage, in a book, in a composition. According to the young Nietzsche, ancient Greek tragedy succeded in doing this by means of music—before classical philosophy, which emerges in its main *logos* through the Socratic figure of Plato's dialogues, began to transform tragedy into comedy, as Nietzsche narrates in the *Birth of Tragedy*.

The most difficult challenge for a philosopher is to give expression to life, without betraying his dynamic nature. Nietzsche (in)forms his philosophy, projecting it for the future searching for a suitable and understandable form which can express life as eternal becoming. This is a crucial issue which emerges in the last book of the *Gay Science* (GS) in a central paragraph called *The ques-*

---

[12] To see deeper in this direction, is Nietzsche's position very distant from Kant's remarks on this topic, defining self-knowledge as an imperative: "[D]er Imperativ, dem der Verstand sich selbst unterwirft (*nosce te ipsum*) ist das Princip sein Subject als Object der Anschauung zu einem Begriffe zu machen oder jenes diesem unterzuordnen" writes Kant in *Opus postumum* (Kant, Opus postumum, AA XXII, p. 22). This means that the subject (Subjekt) of Kant's transcendental self-consciousness makes itself an object (Object) in order to be able to become a concept. In other words, self-knowledge is in Kant not only a moral precept, but also a self-conceptualisation which unifies theoretical and moral aspects, whereas the constitution of the self is for Nietzsche a philosophical-narrative goal, which has to be thought involving the narrative act.

tion of being understandable, when he claims: "One not only wants to be understood when one writes, but also quite as certainly not to be understood" (GS, p. 381). A related remark is also made in the initial paragraph of the new preface to *Daybreak* where Nietzsche depicts the author of his book with a significant metaphor confronting the dark, which represents the obscurity of what is not understandable, with the light of clarification and then he asks the reader rhetorically

> You might call him contented, working there in the dark [...], as though he [the author of *Daybreak*, A. L.] perhaps desires this prolonged obscurity, desires to be incomprehensible, concealed, enigmatic, because he knows what he will be thereby also acquire: his own morning, his own redemption, his own *dawn?* (D, Preface 1, p. 2).

> (Dass er vielleicht seine eigne lange Finsterniss haben will, sein Unverständliches, Verborgenes, Räthselhaftes, weil er weiss, was er auch haben wird: seinen eignen Morgen, seine eigne Erlösung, seine eigne *Morgenröthe*.) (KSA 3, Vorrede 1, p. 12).

This is quite remarkable not because it links without opposing incomprehensibility with comprehension. Nietzsche wants really to be understood, but un-understandability is the base of being understandable for a future interpretation. This enigmatic thought becomes more clear in EH, when Nietzsche affirms:

> I will touch upon the question of their [of his works, A. L.] being understood or *not* being understood. I do it as casually as is somehow fitting: for the time has not yet come at all for this question. My time has not yet come, some people are born posthumously (EH Why I write so good books 1, p. 63).

> (Hier werde, bevor ich von ihnen selber rede, die Frage nach dem Verstanden – oder *Nicht*-verstanden-werden dieser Schriften berührt. Ich tue es so nachlässig, als es sich irgendwie schickt: denn diese Frage ist durchaus noch nicht an der Zeit.) (KSA 6, p. 298).

According to Nietzsche, we read and write not only for the understandability of our own writings, but also for keeping alive the hermeneutic inexhaustibility of our thoughts. Coming readers need not only to receive clear messages, but adequate narrative-philosophical forms for those messages, which the philosopher Nietzsche aims at handing down. In this contest, the relation between life and the art of writing deals with the necessity of remaining "alive"—that is understood and most of all potentially understandable—as a philosopher for the future, which also means to be a classic.

Therefore, it can be affirmed that the need of being interpreted (and self-interpreted) in Nietzsche's work EH goes together with a different way of communicating his own philosophy connected with his notion of the I-person. In his most famous work *Thus spoke Zarathustra*, composed in four parts between

1883 and 1885, (1883 first publication then 1891), Nietzsche describes his philosophical positions through poetic suggestions and unconventional philosophical and narrative images through his main figure Zarathustra. Yet, Zarathustra as a work of art offers an aesthetic reflection about life in as far as it represents a plurality of forms and hermeutical perspectives which correspond to the multiplicity of understandings. In this sense the multiple images and interpretations represented by *Zarathustra* as work not only can be interpreted as a reflection about philosophy, but also as a reflected image thereof. In this sense art is mirror of philosophy and moreover an increase thereof.

Zarathustra's stylistic tendency is more than a formal aspect of the great book: it regards Nietzsche's attitude in the works thereafter. In the programmatic *Beyond Good and Evil: Prelude of a Philosophy of the Future*, first published in 1886, Nietzsche does not only articulate accusations against past philosophers for their dogmatism and of lack of critical sense, but uses—again, but also differently from the past—an aphoristic style whose function and meaning would need to be accurately discussed. In the context of his new compositions next to his self-interpretations, EH cannot be considered as a short appendix, which—at the largest—became a nearly conclusive intellectual autobiography. Yet, reading EH carefully, we are obliged to consider this work more in its stylistic structure highlighting the hyperbolic expressions as well as the parodistic self-descriptions, on the one hand, and the more complex contest of Nietzsche's last writings of the year 1888, to which EH belongs.

The narrative-philosophical experiment of EH can be described as a new attempt based in a narrative self-creating project.[13] Differently from Kant, aesthetics does not link to any moral push.[14] Nietzsche claims that "it was *against* mor-

---

13 The conception of artistic creation opposed to moral constructions roots as leitmotiv in Nietzsche's early work BT (1872) when the philologist Nietzsche questions life from an aesthetical point of view. This attitude still remains years later when in the late Preface to the second edition of this work (1886), Nietzsche writes: "Life is essentially amoral" (BT, Preface 5, p. 9). In this approach the sensible as phainomenon is the only way to discover the inexorable becoming.
14 "The precondition of opera is a false belief about the artistic process; more precisely, it is that idyllic faith that in reality every sensitive man is an artist. In keeping with the sense of this belief, opera is the expression of lay amateurs in art, something which dictates its laws with the cheerful optimism of the theoretical man." So, Nietzsche asks already in 1872 further: "But what can we expect for art itself from the effect of a form of art whose origins do not lie in the aesthetic realm at all but which have, by contrast, stolen from a half moralistic sphere over into the sphere of art and which can deceive people about this hybrid origin only now and then?" (BT, § 19, p. 120). In paragraph 21, speaking about Socrates and Plato, Nietzsche explains why it is difficult to find a moral foundation to create art. But more radically, Nietzsche outlines in paragraph 14 the main features of tragic art, describing how tragic art has to be seen, that is:

ality that" his book on the Classical Tragedy turned to, in so far as it represents a systematic doctrine, a "purely aesthetic valuation" which takes form from the Dionysian character.

Another central question in Nietzsche's aesthetic theory, which might shed new light on the composition of EH and seems to be opposed to Kant's aesthetic thoughts, is strictly related with the conception of the Dionysian. According to Nietzsche, impersonality and universal validity—the essential features of an aesthetical judgement according to Kant's third critique—refer to a conception of aesthetics which is not compatible with the Dionysian frenzy. The two characterisations differ profoundly in conceiving the subject as responsible for the aesthetic experience. According to Nietzsche, aesthetic does not concern the spectator or the observer, but the artist himself. Art represents that which stimulates vital energies, and as such, it involves not only the spectator, but mainly the creator. Nietzsche's Dionysian transvaluation considers this aspect as fundamental and claims critically not only towards Kant, but towards all the philosophers, including Schopenhauer, who did not consider this strict connection between creating and life. It can be said that in the aesthetic experience, it is not a Kantian universal validity, but a personal involvement with the object which concerns directly the subject as mean of the aesthetic experience, even if not as its final cause. The aesthetical subject is not merely as contemplator (or spectator), but the person who is directly *interested*, who is involved as part of the creation himself/herself under the push of his/her drives. This issue plays a role in Nietzsche's late works. In EH, the personal experience is supported and communicated to the reader through a stylisation of the author which involves both philosophy and art (fiction): Nietzsche shows in EH that thinking and writing are a constant recreation of the self, the reformulation of the classical philosophical questions is posed on the ground of the personal, individual experience as writer, as an anti-classic, as becoming a classic for the time we live in.

Bibliography

Baeumler, Alfred (1931): *Nietzsche der Philosoph und Politiker*. Leipzig: Reclam.
Benne, Christian (2005): *Nietzsche und die historisch-kritische Philologie*. [Monographien und Texte der Nietzsche Forschung 49]. Berlin: de Gruyter.

"Something really unreasonable—causes without effects and effects which appeared to have no causes, and the whole so confused and with so many different elements that any reasonable disposition had to reject it, but dangerous tinder for sensitive and susceptible souls." (BT, § 14, p. 98).

Gentili, Carlo (2003): *La filosofia come genere letterario.* Bologna: Pendragon.
Groddeck, Wolfram (1991): *Dionysos Dithyramben.* Berlin: de Gruyter.
Kant, Immanuel (1993): *Opus Postumum.* Ed. Förster, Eckart, trans. Förster, Eckart / Rosen, Michael. Cambridge: Cambridge Unversity Press.
Lejeune, Philippe (1975): *Le Pacte autobiographique.* Paris: Éditions du Seuil.
Lossi, Annamaria (2006): *Nietzsche und Platon. Begegnung auf dem Weg der Umdrehung des Platonismus.* Würzburg. Königshausen&Neumann.
Lossi, Annamaria (2013): "Philosophie als Selbstgestaltung? Umwertung und Selbstverständnis im Ausgang von Nietzsches 'Von den Voruteilen der Philosophen'." In: *Texturen des Denkens.* Eds. Born, Marcus / Pichler, Axel. Berlin: de Gruyter, pp. 107–122.
Magnus, Bernd / Stewart, Stanley / Mileur, Jean-Pierre (1993): *Nietzsche's Case, Philosophy as/and literature.* New York, London: Routledge.
Nietzsche, Friedrich (1967): *Ecce Homo. How one becomes what one is.* Trans. and ed. Kaufmann, Walter (with *On the Genealogy of Morals*). New York: Vintage.
Nietzsche, Friedrich (1988): *Sämtliche Werke. Kritische Studienausgabe in 15 Bänden.* Bd. 1. Eds. Colli, Giorgio / Mazzino Montinari. Berlin / New York: de Gruyter and dtv.
Nietzsche, Friedrich (1997): *Daybreak: Thoughts on the Prejudices of Morality.* Eds. Clark, M. / Leiter B. Cambridge: Cambridge University Press.
Nietzsche, Friedrich (1999): *The Birth of Tragedy and Other writings.* Eds. Geuss, Raymond / Speirs, Ronald, trans. Speirs, Ronald. Cambridge: Cambridge University Press.
Nietzsche, Friedrich (2002): *Beyond Good and Evil. Prelude to a Philosophy of the Future.* Ed. Horstmann, R.-P. / Hormann, J., trans. Normann, J. Cambridge: Cambridge Unverisity Press.
Whitehead, A. N. (1978): *Process and Reality.* New York: Free Press.
Winchester, James (1994): *Nietzsche's Aesthetic Turn: Reading Nietzsche after Heidegger, Deleuze, Derrida.* New York: Suny Press.
Zittel, Claus (2011): *Das ästhetische Kalkül von Friedrich Nietzsches* Also sprach Zarathustra. 2. Aufl. Würzburg: Königshausen&Neumann.

Abbreviations

BGE = Nietzsche, Friedrich (2002): *Beyond Good and Evil. Prelude to a Philosophy of the Future.* Ed. Horstmann, R.-P. / Hormann, J., trans. Normann, J. Cambridge: Cambridge Unverisity Press.

BT = Nietzsche, Friedrich (1999): *The Birth of Tragedy and Other writings.* Eds. Geuss, Raymond / Speirs, Ronald (Ed.), trans. Speirs, Ronald. Cambridge: Cambridge University Press.

D = Nietzsche, Friedrich (1997): *Daybreak: Thoughts on the Prejudices of Morality.* Eds. Clark, M. / Leiter B. Cambridge: Cambridge University Press.

EH = Nietzsche, Friedrich (1967): *Ecce Homo. How one becomes what one is.* Trans. and ed. Kaufmann, Walter (with *On the Genealogy of Morals*). New York: Vintage.

KSA =   Nietzsche, Friedrich (1988): *Sämtliche Werke. Kritische Studienausgabe in 15*
(followed   *Bänden.* Bd. 1. Eds. Colli, Giorgio and Mazzino Montinari. Berlin/New York: de
by vol.)   Gruyter and dtv.

Index

a posteriori 92, 95, 232
a priori 7, 77, 87–89, 92–96, 99–100, 116, 199
Abgrund 9, 181, 184–185, 187, 200, 205
aesthetic 2–9, 14, 22, 25, 28, 60–61, 63, 69–70, 72, 76–78, 103–113, 137, 147–150, 156–57, 161, 163–167, 175, 178, 180–186, 194, 209, 215, 227, 230, 235–236, 238–239
aesthetic state 105, 107, 112, 165–167
analytical 7, 87, 90, 95, 100
anamnesis 131, 136–138, 142, 205
anarchy 164
antagonism 2–3, 7, 9, 14, 175
antagonistic 2
anthropocentrism 214
anthropology 8–9, 91–92, 99–100, 175
anti-classic 228, 239
anti-classicism 7, 25, 69, 71
anti-idealism 52, 103
antithetics 4–5
apodictic 93, 95, 100, 134
apodicticity 95, 97–98, 100
aporia 134, 175
apparent purpose 104–105, 108, 112–113
appearance 28, 59, 74–78, 81, 106, 109, 166, 194, 216
apriority 3, 6, 9, 89, 95, 183–184
arbitrariness 98–99
arbitrary 31, 87, 96–98, 100
Aristotle 191, 196, 204, 206
art 3, 5, 19, 22–23, 30–32, 36, 41, 44, 47, 69–72, 74–76, 81, 90, 103–14, 106, 108, 110–111, 149–151, 154–155, 157, 163,167, 175, 177–179, 182–183, 185, 195–196, 223, 228, 236–239
artist 33, 42, 45, 137, 167, 222, 238–239
artistic 4, 8, 23, 69–70, 72, 76–78, 110, 166–167, 177, 182–183, 185, 216–217, 222, 238
autonomous 4, 61, 73, 110, 124, 127, 164
autonomy 6–7, 29, 45, 47, 116, 122–123, 126, 129, 150, 165–166

beautiful 6, 13–19, 21–25, 27–28, 30–43, 45, 74, 108–109, 112, 138, 150–152, 158, 176, 194, 203
beauty 2, 3, 38, 45, 74, 76, 104, 109, 112, 137–138, 142, 149–153, 158, 161–163, 169–170
Benjamin, Walter 7, 69, 71–83, 180–181, 186,
Bildung 5, 7, 25, 27–30, 33–34, 36, 39, 43–46, 113, 152, 166, 182
Bildungsroman 13–14, 25, 28, 108, 110, 112–113, 161
Blumenberg, Hans 189, 206
body 19, 39, 72, 143, 156, 168, 177–178, 181, 184, 204, 212, 215, 217, 223
Brentano, Clemens 157
Brentano, Gunda 134, 144

Calvinist 17
categorical imperative 3, 4, 8, 103–104, 115–116, 121–127, 130
causality 133, 215, 223
Celan, Paul 70, 84, 185, 200, 206
Christian 15, 26, 39–40, 101, 114, 135–137, 204, 239
Christianity 14, 116, 123–124, 167–168, 171–172
classic 9, 13, 31–33, 151, 227–228, 230, 234, 237, 239
classical 1, 7, 31, 33, 49, 51, 59–60, 63, 66, 147, 149, 150, 155, 159, 206–207, 210, 227–228, 230–231, 233–234, 236, 239
Classicism 5–7, 11, 14–15, 17, 25, 32–33, 60, 63–64, 66, 69–71, 77, 150–151, 180, 227
cognition 7, 9, 53, 57, 87–89, 91–99, 139–142, 190–193, 199, 209, 213–214, 218–219, 222–223
cognitive 4, 9, 96, 108, 132, 135, 141, 151, 177, 209, 211–212, 215, 217–219, 221–222

conscious 91, 97, 99, 135, 139, 141, 143, 156, 195
consciousness 9, 19, 89, 91, 96–97, 99–100, 131–133, 135, 140–142, 144, 156–157, 163, 165, 175, 185, 195–196, 198, 209, 211, 217, 236
convalescence 18, 37
corporeal 3, 6, 8–9, 137, 175–177, 179, 181–184
corporeality 177, 181, 183, 185
creativity 1, 4, 45, 151, 153, 170
crisis 3–4, 150, 219, 221–223, 234
critical 3, 5, 7–9, 42, 52–54, 57, 62, 69, 72, 77–78, 93, 159, 178, 190, 194, 196, 209, 212, 225, 231, 238
criticism 1, 6–7, 13, 15, 17, 25, 39, 40, 87–88, 99–100, 148, 150, 223, 232
critique 2–9, 39, 54, 65, 70–72, 74, 77–78, 85, 87–89, 92–95, 98–100, 103, 108, 114–115, 124, 130, 152, 159, 163, 167, 171, 182, 188–189, 206, 209, 213, 215–216, 222–223, 225

death 1, 8, 18, 21, 36, 39, 92, 135, 142–144, 155, 158, 161–162, 166, 168–171, 177, 179, 181, 220
deduction 91, 94, 97, 100, 118
democracy 165
democratic 164–165
dialectic 77, 136, 138, 156, 162, 164, 190
Diefenbach, Johann Georg 132–135
Dionysus 210
discourse 2–6, 8, 15, 33, 60, 88, 108, 147–148, 150, 155, 173, 176–177, 179, 181–182, 190, 206
discursive 2, 4–5
disinterested 23, 74, 106, 108, 110, 150
disinterestedness 109, 148
divinity 124–125, 166, 169
dogmatic 14, 56, 89
dogmatism 95–96, 188, 238
dualism 2, 76, 143, 152

earth 3, 128, 168, 179, 184–185, 200, 202, 209–214, 216, 219–225, 234
ecocriticism 211–212

ecological VIII, 6, 173, 209, 210, 212, 219, 220, 221, 222, 223, 225
ecology 9, 209–215, 217, 219, 221–223, 225
education 5, 7–8, 13, 24–25, 30, 36–38, 40, 45, 103–108, 110, 112–114, 152–153, 161, 163, 172, 175, 183
embodiment 147, 212, 217
Emerson, Ralph Waldo 38, 47
emotional 33–34, 36, 39–40, 46, 61, 148, 154
empirical 2, 5, 7, 32, 49, 51, 53, 56–58, 60, 62–63, 74, 87, 89, 92–94, 98, 100, 113, 133, 175, 179, 183
empiricism 49–50, 52, 55, 60, 65, 95–96, 100, 150, 182
empiricist 93
Enlightenment 1, 5, 9, 17–18, 26, 29, 48, 103–104, 144, 148
environment 29, 33, 45, 113, 210, 212
environmental 3, 5–6, 171, 209, 211–212, 222–225
environmentalist 9
epistemological 8, 49, 51–52, 55, 59, 62–63, 131–132, 134–137, 139, 193
epistemology 51, 131–132
Eros 8, 64, 131, 136–139, 142, 161–162, 164, 166, 169–172, 177
erotic 138, 157, 177, 181
ethical 6, 44, 181, 236
ethics 17, 26, 166, 190, 223–225
existence 2, 4, 17, 22, 37, 59, 77, 91, 94, 103, 108, 122, 127, 133–134, 139–140, 155, 158–159, 171, 175, 192, 194, 213–214, 221, 233, 236
existential 76, 179, 180
experience 2–8, 15, 19, 23, 28, 43, 46, 51, 56, 62, 65, 72–73, 79–80, 87, 90, 92, 95–100, 107, 110–111, 113, 116, 124, 135, 141, 144, 157, 175, 178, 182, 185, 190–191, 193–194, 202, 205–206, 212, 215–219, 224, 234, 239
experiential 7, 49, 60, 193, 222–223

faith 17–18, 21–22, 52, 129, 164, 171–172, 192–194, 220, 238
fantasy 4, 35, 37–39, 73–75

female 13–14, 25, 28, 30, 34, 43, 46–47, 148, 153–154, 158
feminine 6, 39, 44, 147–148, 152, 155
Fichte, Johann Gottlieb 2, 7, 9, 87, 89, 93, 95, 101, 124, 131, 145, 161, 178
finitude 87–99, 120, 123, 125, 127
Fischer, Kuno 87, 92–93, 100
form 3, 7, 13–15, 19, 22–25, 31, 45, 50, 63, 70, 73–77, 83, 94–96, 100, 103–105, 108, 110–111, 113, 121, 124, 132–133, 135–137, 139, 141–142, 144, 147, 149, 157, 163, 167, 169, 170, 175, 177–178, 180–182, 192, 195, 198–200, 203, 210, 216, 222, 235–236, 238–239
Formtrieb 103, 164
freedom 2–4, 32, 44–45, 47, 91, 106, 110, 113, 116, 119, 124–125, 127–128, 134, 149–159, 164, 166, 175, 182–183, 190, 233
French Revolution 103, 164, 165
Freud, Sigmund 1–2, 15, 33, 38–39, 47, 161–162, 170–172, 198
Freudian 8, 15–16, 162
Fries, Jakob Friedrich 7, 87–101,

Geist 2, 8, 35, 74, 99, 115, 129, 143, 156, 183, 190, 195–198
gender 44–45, 47–48, 147–149, 151–155, 157–158
gendered 46, 148, 150
German 1–2, 5–9, 14, 17, 19, 33, 44, 46–47, 53, 64, 83, 87, 89, 91, 93, 95, 97, 99–101, 117, 145, 147, 151, 158–159, 161, 166, 171–172, 176–177, 187, 189, 196, 204–205, 227–230
God 6, 13, 16, 19, 21–24, 37–38, 91, 116, 124, 133–136, 139–140, 168–169, 183, 190, 192–193, 204, 228
Goethe, Johann Wolfgang 1–2, 5–8, 13–26, 27–48, 49–67, 69–83, 110–114, 127, 154, 156, 166–167, 202, 212, 218, 228
Gontard, Susette 184, 197–198
Greek 32–33, 47, 149, 152, 176–177, 210, 227–229, 236
groundless 175, 188, 193, 202, 205
Grund 9, 18, 37, 76, 187, 189–197, 199, 201, 202, 203, 204, 205–207, 221

Günderrode, Karoline von 6, 8, 131–145, 147–159

Habermas, Jürgen 192, 195, 206
Harmony 31–32, 45, 63, 73, 79, 104, 110, 149, 150
Hegel, Georg Wilhelm Friedrich 1–3, 5–6, 8–9, 35, 48, 93, 100–101, 115–116, 123–130, 145, 149, 183, 187, 196, 206
Heidegger, Martin 2, 186, 209, 224, 229
hermeneutic 236–237
heteronomy 8, 115–116, 122–123, 125, 128–129
historical 5–6, 81, 88, 101, 155, 161, 168, 170, 183, 196, 198, 220, 228, 231
history 2, 5–6, 17–18, 27, 29, 32, 40, 44, 47, 58, 92, 162, 168, 171, 185, 188, 196, 198, 209, 225, 228–230
Hölderlin, Friedrich 1–3, 6, 8–9, 116, 136, 154, 175–186, 189–207, 209–210, 213–216, 219, 222
hubris 178, 219–221
human 3–5, 8–9, 19, 23, 26, 29, 33, 36, 43–44, 51, 54, 60–61, 63, 72–73, 80–81, 87–89, 91, 93, 99, 103–105, 124, 127, 129, 132, 135, 138, 140, 150, 157, 162–164, 168, 171, 175, 179, 181–185, 188, 190, 209–225, 231–232
humanism 23
humanity 5, 17, 23, 116, 122–126, 150, 165, 168, 179, 181, 183, 220–221, 235
humankind 116, 124–125, 127–129
Humboldt, Wilhelm von 15, 40
hypochondria 40

idea 2–3, 5–6, 19, 23, 53, 58, 69, 71, 80, 90, 103–104, 108, 112, 117, 122, 125, 127, 136, 138, 161–163, 166, 169, 176, 178, 183, 190, 192, 194–196, 199, 202, 204–205, 210–211, 213, 217–218, 220, 233–235
Idealism 2, 4–5, 7–9, 49–50, 52–53, 55, 59, 65, 87, 89, 91, 93, 100, 103, 106, 113, 131, 145, 147, 150, 177, 179, 181, 183, 185, 187–188, 207, 215, 222, 227–228

Idealist 2–9, 49, 52, 55, 62–63, 93, 103, 113, 147, 149–151, 155, 157–159, 173, 175, 188, 209, 218
identity 28, 47, 50, 64, 80, 155, 185, 196, 199, 217, 235
idleness 38, 106, 112–113
illness 27, 36–37, 40
illusion 216
image 114, 137, 140–141, 153, 168, 193, 202, 204–205, 214, 216–217, 220, 233–234, 238
imagination 25–26, 39, 53, 70, 73, 82, 98, 109–110, 112, 114, 150, 163, 167, 169, 183, 192, 211, 217, 222, 224
immanence 209
immanent 143, 180, 182
individual 3, 5–6, 9, 27, 29–30, 32, 37–38, 41, 45–47, 50, 62, 131–132, 134–135, 137–142, 144, 162–163, 183–185, 196, 214, 218, 224, 239
individuality 27, 34, 42, 141, 144, 168, 177, 185, 218
intellect 5, 108, 150–151, 158, 170, 212, 214, 216, 223
intellectual 1, 3–6, 19, 24, 29–30, 36, 45, 89, 147–156, 158, 164, 175–177, 182–183, 216, 219, 231, 238
intelligence 3, 24, 34, 154, 163
intelligibility 164
intelligible 3, 5, 7, 175, 177–178, 185, 194
intuition 74, 79, 89, 91, 108–110, 175, 191–194, 216

Judaism 8, 115–117, 119, 121, 123, 125, 128–129
judgement 32, 53–54, 91, 97, 108–110, 112–114, 150, 159, 171, 195–196, 206, 215, 231

Kant, Immanuel 1–9, 45, 49–50, 52–57, 59, 61, 63–65, 69–72, 74, 77–79, 83, 87–93, 96, 99–101, 103, 108–110, 112–114, 115–130, 131–135, 149–153, 159, 163, 171, 182, 186, 187–196, 199, 201–202, 204, 206, 228, 236, 238–240

Kantian 2, 7, 15, 64, 79, 88–91, 93, 95, 100, 113, 115–16, 119, 124–127, 129, 131–133, 135–136, 150–151, 175, 182–183, 196, 202, 212, 215, 236, 239
Kiesewetter, Johann Gottfried 132
Klopstock, Friedrich Gottlieb 197, 206

Lessing, Gotthold Ephraim 1, 142, 144, 149, 192
Liebmann, Otto 87, 93–94, 101
Locke, John 87, 91–93, 191
love 6, 13, 19, 21, 24, 28, 37, 39–40, 119, 136–138, 148, 151, 153, 164–166, 168–172, 176, 197, 199–201
Lukács, Georg 167, 171, 199, 206

male 13–14, 28–29, 40, 46, 148–149, 152–156
Marcuse, Herbert 8, 161–172
masculine 44, 148, 155
material 17, 49, 53, 79–80, 103–104, 108, 119–120, 138–139, 147, 164, 166, 169, 181, 188, 190, 194, 201, 212, 215, 217, 219, 231
matter 151–152, 163, 190, 192, 194–196, 199, 202, 204–205, 230, 233, 235
melancholia 18–19, 21, 36, 40
melancholic 18, 28, 36, 40, 158
melancholy 6, 13, 18, 21, 23, 25, 32
messiah 168–169, 171
messianic 83, 168–169
metaphor 3–4, 31–32, 61, 140, 188, 191–193, 211, 215, 217, 225, 237
metaphoric 213, 217–218
metaphorical 3–4, 187–189, 191–194, 198, 200, 216–218, 235
metaphysical 8, 90, 96, 132, 138–139, 143, 147, 155–156, 170, 178, 181, 183, 189, 210, 215, 219, 235–236
metaphysics 93, 99–100, 117, 130–131, 150, 161–162, 171, 188–189, 222, 229, 235
method 52, 87–90, 92, 94–95, 97, 99–100, 104, 227
methodology 7, 54–56, 58, 88, 94
misogyny 8, 147–149, 151, 153–154

modern 15, 24, 31, 66, 150, 158–159, 164, 167, 189–190, 192, 201–202, 206, 210, 214, 220, 224, 228, 230
modernism 151
modernity 26, 31, 48, 64, 195, 202, 206, 213, 228
monism 135, 143
moral 8, 13, 16–17, 19–21, 23, 29–30, 32, 38, 43, 45, 107, 112, 114–118, 120–124, 126–130, 133–134, 137, 150, 183, 214, 219, 232–233, 236, 238
morality 7, 17, 40, 44–45, 116, 123, 125–126, 149, 154, 162–163, 182–183, 240
mystical 80, 140, 157, 165
mysticism 167

narrative 13, 18–19, 28, 33, 36–37, 39, 41, 46, 131, 136, 185, 187, 190, 230–232, 234–238
natural 3–5, 18–19, 28, 23, 29–30, 33, 38, 44, 54, 56, 58, 61, 63, 69–73, 76, 78, 81, 89, 100, 133–134, 152, 154, 166, 209–213, 220, 232
nature 7, 9, 14–15, 19, 22, 27–28, 34–40, 43–45, 56–60, 64–66, 70–72, 74–79, 81, 89,91, 93, 101, 110–111, 117, 120, 127–128, 131, 133–136, 140–141, 143, 150–151, 156, 177, 180, 182, 185, 188–189, 191, 194, 199–201, 203, 209–214, 216, 218–220, 222–223, 233, 236
necessity 2, 116, 128, 175, 182–84, 216, 237
Nelson, Leonhard 93–101
Nietzsche, Friedrich 1, 3, 6, 8–9, 185, 209–225, 227–241
Novalis 3, 8, 54, 65, 83, 116, 136, 145, 154, 161–172

objective 13, 15–17, 19, 24, 51, 53–56, 59, 81, 106, 118–120, 123, 135, 156, 170, 182, 192–195
objectivity 2, 14, 62, 80, 120, 215, 234
ontological 51, 147, 150, 229
ontology 147, 150
opinion 7, 87, 90, 95–100, 109, 188, 192

panentheism 136

pantheism 136, 144, 192
paradox 8, 131, 135, 140, 144, 177
Pascal, Blaise 214
phenomenal 131, 135–136, 139, 142
phenomenology 1, 6, 51, 64–66, 177–178, 206
philistine 165–166, 170
physiology 212–213, 215
Pietism 14–15, 22
Pietist 17–18, 22–23, 39
Plato 45, 136–138, 144–145, 177, 204–205, 207, 227, 229, 236, 238–240
Platonic 131–132, 136–138, 142, 148, 176, 178, 205, 219
play 3, 7, 17, 19, 37, 51–52, 70, 77, 103–107, 109–110, 113, 142, 161–165, 168–171, 182, 212, 217, 234
playful 8, 74, 107, 163, 166, 169
poetic 2–6, 8–9, 18, 71, 136, 157–158, 136, 175–176, 178–181, 185–187, 197–198, 200, 202, 204, 209–210, 217, 222, 231, 238
poetics 3, 6, 8, 83, 175–186, 191, 204–206, 228
polarity 50, 66, 81
politics 147, 149, 161–162, 164–165, 167, 171, 224–225, 233
practical 2–3, 8, 42–43, 55, 57, 104, 115–118, 120–127, 175, 182–183, 192, 222
practice 4, 8, 24, 56, 148, 197, 201
pre-rational 131, 142, 162
presence 5, 30, 33, 41, 53, 113, 169, 177–179, 186
presupposition 7, 87, 90, 94–98, 100, 167, 194
prima philosophia 189
Promethean 137
psychological 6, 13, 15–18, 27–32, 34, 36, 39, 45, 47, 49, 88–89, 92–93, 98
psychologism 92–93, 98–100
psychology 15–17, 29, 32, 40, 47, 50, 92–93, 98–101, 162
purposeless 104–105, 108, 112
purposelessness 8, 103–105, 108, 112

rational 103–104, 106, 116–125, 127, 133–134, 162–163, 170, 178, 192–194, 206, 218, 233
Realism 6, 167, 209–210
reason 2–4, 40, 50, 54, 65, 87–100, 103–105, 108–110, 117–118, 120–128, 130, 133–134, 150–154, 157, 159, 162–163, 175, 182–183, 188, 190–191, 193–194, 196, 206, 211, 236
reflection 4–5, 19, 28, 54, 56–57, 87, 96–97, 100, 153, 167, 175, 177–178, 181–185, 191, 212, 222, 231, 238
regressive 90, 97, 100
Reinhold, Karl Leonhard 87, 89–90, 95, 101, 132
religion 6, 8, 13, 15, 17–18, 22–23, 33, 36–37, 39, 40, 123–124, 127, 130, 134, 144–145, 165–166, 168–169, 206
religious 1, 6, 13–15, 17–18, 21–22, 25–27, 33, 36, 39–40, 43, 168
representation 19, 50, 61–62, 71, 95, 97–99, 117–122, 180, 183, 193, 195, 200, 211, 235
revelation 124, 132–134, 141, 143–145, 169, 180, 182
Roman 1, 33, 227
Romantic 8, 20, 31–33, 38, 48, 51, 54–55, 65, 83, 131, 144–145, 147–151, 154–155, 157–159, 163, 171, 209
Romanticism 6–7, 31, 51, 64, 66, 83, 145, 147, 149–151, 159, 168, 171
rupture 1, 137, 153

Schelling, Friedrich Wilhelm Joseph 2–3, 7, 9, 87, 89, 93, 95, 101, 131, 145, 156, 196, 207
Schiller, Friedrich 2–3, 7–8, 13–17, 22, 25, 33, 40, 66, 103–108, 112–114, 149, 161–167, 169–172, 175, 182–83, 195
Schlegel, Friedrich 3, 33, 144–145, 147–159, 169
Schleiermacher, Friedrich 144–145
science 6, 37, 39, 44, 48, 51–57, 59–60, 63–66, 83, 88, 90, 96, 98–99, 163, 187–189, 191, 196, 216, 223–224, 231–232, 236

sense 2–3, 5, 13, 15–16, 19–20, 33, 45, 47, 58–60, 80, 90, 95, 128–129, 132, 137, 139–141, 150–151, 154, 163–164, 167, 175, 177–178, 180–182, 184–185, 199, 205, 211–212, 214, 224, 238
sensibility 2, 36, 39–40, 45, 96–97, 127–128, 163, 165, 171, 193, 223
sensitivity 27, 34, 153–154
sensory 51, 65, 135, 141, 185
sensual 153, 157, 165
sensuality 162, 170
sexuality 15, 39, 45, 169–170
sickness 31–34, 37, 39
sign 80–81, 178–179, 181
signification 179
soul 6–7, 13–19, 21–25, 27–28, 30, 32–43, 45, 60, 136–137, 140, 184, 190, 202, 205
speculation 5, 90–91, 97, 188, 193
Spinoza, Baruch de 6, 13, 17–18, 21, 23–24, 26, 57, 136, 139, 192,
spirit 1, 15, 21, 25, 28, 35, 46, 74, 87, 99, 128–129, 136, 143, 145, 152, 156, 165, 176, 184, 190, 195, 197, 206, 225
split 4, 137, 140
spontaneity 98–99
spontaneous 2–3, 80, 170
Stofftrieb 103
Stolberg, Friedrich von 15, 38, 144
subject 2–5, 9, 13–14, 49–60, 62–63, 65–66, 70, 78, 80, 105–109, 113, 121–122, 125, 140, 143, 150, 156, 175, 177–178, 181–182, 185–186, 195–196, 198–200, 205, 215–216, 219, 231, 234–236, 239
subjective 13, 15–17, 19, 23, 51, 53, 56, 61, 63, 105–106, 109, 111, 118–121, 123, 125, 131, 134–135, 182, 193–195, 215, 217
subjectivity 14, 16, 18, 21, 49–51, 54, 141, 167, 178, 181, 202, 215
synthesis 2, 137, 150, 164, 170, 183, 185, 217
synthetic 87, 89, 96

tenderness 8, 175, 177–178, 182–185
Thanatos 8, 161, 169–170

theology 1, 8, 23, 161–162, 170, 204, 206, 230
Tieck, Ludwig 3
topography 185, 209, 211, 224
totality 80, 137, 141, 143–144, 167, 234
touch 178, 184–185, 221
transcendental 2–5, 7–9, 72, 78, 87–93, 99, 151, 166, 175–186, 188, 190–191, 193, 199, 207, 215, 236
transcendentalism 6–7
trauma 3, 36, 137

understanding 1–2, 17, 29, 37, 42, 46, 57–58, 60–61, 70, 77, 87, 91, 95–100, 103, 105–106, 112, 132, 135, 137, 143, 150, 152, 177, 188–189, 194–195, 204, 223, 230, 232, 235–236

unity 67–70, 90, 108, 110, 131, 138, 140, 150, 167
universal 3, 43, 70, 120–122, 126, 133, 138, 149, 168, 217, 239
universality 80, 108–109, 116, 119, 121–123
utopia 46, 112, 171
utopian 25, 163

Weimar 13–15, 17, 22, 25, 63, 65–66, 113, 156, 159, 186
wholeness 13, 63, 167
Windelband, Wilhelm 93, 101
woman 27–28, 30, 36, 40, 119, 148–149, 151–154, 157–158
women 7–8, 14, 27–30, 34, 40, 43–47, 119, 147–149, 151–155, 158

www.ingramcontent.com/pod-product-compliance
Lightning Source LLC
Chambersburg PA
CBHW031806220426
43662CB00007B/542